PULLING THE TRIGGER

Pulling the Trigger

A 25-Year Study of Deadly Force Encounters by Law Enforcement

Larry C. Brubaker

2008

Galde Press, Inc.

Lakeville, Minnesota, U.S.A.

First Edition
First Printing, 2008

Cover photo by Larry C. Brubaker
Drawings by Mike Boss

Galde Press, Inc.
PO Box 460
Lakeville, Minnesota 55044–0460
www.galdepress.com

This book is dedicated to law enforcement officers
throughout the United States, especially the following Minnesota
officers who gave the ultimate sacrifice in the line of duty.

Deputy Ervin Clemons
Carlton County Sheriff's Office
August 26, 1993

Officer Paul Moen
Minneapolis Police Department
July 1, 1995

Officer Melissa Schmidt
Minneapolis Police Department
August 1, 2002

Officer Grant Coyour
Department of Natural Resources
July 11, 1999

Deputy Luther Klug
Dakota County Sheriff's Office
July 17, 1996

Sgt. Gerald Vick
Saint Paul Police Department
May 6, 2005

Officer Brian Klinefelter
St. Joseph Police Department
January 29, 1996

Contents

Acknowledgments

First and foremost I want to acknowledge my family for their support while working on this project. My wife Shiela has watched me cut articles from newspapers, review police reports, fill one filing cabinet with research material and spend hours on the computer. My son Jason, a police officer in Saint Paul, has had to contact Saint Paul officers for me to interview and listen to my frustration of getting the book completed. Lastly, my youngest son Brett, a Sergeant in the Army, provided suggestions during my research. He also assisted Dr. Bill Lewinski while at University of Minnesota-Mankato in his research of police officer's reaction and movements during shooting scenarios.

The following individuals from the Minnesota Bureau of Criminal Apprehension:

Special Agent in Charge John Fossum (Retired)
Special Agent in Charge Terry Smith (Retired)
Special Agent in Charge Jeff Hansen
Senior Special Agent Dennis Fier (Retired)
Senior Special Agent Joel Kohout (Retired)
Senior Special Agent Gene Leatherman
Special Agent James Boyer
Special Agent Jan May
Forensic Artist Marcia Cummings
Special Agent Janet Nelson
Administrative Assistant Deb Remackel
Criminal Justice Information Systems Analyst Kathy Leatherman

The following individuals from Hennepin County Sheriff's Office:

Sheriff Rich Stanek
Captain Patrick Moe (Retired)
Sgt. Charles Kelly

Senior Support Supervisor, Detective Division, Jacqui Albright

The following individuals from the Minneapolis Police Department:

Chief Timothy Dolan

Inspector Robert Skomra

Lt. Lee Edwards

Lt. Robert Kroll

The following individuals from the Saint Paul Police Department:

Chief John Harrington

Comdr. John Vomastek

Comdr. Tim Lynch

Comdr. Don Winger (Retired)

Sgt. Tom Bergren

Sgt. Richard Munoz

Administrative Assistant Lisa Drake

Major Michael Asleson, Minnesota State Patrol

Chief Deputy David Bellows, Dakota County Sheriff's Office

Chief Scott Johnson, Apple Valley Police Department

Inspector Dan Votel (Retired) Ramsey County Sheriff's Department

Executive Director Neil Melton, Minnesota Board of Peace Officer Standards and Training

Ms. Susan Vlasek, Lakeville, MN (Proofreader)

Ms. Sharie L. Larson, Maplewood, MN (Proofreader)

Lastly, I want to acknowledge all of the officers that took time from their busy schedules to allow me to interview them. Your personal recollection and insight to the actual event is greatly appreciated. Your candid comments gave me a better understanding of your feelings, perceptions and actions during and after the incident.

Introduction

There are probably two events in law enforcement that an officer would rather never have to experience: attending the funeral of a fellow officer killed in the line of duty or taking the life of a person while acting in one's official capacity. My purpose is to address the latter. When a shooting results in the death of a citizen, emotions erupt from the public, media, the decedent's family, and the law enforcement community. Sides are taken and opinions are abundant.

An officer is given the duty to protect members of society. Officers take a sworn oath to carry out their duties. Occasionally one must resort to the use of deadly force when the circumstances call for it. It is at that time, often within a split second, that the officer must draw upon his or her training in many different disciplines to make the right choice. That quick decision may result in months to possibly years of criminal or civil legal proceedings.

The State of Minnesota has experienced 110 fatal shootings by officers during the twenty-five year period 1981 through 2005. Those officers, while acting in an official capacity, used deadly force that resulted in the death of 112 citizens. This book is restricted to peace officers in Minnesota. It should be noted that the experiences of officers involved in a shooting incident are universal. While at the FBI Academy, I was able to interview officers from throughout the United States who used deadly force. Those officers related the same emotions as those officers in Minnesota. In 1981, when the first shooting occurred, there were approximately 7,400 active sworn officers in the State of Minnesota according to the Minnesota Peace Officers Standards and Training (POST) Board. In 2005, there were approximately 9,800 sworn officers. Information in this book relates to the small population of 191 officers (nine officers were involved in two separate shootings) who fired a weapon during these twenty-five years resulting in 112 individuals dying.

This book includes *all* officers who shot during an incident resulting in death, although that officer may not have fired the fatal shot or even hit the person. The officer initiated the use of deadly force. One hundred eighty male officers (nine male officers were in two fatal shootings) and eleven female officers shot a weapon during an incident that resulted in death. The experience level of the officers was significant. These officers were not "rookies." The average experience at the time of the event was slightly over ten years. The assignment of the officers was overwhelmingly that of uniform patrol.

Of those involved in fatal shootings, police departments employed 166 officers; thirty-four were sheriff's deputies. There were four State Patrol officers and one officer from the Department of Natural Resources firing their weapons. One hundred sixty-two of the officers shooting were from the seven-county metropolitan area. Larger organizations, specifically Minneapolis and Saint Paul Police Departments, had a higher frequency of shootings. Over half, 122, were employed by departments with over one hundred officers.

Minnesota peace officers routinely used three types of weapons in the performance of their duties: a revolver, semiautomatic handgun, or a shoulder type weapon. The standard weapon into the mid-1980s was the revolver. The caliber was either .38 or .357. The semiautomatic has gained popularity and is the issued weapon for almost all departments. Initially, the 9-millimeter caliber was the most common. However, more recently some departments are using the .40 and .45 calibers. The common shoulder weapon is the .12-gauge shotgun. The usual round is the 00 buckshot. This was used in all except one shooting. That incident used a rifle slug in the shotgun. Additionally, tactical teams have used the MP-5 shoulder-type weapon firing the 9-millimeter round. Three officers on tactical teams used a .308 sniper rifle to shoot the individual. In 1999 and 2005, deputies from different departments fired a .223-caliber round during a shooting. Three officers changed weapons during the incident. During two of those occasions, officers had difficulty ejecting a spent round from a shotgun, so the weapon was changed by the officer. The other officer changed weapons after he had fired all of his rounds from the shotgun.

Other than retirement, twelve officers have left the law enforcement profession. One officer left for a new career in a field that he had been pursuing on a part-time basis prior to the shooting. Two left to pursue another career path. One officer had to leave as his existing medical condition intensified and made him unable to continue in law enforcement. Another officer left a department in a dispute over a separate matter and sued that agency. Seven officers (four males and three females) quit as a direct result of the shooting incident. Four of the seven officers continued working for a period of time before leaving their agency.

Unfortunately, two officers have lost their lives during an incident where the suspect was also killed. The first incident was in August 1993. Sheriff's deputies had arrived at the residence of a known paranoid schizophrenic who had quit taking his medication. He was shooting a weapon outside the home where he lived with his father. A four-hour standoff began. The suspect shot and killed a deputy who was trying to assist in leading the father away from the house. Officers returned fire and killed the suspect.

In August 2002, a female officer from Minneapolis escorted a female to a restroom in a high-rise building after receiving a call regarding a woman with a gun. This woman was searched and then she requested to use the restroom. It is believed the woman had secreted a small .38-caliber revolver in her buttock area. She fired one shot that hit the officer in the lower stomach under her ballistic vest. The bullet traveled in an upward track. The officer returned fire fatally wounding the assailant. The officer died in the operating room.

Four additional officers who had been in fatal shootings later died while working in their official capacities. A Department of Natural Resources officer was killed in an aircraft accident six years after his shooting incident. A Minneapolis officer died of a heart attack while assisting another officer two years later. A Dakota County sheriff's deputy was hit and killed in his patrol car by an intoxicated driver in 1996, only two years after his shooting. An officer from the Saint Paul Police Department was killed by gunfire eight years after his shooting in 2005.

Of course, every case is classified as a homicide and investigated thoroughly. Usually the larger departments, such as Minneapolis and Saint Paul, had their respective homicide units investigate the shootings. In 1999 the Minnesota Bureau of Criminal Apprehension (BCA) investigated both of the Minneapolis Police shootings. The Hennepin County Sheriff's Office investigated two Minneapolis Police Department shootings in 2000 and investigated all Minneapolis police shootings through 2003. Another Minneapolis police shooting in 2000 was in the City of Saint Paul and the Saint Paul Police Department homicide unit investigated that case.

Minneapolis Police now investigate their own shootings, whether fatal or not. Saint Paul Police independently conduct the investigation of all their officer-involved shootings. Smaller local departments typically have the BCA and/or the county sheriff where the shooting took place investigate such shootings. Sheriff's departments will have the BCA investigate. On occasion, the FBI has been requested to conduct a separate investigation to determine if the person's civil rights were violated. Additionally, every case is either presented to a grand jury in the county where the shooting occurred or the county prosecutor makes the determination that the shooting was justified and directs the investigative agency to close the case. There have been some civil awards given to families of the deceased.

There have been advancements in the use of fewer lethal weapons since the beginning of this study in 1981. Some departments use bean-bag-type shotguns. The biggest advancement has been the development of the stun gun. The company leading in this technology is TASER®. It has been very successful. However, as reported in this book, using the stun gun does not always stop every offender.

This book is divided into chapters with various types of police responses.

The chapters are not all distinctive. You may find (or argue) that a SWAT team was called to a domestic situation. Someone with a replica type weapon, simulated weapon or knife was actually a "suicide by cop." The subject matter for each chapter was written as I believed best described the event.

The following terms are defined to give readers a better understanding of legal definitions regarding this topic:

Grand Jury: A body of persons returned at stated periods from the citizens of the county before a court of competent jurisdiction and sworn to inquire of public offenses committed or triable in the county. It shall consist of not more than twenty-three nor less than sixteen persons, and shall not proceed to any business unless sixteen are present. (Minn. Stat. § 648.41, Subd. 1 [2007]).

Indictment: An indictment is an accusation in writing presented to a competent court, charging a person with a public offense. (Minn. Stat. § 628.01 [2007]).

No Bill: A grand jury's notation that insufficient evidence exists for an indictment on a criminal charge. (*Black's Law Dictionary*, 8th Edition, Bryan A. Garner, Editor in Chief, Thomson West Publishing, Saint Paul, MN, 2004, page 1073).

Deadly Force: Force which an actor uses with the purpose of causing, or which the actor should reasonably know creates a substantial risk of causing, death or great bodily harm. The intentional discharge of a firearm, other than a firearm loaded with less lethal munitions, in the direction of another person, or at a vehicle in which another person is believed to be, constitutes deadly force. "Less lethal munitions" means projectiles which are designed to stun, temporarily incapacitate, or cause temporary discomfort to a person. (Minn. Stat. § 609.066, Subd. 1 [2005]).

Peace Officer: An employee or elected or appointed official of a political subdivision or law enforcement agency who is licensed by the board (Minnesota Peace Officer Standard and Training Board), charged with the prevention and detection of crime and the enforcement of the general criminal laws of the state who has the full power of arrest, and shall also include the Minnesota State Patrol, agents of the Division of Alcohol and Gambling Enforcement, state conservation officers, Metropolitan Transit police officers, Department of Corrections' Fugitive Apprehension Unit officers, and Department of Commerce and Insurance Fraud Unit officers. (Minn. Stat. § 626.84, Subd. 1(c)(1) [2005]).

Great Bodily Harm: Bodily injury which creates a high probability of death, or which causes serious permanent disfigurement, or which causes a permanent or protracted loss or impairment of the function of any bodily member or organ, or other serious bodily harm (Minn. Stat. § 609.02 Subd. 8 [2005]).

Reasonable: Fair, proper, just, moderate, suitable, under the circumstances. (*Black's Law Dictionary*, 2004, page 1293).

Firearm: A weapon that expels a projectile (such as a bullet or pellets) by combustion of gun powder or other explosive. (*Black's Law Dictionary*, 2004, page 666).

Unauthorized Withdrawals
aka Bank Robberies

I

On Friday, August 3, 1984, thirty-five-year-old Deputy Steven Peterson decided to get an early start on the day. The thirteen-year veteran of the Hennepin County Sheriff's Office needed to go to the Riverside Bank near downtown Minneapolis to serve legal papers on a matter assigned to him. He arrived at the bank shortly after 9:00 a.m. He soon realized that the bank was being robbed.

The question that goes through the mind of all law enforcement officers became a reality to him: "What would do I do if I was in the middle of a robbery in progress?"

The lone robber was a forty-three-year-old white male named Gerald Edwin Heft. He had entered the bank around 9:10 a.m. He immediately jumped onto the teller's counter and announced that he was robbing the bank. He had a snub-nosed .38-caliber revolver he was displaying to show that he meant business. He then climbed over an eight-foot glass barrier into the tellers' area. Once in the tellers' area, he demanded that a teller open the vault. When it was determined that the keys to get in the vault were not readily available, Heft ordered several tellers to open their teller drawers and move away from them. Heft proceeded to walk down the teller line retrieving money from each drawer. It was evident to the tellers that this robber knew what he was doing as he discarded the security dye pack from each of the drawers.

Heft placed just over ten thousand dollars in United States currency in the rust-colored backpack he had brought with him. He seemed very comfortable as he walked from behind the teller counter through a locked glass door into the main area of the bank lobby. He immediately walked toward the bank exit. He had to go through two sets of doors then down a few steps to a busy business area on Riverside Avenue.

Unknown to Heft, Deputy Peterson had entered the bank soon after the robbery began. Peterson was in civilian clothes—a sports coat, slacks, shirt, and tie. He appeared to be just another bank customer. The thirty-five-millimeter security cameras were activated immediately and provided a moment-by-moment view of the entire robbery.

Deputy Peterson and a bank officer were intently watching the area where the teller windows were located. There were two other customers also watching the drama of the robbery. One of those later said, "I found myself denying the reality of it (robbery)." Almost comically, two elderly customers were sitting at a preparation table apparently completing bank forms for conducting a transaction. These two appeared oblivious to what was happening.

At one point during the robbery it appeared as though Peterson was going to draw his weapon. He turned sideways from the tellers' area and pulled back his sports coat, exposing his holster. He covered his holstered weapon and turned back again to watch the robbery. I later asked Deputy Peterson if he had thought about drawing his weapon at that time. He told me, "I was unsnapping the loop on the holster so I could draw easier."

The next thing on the surveillance camera showed Heft carrying the backpack and weapon, going out the first set of doors, the second set of doors, and then lastly out of sight down the steps. Peterson waited until Heft exited the outside set of doors. Peterson is next seen going through the first set of doors and opening the next door to the street with his left hand. It is obvious that he is extending his right hand with a weapon in a shooting stance and firing at Heft. Heft is not seen in this photograph from the surveillance cameras. Peterson is then seen returning to the bank and going out of sight into the tellers' area through the same door that Heft had used to exit moments before.

While Peterson was shooting at Heft, customers and the bank officer were running away from the door for cover behind desks. The man at the preparation table took a few seconds to move. The lady at the table, who appeared to be hard of hearing, finally moved away from the door after Peterson had already returned and others had sought cover.

Deputy Peterson stated that he waited for Heft to almost reach street level and then announced his identity. Heft turned and shot toward Peterson with a single shot from his revolver. Peterson immediately fired all of the rounds from his .38-caliber revolver.

Witnesses outside on the street and others in a restaurant across the street described the shooting scene. They said Heft dropped the backpack containing the money a short distance from the bank. He then turned back toward the bank and fired his weapon. Someone was shooting at him from the door of the bank. Witnesses thought he was trying to go to get his backpack and money before collapsing on the sidewalk.

Police immediately responded to the scene. However, they did not approach Heft or go into the bank. Officers positioned themselves outside the bank with weapons drawn, using their vehicles for cover. After police dispatchers made calls to the bank, Peterson came to the door and held out his badge and identification. His revolver dangled from the little finger of his other hand as he called out his identity to the uniformed Minneapolis officers.

Crime scene investigators found two bullet holes across the street. One went through a window of a hardware store and the other hit a partition between the two businesses. One citizen walking across the street was grazed by a shot from Peterson, but he refused medical attention.

In a related incident during the crime scene investigation, Minneapolis police arrested a longtime area activist. He used profanity as he complained that police jeopardized innocent lives by provoking a shootout at a busy intersection near the bank. That individual confronted police as they were examining the bullet hole in the hardware store. He was charged with disorderly conduct.

Heft's identity was not immediately determined. His vehicle, a 1973 AMC Gremlin, was located approximately two blocks from the bank. The vehicle had Illinois license plates and a sixteen-channel radio scanner that contained numerous police frequencies. Further investigation determined that Heft had registered at the Minneapolis YMCA on July 21, 1984, using an alias. The room was searched and numerous fictitious identifications were found.

Once Heft's identity was made, it was determined that he was a fugitive wanted by the U.S. Marshals Service for parole violation. Heft had been released from the U.S. Penitentiary at Fort Leavenworth, Kansas, on June 13 and was to report to a halfway house in Grand Rapids, Michigan. Miscellaneous papers in Heft's YMCA room indicated that he had been in Milwaukee and Green Bay, Wisconsin, prior to arriving in Minneapolis. It was suspected that he had robbed a bank in Madison prior to hiding out in Minneapolis.

Deputy Peterson received the Minneapolis Police Department's "Medal of Valor" regarding his actions during the robbery. Minneapolis Chief Anthony Bouza described Heft as "a vicious, dangerous criminal" and said that Peterson "made society safer through his actions."

A Hennepin County grand jury was presented evidence in this shooting to determine if Deputy Peterson should be charged with a crime by indictment. After evaluating the evidence, the grand jury returned a no bill in the case on August 30, 1984. This action exonerates the officer from criminal charges and indicates to the officer that unbiased citizens believe he correctly used deadly force in the incident. This action does not eliminate the possibility of civil charges.

II

On Monday, April 16, 1990, thirty-six-year-old plain clothes Deputy Willis "Will" Purvis of the Blue Earth County Sheriff's Office, Mankato, Minnesota, reported to work at his normal starting time of 7:00 a.m. An officer from a nearby small town had briefed Purvis about a person trying to pick up a young child the previous day. Law enforcement throughout the State of Minnesota was very alert to any information about any attempted child abduction. A young boy named Jacob Wetterling had been kidnapped in a small community in central Minnesota only six months before and had not been found. The FBI had a lead role in the investigation of the Wetterling disappearance, and Purvis wanted to get the information to the local FBI office.

Deputy Purvis called the Mankato FBI office and arranged to have lunch at a convenient place for both parties at 11:30 a.m. Everyone was running late that day and they eventually met at Bobbie Jo's at approximately 11:45 a.m. Bobbie Jo's is located next to the Valley National Bank. FBI agents Dan Hoffman and Dan Miller settled in with Purvis for lunch and to discuss a possible lead in the Wetterling matter.

Typically, as law enforcement officers usually do, they sat in the back of the establishment. Just as they were finishing eating, a young man came running into the back door of Bobbie Jo's shouting, "Someone is robbing the bank." Purvis and Agent Miller ran toward the bank while Agent Hoffman went to the telephone to call 911.

Events leading to this robbery began earlier in the day. A sixty-year-old owner of an automobile garage in Mankato parked his 1980 Ford F100 pickup truck on the street outside his business. He occasionally looked out the window and last recalled seeing his vehicle around 11:00 a.m. He went out to use the truck around 12:20 p.m. and discovered it missing. Unfortu-

nately for him and conveniently for the thief, he left the keys in the overhead visor on the driver's side. He inquired at other business nearby to see
if anyone had seen the truck leave. All responses were negative. On his way
back to his business a business owner stopped him and told him he had just
heard about a bank robbery on his police scanner. When he heard that the
robber had a truck, he thought maybe his truck might have been used. He
called police. He was right. His vehicle was being used for the getaway.

Meanwhile back at the Valley National Bank, twenty-five-year-old
Daniel Joseph Lynch was making his withdrawal by gunpoint. He had
parked the stolen truck just outside the "front" side door to the bank only
a few feet from three drive-up teller lanes. He had entered the bank through
that side door and proceeded to demand money from the tellers working
at the drive-up windows. As he was obtaining money from those tellers,
a customer pulled into a drive-up lane and observed the robbery. He went
on through and parked. He was the person who ran into Bobbie Jo's to
report the robbery.

Purvis and Miller came around the corner of the bank where the drive-
up lanes exit. They entered a door on the backside of the bank. Miller shouted
to the tellers, "Where did he go?" He was told that the robber had gone out
the front door. Miller continued into the bank to follow the robber out the
front door. Purvis went back outside to run past the drive-up teller lanes to
the front door.

Communication is always a problem in any stressful situation and this
was no exception. The "front door" to the bank employees was the side door
where Lynch had entered and had his stolen getaway vehicle waiting. The
"front door" to the two responding officers was the door facing busy Belgrade Avenue.

Deputy Purvis proceeded outside, with his 9-mm handgun drawn, past
the drive-up lanes toward Belgrade Avenue. Agent Miller proceeded through
the bank lobby toward the Belgrade Avenue exit. Purvis saw a blue Ford
truck parked directly outside the side door with the engine running and no

one in it. As he was passing the truck, he observed an individual wearing a disguise and carrying a revolver exit the side door. Purvis stopped and called, "Police, drop it!"

Lynch immediately responded by firing at Purvis. Purvis fired one shot that missed Lynch. Purvis stood by the front passenger side of the truck for cover. Lynch appeared to be trying to get in the driver's door. While attempting to do so, he fired two more shots from his .38-caliber revolver at Purvis. Neither hit Purvis, as they were too high. Purvis could see Lynch crouch down just behind the driver's door using the side of the truck box as cover. All Purvis could see was the top of Lynch's head.

Purvis had just recently attended a training session regarding different types of high-risk situations and shooting scenarios. One thing he vividly remembered was that you did not have to see a person behind cover to shoot. He shot his weapon into the side of the box where he believed he would hit body mass. He fired twice. One round never penetrated the double side of the box. The second one did. Lynch shouted some obscenities, and Purvis knew that he had hit him.

Agent Miller came running around from the Belgrade entrance to the bank when he heard the shooting. Lynch was still crouching on the pavement and had his weapon in his hand when Miller approached him. Miller thought Lynch looked somewhat incapacitated. Miller tackled Lynch and struggled with him. Miller was subsequently able to force Lynch to release the weapon. Purvis came to assist and kicked the weapon away from Lynch.

Purvis went to handcuff Lynch, but he discovered his handcuffs had fallen from his carrying case. He retrieved them a short distance away and gave them to Miller. Purvis then ran to Bobbie Jo's to call 911 on the pay phone just inside the door. He passed Hoffman who was on his way out. Purvis told Hoffman twice, "I shot him!" Nothing else was said as they passed, and Purvis also called 911.

Hoffman ran to assist Miller. Hoffman took the handcuffs from Miller and proceeded to cuff Lynch who was on his stomach by this time. Lynch was turned over on his back, and Hoffman asked him if he was okay. Lynch did not respond.

Hoffman then attempted to go back into the bank to see if there was an accomplice or injuries to any bank personnel. The door was locked. After gaining entry and determining that everyone was safe, Hoffman gave instructions to the employees to close the bank and for each person to write a separate statement about their observations during the robbery. Two months later, Hoffman related that he was asked to be a guest at the bank to discuss what to do during robberies. The bank employees told him that he had shouted the instructions to them the day of the robbery. "I thought that I was speaking in a calm, normal voice" Hoffman later said. He added, "Stressful situations can alter your perceptions."

Lynch was rushed by ambulance to a local hospital where he subsequently died during surgery at 1:33 p.m. He had no identification on him. His only possessions were a wristwatch and a wedding band.

His identity was determined later in the afternoon. It all began with a telephone call to the hospital from a woman identifying herself as Tammy Lynch. She was inquiring about possible treatment to her husband. She was concerned that her husband might have been injured somehow and was at the hospital for medical treatment. She had expected her husband home for lunch at noon. She had called his work and determined that he had left the business for lunch and had not returned. She was concerned for his well-being.

North Mankato Chief Les Ennis and Agent Hoffman proceeded to Lynch's employment with photographs of the unknown robber after the call from Tammy Lynch. Several of the employees at the business positively identified the photograph as that of Lynch. It was determined that Lynch had no criminal record. The inquiry revealed only minor traffic violations.

Following the positive identification of Lynch, law enforcement began a search for Lynch's 1983 Ford Ranger. Officers in the City of Mankato located the Ranger on a street near the business where the getaway vehicle was stolen. The driver's door was unlocked. A leather jacket with numerous keys in the pocket was in the vehicle. A billfold with identification in his name and a checkbook were also located in the truck. The checkbook was for an account at the Valley National Bank in the names of Daniel and Tammy Lynch. The key for the Ranger was not on the key ring in the jacket and was never located.

An autopsy revealed that Lynch died from a gunshot wound to the upper right chest area. Further investigation determined that Lynch did not spend excessively or live beyond his means. He did not abuse alcohol, did not smoke or use any illegal controlled substances. He had attended a technical school and majored in bookkeeping.

He had been employed for five years as a bookkeeper. Apparently, the weapon used in the robbery had been purchased from an acquaintance about a year and a half before the incident.

On May 31, 1990, a grand jury in Nicollet County, Minnesota, heard testimony and received evidence regarding the robbery and shooting death of Lynch. On June 1, 1990, the grand jury reported that no indictment was returned against Deputy Purvis relative to his role in the death of Daniel Lynch.

III

What seemed like an innocent call to the New Brighton (Minnesota) Police Department to report a missing person subsequently resulted in a shooting death by a deputy two months later. On July 7, 2000, the wife of fifty-two-year-old Walter James Kangas reported to police that she and her husband were going through a separation. However, she was concerned for his well being. They had been living together and had agreed to "sit down and talk" on July 3 when she arrived home from work at 5:00 p.m. She had a message that day on her telephone recorder when she arrived home on time from Walter stating, "I thought you were going to be home to talk."

Two days later, on July 5, she received a telephone call from Walter at her residence. During that call Walter told her that she should "throw my bowling balls away in the garbage." (Walter was an outstanding bowler and had won many local tournaments.) He also indicated to her that she was "talking to a dead man" and that he was "going to kill himself by the end of the month." He told her that he was calling from Albert Lea, Minnesota, a city about one hundred miles south of the Minneapolis metropolitan area near the Iowa border. He also told her that he "may call her the night before (taking his life) so she can pick up the car." The police report also indicated that she thought he had a small-caliber handgun with him.

Kangas's wife further informed the police that Walter had been extremely depressed since he had lost his job as a mechanic at a local automobile dealership earlier in the year. He was an alcoholic and could have had his job back with some effort. However, he refused to do so. He had filed for bankruptcy in March 2000. It was later determined that he had almost a thirty-thousand-dollar gambling debt. As with many depressed individuals, Kangas was not prudent with his hygiene. He only showered or bathed once every three to four months.

The whereabouts and actions of Kangas for the next two months are a mystery. The only knowledge that Walter was alive, according to his wife, was reported to the police on July 27. She notified the police that she had been called by the bank and informed that his bank account was overdrawn. She had no telephone contact with him.

September 11 was the next time that anyone would definitely know what Walter was doing and where he was. It was a routine day for the owner of a liquor store in the small town of Waterville, Minnesota, located about sixty miles southwest of the Twin Cities. He parked his 1983 GMC pickup alongside his business about 1:00 p.m. He always parked on the side of the building to allow customers to park in front. He parked next to a 1998 white Chevrolet Astro van. He saw a white male with uncombed messy hair sitting in the van. He did not think much of it and left his keys in the ignition as he always did and went into work. When one of his employees arrived for work at 2:00 p.m., he was asked where his truck was parked. The owner went out and determined that his pickup truck was gone and the van was still there. He immediately reported the theft to authorities. It was further determined that the van had been left outside at a dealership in a southern Minneapolis suburb on Friday, September 8. When mechanics went to the parking area on September 11, it was missing. Kangas apparently stole the van and drove it to Waterville on Monday. He then proceeded in the stolen truck to Hayward, Minnesota, about fifty miles southeast of Waterville and a few miles from Albert Lea.

About 2:00 p.m. Kangas entered the American National Bank, a small branch bank of a larger bank in Albert Lea. There was only one female employee at the bank and he was the only customer. The bank had no surveillance cameras of any kind. He initially approached the teller and then turned his back to her. When he turned back around, he tossed a plastic grocery sack on the counter and said in effect, "We've got a problem!" When the teller asked what he meant, he reached down toward his belt area and produced a small handgun. The teller claimed that it was so small it almost fit entirely into his hand. He then demanded that only fifty and one-hundred-dollar bills be put into the plastic bag. She put some five-dollar bills into the bag, and he again told her that he wanted big bills. She complied.

Kangas exited the bank and entered the stolen truck. The teller was able to get the license of the truck and immediately reported it to the police. A statewide alert went out for the vehicle and related the circumstances of the robbery. His whereabouts was unknown until about 5:00 p.m. A county north of Hayward received a report of a "drunken driver" in a vehicle matching the description of the alert. The license plate for the vehicle was obtained and verified as the stolen getaway vehicle.

Two deputies from the Dakota County Sheriff's Department, the next county north toward the Twin Cities, were notified that the vehicle was proceeding northbound in their direction on a main two-lane highway. The vehicle had last been seen about nine minutes prior to the radio dispatcher advising the deputies. Thirty-four year old Deputy Tom Hooper radioed that he would be heading southbound on that highway. Immediately thereafter, twenty-six-year-old Deputy Jennifer Lenarz advised she had been contacted by a citizen that a vehicle matching the wanted vehicle was driving all over the road and she was going to go north in an attempt to catch up to it.

Lenarz next radioed that she was behind the vehicle and had activated her lights. The truck pulled over near a salvage yard a few miles south of the city of Farmington. Lenarz stayed back from the vehicle as she saw Deputy Hooper coming south toward her location. She was going to wait for him to turn around and assist in the felony traffic stop for safety reasons. The suspect vehicle started back on the road before Hooper got there to assist on the stop.

Deputy Hooper was already accelerating before Lenarz got into the chase so he was able to get in behind the suspect vehicle first. Lenarz was close behind Hooper. Both had their lights and siren activated. They were proceeding about seventy miles per hour toward the City of Farmington. Law enforcement agencies further north were monitoring the chase and readying to place "stop spikes" on the highway at two different locations. When Kangas reached the first set of spikes, he swerved to the right, missing them. The Farmington officer pulled the spikes so the deputies would not run over them.

Kangas continued north until he reached an intersection at the south end of Farmington. He took a right turn onto a paved county road. He then made a quick turn into a driveway of a home in a residential neighborhood and stopped. Both officers chasing him did likewise.

Deputy Lenarz related that she exited her patrol car and saw Kangas a few feet away with a gun drawn. She heard Hooper yell at Kangas. She saw Kangas moving up and down by his vehicle pointing his handgun at Hooper. She then heard one shot. She looked at Hooper and then toward Kangas. She could see that Kangas has fallen down and there was blood on his shirt. Both of them tactically approached Kangas. Hooper kicked a .38-caliber handgun from Kangas' immediate reach and told her not to touch the gun.

Hooper checked for a pulse and Lenarz went to retrieve her medical kit from her vehicle.

Hooper recalled that while he was following Kangas, he could see that he was drinking something. He assumed by his driving that it was alcohol. When Kangas pulled into the driveway of the house, Hooper pulled in about two car lengths behind him. Hooper immediately exited his Dodge Durango. He stopped momentarily while still by the door and reached in and turned the siren off. He drew his .40-caliber handgun. He observed Kangas exit the truck in a peculiar way. Kangas put both feet on the ground and then put his right arm on top of the open door. He appeared to lift himself out of the truck. Hooper then shouted at him, "Put up your hands. Put up your hands!"

Kangas had his right hand up at that time, and Hooper thought the left hand would follow in a similar fashion. He was wrong. Kangas had a .38-caliber revolver in his left hand pointed directly at Hooper. Hooper fired one shot.

Kangas was still there. Hooper had missed and tried to shoot again. The weapon jammed. As Hooper racked the slide to make the weapon operable, Kangas shouted, "You missed." Hooper fired again, and this time he did not miss. Hooper saw Kangas slump down and fall to the ground. He reached into his squad and radioed to "Send an ambulance. One is down." He and Lenarz then approached Kangas and Hooper kicked the handgun out of reach. He asked Kangas twice, "What is your name?" He did not get a response. He immediately asked Lenarz to get the defibrillator while he applied pressure to his chest with a towel from the stolen truck.

Hooper, Lenarz, and a Farmington officer continued to provide medical attention to Kangas. Hooper tried to determine the condition and identity of Kangas through questions, but Kangas did not respond. Paramedics then arrived.

Hooper recalled that he saw "a large wad of money" in Kangas' getaway vehicle when he took out the towel. He did not recall any alcohol containers. Hooper also remembered two individuals standing in the garage of the residence they pulled into. He knew they were not in his line of fire.

An officer from Farmington asked Hooper if he should mark the area with crime scene tape. Hooper answered affirmatively. He then went and stood by his vehicle. He saw that Lenarz was standing by the gun that he had kicked away. A Minnesota State Trooper arrived and went over to the gun also. Numerous officers from other jurisdictions began to arrive.

Investigators found numerous beer cans on the floor of the getaway vehicle. There were also over three thousand dollars, a holster, and a beer can in a plastic sack on the seat of the pickup. An FBI agent at the scene took the money because the bank robbery was in federal jurisdiction.

Kangas was transported to a nearby trauma center where he subsequently died in surgery at 10:08 p.m. An autopsy report indicated that Kangas died from exsanguination due to a single gunshot wound to the chest. The manner of death was homicide. Kangas had a blood alcohol level of .20—twice the legal limit in Minnesota to operate a motor vehicle.

Follow-up interviews are always important in these cases, if only to verify the information provided by the officers involved. The two witnesses in the garage saw the entire incident but were at different angles to the vehicles. The owner of the house was a seventy-year-old retired lady. She described the truck rapidly pulling into her driveway and two police cars "zooming in" right behind it. She recalled the man in the truck staying in the vehicle, but the "policeman" and "policewoman" got out of their vehicles with handguns drawn. She saw the driver's door of the truck open and heard the male officer shout something twice to the man in the truck. She next heard one shot followed momentarily by another. She then saw both officers go to the truck. The male officer said something to the female officer, and she ran to her vehicle. She took something in a container back to the area where the man had fallen. She did not see the man in the truck display a weapon as she could not see him completely.

The other witness in the garage was a sixty-six-year-old man who was working on a lawnmower for the female witness. He also saw the three vehicles arrive. However, he was at a better angle to the getaway vehicle. He saw Kangas exit the truck with a handgun and point it at eye level at the officers. He saw the officers with their guns drawn and the male officer call out, "Put your hands up" twice. He heard the two shots a few seconds apart. He then saw the two officers go to the man who was shot. He saw the female officer return to her vehicle and returned with a "medical bag."

A younger man, somewhat farther away, was training his dog and also substantiated the other two witnesses regarding the demands by the male officer. Another person helping him train the dog basically told the same account.

This matter was presented to a Dakota County grand jury, and a no bill was returned on December 18, 2000, regarding the homicide charge against Deputy Hooper.

IV

Thirty-year-old David Lincoln White grew up in the exclusive area of Shaker Heights, Ohio. Little did his hard-working parents know that he was apparently making his living as a cross-country bank robber. His brother had no idea he was doing anything illegal. White told family members that he had to go on business trips for his clients and could not give them any information in order to protect the clients.

White was familiar with firearms as he had completed the basic police skills training course at Shaker Heights Police Department, according to Chief Walter Ugrenic, but he never applied to become an officer there. Within six months of that training, he applied and was accepted as a recruit at the Cincinnati Police Department (CPD), Ohio. White listed two previous employments on his application to CPD. Both were with investigative firms. One was as a corporate security guard and the other as an investigator involved in undercover and surveillance assignments for a company.

The training at CPD did not go well for White. Officers running the academy requested White's termination in a letter to the chief. They said that White twirled his pistol on his finger like cowboys in western movies and actually pointed his pistol at other recruits soon after the firearms training began. Officers were taught to shoot at body mass, but White continued to shoot head shots even though instructors directed him not to do so. White clearly indicated to trainers that he wanted to take the "kill shot." White refused to follow other directions from instructors and would not assist other classmates. On one occasion a police-training commander saw him beating a heavy dummy in a "violent manner" with his baton during breaks. The letter said, "Again recruit White shows signs of aggression which indicates a potential for a more serious underlying problem." The final determination to remove White from the academy came from the department's psychologist who wrote, "Recruit White does not have the mental stability necessary to face the pressures of law enforcement" (Graves, C. November 21, 2000, "Before Robberies He Dreamed of Police Career," *Star Tribune*, Minneapolis, Minnesota, pp. B1 and B11).

White became the person responsible for what turned out to be the most violent day in the history of the Edina Police Department (EPD). Edina is an upscale suburb of Minneapolis. Just before 10:00 a.m. on Thursday, November 16, 2000, Edina received a call from a citizen with a cell phone that a ski-masked man with a handgun was robbing the Firstar Bank, 6900 France Avenue, near a shopping center and busy business area.

Inside the bank a professional was perpetrating a robbery. White walked in wearing a long leather coat and calmly announced the robbery. He then racked the slide of his semiautomatic handgun to get everyone's attention. He next removed plastic bags from a black and green duffle bag. He told the teller to fill it with money and include no dye packs. After getting money from the first teller, he proceeded down to the next teller and gave her the same instructions. She could not get her cash drawer unlocked due to nervousness. He made her go to the drive-up teller window and get the cash from there. He placed all of the filled bags in the duffle bag and instructed the people to stay in the bank because he did not want to hurt anyone.

He fled the bank and crossed the parking lot to his getaway vehicle, a rented 2001 Ford Explorer. As White approached his vehicle, he spotted twenty-three-year veteran Officer Michael Blood approaching in his marked squad car. Blood, just days from his fifty-third birthday and announced retirement in two months, told the Edina dispatcher at 9:59 a.m. that he was "in the area." He also reported that he had observed a Ford Explorer with no license plates. Officer Shelby Lane also transmitted that she was in the area. About twenty seconds later Officer Blood came on the radio exclaiming, "Officer hit, officer hit, officer hit!" The next transmission was "shots fired."

White had removed a scoped .223-caliber rifle from under his coat and began firing at Blood before he could exit the vehicle or even get his weapon out. Blood was hit in the leg and abdomen. Shelby Lane, only on the department for eight months, rendered aid to Blood. The next call out to dispatch was "officer down." Response was "ten-four, medics en route."

Meanwhile, another twenty-three-year veteran of EPD, Bill Moir, spotted the Explorer about a block away. The forty-nine-year-old officer turned on his lights and siren. White complied by stopping. Moir thought he would just wait with his weapon sighted on the vehicle and "the cavalry (other officers) would arrive." Again, this robber did something the law enforcement officers did not expect. White came out of his vehicle shooting. Moir, using the engine and vehicle as cover from the driver's door, returned fire. Moir stated later, "He was blowing me up!" He also later said that he thought, "What am I doing here?" Moir had the spotlight of his vehicle blown apart by one shot. It was on the door that he was using for cover. He said to himself, "Boy that was close!" Both Moir and White emptied their weapons during this battle.

White entered his vehicle again and sped away. Moir put his car in gear and was surprised to discover that the .223-caliber rounds from White had damaged his engine, rendering it inoperable. Moir was able to radio a good description of the Explorer, saying that he had shot out the rear window. Also, this was the first radio transmission letting other officers know that the robber had a high-powered rifle.

Two other uniformed Edina officers took chase. Thirty-six year old Sgt. Scott Kupyer and twenty-nine-year-old James Rygg pursued White at high speeds for about one and a half miles into a residential neighborhood. The right rear tire of the Explorer blew out and caused the vehicle to spin out of control. White's vehicle stopped crossways in the street. The officers came upon him and stopped parallel to each other facing the passenger side of the Explorer. Kuyper was on the left and Rygg on the right.

Sergeant Kuyper, undoubtedly the best shot on the EPD that day, saw White exit and put the scoped rifle to his chin. Kuyper stated, "I opened up!" White's rifle was empty, and he threw it to the pavement. He fired one round from his 9-mm handgun toward the officers. It was later determined that the 9–mm handgun jammed because of a double feed.

The next series of events are not certain. However, it appears as though White decided to go back to the vehicle to get another weapon or another magazine for the .223-caliber rifle. The duffel bag he used in the robbery was sitting on the front passenger seat of his vehicle. In the duffel bag was another twenty-round magazine for the rifle and the money from the bank robbery. There were also other weapons in the vehicle. The front passenger window of the Explorer had been shattered during this gunfight. Sergeant Kuyper could only see the top of White's head leaning across the vehicle toward the passenger seat. Kuyper took careful aim with his .40-caliber handgun and fired one round. There was no more firing coming from the direction of White's vehicle.

Officer Rygg, with his patrol car as cover, went to the right front of the car and was able to see White lying face down next to the driver's front door. The .223-caliber rifle was out of his reach. The officers tactically approached White. As soon as it was determined that the officers were safe, the next radio transmission was, "Officers ten-four [okay]. Get a medic here now!"

Seven minutes after the call of the robbery and five minutes after the first shots were fired the event was over. The robber was down and incapacitated. Officer Blood was being provided medical assistance and clinging to life.

This bizarre incident did not end with White's death.

A search warrant was executed for the rented Explorer. Recovered in the Explorer was the cash taken from the bank that included prerecorded "bait bills" from the Firstar Bank. His Colorado driver's license was in his wallet, indicating that his address was an apartment in Boulder, Colorado. Several identifications, credit cards, and student identification were also in the wallet. Numerous clothing items, weapons, ammunition, a laptop computer, and miscellaneous notes and journals were found. One page of the journal revealed a list of twelve cities located throughout the country with corresponding dollars amounts next to the cities. What was interesting was a notation and dollar amount next to the city of Edina two years before.

On December 11, 1998, a Twin Cities Federal Bank, located about two miles from the Firstar Bank, was robbed. This robbery was investigated by the FBI and Edina Police and remained unsolved until the events of November 16, 2000. During the 1998 robbery a lone black male entered the bank about 9:15 a.m. wearing a Fedora and ski mask. He racked the slide of his semiautomatic handgun and yelled something to the effect of: "Merry Christmas. This is a robbery. Everybody put their hands up!" This robber continuously shouted orders to the tellers and was very emphatic that he wanted "big bills and no dye packs." A large amount of money was obtained during this robbery. A United Parcel Service driver who had entered the bank during the robbery followed the robber out of the bank. Unfortunately, he lost sight of him. He was able to determine that the robber fled in a bright red Ford Explorer.

Additional items were recovered at Edina. A chrome plated Taurus 9-mm handgun and Sig-Sauer P 220 .45-caliber handgun were found in the Explorer. The most devastating weapon used to injure Blood and destroy Moir's car engine was the chrome Ruger Mini-14 rifle with a folding stock, compensator and scope. Items indicative of changing one's appearance were also located. These included a tan Fedora-style hat, fake mustache, and fake beard.

A search warrant conducted at White's Colorado residence found large amounts of red dye-stained money. The money was most likely obtained during bank robberies he had committed. It was verified from his list of cities that robberies had occurred and dye packs taken. The FBI determined through White's journal and investigation that his bank robbery career more than likely began on April 3, 1998. His robberies were basically carried out in the same manner. He would enter a bank and announce his robbery to everyone there. He always displayed a handgun, wore the same type of disguise, used a duffel bag, and directed that no dye packs be given to him. He was very aware of his surroundings and where police were patrolling. This was evident at a city in Wisconsin. The police in that city had been tipped by an informant that a local person (not White) was planning to rob a bank. The police had surveillance at every bank except one. You guessed it. That bank was robbed. White's journal listed the city and the exact amount of money taken in the robbery. That amount had never been released to the public. The FBI determined that White had robbed at least thirteen banks in California, Minnesota, Ohio, Oregon, and Wisconsin.

Officer Blood's condition was followed closely in the local media. Within the hour prior to the shooting, he had been talking to the dispatchers at the police department about his retirement. The same dispatchers he was joking with handled the transmissions securing the medical assistance for Officer Blood on the radio. It was a very emotional situation for all of them. Blood had been hit four times with rounds from the rifle. He had to have two separate operations of three hours each within the first two days of his hospitalization. He had an additional five operations by the end of the first week. Over seventy pints of blood were needed during all of these surgeries. More than one hundred officers and citizens, some from over two hundred miles away, came to donate blood in honor of him. Edina Police received over two thousand cards from people wishing Blood a speedy and complete recovery.

On June 5, 2001, a Hennepin County grand jury cleared all officers of any charges relating to this incident.

Chapter Two

A Team Effort
aka SWAT Operations

I

Gerald Giesler was no stranger to law enforcement in Dakota County. The thirty-seven-year-old white male had numerous occasions where he was involved with the legal system. On May 11, 1979, he was arrested on a three-count complaint for drug possession (marijuana, cocaine, and LSD) with intent to sell. Later that year he pleaded guilty in a plea agreement to possession of cocaine. The condition of the plea was that he be placed on probation for three years and pay a one-thousand-dollar fine.

Giesler was arrested in July 1987 for possession of hashish. Another plea agreement in February 1988 was negotiated and he received probation for two years. He had to reimburse the Minnesota Bureau of Criminal Apprehension Drug Buy Fund $250 and pay a fine of $330. In April 1989 he entered a plea of guilty to Driving Under the Influence (DUI). He was given one-year probation with four conditions: (1) pay a $440 fine; (2) remain law abiding; (3) evaluation and aftercare; and (4) pay a seventy-six-dollar assessment fee. A note in the record later revealed that the assessment fee was waived. In total, he had four felony drug convictions from 1975 to 1988.

It was no surprise to the Dakota County prosecutor's office when a request was made by a member of the South Metro Drug Task Force in 1994 for a search warrant for illegal possession and distribution of drugs at the Giesler residence. The affiant on the search warrant had information from a confidential informant that Giesler was selling up to a pound of marijuana and hallucinogens from his residence. The source stated that Giesler was being assisted by a friend and his brother Robert Giesler. All three supposedly resided at the residence.

The source also informed officials that Giesler kept trained attack dogs and loaded weapons at his house. Giesler made threats that he would never go back to prison. Investigation also determined that Giesler's friend had controlled substance violations dating back to 1979 and had been arrested for weapons violations, although he was never convicted of that charge. A controlled purchase of illegal drugs was conducted in support of the warrant. A search warrant authorizing entry without announcement and nighttime outside of the hours of 7:00 a.m. to 8:00 p.m. was signed by the District Court Judge.

Careful planning took place prior to executing the search warrant due to Giesler's proclaimed hatred for law enforcement and his possession of weapons. The decision was made to use the Dakota County SWAT team, in assistance to the Task Force. On January 31 the SWAT team leader met at the sheriff's office in order to be briefed on the search warrant. The plan was to meet at the sheriff's office at 4:00 a.m. and proceed to the Giesler home to be searched. It was noted in the file that surveillance of the residence on January 31 observed numerous vehicles coming and going during the evening hours until 9:30 p.m.

The SWAT team met at 4:00 a.m. and proceeded to the residence at 5:45 a.m. A coordinated entry was made at 6:15 a.m. by using a battering ram to break open the main door. Entry was made immediately after a flash bang diversion grenade went off. Deputy Luther Klug was the body bunker person. Following him was Deputy Brad Jeska. Deputy Todd West was immediately behind Jeska with Sgt. Tim Ernst behind him. The assignment of that group, Team One, was to secure the first floor. Team Two was to follow and proceed to the second floor. Jeska was close to Klug, who was illuminating the room with the large quartz light on top of the bunker. In addition to that light, Klug had a flashlight strapped to the bottom of his arm so it would shine wherever he pointed his handgun. After clearing the entry and giving a cursory look in the living room, Team One proceeded to the bedroom, continuously calling out, "Police! Search warrant."

When entry was made into the bedroom, a male later identified as Giesler, was lying on the bed. Jeska repeatedly called, "Police. Search warrant. Put your hands up!" Giesler reached for something with his right hand and momentarily produced a handgun. He did not respond to the commands of the officers and pointed the weapon in the direction of the deputies. Klug fired one round from his .40-caliber handgun. Jeska fired a burst from his MP5 automatic 9-mm. Giesler was still not complying with the demands of the officers and began making movements as if to get up. West fired one round at Giesler from his .45-caliber handgun. Giesler fell. Commands to show his hands finally resulted with him extending his right arm palm up. Following further demands, he extended his left hand exposing the handgun which had been hidden. At that point, Jeska saw Giesler move his hand away from the gun.

Tim Ernst, the supervising sergeant, followed behind team members Brad Jeska, Todd West, and Luther Klug in the search of the main floor, while another team went to the second level of the home. After quickly checking the small entry area of the main floor, the three-person team proceeded to the bedroom, as intelligence indicated Giesler used that room and was not likely to be awake early in the day. Ernst checked the living room next to the bedroom in the event someone was sleeping on the couch or trying to hide. Ernst heard shouting from the bedroom: "Drop the gun, drop it, drop it!" He heard one shot and more commands to "drop it." He then heard more shots.

Ernst then entered the bedroom and observed Giesler lying partly on the bed face down. The three deputies were pointing their weapons at him. Ernst, with his gun in his hand, called to Giesler to put his hands behind his back. Ernst, who then had cover by the other deputies, pulled back Giesler's right hand and observed a pool of blood underneath him. Giesler was groaning as Ernst requested his other arm. An ambulance which was on standby near the home was called to come to the scene. Ernst found a weapon believed to belong to Giesler on the bed. Deputy Jeska removed the weapon, a .22-caliber High Standard revolver, from the bed and placed it on the bedroom dresser.

Robert Giesler was upstairs and gave up without any type of confrontation. Robert claimed his brother did not like guns but kept a low-caliber handgun under his bed. Robert also claimed they only had "a little pot for ourselves." According to Robert, he and Gerald owned ten acres, grew crops, raised chickens, and were trying to breed Rottweiler dogs.

An autopsy determined that Giesler died from gunshot wounds. A Dakota County grand jury returned a no bill regarding this matter. Giesler's father filed a lawsuit regarding the shooting death of Gerald. However, no money was awarded.

Unfortunately, on July 16, 1996, Deputy Klug died in the line of duty. Klug was a defensive tactics instructor, firearms instructor, SWAT team leader, and field training officer. He led the Dakota County Sheriff's Office in Driving Under the Influence and traffics citations. Deputy Klug was within minutes of ending his shift that night when an intoxicated driver looking for a casino hit Klug's squad car. Klug, thirty-six at the time of his death, is survived by his wife and four-year-old son.

II

The rural area of Mille Lacs County, Minnesota, had a fatal shooting on Saturday June 23, 2001. The day began rather innocently with Robert Crawford, a seventy-two-year-old man, attending an auction with his daughter Leslie Holt. Also going to the auction was Leslie's husband, her sister Laurie, and a friend. They returned home around 4:00 p.m. Holt lived in one of the two residences located on the property, the smaller of the two houses west of where her father lived.

After being home for some time, her father came running into her house ranting and raving that he was going to kill her son Michael. He called Michael a "son-of-a-bitch" and stated that he was "going to break his fucking neck." Leslie then went to where Michael was taking down some old trees and planting some other trees. Michael told Leslie that his grandfather threatened him and drove a tractor with a bucket on the front toward him, causing him to jump out of the way to avoid being hit. Crawford began screaming at the two of them, so she told Michael to go to the house. Leslie called 911 regarding his behavior. A deputy from the Mille Lacs County Sheriff's Department responded.

The deputy spoke to Crawford. Paramedics were called because Robert told the deputy that he was not going to take his prescribed medication any longer. It was determined by the deputy that Robert could be taken into the hospital for a seventy-two-hour hold and examination. The ambulance crew was asked to come to the house. Leslie had advised the deputy that she had power-of-attorney for her father and that she was also designated as his health-care agent. She could sign the form to have him taken for the hold. She indicated she feared that he would physically and/or mentally abuse her when he was released.

When the ambulance crew went up to Robert's house, he told them to "get off his fucking property." He continued to tell them that he was not going anywhere. He kept shouting profanities and appeared totally out of control. Leslie observed his behavior and became very distraught over his verbal abuse. The ambulance crew and deputy kept telling him that he was only going to the hospital. Crawford went into the house and nailed his door shut.

The Mille Lacs Special Emergency Response Team (SERT) was called, and preparations were made to enter Robert's house to remove him, as numerous calls to Crawford's cell phone had gone unanswered.

SERT member Bill Hawley, a forty-year-old deputy, would be the first deputy to enter. He would be holding a ballistic body bunker and carrying his 9-mm handgun. Behind him would be Deputy James Osowski carrying an MP5 9-mm, Deputy Terry Boltjes with the flash bang diversionary device, and, lastly, Deputy Reed Bye with a handgun and flash bang. It was decided to use the flash bang outside of the house rather than inside because of Crawford's use of oxygen for his emphysema. The same reasoning was used for the decision not to gas the residence, as Leslie told the deputies that Robert had numerous tanks of oxygen in the house.

Hawley was the first to enter. The first thing he recalled hearing was, "I'm going to kill you!" Everything seemed to be in slow motion as he entered. He saw Crawford sitting back almost as if on a counter. Hawley could see through the shield on his body bunker that he was holding a shotgun. Hawley called out, "Sheriffs Department! Drop the gun." Crawford shouted back very loudly, "I'm going to kill you!" Hawley moved to his left as he entered. He could see Crawford "tracking" him with the shotgun as he moved. Hawley shouted at him to "drop the gun!" When Crawford failed to comply with the order, Hawley, fearing for his life, fired his weapon at Crawford. Crawford fell to the floor, with the shotgun falling away from his reach.

Hawley dropped his body bunker over the shotgun and placed himself in a guarded position over Crawford. He then began shouting for the paramedics to come in to attend to Crawford. He did not hear anyone else fire. However, he later discovered that Deputy Osowski also fired his weapon.

Deputy Osowski, the thirty-eight-year-old team leader of SERT, told investigators that when he entered the residence he observed a white male matching the description furnished to him of Crawford tracking a shotgun at Deputy Hawley. He heard Hawley call for him to drop the gun and then heard a shot from Hawley. Osowski then fired two bursts from his MP5 at Crawford.

Leslie told the investigating officers of the shooting, "I wanted to keep my father around for a long time and I feel sorry for the officers who had to shoot him because I think my father was on a suicide mission...he had watched my mother die; she had cancer and so he watched her die, and he was not going to go that way."

This situation matter was closed by a grand jury no bill.

III

Thirty-four-year-old deputy Dennis Lasher of the Crow Wing County Sheriff's Department began his shift approximately 9:45 p.m. on Friday, July 24, 1998. Lasher had six years' experience as a deputy and was an MP in the Army for three years prior to his employment as a deputy. He was to respond to the same City of Crosby (population three thousand) to execute a search warrant for narcotics and firearms. Investigation by Officer Nicole Yarke-Redding of the Crosby Police Department determined that there was probable cause to believe that forty-one-year-old Michael Truchinski was involved in illegal drug activities and stolen firearms.

When he arrived in Crosby, an individual familiar with the residence briefed the entry team of the house layout. The residence had a split entry. There was a small landing just inside the front door. There was a staircase on the right going immediately upstairs and there were stairs to the left that went to the basement. Lasher was to be the first to enter of the six-person entry team. His assignment was to go upstairs to clear the rooms. Two additional officers were to accompany him to the upstairs area.

Deputy Lasher went to the door and determined that he could not turn the handle. He decided to kick at the door to open it. The door was very solid, and he did not open it with his first kick. He and the next officer, Dean Savor, both began kicking at the door. The door eventually opened and Lasher proceeded in and up the stairs as his assignment dictated. He yelled twice, "Sheriff's Department. Search warrant," as he was proceeding up the stairs. The residence was completely dark, and his only light was his flashlight. Two officers were following him. At the top of the few steps was the living room area.

Lasher scanned the living room to make sure it was clear before he proceeded down the hallway to the bedrooms. Lasher saw a white male, later identified as Michael Truchinski, on a couch lying on his right side. Lasher believed at that moment that it was Truchinski based on the description furnished to him. Truchinski was a large man, only five-foot-nine but weighing 270 pounds. Lasher called to Truchinski, "Let me see your hands." Lasher had his flashlight on Truchinski, but his hands were underneath a coffee table in front of the couch. Lasher continued to request to see his hands. Truchinski raised his right hand in the air but kept his left hand out of Lasher's sight.

Truchinski began to sit upright, and it was at this point that Lasher observed what he believed to be a Colt .45 semiautomatic handgun in his left hand. Lasher shouted for him to "drop the gun!" Truchinski said something to Lasher. However, Lasher did not recall or understand what he said. Lasher continued ordering him to drop the weapon. Lasher told investigators that he next remembered looking "directly inside the barrel of the gun." That is when Lasher decided to fire his .40-caliber Glock handgun at Truchinski.

Truchinski dropped the weapon, doubled over, and rolled off the couch. Lasher and Chad Visser of the Crosby Police Department approached Truchinski. The weapon was a good distance from Truchinski, and Visser appeared to have control of the scene. Lasher immediately turned and went down the hallway to check the bedrooms. He recalled Visser calling over the radio at this time that shots had been fired and requesting an ambulance. After determining there no other occupants in the area, he returned to check the status of Truchinski.

The downstairs area was still being checked by Sgt. Tim Leonard of his department. Lasher assisted him in clearing that area. Lasher then returned to his vehicle for approximately two minutes. Sergeant Leonard then came to him and requested that he go to Crosby City Hall. Lasher asked Leonard if he wanted his weapon and Leonard said, "Yes." He did as directed and then went to the hospital to provide blood and urine samples.

It was determined that Truchinski was shot once in the right chest area. He was unconscious when medical responders arrived. He was later transported to the Hennepin County Medical Center trauma unit in Minneapolis. He died from the wound on Sunday, July 26.

The weapon in Truchinski's possession was a Browning semiauto 9 mm. Lasher's one shot hit him in the chest. The BCA crime scene investigation found the one .40-caliber shot from Lasher's gun. Other officers at the scene told BCA investigators that they had heard Lasher shouting, "Show me your hands," before they heard one shot.

In August, 1998, a grand jury heard evidence in this matter and did not return an indictment against Deputy Lasher.

IV

This next incident is true, as a fiction writer could not have imagined anything so bizarre.

I was at the Minneapolis Police Department homicide unit discussing a case with the supervising lieutenant on March 17, 1989. Sometime after 9:00 a.m. one of the homicide detectives came into the lieutenant's office with information regarding an escapee from the Stillwater State Prison. Larry Hill, a forty-nine-year-old inmate serving a twenty-seven-year sentence for killing his girlfriend, had escaped custody while at the Medical Arts Building in downtown Minneapolis. To make this even more unbelievable, Hill is blind and he was at the clinic to be fitted with prosthetics for his eyes. Of course, he could not do it by himself; he had an accomplice. Forty-seven-year-old Willie Johnson, who had been incarcerated with Hill, was aware that Hill was coming to the clinic to be fitted for the prosthetics. Johnson approached two unarmed correctional officers with a gun at the clinic. He demanded Hill's release, and they made their escape.

Hill had been in and out of prison for over twenty years and had previously escaped from correctional facilities three times. Before moving to Minneapolis from Chicago around 1975, Hill had served a year in an Illinois prison for rape and robbery. In Minnesota, he served time for burglary, raping a woman at knife point, illegally possessing a handgun, and murder of his fiancée in 1982. He became legally blind in 1980 from glaucoma. His criminal record revealed that he strangled his fiancée and stuffed her into a closet. It should also be noted that Hill was a large man—standing six-foot-four and weighing almost three hundred pounds.

Hill and Johnson then drove approximately twenty miles to the southern suburb of Apple Valley so Hill could visit Lois Platt, a former pen pal while he was incarcerated. Platt related to *Saint Paul Pioneer Press* reporter Kate McEnroe (March 21, 1989) that she became acquainted with Hill in 1987. A friend who had a boyfriend at Stillwater Prison asked her if she would talk to Hill. Platt talked to him over the telephone, wrote him letters, and visited him at Stillwater. Her daughter Cameo, age six, and son Dominic, age nine, had met Hill, as Platt had taken them to the prison when she visited him. Platt said that she assumed he was in prison for having a handgun. She called the prison regarding his release date and discovered it was scheduled for the year 2000. The prison official told her about his conviction for the murder of his fiancée. She decided to terminate her contact with Hill at that time, late 1987 or early 1988. He told Platt, "If she couldn't see me, no one else would." He would occasionally call her, and she thought it would do no harm as "he was locked up."

Platt told investigating officers after the ordeal ended that around 10:15 a.m. that Friday morning her son Dominic called at work and said Hill was at her townhouse in Apple Valley. She told her boss she had to go home because someone she knew had been released from prison. Platt assumed Hill somehow had been released on parole and had no idea that he had escaped. She arrived at her house only to discover Hill along with Willie Johnson. Hill put a knife to her throat and took her to the upstairs bedroom where he forcefully assaulted her.

Her fiancé came home about 4:30 p.m. that afternoon and encountered Johnson and Hill. Johnson threatened him with his gun. He quickly determined what was happening and was able to escape. He immediately called Apple Valley police.

Apple Valley police quickly responded and determined that there was a hostage situation in their city. Telephone contact was established and at-tempts were being made to get Platt and her children released. SWAT teams from the area and additional negotiators were called to assist. Television crews and mobile satellite trucks were rushed to scene. The nightly news on all of the channels was live at Apple Valley with Apple Valley Police Captain Terry Cook as the spokesperson.

As a crisis negotiator for the FBI, Agent Mike Goergen and I had trained the officers who were actively negotiating with Hill. It appeared on the news reports that they were doing everything to peacefully and safely resolve the situation. It was interesting as a negotiator to hear on the news that the power to the house had been turned off in attempt to get them to surren-der. This is a ploy which is often used by negotiators to get the hostage taker to surrender or to give up a demand or a hostage in order to get the power restored. The temperature was about zero and there were approximately eight to ten inches of snow on the ground.

On Saturday morning the media reported from the scene that the power had been restored. However, there had been no progress. I received a call from the FBI office around 4:00 p.m. that the Apple Valley police had requested as-sistance from the FBI negotiators and SWAT team, as time was taking a toll on the local teams. I responded, as did Agent Goergen. The Command Post was located in the same townhouse complex. This was the residence of a trooper with the Minnesota State Patrol. It was a two-bedroom home. The negotiators were in one bedroom, and the technical experts were in the other bedroom recording the conversations with Hill. The living room/family room was the location where the commanders of nearby police departments and Dakota County Sheriff's Department held discussions and strategy decisions. There were SWAT officers around the perimeter of the townhouses and one in a second level townhouse who had a visual of the Platt townhouse.

It was decided that this would be a good time to introduce Agent Go-ergen as the lead negotiator, with me acting as his secondary. Also present in the bedroom of the negotiators was Steve Gieger, a former police officer and psychologist, who was an advisor to the Minneapolis FBI and Minneapolis Police Department's negotiation teams. Goergen was able to establish telephone dialogue with Hill around 5:00 p.m.

A significant development had occurred during the day. Negotiators were able to convince Hill (who was doing ninety-nine percent of the talking) around noon to let Platt come out to the garage area to get her car. The garages for the townhouses were located in a separate structure not attached to the building of the townhouses. The plan was to disable the car and get Platt out of the situation. Hopefully, Hill would then decide to give up. The plan worked to an extent. Platt was able to be freed and under police protection. Unfortunately, Hill became very agitated. Negotiations were strained with Hill for some time.

Hill was upset with the way things had been going for him. Negotiations with him were mainly about his being treated unfairly by the Minnesota Department of Corrections and law enforcement in general. We all recalled how upset he was about the prison not allowing him to attend his mother's funeral in Chicago. (We were all surprised when his mother was interviewed by reporters in Chicago on the Sunday after his death). It was very obvious that he had lied.

At one point Goergen asked to speak to Willie Johnson. When asked by Goergen what he thought of the situation, he replied that he was behind Hill one hundred percent and wanted the police to start meeting his demands. This statement by him (the conversation was recorded) was a deciding factor during his trial in Duluth as he tried to convince the jury that it was all Hill's idea. It did not work, and he was found guilty.

Goergen arranged to have a car come to the front door to allow him to leave with Johnson. Of course, a "kill switch" would be attached to the vehicle so it could be stopped before they got away. Everything seemed to be in order, and then Hill changed his mind. It seemed that every time Hill agreed to something (a getaway car or release of a hostage), he would change his mind just before it happened.

The commanders and negotiators decided to end the situation. The plan was to offer him some food as a "good faith" attempt. Hill quickly agreed to the delivery of some pizza. A SWAT member would place the pizza box about six feet from the front door. When Johnson exited to get the pizza, SWAT would grab him and other members would quickly enter the house and get Hill before he could react. Unfortunately, the SWAT member slipped on the ice around the side of the house and Johnson got back into the house before he was captured. Luckily, Johnson did not see the SWAT person slip or attempt to get him.

Now we had to address the situation again. It was after 1:00 a.m. on Sunday (actually Palm Sunday). The negotiating team discussed alternatives with the commanders. It was decided to see if we could get Johnson to come out to get a can of soda. Goergen called back and asked Hill if he would like some soda as we had forgotten to include them in haste during the delivery. Of course, he was more than happy to get something else from us. The decision was made to separate the six-pack so Johnson would have to pick each one individually and give the SWAT person more time to secure him.

The cans were delivered, and Johnson came out to retrieve them. The SWAT member came around the corner and grabbed him. Unfortunately, he was able to break away. The decision had been made that if that happened, we were committed to carry out the assault. Other SWAT members hit the door with a battering ram. It opened immediately and a diversionary device (flash-bang) was thrown into the residence.

Johnson gave up right away. Hill, who had been talking with Goergen during all of this, dropped the telephone and grabbed Cameo, as he was right next to him. He backed away from the commotion of the shouting by Johnson and the SWAT members. He was holding her up to his chest with his left arm and holding a knife to her throat with his right hand. He shouted at officers to stay back. Dakota County SWAT deputy Todd West fired once with his .357-caliber revolver. He hit him directly in the head, killing him instantly. Cameo was not injured. Momentarily a SWAT officer transmitted that the kids were safe and unharmed, one was in custody, and medics were needed as one of the subjects was shot. Cheers went up in the command post because of the safe recovery of the children.

A Dakota County grand jury cleared West in April 1989 as a no bill was returned. Johnson stood trial in Duluth because of a change of venue. He was convicted of numerous felonies relating to the incident and returned to Stillwater prison where he and Hill had become friends.

V

Occasionally a SWAT team will be asked to assist other jurisdictions. This was the case on August 6, 1999. A search warrant had been issued in U.S. District Court by the Honorable Earl Cudd on August 5. The warrant was to search the farm and surrounding out buildings of Robin M. Emmert, a thirty-seven-year-old white male living in Hancock, Minnesota, in rural Pope County. The warrant was for drugs, specifically the manufacture of methamphetamine.

The intelligence received by an investigator was that Emmert had mental health issues. Neighbors described him as a good neighbor when he was "stable." Unfortunately, he did not always take his medicine and would do things out of the ordinary. Neighbors would hear gunfire from his residence. Emmert would tell neighbors he was only shooting stray dogs. He was known to own weapons and actually displayed a .357-caliber revolver to a neighbor which he kept under the seat of his pickup truck.

Other rumors had him cutting the head off one of his cows with a chainsaw. He believed there were people spying on him, and he was described as "shooting at shadows." Emmert also related to others that he saw flashing lights in his silo that people were using while they were loosening the bolts holding the silo together. He had actually climbed into the silo and used a welder to spot weld each nut on the bolts so the silo would remain stable.

Family members were aware that Robin had threatened bill collectors and feed dealers with a handgun to get them to leave his residence. It was also rumored that he stole a tank of anhydrous ammonia from the local

Farmers Union. With this in mind, the Minneapolis Police Department SWAT was requested to assist in securing the residence in order for the warrant to be executed. Members of the team were briefed and advised that Emmert might be armed with a .357-caliber revolver and/or shotgun. The SWAT team traveled to Morris, Minnesota, and had a final meeting regarding strategy at 6:00 p.m. on August 5.

An advance team was dropped off at 2:50 a.m. near the property. There were two three-person teams. One team consisted of Officers Tim Hanks, David Clifford, and Team Leader Sgt. Mike Young. The purpose of this team was to attempt to determine if Emmert was present at the residence. Officers Hanks and Clifford set up in an area on the south side of the feed barn located on the property near the house. Sergeant Young was continuing his reconnaissance of the area. Hanks had night vision goggles and moved to get a view of the front door of the house.

Sergeant Young was going to meet the other three-person team and inform them of the situation at the house. Young left Hanks and Clifford around 5:20 a.m. to walk southbound toward the entry to the driveway from a main road. Young was checking out the area of the driveway, and the sun was just beginning to come up.

Officer Clifford had a twenty-power scope on the .308-caliber rifle which he had in addition to his Beretta 9-mm pistol. He could see the front porch of the house. Sergeant Young was out of his view for about five minutes. Suddenly, Emmert came out onto the front porch. Emmert appeared irate and was yelling, "What are you doing here? What do you want?" Clifford was not certain where Young had gone; but he knew the general area. Emmert then went back into his house. Clifford informed the other members of the situation and that they had possibly been compromised.

The officers stayed in their location. Several minutes later Emmert came back out of the house carrying something. Clifford was not initially certain what it was, but believed it to be a long-barreled weapon. Emmert was again shouting, "What do you want? What are you doing here?" He seemed more agitated than before. Emmert walked back and forth on the porch. Clifford looked at him through his scope and described him as having a "confused, mean look." Emmert was screaming at that point and then suddenly returned into the house.

Sergeant Young advised via radio that he did not believe he could get out of his location without being seen by Emmert. The second team on the road was also aware of the situation. The ideal situation would be for the second team to drive to the edge of the driveway and Young to sprint to the police van, escaping undetected. It was decided that this is what Young would do.

Just then Emmert came back out; it was certain he was carrying what appeared to be a shotgun. Clifford immediately advised the other team members. Young let everyone know that he was pinned down and could not get away from his location. He related that Emmert would be able to see him if he came to where he was hiding in some high weeds. Emmert shut the door to his house and locked it. He appeared to be manipulating a series of locks on the door as if he were setting booby traps or some type of alarm.

Clifford was able to see that Emmert was waving the shotgun around with one hand on the pistol grip. He was pacing and pointing the shotgun in the direction of Young's hiding place. It appeared he was certain someone was located there and he was going to find out for certain. Suddenly Emmert turned and began walking toward Clifford and Hanks. They had no avenue of escape, as they were trapped inside an outside building. If they tried to exit, Emmert would see them. Clifford got up with his 9-mm pistol in his hand and called, "Police, search warrant. Drop the gun! Drop the gun!" Emmert and Clifford apparently fired simultaneously. Clifford believed he had been shot, as he was hit by the shotgun wad and "could feel the rush over his head of pellets" as they went by him.

Clifford saw Emmert fall backwards to the ground and immediately get back up and shoot at him again. Clifford radioed that he thought he was hit. He saw Emmert get behind a large steel barrel located in the yard. Clifford heard him say, "Hey."

Clifford responded by saying, "Police, I don't want to kill you. Drop the gun!" Clifford then heard Hanks fire his weapon. Hanks told investigators that he saw Emmert attempting to rack his shotgun so he fired his 9-mm weapon at Emmert.

Clifford waited a few seconds and, with Hanks covering, approached Emmert. Clifford could see Emmert slumped on the ground with his back to him. He could also see the butt stock of the shotgun pointing away from Emmert and his finger not on the trigger. Clifford pulled the shotgun far away from Emmert's immediate reach. The chamber of the shotgun was open as if Emmert was attempting to chamber another round. They waited for backup from other officers, as they were not certain if there was anyone else in the house. Other officers and medical assistance arrived momentarily.

Emmert was dead at the scene from multiple gunshot wounds. It was determined that Clifford had only been hit with the shotgun wad. Minnesota Bureau of Criminal Apprehension agents investigated the shooting and presented the case to the Pope County Attorney Belvin Doebbert. Doebbert declined prosecution on October 21, 1999, as "evidence is insufficient to warrant charges against officers Clifford and Hanks, it is also concluded that the State lacks evidence sufficient to support a finding of criminal culpability on the part of any other officer present on the scene August 6, 1999."

VI

Just after midnight on September 27, 1995, officers of the Itasca County Sheriff's Office and Grand Rapids Police Department attempted to serve a federal search warrant at the residence of Gregory Glynn, a thirty-seven-year-old ex-con, who was suspected of a recent bank robbery in Minnesota. Also present at that time was FBI Agent Bob Harvey. Sheriff Pat Medure called Glynn in an attempt to get him to open the door. Glynn refused and indicated to Sheriff Medure that he had an "arsenal." The upstairs of the dwelling of the apartment building was evacuated as negotiators began to attempt to talk Glynn from the residence. A perimeter was established by the two agencies. Around 4:00 a.m. the Emergency Response Team from the Saint Louis County Sheriff's Office from Duluth came and set up in the area also. A total of six officers, from three separate jurisdictions, were located on the perimeter.

Negotiations continued with Glynn to convince him to come out of the apartment. The negotiators had the phone changed so no calls could be received on the phone except from the negotiators. Glynn became very upset over this arrangement as he wanted other people to be able to call in to him. He demanded that the phone be activated to operate normally or "something's gonna happen." He also told negotiators that he wanted to talk to his sister. He wanted his sister to give him his last rites and then he would call the negotiators back. Previous contacts by law enforcement with Glynn made it known to them that he was armed and dangerous and also suicidal. Negotiators determined through calls to him that he claimed to have a SKS assault rifle, a shotgun, and a pistol. Glynn kept telling officers that he was not going to be taken alive. Glynn claimed that if he was shot and wounded, he would shoot himself so the "Feds" could not. Because of his threats to shoot officers and/or himself, the officers on the perimeter were advised that deadly force could be used if felt necessary. Between 4:30 a.m. and the break of daylight the officers on the perimeter radioed that a person (Glynn was believed to be the only person in the building) would open a blind on the window and look out. That happened several times. On one occasion the door inside the storm door opened approximately two inches. After a few minutes, it closed again.

At approximately 8:10 a.m. the inside door opened all the way, and immediately the storm door opened. Glynn, wearing a long black trench coat and long hair tied into a ponytail, came out the doorway and onto the sidewalk in front of the building. He pulled a large-caliber handgun from behind his back in his right hand. Officers shouted three to four times, "Police. Drop the weapon. Put your hands in the air!" Glynn just stood unresponsive to the commands. Momentarily, he began walking toward a major traffic avenue in the city. Daylight had come, and people were starting to move about. One man close by appeared to be getting his boat ready to go fishing. A major U.S. highway was only a block away, and officers on the inner perimeter could see onlookers beginning to gather. Additional officers were called to direct traffic away from the area.

Glynn started bringing his weapon up toward the officers. The lead officer gave the command to shoot. The sniper, about seventy-five yards away with his .308-caliber rifle, heard the command and fired his weapon once. The shot hit Glynn in his lower neck area. He was still moving when five other officers on the inner perimeter began firing. Glynn went down and was pronounced dead at the scene. Officers Brent Bradley, Frank Scherf from Grand Rapids Police Department, Dean Scherf from Itasca County Sheriff's Office, Joseph Skofich, William Henegmon, and Randall Lehman from the St. Louis County Sheriff's Office all fired their weapons during the indicent.

Itasca County Prosecutor Jack Muher declined prosecution of the officers involved in the shooting.

VII

Forty-nine year-old Donald Gross was often unemployed and had difficulty coping with the normal routine of life. He continually failed to make child support payments for children whom he had fathered with two women. When his first wife took him to court in 1986, he told the Hennepin County court referee that he never intended to work again so he would not have any income to pay child support. When his second wife said she was divorcing him, he told people he was not only losing a wife but also his source of income. Ironically, this wife's income came from a company called Varitronics Systems—the place where he would be shot to death by Brooklyn Park Police Department SWAT members.

The events of July 29, 1992, actually began on Tuesday, July 28. Gross took his wife hostage and raped her at her apartment around 6:30 a.m. He finally released her near 11:00 a.m. She immediately called the Brooklyn

Center Police Department to report what had happened. Her apartment was located in the City of Brooklyn Center. Police set up surveillance on Donald Gross's apartment on the north side of Minneapolis.

He picked up his fourteen-year-old son from a neighbor's house around 2:00 p.m. Police saw him in his pickup truck and attempted to stop him. He fired at police, and one round "exploded" the spotlight on the driver's side of the patrol car during the chase. The chase and shots fired were broadcast, and adjacent departments became involved. The chase went for about five miles. A roadblock was set up by Brooklyn Park Police, and when Gross came upon them, he fired at them and avoided being stopped.

Gross continued and eventually drove up to the main doors of Varitronics Systems in Brooklyn Park. He held his son as a shield and was holding his revolver when he entered the main doors of the building. His wife had already been removed from the building by police, and 120 additional employees immediately fled upon hearing of his entry. Other employees who had been hiding left in small groups when circumstances allowed. Police also assisted others in various locations throughout the building to flee. The building was surrounded by officers from several adjacent police departments as well as deputies from the Hennepin County Sheriff's Office.

Negotiations were established with Gross. Attempts were made to get him to release his son and surrender. The conversations with him were brief and without much progress until around 10:30 p.m. At that time he allowed his son to come out. His son had with him his father's wallet and glasses. Unknown to law enforcement, there was also a note to his family. The plan was to just wait it out and he would eventually surrender. However, a shot rang out from inside after midnight. Police were not sure if he had shot himself or some other unknown employee remaining in the building.

A six-man team of the Brooklyn Park Police SWAT team was already in another part of this large building. They heard the shot and a moan. They began going room to room, and eventually around 1:30 a.m. came to the company's chemical lab room. They found that it was barricaded. They were able to open the door and introduced tear gas. Requests were made for Gross to come out to them and surrender.

Gross failed to come out so the SWAT team entered. Two of the officers held body bunker shields in one hand and 9-mm pistols in the other. The other four members of the team carried an MP5 9-mm automatic weapon. Gross was spotted lying on his back, eyes closed, and his hands folded over his .44-caliber revolver on his chest. They began calling for him to raise his hands. He did not move. Initially thinking that he had killed himself, the members were shocked when team member Wade Setter yelled, "He's alive."

Gross opened his eyes and sat up. Some members of the team thought he was going to make them watch him kill himself. Rather than doing that, Gross turned the gun away from himself toward the officers. Five of the six members fired their weapons, killing Gross instantly. One officer with an MP5 did not shoot. The Brooklyn Park officers involved in the shooting were Terry Huntington, Jeff Jindra, Steve Pearson, Kent Blum, and Steven Baker.

An autopsy revealed that Gross died of multiple gunshot wounds. He had caused over one million dollars worth of damage in the Varitronics building, and it was closed for a week. After the shooting took place the note brought out by his son was revealed to the police. The note in part read as follows:

> *I'm at Sharon's job and the cops are all around the place. I can't get to jail any more. I'm to old. Thanks a lot Sharon for call the cops on me. I never thought that you would do this. I love you all and well see you in Heven with god.*

A Hennepin County grand jury returned a no bill on October 20, 1992.

VIII

SWAT teams and the department's negotiators often train together so the use of deadly force does not have to be instituted. On Sunday, August 25, 1996, the Saint Paul Police negotiators and Critical Incident Response Team

(CIRT) responded to a Command Post that had been established to await instructions regarding Freddie Lee Bowen, a fifty-five-year-old carpet installer who had just killed his girlfriend. He had fled to the area of Snelling Avenue between Portland and Summit on the far west side of Saint Paul.

Information received at the Command Post was that Bowen had killed forty-one-year-old Yvonne Thompson in the hallway of her nearby apartment building. A witness at the apartment visiting a friend told responders to the apartment that she heard high-pitched screams. She went into the hallway and came upon Thompson. Thompson told her that she needed help and related that someone was after her with a gun. The witness was with Thompson when Bowen cornered them. The witness was able to get away but then heard five gunshot rounds. Thompson had been shot in the arm and head.

Bowen ran from the apartment after shooting Thompson. He was running through traffic on busy Snelling Avenue. Police were responding to the area on a report of a domestic when a Saint Paul squad confronted Bowen. He had his weapon displayed, but the police were able to isolate him on the street. A six-block area was then cordoned off by police.

The initial response of two teams (one negotiator and one CIRT) was established at 2:07 p.m. The CIRT team deployed as four separate teams of four officers. Their specific duties were to observe Bowen and report his activities. Discussion with the negotiators related that Bowen had specific options: (1) commit suicide; (2) surrender and go to prison; or (3) force the police to shoot him (suicide by cop). The negotiators further stated they believed he would not surrender.

The following are selected narratives of the events recorded by police:

2:45 p.m.—Bowen crawling around on the ground.

2:53 p.m.—Bowen puts his gun in mouth.

3:05 p.m.—Negotiators report that TV helicopter was orbiting the area. The noise was preventing negotiators from talking with Bowen and was agitating Bowen.

3:10 p.m.—Call made to TV to get helicopter out of area.

3:15 p.m.—Helicopter departed.

3:35 p.m.—Bowen crawling around on ground with gun in hand.

3:40 p.m.—Bowen standing with gun in hand.

3:50 p.m. —Negotiators report that they were at an impasse with negotiations.

3:52 p.m.—Bowen threw bag at one of the CIRT teams and asked them to read the contents.

3:53 p.m.—CINT could not safely retrieve bag. Negotiators asked Bowen to put his gun down. He would not do so.

4:05 p.m.—Bowen puts his gun to his head.

4:15 p.m.—Negotiators ask Bowen to move further north so they would not have to shout at him—he refused.

4:17 p.m.—Bowen appeared to be trying to go to sleep.

4:18 p.m.—Negotiators said they would stop trying to negotiate with him for thirty minutes to let him sleep.

4:20 p.m.— Bowen not sleeping, would pop head up and look around.

4:28 p.m.—Bowen stood up and looked around, then lay back down.

5:10 p.m.—Bowen walking around for seven minutes pointing his gun in various directions.

5:22 p.m.—Bowen puts gun to his head and will not talk to negotiators.

5:30 p.m.—Bowen identity officially determined.

5:40 p.m.—CIRT begin practicing arrest procedure.

5:50 p.m.—Attempts to negotiate negative: Bowen will not respond.

5:55 p.m.— Bowen shouts, "It's not going to be long now."

6:04 p.m.—Command Post orders CIRT to activate arrest plan.

6:05 p.m.—Diversion device delivered and shots heard. Medics requested by CIRT team leader Jeff Winger.

6:06 p.m.—Scene secure. Suspect with medics and leaving area.

6:32 p.m.—Command Post notified that Bowen was dead on arrival at Regions Hospital.

CIRT members on the arrest team began to approach Bowen from a distance of approximately thirty yards. There were four approaching officers: Steve Anderson carrying a body bunker and a .40-caliber Glock pistol; to his right was Sgt. Jeff Winger using a .12-gauge shotgun; to Anderson's left was John Wright carrying a body bunker and .40-caliber Glock pistol; to Wright's immediate left was Carl Schwartz, also using a .12-gauge shotgun. Two distraction devices were deployed. Bowen, who had been lying on his stomach, began to get up to his feet and turned toward the CIRT team.

Anderson saw a black handgun in Bowen's right hand and called for him to drop the gun. When it appeared that Bowen was going to fire toward the team, Anderson fired his pistol three times. The other three officers also called for Bowen to drop his gun. Sergeant Winger saw Bowen's movement with the gun and fired his shotgun from a distance of about fifteen yards. Officers Schwartz and Wright responded to the threat and also fired their weapons. Bowen fell to the ground.

When it was determined safe, Sgt. David Korus began to perform first aid. Medics immediately came in and removed Bowen.

An autopsy determined that Bowen died from exsanguinations due to multiple gunshot wound. Bowen had a Lorcin 9-mm pistol with one round in the chamber and four in the magazine.

A Ramsey County grand jury cleared the officers in September 1996.

IX

Unfortunately, domestic situations boil over to involve law enforcement. Occasionally SWAT teams have to be called and deadly force is necessary. This happened again in the southeast area of Duluth, Minnesota, on Friday, May 26, 2001. The history of this relationship is important to understand this incident.

James Balen was introduced to Patti Ward by a mutual friend in 1991. This relationship was not romantic until 1998. Balen moved into Ward's house. He was unemployed, but had been receiving workers' compensation and Social Security disability as a result of a construction accident while employed in Colorado. The relationship was described as "normal" and "peaceful." At times, Balen's son, Michael Balen, lived with them. Supposedly Michael was abused by James and placed in a Duluth shelter. He then returned to live with his mother in Colorado. Balen also had a daughter living in Colorado.

The relationship was going well for Ward and Balen until she became pregnant in March 2000. Balen supported her decision to have the baby. However, he had begun to abuse prescription drugs and alcohol. On December 13, 2000, their son, Chance Allen Ward-Balen, was born. Three days after his birth, Balen moved out of her house. In February 2001, she had an Order for Protection filed against him.

On May 22, 2001, she received a call from Balen who was in the Sterling County Sheriff's Office, Colorado. He told her he had been arrested regarding a violation of an Order for Protection and burglary. Balen wanted her to wire money to him at the jail for bail. She attempted to transfer the money. However, she was unable to do so because the account was in his name only.

There was no communication with him after the failed attempt to transfer the money on the May 22 or 23. On Thursday, May 24, he called her and told her that he was back in Duluth. She received numerous calls from him between 4:00 p.m. and midnight relating to the custody and visitation rights of Chance.

Calls began again on May 25 between 10:00 a.m. and 9:00 p.m. The calls became very harassing. He called her derogatory names such as "bitch" and others. The calls were either from his cell phone or "C J's," a tavern across the border from Duluth in Oliver, Wisconsin. During one of the calls, Ward's roommate, Barb Lewandowski, talked to Balen. Balen threatened to break Lewandowski's arms. When Lewandowski had to go to work that afternoon, Kurt Olson, a good friend, came to her house for Ward's protection.

Lewandowski returned to the house when she finished work. Other friends (a married couple) also arrived. The couple said that they had been to C J's and had seen Balen. They described him as "pretty looped."

Sometime around 9:30 p.m. as the group was sitting in the kitchen, Ward noticed Balen attempting to break through the two front doors that faced the street. There was a far exterior steel door that was always locked. Next was a porch area that separated the steel exterior door from an interior door leading into the living room of her house. When Ward saw what he was doing, she grabbed five-month-old Chance and ran downstairs to her basement. She then fled from the basement via her tuck-under garage to the residence of a friend and called 911 at 9:33 p.m.

Ward told 911 that while exiting her home she could hear what she described as "an assault type" commotion. She believed Olson might have encountered Balen on the stairs to the basement. Olson had gone to the basement to watch television while Ward was upstairs with the others. She also described what she believed to be Lewandowski screaming.

Balen left the area, and Ward retuned to her house, where police interviewed her. The couple and police left around 11:25 p.m. She then received another call from Balen. He asked her if the police were still there. She said, "No."

Balen told her, "You have five seconds to evacuate the house. I'm coming in and someone's going to end up dead." Ward immediately gave her cell phone to Lewandowski and told her to call 911. She again grabbed Chance and told everyone to leave. Lewandowski's call to 911 was recorded at 11:42 p.m.

Ward, Chance, and Olson fled and hid in some bushes next to the house. Ward was able to see Balen kicking in the front door as the street light and her porch light provided her a good view. As Balen kicked in the door, she heard a firearm discharge. She described it to police as a "foot long" handgun that he held in his left hand. After gaining entry to the house, she heard two additional shots. Lewandowski had still not joined them yet, and she feared that she had been shot. Moments after the last shots, Lewandowski joined them. The four then fled to a neighbor's house and waited for the police to arrive. Responding police took them away from the area to safety.

When interviewed by police at this time, she told them that Balen had approximately twenty-five weapons that included handguns, rifles, and shotguns. She related that he had ten to fifteen military type "ammo cans" containing ammunition for the variety of his weapons. She said that he had kept some at her residence, but she made him take them to a residence that he owned in Douglas County, Wisconsin. Ward drew a diagram of the two floors to her home for police.

Lewandowski was also interviewed by police at this time. She described basically the same information as Ward. However, she stayed in the house on both occasions longer than Ward. She stated that during the first incident (9:30 p.m.), she confronted Balen after Ward had left with Chance. Balen grabbed Lewandowski in the kitchen and slammed her head against the kitchen cabinet twice. He went downstairs looking for Ward and confronted her male friend. He was mad when he came back as he did not find Ward. She showed Balen the cordless phone in her hand and told him, "The police are on their way. I've called 911. They're gonna be here any minute." She kept backing up around the room with Balen coming toward her. He suddenly stopped and just walked out the front door.

Lewandowski stated that after Ward came back to the house, the police arrived. They told the police how fearful they were of Balen. Ward had actually called the police just minutes before Balen arrived the second time to see if he had been arrested. When the phone rang around 11:40 p.m., Lewandowski yelled that it was Balen and they had five seconds to get out. Ward told her to call 911 as she fled again.

Lewandowski claimed that she called 911, and the next thing she knew Balen was in the house and "was on me." Balen pinned her to the floor and was pointing a gun with a red laser dot at her. He told her, "You're gonna fucking die, bitch. You don't fucking believe me?" He held the gun to her head and said, "You got five fucking minutes to get out of this house."

She asked him, "Jim, what have I done to you? I have done nothing to you."

Balen then said, "You don't fucking believe me, do ya?" He then fired one shot past her head. He threw that gun down and then grabbed another one that he had with him. He then fired another round and said, "You've got five fucking minutes to get out and run. Start running now." Lewandowski got up and ran out the stairs to the back of the house and found Ward, Chance, and her friend in the bushes. She added that Balen kicked her in the head while she was on the floor. He would put the red laser dot between her eyes before he changed weapons. She said that he had two handguns and what appeared to be a rifle. She showed police the bruises to her head from the kicks Balen had inflicted on her.

Olson told police that he initially went to Ward's house around 2:00 p.m. because Balen was calling and harassing her. Around 9:00 p.m. he went downstairs to watch television because Lewandowski had returned along with a couple that he did not know. At approximately 9:30 p.m. Ward came running down the stairs with her baby shouting, "You've got to stop him." He assumed that it was Balen.

Olson met him at the top of the stairs and said to him, "What the hell do you think you're doing?" They began fighting and fell to the bottom of the stairs. Balen was kicking him in the head and ribs. As Olson was down, Balen searched the bedroom and bathroom for Ward. He then went upstairs and left the house.

Olson said that after that confrontation, Ward came back and the police interviewed them. She then went back to the neighbor's house and brought her son home. They were all sitting at the kitchen table when Balen called. That is when he, Ward, and Chance fled again. They hid, but were able to watch the front of the house. It appeared to Olson that Balen was carrying a long rifle as he approached the front door of the house. Balen kicked at the door and Olson thought that a handgun fell from his hand or belt, discharging. Balen picked up the weapon and entered the house.

Olson said that he jumped a fence and went to a neighbor's house while Ward stayed hidden in the bushes. He told the woman to call police and to tell them that there was a crazy man shooting a gun. When he got back to Ward,

Lewandowski had arrived. He heard six more shots coming from the house.

Numerous law enforcement officers from Duluth Police, St. Louis County Sheriff's Office, and the Minnesota State Patrol responded to the last 911 call relating to shots being fired. A total of twenty-three officers and medics arrived.

When officers arrived at the scene to set up a perimeter, they could see the front porch light flickering on and off. A man could be heard shouting and challenging officers to come and get him. A shot was fired at 12:05 a.m. A negotiator arrived at 12:06 a.m. Just then, Balen went outside by the alley and cried, "I'll do it myself." He fired one round into the air and returned back into the house. He was yelling and officers could see him pointing the red laser dot out toward the alley. He was contacted on his cell phone at 12:47 a.m. by a negotiator when he said that he was hiding upstairs.

At 1:05 a.m. three shots were fired from the back of the house. One shot was fired at 1:11 a.m. Dialogue back and forth continued with Balen and the negotiator, with Balen saying that he was going to "run and go out in a blaze of glory." At 1:34 a.m. he told officers that he was "going to load up and go out the front door" so they "can take a shot." He did not come out; but fired two shots. More shots were heard at 1:36 a.m.

Balen talked on the phone to the negotiator at 1:50 a.m. He was crying and complaining about custody issues and the laws relating to them. He said at 1:55 a.m. that he would come out to the porch so "no one gets hurt." He immediately changed and said that he would come out through the front door. He said if he did, "It's war!" At 2:15 a.m. he said, "It's time to die." For the next hour or so Balen went from the upstairs to the downstairs turning lights off and on. Observers could see lights being broken and hear loud banging on the doors and walls. At 3:11 a.m. flames were visible inside the house. A decision was made by the commanders on scene to use deadly force against Balen if he was seen with a weapon and advanced toward them.

Sgt. Martin LeRette, a forty-nine-year-old SWAT team officer with eighteen years' experience, was at home when his phone rang around 1:00 a.m.

early Saturday morning. The call related that there was a barricaded suspect situation and shots had been fired by the suspect. LeRette stopped at police headquarters and picked up additional supplies for officers at the scene. After a briefing near the scene, LeRette went to his observation site.

LeRette set up in the open box of a pickup truck east of the Ward residence. He was about sixty yards away and had a direct view to the back of the house. It was drizzling rain and a fog had rolled in at that time; visibility had diminished somewhat. He was aware that Balen had a rifle and handgun with a laser sight. LeRette was one of two precision marksmen on the tactical team. His weapon was a Remington Model 70, bolt action .308-caliber rifle with telescope sight. He also had an M16 rifle and his department-issued .40-caliber handgun.

LeRette was monitoring radio traffic indicating that Balen was banging on doors and walls in the house. He could also hear muffled banging from his location. Because of the shots being fired and the type of weapon in Balen's possession, he was advised that he could use deadly force. About 3:35 a.m. Balen came to the back porch area. LeRette heard him say, in effect, "It's time to get going; we're going to make this happen." LeRette then heard what sounded to him to be a round chambered into the weapon. He could see through his sight that Balen had his weapon in a port arms position. LeRette later told investigators that this reminded him of the recent North Hollywood bank robbers who had been seen on the news. Balen was silhouetted by what he believed to be flames inside the house. Balen turned with his weapon pointed toward LeRette. He felt in harm's way for himself and other officers. He lined up his crosshairs on the midsection of Balen and fired one round from the .308-caliber rifle.

Balen said very clearly, "You got me."

An autopsy determined that Balen suffered a single gunshot wound to the left forearm that fractured the ulna and radius. The shot then entered the abdomen with laceration of the colon, superior mesenteric artery, and liver. His blood alcohol was .176.

Investigation by the Minnesota Bureau of Criminal Apprehension determined that Balen had fired a total of twenty-one shots with three firearms—a Norinco SKS assault rifle, a P38 9-mm pistol, and a .45-caliber Colt handgun. Law enforcement fired one round: the fatal .308-caliber round by LeRette.

In a news release on August 2, 2001, the St. Louis County Attorney's Office issued a statement that the shooting death of Balen was justified under Minnesota statue and no charges would be filed against LeRette. It is also noted that the investigative file regarding this matter was 575 pages.

Chapter Three

"This Is a Stickup"
aka Armed Robberies

I

The south side of Minneapolis was experiencing a string of armed robberies at convenience stores during August 1981. The problem was getting so out of hand that a decision was made by Minneapolis Police Department's administrators to set up surveillance in the area of the stores.

Officer Ted Boran (age thirty-eight), Officer Art Gooselaw (age thirty-five), Pete Heeren (age thirty-five), and Tom Peterson (age thirty-one), were assigned to two separate surveillance vehicles. Their assignment was to each set up at one of the most recent robberies to determine if the robbers would come back to rob the same store. There were two separate stores that the teams were watching. One of the stores, Knudsen's Country Boy located at 42nd Avenue and East 45th Street, was being watched. The manager of the store was aware of the surveillance.

Around 8:35 p.m. on Wednesday, August 26, two men were observed by officers entering the store. The men, and their vehicle, matched the description police had compiled in seven convenience store robberies—including a robbery at Knudsen's the previous week. The officers saw the men walk into the store as they were putting on ski masks. (Minnesota gets cold, but in August?) They were inside for about one minute.

An interview with the store manager revealed that he gave two hundred dollars to the pair. One of the robbers had a handgun and the other had a knife. The manager pulled down a window display, as previously discussed with the officers, to indicate that he had been robbed. The officers also saw one of the robbers with a revolver when he left the store.

They had robbed the store again. They fled the scene, and the two unmarked surveillance vehicles tracked them. Apparently they realized that they were being followed and increased their speed through Minnehaha Park. The officers called for additional help. A chase ensued, and shots were fired at the lead surveillance vehicle. As the car (a Ford Pinto) crossed the bridge, near the Old Soldier's Home in the park, other police officers had arrived, stopping them from getting across the bridge.

The robbers continued firing from the car. However, they were no match for the four officers. Each officer was armed with a .12 gauge shotgun or .38-caliber revolver. One of the officers fired both a shotgun and revolver. Numerous rounds were fired at the Pinto. The officers shouted, "Freeze. Throw out the gun. Raise your hands. Come out!" Shots rang out at the officers. Officers returned fire at both the driver and passenger. The passenger, later determined to be twenty-year-old Eugene Mehl, was the one who had been firing at the officers. The driver, twenty-year-old Joseph Tornio, was also directed to "freeze." He continued to appear to be making offensive movements, and one of the officers fired, hitting him.

Both robbers were immediately taken to Hennepin County Medical Center. Mehl was placed on life support due his gunshot wounds. He expired around 9:00 a.m. on Thursday, August 27, 1981. Tornio was listed in critical condition. However, he survived and was charged with the armed robbery and assault on the officers.

None of the officers were injured. The officers were on heightened awareness on the night of the shooting. Officer Richard P. Miller had been shot and killed on Tuesday night of that week, and officers throughout the city were looking for the suspect.

A Hennepin County grand jury determined that the shooting of Mehl was justifiable homicide.

II

One never knows what to expect when responding to a robbery call. At 12:16 a.m. on Monday, April 28, 1997, Saint Paul Police officers responded to an apartment on Saint Paul's east side.

Thirty-three-year-old Gerald Vick and Officer Josh Lego, a twenty-four-year-old new officer who was still in field training, contacted the victim of the robbery. This person informed the officers that he had come to the apartment to visit a friend. While just sitting on the back steps by himself, a person that he had only known for two weeks by the name "Meechie" appeared and was pointing a silver semiautomatic handgun at him.

The victim thought that Meechie was only joking as he was smiling. He soon realized, however, that Meechie was not joking when he ordered him to the ground. He robbed the victim of $150 in cash, a gold watch and gold bracelet. Meechie pulled the trigger three times. The victim heard the trigger click three times. The victim told police, "The stupid mother fucker didn't know that the safety was on." Meechie ran east toward Westminster Street from the apartment. Meechie was described as a black male, eighteen-years-old, five-foot-seven, and around 160 pounds. He said that Meechie would be easy to pick out as he had a "bunch of pony tails" in his hair and was wearing a gray sweatshirt with stripes.

Further investigation by the officers at the apartment determined that a woman also witnessed the robbery. She stated that she was going to her apartment on the second floor when she heard voices in the hall downstairs. She walked toward the voices and saw Demetrius Hill, also known to her as "Meechie," standing with a gun on Kenny (the complainant and victim).

This took place directly in front of the door to the apartment building.

She heard Hill say to Kenny, "You know what this is?" Hill pulled the trigger at least twice according to her. She heard a click and saw bullets fall to the floor. She saw Hill "jerking" at the handgun.

She told Hill, "Please, Meechie, don't do that in front of my door, my kids are in there." Hill turned and pointed the gun at her. Hill then turned and ran out of the apartment building. Kenny went into her apartment to call 911. The officers took his statement in her apartment.

Another witness at the apartment saw Hill point a gun at Kenny's face and say, "Come on, nigger, break yourself, come on with all of it, break yourself, drop everything, drop." This witness thought Hill was just joking, but he soon realized that it was not a joke. This witness ran toward his nearby apartment as he heard Hill say, "I ain't playing, nigger, now drop." This witness saw the police arrive and talk to Kenny. Then he gave his statement.

Officer Lego interviewed other witnesses in the apartment building and confirmed the identity of Hill. Vick told Lego that Hill would probably return as he had family members in the building. Lego moved the police squad car from sight and Vick waited inside the building on the second floor landing. About five minutes later Vick heard the door open. He drew his 9-mm pistol and held it to the side of his leg. Two males were at the door. The first male matched the description of Hill. Hill walked about two to three feet into the building.

Vick made eye contact with the first male and yelled, "Police. Meechie, get on the ground, get on the ground." As Vick was saying this, Hill reached into his waistband and pulled out a silver semiautomatic handgun. He started to raise it in Vick's direction. Vick fired several shots and jumped left out of Hill's path of fire. Vick saw Hill move slightly to his right and fall to the floor. The other man ran out of the building west toward Mississippi Street.

Vick then went to Hill and moved the gun about two feet from his hand. He immediately called on his radio for assistance and medics. He also radioed the other individual's direction of flight. Medical personnel arrived and transported Hill to nearby Regions Hospital where he was pronounced dead. The other individual was located and questioned by police. That man had $275 cash on his person and a gold bracelet matching the one stolen from Kenny. This individual said that he knew Hill and had just bought the bracelet from him. He also claimed that he was outside the building when he heard the shots and ran out of fear. He also said that he did not see a weapon in Hill's possession.

The handgun in Hill's possession was traced by Saint Paul Police investigators. It was a Ruger 9-mm purchased in Minneapolis on December 24, 1993. The gun was sold to an individual who reported his car stolen in 1996. The gun was in the trunk of the car when it was stolen; however, he did not report to police that there was a weapon in the car. The original report of the stolen car was reviewed. The owner had reported that he went to a Speedy Mart and parked next to a four-wheel drive Ford Explorer with a lone man sitting in it. When he came out of the store, the Ford Explorer and his car was gone. A further check by the police revealed that the towing company searched the car when impounded and noted there was an empty Ruger handgun box in the truck. When told that the gun had been recovered during a robbery and police shooting incident, the owner told them about the gun and furnished the police with a copy of documents regarding his purchase of the weapon. That person said that he did not report the gun stolen as he was "embarrassed" for leaving the gun in the trunk.

The Ruger was taken to the Saint Paul Police range, and it was found to be fully operational. It was also determined that it had a fully operational external safety which allows the trigger to be pulled in a full range of motion without firing. The external hammer on the weapon falls on the safety when put in a safe position. A clicking noise can be heard from the trigger mechanism if the trigger is pulled when the safety is on. The safety was more than likely in the on position when Hill pulled the trigger at the robbery victim.

It was determined that Hill died from four gunshot wounds. There were no drugs or alcohol found in his system at time of the autopsy.

Officer Vick was cleared by a Ramsey County grand jury on July 18, 1997. Tragically, Vick was killed in the line of duty on May 6, 2005. His assailant was convicted and sentenced to life without the possibility of parole. Vick, who had been promoted to Sergeant, was, and still remains, the only Saint Paul Police officer ever to receive two Medals of Valor.

III

Minneapolis and Saint Paul are nationally known as the Twin Cities—even the baseball team is called the Minnesota Twins. It goes without question that the two cities will have individuals known to both police departments, and criminals will go back and forth between the two cities committing criminal acts.

Rigoberto Prieto Cuellar, a twenty-three-year-old Cuban immigrant, was well known in Saint Paul. He was charged in an assault on January 13, 1983, in Saint Paul and with possession of a martial arts weapon. When he failed to appear in court on this charge, a bench warrant was issued for his arrest. Cuellar was also being sought for questioning in a knife attack against a man dressed in woman's clothing on January 27, 1983. Cuellar had been living in Saint Paul at that time. However, he had moved and his whereabouts was unknown until Saturday, December 17, 1983.

Thirty-one year-old Minneapolis officer Charles Dodge and thirty-four-year-old Mike Green responded to investigate the claim of an armed robbery in their city. Just after 9:00 p.m., on December 17, they met the complainant at a liquor store near downtown Minneapolis, at 12th and Hennepin Avenue. The victim told the officers that two armed men had robbed him of forty dollars in cash and his coat in an apartment located in a building nearby at 1205 Hawthorne Avenue.

The two officers took the victim to the third floor of the apartment building where the apartment in question and robbery took place. The plan was to identify the individuals in the apartment and have the victim point out the robbers. The officers knocked on the door and identified themselves as "Minneapolis Police!" Cuellar opened the door and pointed a handgun at the officers. He slammed the door shut and fired two rounds into the door.

Dodge and Green responded with shots from a .12-gauge shotgun and .38-caliber revolver. The door flew open as Cuellar was falling to the floor. He had a .25-caliber semiautomatic pistol in his hand. Emergency medical personnel arrived and pronounced him dead at the scene. Two additional individuals were arrested. One person, Ramon Julia, was in the apartment when the shooting occurred and was hit in the right shoulder by one of the officers' shots. A third man jumped from the third floor window and was arrested soon after.

The shooting by the officers was determined to have been in self-defense by a Hennepin County grand jury.

IV

One department's armed robbery can later turn another department into action. This happened in January of 2004. Around 9:05 p.m. on Sunday, January 18, 2004, the Rainbow grocery store in Roseville, Minnesota, was robbed by a lone male. The robbery suspect was armed with what appeared to be a serrated knife with a brown handle. During the robbery a female employee at the store was cut on her hand during a physical struggle with the robber. The suspect was able to get a large amount of money and flee the store on foot. The robber was described as a black male, six feet tall, average build, goatee/beard, black knit hat, and dark clothing.

Witnesses followed the suspect on foot for a short distance to a neighborhood north of the store. They lost sight of him in the darkness. Roseville police responded to the scene and began tracking the suspect. They found cash outside of an open shed nearby. About two-thirds of the stolen loot in small denominations was in the same type of bag used during the robbery. They were unable to locate the suspect.

On Tuesday January 20, local television stations broadcast still images of the suspect taken by surveillance cameras at the store. A citizen called a Hennepin County probation officer stating that the person looked like Johnnie Berry Rodgers, a fifty-four-year-old black male from Minneapolis. The probation officer requested more still images from the robbery as he was the officer in charge of Rodgers while on probation. He identified the photos as that of Rodgers. It was learned that Rodgers had recently been released from the Minnesota Department of Corrections for a series of aggravated robberies.

An officer from Roseville made telephone contact with Rodgers on four separate occasions in an attempt to get him to turn himself into authorities. He admitted to robbing the store during one of the calls. He was asked about the remaining cash taken during the robbery. He said that he had no additional money and claimed that he left all of the money stolen in the shed. Rodgers told the Roseville officer that he was too old to go back to prison and had no reason to live. He told police that he had said goodbye to his friends and would not go back to prison. Roseville police alerted metro area police departments of Rodgers' fugitive status.

Thirty-four-year-old Saint Paul Officer Charles Sims and his partner Ruby Diaz were working their 7:00 a.m. to 2:30 p.m. shift. Later that day they went to a parking lot in Saint Paul to meet Roseville detectives. The Roseville detectives gave a photo of Rodgers to them and information regarding the robbery. They also said that they had a warrant for his arrest and his claim that he would not to be taken alive. They were told that recent cell calls had him in the area of University Avenue and Dale fifteen minutes prior to their meeting. The Roseville officers were attempting to locate Rodgers by tracking his cell phone calls. Rodgers' vehicle description and license number was also supplied.

Diaz left for the day, but Sims continued looking in the area for the green Dodge Intrepid that Rodgers was supposedly driving. Roseville police notified Saint Paul police again that Rodgers was using his cell again during a fifth call to Roseville police. His location was near the capitol building in

Saint Paul. Sims was nearby.

Around 3:30 p.m. Sims saw a car matching the description. He observed an older black male driving the car along with a black female in the front passenger seat. He began following the vehicle. He was unable to see the complete license plate because of snow covering part of it. The numbers and letters that were visible matched the car he was seeking. As he was following it, it "blew" right through a stop sign. Sims notified dispatch that he was following the suspect vehicle.

Officers did not know that Rodgers had picked up a female friend and was taking her to the Sears store in Saint Paul so she could pay her credit card bill. The vehicle drove into the south side of the Sears parking lot. Sims pulled in behind and activated his light bar. The car stopped in the driveway of the parking lot. Sims related that the female passenger began to get out of the car. When she got out, Sims shouted at her, "Get back in the car." As she was getting back into the passenger seat, the driver began getting out of the driver's side. The man matched the description of Rodgers. He stood outside of the car facing to the front of the car. Sims heard the woman say, "Johnny, no, get back in the car."

Sims had exited his vehicle with his .40-caliber Glock handgun drawn and was moving toward the vehicle to get a better look at the license plate. Rodgers turned and looked at Sims. Rodgers' body was bladed and Sims could only see the left side of his body. Sims directed him to "get down on the ground."

Rodgers called back, "I'm not getting down on the ground," as he raised both hands. Sims saw a long, silver, butcher-type knife in Rodgers' right hand. Rodgers moved to his right and Sims countered with a move to his left. Sims did not want Rodgers moving at all as people were coming out of the Sears entrance. Sims did not want to give him an opportunity to take someone as a shield or hostage.

Sims pointed his weapon at Rodgers and shouted, "Drop the knife. Drop the knife." Sims yelled the command at least two more times, elevating his voice each time so innocent bystanders could hear him. Sims could see that there were people off to Rodgers' right. Rodgers was about five to six feet from his vehicle and Sims positioned himself away from his squad.

Rodgers started to move toward Sims and said, "I'm not going to prison." Sims, fearing for his well being and that of others, fired his weapon three times.

Rodgers dropped the knife and spun away from Sims, falling to the ground on his stomach. Sims radioed dispatch that shots had been fired and the suspect was down. He could see other squads from Saint Paul arriving, but he remained focused on the female passenger as he was unsure what she would do. Once the other squads were on the scene, Rodgers was handcuffed and the passenger secured. Medics arrived shortly thereafter and attended to Rodgers. A knife with a ten-inch blade was recovered near him.

Rodgers was removed from the scene and was pronounced dead at Saint Paul Regions Hospital. An autopsy revealed that he died from gunshot wounds to the chest.

Investigators determined that Rodgers had a long criminal history in Arkansas and Minnesota. His first arrest was for grand larceny of an automobile in Little Rock at the age of sixteen. There was no disposition of that charge as he was adjudicated in juvenile court. The next arrests and convictions in Arkansas in the 1960s and 1970s were for burglary and armed robberies. He was eventually paroled in 1978.

Rodgers found his way to Minnesota and was arrested for the State of Arkansas in Minneapolis. He was subsequently sentenced to 97 months at Minnesota's Stillwater prison on December 6, 1982. His parole was given to Minnesota as an "Interstate Transfer." He was arrested while on parole in 1988. He entered a guilty plea in April 1989, and sentenced to one hundred months to run concurrently with his previous sentence. His record showed that he was convicted of eight counts of aggravated robbery and two counts of first-degree assault.

Sims was cleared by a Ramsey County grand jury on June 23, 2004. He was later awarded the Saint Paul police Medal of Valor for bravery regarding the incident.

V

This next incident sounds like something from a movie. Some people go shopping for Christmas presents, and some like to steal. The Rogers jewelry store in Saint Paul is located in the downtown business area. It was around 10:40 a.m. on Tuesday, December 17, 1985, when two men wearing ski masks entered the jewelry store. One had a handgun and the other a sawed-off shotgun. One of them went directly to the man in charge and grabbed him by his tie and told him, "This is a mother-fuckin' stickup." He proceeded to pull him to the store's safe which was in view behind the counter. He ordered him to put all of the diamonds in a duffel bag he had brought with him. The telephone line was cut, and one of the glass display cases was shot out by the robbers. There were three customers and three employees. They were all herded into the back room and ordered to lie down.

The dispatch center began receiving 911 calls. The first call was from a nearby business. The call reported, "Ah yes, I was just trying to get a hold of Rogers Jewelers. The phone was taken off the hook. It sounds like they are in the midst of a robbery." The next 911 call was, "Rogers Jewelers. We were just robbed at 7th and Wabasha, two black guys ran up Wabasha toward 6th Street…they left thirty seconds ago." The call was transferred to the duty officer at the Saint Paul Police Department.

The call of the robbery was dispatched to thirty-year-old Officer Richard Munoz, who was working in an unmarked vehicle and in plain clothes only one block away. Munoz pulled close enough to observe a black male pacing back and forth with a hooded sweatshirt pulled tight around his head. Munoz could see the other suspect kneeling by the front door of the building as a lookout. Munoz radioed that it looked like a robbery was in progress and waited for backup. Munoz observed the two leave, with one of them carrying a navy blue duffel bag. The two then entered another building in the area. A marked squad arrived. Munoz advised them and dispatch of the situation.

Munoz entered the building and found that the suspects were not in sight. Munoz was joined by Ken McIntosh, a thirty-seven-year-old uniformed officer. They both ran up the escalator to the second floor. The other responding officers were searching the area of the first floor. When they reached the second floor, a woman in an office pointed and mouthed to them, "They went that way." Munoz and McIntosh separated.

McIntosh went to check the restrooms and Munoz continued down the corridor. Munoz could see one of the robbers as he started back down the stairs to the lobby of another building. Munoz went down the stairs to confront the man. Munoz, with his revolver out, identified himself and told the man to "freeze." The suspect, later identified as thirty-six-year-old Earl Gilchrist from Omaha, Nebraska, pointed his weapon at Munoz. Munoz fired one shot and jumped back down a staircase for cover. When he hit a step on the staircase, he twisted his knee and fell to the floor. Munoz radioed McIntosh that it appeared the robber was returning to the second floor toward McIntosh. Gilchrist apparently heard the radio transmission and headed to the doors that exited onto St. Peter Street.

Officer Frances Jacobs saw Gilchrist walk from the building and throw a duffel bag into a 1975 blue Dodge that was parked in a fifteen-minute zone. Jacobs pointed a shotgun at Gilchrist and ordered him away from the vehicle. Sgt. Bob Paskett arrived and assisted Jacobs. Gilchrist was placed into custody and hauled away in a squad car. The money and jewelry stolen during the robber was recovered from the Dodge.

Meanwhile, Officer McIntosh was on the second floor attempting to locate the second robber. After checking the restrooms, he returned to the corridor. Munoz was gone so he took the skyway to the next building. He heard a shot. He was then radioed by Munoz that at least one suspect was coming his way. McIntosh saw one of the suspects, later identified as twenty-six-year-old ex-con Erik Ware from Des Moines, Iowa, on the first floor. When

McIntosh reached the first floor lobby, people in the area were shouting and pointing in the direction Ware was fleeing. McIntosh looked out the door and saw Ware enter a building across the street.

McIntosh ran across the street and carefully entered the building. His radio was blaring quite loudly. He turned it off and started toward the back of the lobby area of the building. He saw a beauty parlor with sinks and large mirrors. He saw Ware in a mirror holding a gun in his gloved hand. Ware was moving along the wall toward the door that McIntosh was about to enter. It was McIntosh's feeling that Ware was moving to "sneak up on me." McIntosh rushed through the door into the room across from Ware. Ware looked at McIntosh and pointed his gun at him. McIntosh fired twice from about six feet and ducked back out of the room. McIntosh then quickly jumped back in the room and fired at Ware a second time. McIntosh then "ducked back out again." He went back in again and fired the remaining two rounds from his .38-caliber weapon as Ware was still standing. Ware then said, "Hey man, you shot me, you won. I quit."

Ware began walking backwards into the reception area of the beauty parlor. McIntosh followed pointing his empty weapon at him. Ware then collapsed to the floor and dropped the gun. McIntosh secured the weapon and quickly searched him. He found gold jewelry in his pockets containing Rogers Jewelry price tags. He then began to administer first aid to an obvious wound to his right shoulder area by applying pressure with a towel found at the beauty parlor. Two other uniform officers arrived and assisted him. Ware asked McIntosh, "Am I going to die?"

McIntosh responded, "I'm a lousy shot." Paramedics arrived and removed Ware from the scene. He died two and one-half hours later at the hospital.

Three employees at the beauty parlor substantiated McIntosh's description of what happened at the scene. When the shooting started, the three huddled in a closet and listened to what one described as six gunshots. One said, "We didn't know who won—the good guys or bad." When one employee heard the sounds of police radios, he opened the door and saw a Saint Paul officer pointing his weapon toward the closet and them. He and the other two in the closet were quickly identified as witnesses.

Ware had a warrant outstanding in Des Moines for rape and robbery at the time of the shooting. His past record included kidnapping, armed robbery, burglary, resisting arrest, assaulting a police officer and numerous misdemeanors. His juvenile record began at age fourteen. An autopsy determined Ware died from three gunshot wounds to the right chest area. Munoz had to have surgery to repair his injured knee from the fall. He returned to work and was assigned to the homicide unit until his retirement in 2008. McIntosh has also retired.

VI

When you make your living by stealing from others, make sure your getaway vehicle cannot be traced immediately to your address. In this incident a witness was able to get the license number of the getaway vehicle. This shooting event by Minneapolis police actually began in Saint Paul shortly after 1:00 a.m. on Tuesday, January 19, 1982. The Vickers gasoline station on University Avenue was robbed of $125 by gunpoint. The station attendant gave the Saint Paul officers a description of the robber and said that he saw another man sitting behind the wheel of the getaway vehicle. He furnished the license plate number that was identified as a Chevrolet.

The Saint Paul police were able to trace the Chevrolet back to an apartment complex on the north side of Minneapolis. Minneapolis officers were notified and squads responded to the area. About 1:45 a.m. the Chevrolet with two occupants pulled into the parking lot of the apartment building. One officer approached the car and ordered them from it. Instead, the driver of the car, later identified as thirty-two-year-old Donald J. Haynes, pointed a gun at the officer and sped away. No shots were fired by either Haynes or the officer.

Minneapolis police then began a chase of the vehicle. One of the officers described it as "a high speed chase at ten miles per hour." Weather conditions that night were extreme. It was very cold and the streets were slippery due to recent snow and ice. A few streets away, Sgt. Jerry Larson was standing alone behind his open squad door with a shotgun. The Chevrolet came directly at Larson as if attempting to take off the door. Sergeant Larson ran around behind the squad for cover. Someone from the Chevrolet fired two shots at him. Larson fired three rounds from the .12-gauge shotgun at the vehicle. The rear window of the Chevrolet was blown out. Larson did not receive any injuries.

Additional Minneapolis officers were waiting nearby and had seen the encounter with Larson. Haynes again drove the car directly toward these officers. One more shot came from the Chevrolet as it slammed into a squad car at the scene. Officers Greg Zipoy and Ron Johnson began firing at the occupants of the car. Haynes was struck by shots from Zipoy and Johnson and died at the scene.

The passenger, twenty-two-year-old Stacey E. Barrow, jumped from the car but was captured a short distance away. He was taken to Hennepin County Medical Center with wounds to his neck and wrist. It was determined that his wounds were probably a result of shots fired from Larson's shotgun. He recovered.

Officers located two weapons in the car: a .22-caliber revolver and a .32-caliber semiautomatic pistol. Only the .32-caliber was determined to have been fired. The dollar amount taken during the robbery was on the front seat of the car. Haynes, a former Saint Paul resident, only had one arrest record: driving while intoxicated in 1979. A search of Haynes' apartment recovered stereo and camera equipment from a Saint Paul robbery occurring a week before the shooting.

A Hennepin County grand jury cleared the officers in March 1981.

Chapter Four

Catch Me If You Can
aka Police Pursuits

I

Mother's Day is different for everyone. Some drive a few miles to spend time with their mother. Others, who are hundreds of miles away, can only call. Apparently, thirty-four-year-old Sean Hayes, who was cruising up and down streets in south Minneapolis in his yellow Cadillac, caused enough concern for residents in the area on Mother's Day, May 14, 2000, to call 911 three times. Eventually, a call to 911 furnished his license plate and indicated there were two people in the neighborhood who were following the car in their own personal vehicles.

Interviews by police of witnesses following the shooting determined that a white male, balding and about thirty years old had been driving an older yellow Cadillac very slowly and suspiciously around their neighborhood for the past two months. One witness told authorities that the same person pulled into an alley near his house and approached several children. This witness had not previously reported the events to the police. Even another witness said that she had seen the same vehicle for the past month or so and described it as "casing the neighborhood." She said several people had heard rumors that the person in the car was a convicted child molester.

The person calling 911 told police that she initially called around 7:50 p.m. when the Cadillac drove slowly by her residence numerous times. She said the car would almost stop in front of her house and just stare at her sister-in-law who was in the front yard. The car would proceed down a block, make a U-turn and come back down the street slowly in front of her house again. Her children had just gone to a nearby store, and she was concerned about their safety, so she called 911. After making the 911 call, she saw the car go by again, and she was able to get the license number. She then called 911 again with the number.

This same person added that sometime later her children and some friends came running into her house. Her eleven-year-old daughter told her that a man in a yellow Cadillac had approached her and attempted to get her to go into the car with him. Her son was with the group of kids and verified what had happened.

Officers spoke to the children. The daughter said that the man stopped his car at a stop sign and just stared at them. He then rolled down his window and waved at them. He stated, "Come here, I have to give you a treat." He waved again and winked at them. She definitely felt like he was trying to get her into his car. Her brother stated he was sitting on his bike with the group watching what was happening. He thought that the man asked his sister to "Come get in the back seat" of the car. All of the kids were scared and went directly home to tell his mother what had happened.

The children's father said he questioned his children about what had happened. He wanted to make sure the children had not misinterpreted what the man was doing. He told police, "There's no doubt in my mind that he was trying to lure my daughter into his car."

The father saw the car go by his house again. He saw that a friend of his was following the car in his blue Mazda. He then jumped into his white van in an attempt to follow the Cadillac and detain it for the police. He determined that another vehicle, a Chevrolet pickup, was also following the Cadillac. The father said he could not keep up with the other three vehicles by driving within the traffic laws.

Minneapolis police squads responded. At the intersection of 46th Street and Bloomington Avenue South the suspect vehicle was located. Officers determined that the person driving matched the description previously given by witnesses. There was a Chevrolet pickup parked behind the Cadillac, and the driver was flashing his high beams on and off. He also pointed to the Cadillac to get the officer's attention. The officer activated his emergency lights and pulled through the intersection in front of the Cadillac. Just as the squad did this, a blue Mazda pulled around the southbound lane into the northbound lane and stopped. The driver also pointed toward the Cadillac, and it appeared as if he was trying to block the Cadillac from leaving.

Officer Brian Thurson, in full uniform, immediately exited his squad and drew his weapon. He stood at the left front fender and caled very loudly and clearly several times, "Police. Don't move." Hayes looked directly at Thurson, and it was clear to Thurson that Hayes knew who he was and understood his commands. Hayes looked at Thurson and accelerated. Thurson had to jump out of the way to avoid being struck. Thurson notified dispatch of the location and that he was behind the Cadillac attempting to stop the car. Strangely enough, Hayes was going the speed limit and stopped at every intersection. He even signaled his turns. He was doing this while Thurson was behind him with the lights and siren activated. All of a sudden Hayes sped up to forty-five or fifty miles per hour and was going directly through stoplights. Hayes was driving very erratically. Thurson was afraid Hayes would hit other cars or pedestrians.

Thurson radioed to ask permission to "take him out." This meant to ram the car with the approved Minneapolis techniques. Sgt. Rob Goodsell came on the radio and stated that he would take over as the primary (first) squad. He advised that he would use the Pursuit Intervention Technique (PIT) to stop him. Goodsell was able to get in the lead and use PIT. The Cadillac spun around and stopped. Thurson jumped out and ran to the left front of the Cadillac. He shouted for Hayes to "get out of the car." Hayes accelerated and Thurson had to again jump out of the way to avoid being hit.

Sergeant Goodsell was still driving the primary car. When Hayes tried to turn back on 2nd Avenue, Goodsell again used the PIT maneuver. The Cadillac spun around again and other squads that had joined the chase were in the area. Thurson again exited his squad with his weapon drawn. Hayes rammed his Cadillac into Goodsell's squad. There were several other officers outside their squads yelling at Hayes to stop and get out of his car. Hayes put his car in reverse and hit another squad behind him.

Thurson was standing between Goodsell's squad and the Cadillac when Hayes put his car in drive and came at Thurson at a high rate of speed. It was obvious to Thurson that he was going to be hit by the speeding car and possibly killed. Not having time to get out of the way, Thurson holstered his gun and prepared to jump on the hood if necessary. Thurson was able to brace himself for the impact as the car hit him above the left knee. The impact caused him to fly on the hood and roll off the driver's side away from the car. Immediately after rolling away, he heard several shots. He then observed the Cadillac going in reverse eastbound across East 36th Street. The car came to rest in the front yard of a house on the south side of 36th Street.

Several officers who had arrived to join in the chase fired at Hayes when they saw Thurson fly over the hood. In total, five officers carrying Beretta 9-mm handguns, fired at Hayes. Twenty-four-year-old Jeff Kading had only four days on the street when the shooting occurred. Other officers firing were twenty-eight-year-old Gene Stuker, twenty-eight-year-old Jeff Werner, twenty-five-year-old Tim Costello and twenty-eight-year-old Brandy Steberg.

Hayes was determined to be dead at the scene from numerous gunshot wounds. A good friend of Hayes described him as a "good crook" and that he would never have harmed children. The friend believed that Hayes may have been in the neighborhood to buy drugs. The friend claimed Hayes may have wanted the kids in the car to divert attention from the police regarding his real intention in the area. Hayes had ten felony convictions on his record, including theft of a motor vehicle and receiving stolen property. He had fled from the police two years before this incident. He was out of court on bond regarding an auto theft charge. There were no sexual offenses on his record.

A Hennepin County grand jury returned a no bill regarding the officers on September 26, 2000.

II

You steal a vehicle from a car dealership and lead the police on a short chase. When you eventually stop, why not give up—it's only a stolen car. Thirty-three year-old Duane T. Breitbach decided that he was going to go down with a fight against the police. It all started on Friday, July 23, 1993, in Cold Spring, a small town near St. Cloud, Minnesota. A dealership reported a 1987 Ford Taurus had been stolen. Area law enforcement was notified to be on the lookout for it.

At approximately 8:40 p.m. that night, St. Cloud police stopped the vehicle, and a short chase took place. Breitbach abandoned the vehicle and ran into a wooded area. Several residents in the area reported to police that they saw an individual run from the car and also noted that he was carrying a long-barreled weapon. (Note: It was July and still daylight).

Over the next hour and a half, law enforcement officers from St. Cloud and Stearns County Sheriff's Office surrounded the wooded area. Officer Arlan Schermerhorn, a thirty-year-old Waite Park police officer, was called to the scene with his canine Toby. Schermerhorn was armed with his Beretta 9-mm. Thirty-one-year-old St. Cloud officer Tom Schlieman was called at home that night as he was a member of the Emergency Response Team. He arrived at the scene around 9:30 p.m. and was carrying his department-issued Remington .12-gauge shotgun. St. Cloud officer twenty-eight-year-old

Mark Moline joined Schermerhorn around 10:25 p.m. Schlieman was instructed that he and officer Moline were to supply cover for Schermerhorn and his canine. The area to be searched by them was surrounded by an eight-foot metal mesh fence with several barbed wire strands on top. The officers entered the area through a hole in the fence.

The area to be searched was one block wide and four blocks long. It was overgrown with weeds and brush. The area was centrally located in St. Cloud and surrounded by residential housing on all sides. Law enforcement was concerned that Breitbach would escape and possibly take a hostage or create some other type of crisis with an innocent citizen. The search was conducted during the hours of darkness without lights because of tactical considerations. The night was hot, humid and mosquito infested. Just after 11:00 p.m., Breitbach was flushed from the brush on the east side of the area by officers and the canine.

The three decided to work their way back and forth in a zigzag pattern hoping to locate Breitbach's scent. They went in all directions and were unable to find anything positive in their search. This took almost forty-five minutes. Canine Toby was hot and thirsty so they stopped at a Schermerhorn's squad to give the dog water and a short rest. They were informed at this time that Breitbach had been wearing a yellow rain jacket when he initially fled. He had discarded it during his flight. The canine was given a sniff of the jacket to get a better scent. They went back through the hole in the fence. However, they were still unable to get a good tracking of him. As they came out of the hole, the wind came up, and it appeared that Toby seemed to be picking up on a scent.

The three officers, still not using flashlights in the now dark conditions, went along the fence for approximately one hundred yards or more. Toby seemed very alert with his ears perked up. Schlieman was aware there was another hole in the fence at this point as he had worked that area previously. Inside the fenced area was a bus garage. Toby went on alert in the brush area by the hole. The officers were in the dark so as not to be silhouetted. There were lights on one side of the bus garage. They then saw the silhouette of someone standing in the brush outside of the fence.

It first appeared as though the person was coming toward them. However, he turned and started going away from them. All three officers repeatedly commanded, "Police. Stop!" They went through the hole and took chase. Schlieman was the last officer through the hole. When Schlieman came through the hole, he saw Sergeant Biese from the St. Cloud police. Biese had been part of the perimeter; but he was now joining in the chase. Breitbach was running with a shotgun in his right hand. As he ran under a light, Schlieman could see that Brietbach had on a brown plaid shirt and blue jeans.

Schermerhorn and canine Toby were leading the chase. Toby was on a leash of about ten feet. Moline was next to Schermerhorn. Sergeant Biese caught up to the other two with Schlieman about ten to fifteen yards behind. They all continued chasing Breitbach. There was an open area between two bus garages about fifty to seventy yards. Breitbach ran under a street light in the middle of the bus parking lot. The officers continued shouting for Breitbach to stop during the chase. When Breitbach was crossing the parking lot in the light, Schermerhorn released the dog and said, "Get him." Breitbach looked over his shoulder at the dog. He turned back and continued running without firing. Breitbach abruptly turned and fired one round in the officer's direction. Investigation later revealed that shotgun projectiles struck the metal overhead doors of the garage where the officers where located. The dog fell and rolled. Schlieman yelled, "Shoot him!"

Breitbach turned as if to flee; but then turned back and fired at the officers. Simultaneously, Moline and Schermerhorn fired at him. Sergeant Biese fell to the ground, and Schlieman believed he had been shot. However he had only gone down to the ground to make himself a smaller target. Breitbach turned and ran away with the shotgun in his hand. It appeared he had not been hit by any of the bullets fired by the officers. Neither Biese nor canine Toby had been hit. The officers ran to the corner of the bus garage where Breitbach had disappeared. They stopped there as proceeding would have been very dangerous due to the possibility of an ambush.

The officers carefully went around the corner and could see residential houses with lighted security lights. Officer Moline stated that he had seen a security light, possibly motion activated, come on just after Breitbach fled around the corner. The officers decided they had to search the immediate area near the garage first. They did not locate him.

The officers radioed to the chief of police and the other sergeant at the command post advising what had just occurred. A new perimeter was established and the search continued. Schermerhorn, Moline, and Schlieman went back to the area where Breitbach was last seen. They followed the course they believed he had taken. The area was littered with brush, fences, small storage buildings, garages, boats, and cars. They reached the house where Moline had seen the light go on. It came on again as they walked under it. This was about ten minutes after Moline had seen it activated. They were now in a residential area. Toby was on leash and had his nose to the ground as if on scent. This was even more certain as they passed a house with a Husky dog tied up in the backyard. Toby went past the dog without looking up or taking his nose off the ground. The husky was at the end of his chain and as close as three feet to Toby.

They continued and went across an alley to a residence. There was a garage and bushes along the south side of the house. Toby continued to track on the south side of the house until he reached the front corner of the house. As they went along the house, they noticed there was a fence about eight to ten feet on the property line. The area was tight because of the large bushes along the side of the house and the fence. Toby continued around the front of the house, to the sidewalk and steps, and then to the front door of the house.

They were still not using flashlights. The only light available was from streetlights on the corners of the blocks. There were two shrubs next to the south side of the steps. Schlieman later said that he "had a gut feeling" that Breitbach was there. He took out his flashlight and shined it toward the shrub. He saw a pair of tennis shoes and Breitbach's legs. He could see blood on the jeans just below the knee. Schlieman shouted, "There he is," as he kept his light on the legs.

Schlieman had the flashlight in his left hand that was holding the forearm of the shotgun. He took one step forward and could see Breitbach's face. Breitbach was on his back slightly propped up at the shoulders. He rolled toward the three officers with his left hand on the forearm of the shotgun and his right hand on the pistol grip and trigger area. The shotgun was in an upward position toward the sky. All three of them yelled, "Drop it! Do it now," over and over. Breitbach was shaking and never acknowledged them. They were approximately six feet from him. Schermerhorn was to Schlieman's right and Toby was attempting to get to Breitbach. Schermerhorn was pulling Toby back when Breitbach lowered the shotgun.

Immediately there was a loud bang and a flash from the muzzle of Breitbach's shotgun. Schlieman fired his shotgun at Breitbach. Schlieman fired two more shots as he took several steps back. Moline fired his shotgun and Schermerhorn fired his pistol. The shooting stopped and Schlieman picked up his flashlight which had fallen from his left hand as he fired his weapon. The flashlight was still on.

Schlieman moved forward to check on Breitbach. He observed the butt of the shotgun near his left shoulder and the barrel down around his right hip. Breitbach was attempting to lift it off his chest, and Schlieman ordered him three times to "drop it." Breitbach was bleeding from his midsection. Breitbach took his hand off the shotgun and said, "I'm dead." He dropped his hands to his side.

Moline provided cover, and Schlieman pulled the Maverick brand shotgun away. Schlieman pulled Breitbach from the shrub and called for an ambulance. He then began to administer CPR and oxygen. The radio transmission regarding the shooting was at 11:23 p.m. An autopsy determined that Breitbach died from multiple gunshot wounds.

It was determined by the county attorney that the officers acted in self-defense.

III

Leslie S. Fredrickson, a fifty-two-year-old man, was well known to the Fergus Falls Police Department. He was a former mail carrier with a criminal history of assaults, kidnapping and weapon violations. He had threatened family members and co-workers in the past. In 1993 he kidnapped his thirteen-year-old son and used him as a hostage during a disagreement with his wife. He used a .22-caliber rifle during that situation. He had demanded that his wife and mother-in-law come to where he was holding his son. He even fired one round past his son's face to demonstrate that he was serious. The two never responded, and Fredrickson passed out drunk. He was arrested and convicted of false imprisonment.

Three times during the following years he would be released from custody only to be arrested within a few days and returned to prison. In 1998 he was out on probation. He was soon arrested with a gun and sent to the federal prison at Oxford, Wisconsin. Authorities in Fergus Falls were so concerned about his release to a halfway house in nearby Fargo, North Dakota, scheduled for January 7, 2004, that arrangements were made to immediately notify them if he violated the conditions of his release by not returning to the house at the end of the day.

Fergus Falls Police Chief John Wagner was so concerned of the volatility of Fredrickson that he made a 68-page manual regarding him. There were photographs of Fredrickson, family members, houses and other pertinent information. There was a "calling tree" to notify individuals if Fredrickson's whereabouts were unknown. Fergus Falls police were notified at 6:05 p.m. on January 29, 2004, that Fredrickson had failed to return that afternoon. The police department and Ottertail County authorities went on alert status regarding him.

Fredrickson apparently took the bus from Fargo to Fergus Falls and checked into the small Jewell Motel sometime between 7:00 and 8:00 p.m.

Law enforcement had notified the local area lodging facilities and relatives of Fredrickson's fugitive status. However, the motel owner, seventy-one-year-old Lois Knutson, did not recognize him when he checked into the motel. He told her he had no vehicle because he had taken the bus. He checked in using the name Bob Fail.

At 5:45 a.m. on Friday, January 30, Fredrickson brought the key and television remote back to check out. He then produced a gun and told Knutson to get dressed and get in her car. It was 25 degrees below zero that morning. She had her car plugged in so it would start in the frigid weather. Fredrickson had her drive out into the country while he gave her directions from the backseat. He eventually told her to stop the car and get out. She heard him drive away. It was still dark; but she saw a light in the distance. She walked as fast as she could and was able to reach the residence which was later determined to be about three-quarters of a mile away. She was fortunate to find someone home as she was rapidly getting cold. She was clad only in blue jeans, a light coat, scarf and tennis shoes in the bitter cold. She called 911 at 7:32 a.m. as she was able to determine the identity of her captor during the time with him.

Law enforcement received another call regarding him. This one was from a sister-in-law who was calling from a closet. She saw him approaching and hid to make it look like no one was home. He had left when he thought no one was home. Officer Paul Peterson located Knutson's stolen vehicle, a 1991 Cadillac, north of the city of Fergus Falls at 8:25 a.m. The vehicle began heading toward Fergus Falls at a high rate of speed. The windows of the Cadillac were "fogged up" and Fredrickson was actually driving with his head out the window.

Meanwhile, back at police headquarters, two officers had been called in to assist. Officer Jess Schoon, thirty-year-old officer on the job for seven years, had been paged because he was a member of the Special Response Team. He had been notified the previous night that Fredrickson had failed to report to the halfway house and it was possible he would get called out if he was located. When Schoon arrived at the Law Enforcement Center, he was informed of the events which had occurred that morning and of the fact that officers were attempting to locate the stolen Cadillac. Radio transmissions were then heard that the Cadillac had been located and a chase had begun. Sgt. Kile Bergren came running through the parking garage and told him to jump in a marked squad to join in the chase.

The chase was coming toward the high school and middle school area. There was a radio transmission to put out "stop sticks" to flatten the tires and get the vehicle to stop. Bergren and Schoon were proceeding in a direction to head off the Cadillac. As the vehicle came in the direction of the local Pamida store on the edge of town, Chief Wagner gave the order to stop it and not let it into town if possible. As the squad came around a corner, Schoon saw the red Cadillac coming at them. The vehicle went through a stop sign without slowing down or having any regards to traffic or pedestrians. The Cadillac was not able to make the corner due to the excessive speed. The car skidded across the intersection and eventually jumped the curb and sidewalk, going into the parking lot of the Pamida store.

Bergren and Schoon's squad hit the curb of the parking lot and proceeded over the boulevard into the parking lot. Another marked squad was following the Cadillac and bumped it causing the Cadillac to spin out of control. It then came to a stop. Their squad stopped not far from the Cadillac with the front of it pointing directly at the passenger door of the Cadillac. A sheriff's squad bumped the back of Bergren's vehicle as they exited it. Schoon had his .40-caliber H&K MP5. Schoon came around more to the front of the Cadillac so he could see through the front windshield. Schoon could see movement as if the driver was getting ready to exit the vehicle.

Schoon could hear Sergeant Bergren shouting commands to the driver about showing his hands. As Schoon moved toward the vehicle, he heard Bergren yell something about a gun. He then heard a "pop" that sounded like a shot coming from or near the Cadillac. He heard Bergren begin firing his weapon. Fearing that either he or Bergren would get shot, he began firing his weapon into the windshield toward the driver's side. Schoon then retreated back to their squad. He could see that the passenger window was shot out and could see into the car. He and Bergren both signaled and called for no one else to fire. Schoon approached the car and used his weapon to rake out all of the glass that covered Fredrickson. Ottertail County Deputy Darren Kunz then went up to the driver's door and handcuffed Fredrickson.

Thirty-year-old Sergeant Bergren, with nine years' experience, told investigators later that he arrived at the Law Enforcement Center at 8:10 a.m. as Fredrickson was "on the loose." When he arrived, he heard the radio transmission that he was heading toward Fergus Falls at speeds nearing seventy miles per hour and that officers were in pursuit. He heard Chief Wagner tell Sgt. Steve Adams to use deadly force if necessary as he did not want him to reach town.

Bergren went to the basement of the parking garage to get a marked squad. He called for Schoon to assist him. He continued to monitor the radio traffic. Fredrickson had gone over the spike strips, but he continued toward town. The chase ended as Schoon had described in the Pamida parking lot which was quite icy.

Bergren stated that after they all stopped, he jumped from his squad and called, "Police officer. Let me see your hands" several times. Bergren was looking through the front passenger side window. He saw Fredrickson turn back to his left as his hand came across with what appeared to Bergren to be a handgun. Fredrickson was pointing at Officer Paul Peterson who was also in the parking lot. Bergren shouted, "Drop the gun. Drop the gun!" Bergren heard a "pop" from within the car. Bergren then fired all six rounds from his .357-caliber revolver into the car at Fredrickson. He then raised his arms yelling, "Hold your fire" twice. Bergren could see that Fredrickson was "kind of leaning out the driver's side window." He was not moving. Schoon covered as a deputy came up and handcuffed him.

Fredrickson was declared dead at the scene by medical personnel responding. He had two .22-caliber handguns in the car. One was determined to have been fired. Investigation after the shooting determined that Fredrickson had purchased the two weapons and ammunition via an ad in a Fargo newspaper. Letters to the editor of the local paper after the shooting described Fredrickson as a "normal" person until 1993 when his marital difficulties began in the early 1990s. He had played softball and was a reliable mail carrier. What caused him to remain so angry and threaten people for such a long period of time will never be known. We know for certain that he was very violent at the end of his life and caused a great amount of fear in the area.

Both officers were cleared, as the shooting was determined to be justified.

IV

Forty-seven year-old Mohd Ahmad Hasan robbed the Northern Star Bank Avenue in Roseville on Wednesday August 10, 1994, at 9:30 a.m. Almost immediately after the robbery, a seventy-seven-year-old witness gave police a perfect description of the getaway vehicle. An unmarked Roseville squad saw the vehicle on a lesser traveled state highway. He caught up to the car and the chase was on.

Hasan went to I-694 and then to I-494 as it looped around the east side of the Twin Cities. Numerous squads from many jurisdictions joined in the chase that went on for almost twenty miles. Speeds went to approximately seventy miles per hour.

Kenneth Drevnick, a thirty-six-year-old Minnesota State Trooper with fifteen years' experience, joined in the chase. He was sitting in the median of I-694 when he saw police squads with lights flashing approaching him. He was able to pass other squads and became the second vehicle in the chase. He had a camera in his vehicle and caught the chase on video. He was directly behind the Maplewood police who had joined the chase as it went through that city. Drevnick heard over the state radio system that Hasan was armed with a shotgun and had pointed it at officers. The Maplewood unit radioed that the officer in the passenger seat was waiting for a "clean spot" to shoot the tires out. He saw the officer hanging from his vehicle shooting at the car. A radio transmission was called out "shots fired."

Twenty-nine-year-old Trooper Scott Trautner joined in the chase just barely into Dakota County and before a long bridge that crosses the Mississippi River. Drevnick saw Hasan lift what he thought to be a shotgun and point it at Trautner. Trautner could be seen on Drevnick's video allowing Hasan pass him and then falling in directly behind him as the first car in the chase.

The left rear tire of Hasan's car was flat, and he was driving on the rim. It was decided to use a PIT maneuver to get Hasan to stop. Trautner, who was just starting his first shift on days, was the trooper to institute the PIT. The radio transmission was "take him out," meaning use the PIT. It took two attempts by Trautner before he was successful in getting the car pushed off the road down into a deep ditch.

Hasan jumped out of his car and grabbed his weapon. He turned and pointed it at the officers who had arrived. Six officers begin to shoot at him— one shot killing him instantly. The shooting is not seen on the video as the squad with the camera was pointed slightly away from Hasan's car. You can see officers from the City of South Saint Paul located at the exit, just past the bridge, scattering as the officers firing at Hasan were shooting in their direction.

Six officers fired their weapons at Hasan. Oakdale police officer Eugene Johnson used his 9-mm pistol. Roseville officers Loren Rosland and Robert Ebert each fired their .40-caliber Glock pistols. Maplewood officer David Arnold fired his .12-gauge Remington shotgun. Troopers Trautner and Drevnick used their issued .40-caliber handguns.

The weapon in Hasan's possession was later determined to be a Desert Eagle paint pellet gun that resembled a .50-caliber pistol. One of the witnesses at the bank described it as a shotgun. Another bank witness thought it looked like an older weapon that might have been a toy. That same witness also described Hasan as a "black man." Witness who had seen the chase by police described it as an "O. J. Simpson" chase.

A Dakota County grand jury returned a "no bill" regarding the shooting on October 6, 1994.

Trautner, one of the troopers in the shooting, later made news. He was charged with sexually assaulting his fourteen-year-old niece on Christmas Eve, 2004. His received a medical retirement from the Minnesota State Patrol while he was out on bond prior to the trial. He was found guilty and was sentenced to one year in jail and thirty years' probation.

Tragically, the victim of the sexual assault was killed in a car accident on October 28, 2005, on the same bridge about a mile from the shooting event. She was stopped in her own lane due to an accident when a drunk hit her car. She was pronounced dead at the scene.

V

On Wednesday, November 1, 2000, around 7:00 a.m., an Augsburg University security officer reported seeing a vehicle driving on the sidewalk at Franklin Avenue and 22nd Avenue South in Minneapolis. It was reported to Minneapolis 911 dispatch. As officers were responding to the area, numerous other 911 calls were received regarding the vehicle. The vehicle was described as a dark blue Hyundai Elantra.

Minneapolis Officer Valerie Goligowski recognized the name of the registered owner when the license plate was run. She had responded to a call on the registered owner, Alfred Sanders, the previous day. Sanders was a large man—six-foot-four and 295 pounds. On October 31, 2000, a call had been received by 911 that there was a suspicious person driving a white Jeep back and forth on a Minneapolis street for twenty minutes. That vehicle was registered to Sanders at the same address as that of the Hyundai. When Goligowski arrived in the area on October 31, she could not locate the Jeep or Sanders.

Officers Hein Dinh and Matt Blade advised Goligowski that Sanders could possibly be a "crisis candidate" from a dispatch call that they had also handled on October 31, regarding Sanders. Goligowski, the passenger in the squad, driven by Officer Lupe Herrera, proceeded to the area where the Hyundai was last seen. Radio transmissions indicated that the vehicle was backing up traffic on the busy east/west Lake Street. Dispatch told the officers that the Augsburg security officers had lost sight of the Hyundai at Lake Street and Park Avenue. Goligowski notified dispatch that they were going to proceed to Sanders' home address from the registration to see if they could locate him or the vehicle.

As they proceeded toward the address, a female in a white Mercury Mountaineer began honking her horn and waving her arm out her window to get their attention. As they turned around in the intersection to speak to the woman, a person who identified himself as a Minneapolis fireman jumped out of his vehicle and waved them down. He told them, "There's a guy out here driving like a maniac. I just saw him drive on the wrong side of 38th Street for a least two blocks and he just hit and run that lady in that white vehicle."

They proceeded to the woman who was pulled over in the Mercury. She was standing outside her vehicle crying. She told the officers, "He deliberately hit me." After telling the officers that she was not physically hurt, she gave a description of the person driving and the vehicle. She gave the same license number of the Hyundai. She added that there would be a large dent on the passenger's side of the Hyundai due to the accident with her. She added that after the collision, the large black man driving looked directly at her and shook his finger. Another witness who was immediately in front of the woman informed the officers that he had seen the Hyundai proceeding eastbound on 36th Street.

Goligowski and Herrera proceeded eastbound on 36th. They were then notified that an Augsburg security officer had located the Hyundai six blocks north of 36th Street on Lake Street proceeding east. They rushed via lights and siren to the area and were on 31st Street when notified that the Hyundai was on 31st Street. They waited for the vehicle.

The vehicle did not go by their new location. They were then told that the Augsburg officer was following the Hyundai south on Chicago Avenue crossing 33rd Street. They activated their lights and siren in an attempt to catch up to the security vehicle. When they turned onto Chicago Avenue, they were unable to locate the Hyundai. They were soon notified that the Hyundai had stopped in the alley behind 3428 Chicago. They saw the Augsburg security vehicle facing south in the alley with the officer standing outside of his vehicle next to a green and white garage.

The Hyundai was in a parking lot behind 3428 Chicago facing east. The driver, later positively identified as Sanders, was sitting behind the steering wheel. He was alone in the car. Goligowski exited her squad and approached the passenger side of his car. The window was halfway down, and she shouted at Sanders show his hands. She had drawn her handgun but was not pointing it at Sanders. He did not respond to her commands.

After the third command, Sanders appeared to be reaching down to the area between the front seats. He then began backing up toward the security officer. Goligowski yelled at the security officer as she was afraid that he was going to get pinned against the garage. The officer was able to move away. Sanders then turned his vehicle and slammed into the security officer's vehicle.

Goligowski felt that the crash would stun Sanders long enough for her to run to his vehicle and pull him from it. After slamming into the security vehicle, his car bounced about four or five feet forward. She heard him shifting gears. He looked directly at her and she felt that he was then going to run over her.

She put her weapon in her holster. She saw his tires were spinning. She believed this would give her a chance to get to the driver's door. She was able to grab the door handle, but discovered it was locked. At that point, the wheels grabbed traction and the vehicle began moving toward Officer Matt Blade who was a few feet in front of Sander's vehicle. Goligowski pulled her weapon. She told investigators later that she feared for the safety of other officers at the scene and wanted to shoot Sanders. However, she did not shoot, as Herrera was in her line of fire on the passenger side of the vehicle.

Goligowski heard two shots and saw that there were immediately two holes in the front driver's windshield. The Hyundai then veered off to the right toward Herrera. Goligowski fired two shots though the driver's side rear window. She moved along with the moving vehicle and continued firing. She fired a total of seven shots. She believed she was hitting the headrest of the driver's seat. She later told investigators that all of the officers at the scene began firing after the first two shots hit the windshield. When Sander's vehicle ran into Goligowski's squad car, the shooting stopped.

After the Hyundai struck the squad, it continued to rock back and forth across the bumper as if Sanders were attempting to free the car. Sanders could be seen reaching down between the front seats. Officer Hein Dihn shouted for the officers to be careful in the event Sanders had a gun. Goligowski radioed that shots had been fired and requested emergency/medical personnel, Code 3. About fifteen seconds after the shooting stopped, the front tires were spinning so fast on the Hyundai that smoke made it difficult to see what direction they were spinning. Officer Blade ran and reached into the car and was able to shut it off. Goligowski went up to the car to determine if Sanders had a carotid pulse. She could not find one.

It was determined following the shooting that five officers shot at the Hyundai. Blade, Dihn, and Steve Manhood were all on the driver's side with Goligowski. Herrera was the only officer on the passenger's side. All of the officers had 9-mm handguns except for Herrera. She had a .38-caliber revolver. There were twelve separate projectiles recovered from Sanders' car. They were so mutilated that only one could be determined to have been shot from a certain weapon. The autopsy reported that Sanders died from multiple gunshot wounds.

Family members had sought to have Sanders committed for a mental evaluation on October 31, 2000. He had been committed to Hennepin County Medical Center in 1998. He had recently been a patient at Saint Paul

Regions Hospital. Delores Sturgeon, mother of one of Sanders' four children, told the *Star Tribune* that Sanders had recently exhibited bizarre behavior. He apparently was suffering from bipolar disorder. (*Star Tribune*, November 2, 2000, Estrada and Chanen).

On Saturday November 18, 2000, about 180 people gathered at the Sabathani Community Center in south Minneapolis to protest the shooting. They shouted, "No justice. No peace." One protestor claimed that race was a factor in the shooting. She commented, "I do not believe that it was because he was mentally ill. He was black." (*Star Tribune*, November 19, 2000, Ison).

A Hennepin County grand jury cleared the officers on May 15, 2001.

VI

Usually on Christmas Eve people are doing last-minute shopping or traveling to visit relatives for a Christmas family gathering. This was definitely not the case for Rodney Allen Miller on December 24, 2004. Miller, who had an extensive criminal record, decided that he would spend the day stealing a few vehicles and having his own version of "bumper cars."

This event began around 9:45 a.m. when a citizen just north of Waseca, Minnesota, reported that his 1996 Ford Taurus had been stolen from his residence. Waseca is located about forty-five to fifty miles southwest of the Twin Cities. Just prior to that call, another call to authorities in the area reported that a 1992 Ford Crown Victoria was found abandoned in a farm field.

Starting at 10:30 a.m., authorities in rural Waseca County received two calls about a person "snooping" around vehicles at residences southwest of Waseca. At 10:40 a.m., a person in a vehicle on County Road 30 south of Waseca reported that a black Ford Taurus had just rammed into the back of his car. The driver drove away. The twenty-five-year-old driver and his eighteen-year-old passenger were treated and released from the Waseca Hospital for minor injuries. More vehicles called 911 to report that they were forced off the road, but luckily the two were the only ones slightly injured.

The next call to authorities was at 10:52 a.m. to report a tow truck had been stolen in New Richland. New Richland is located south of Waseca. The tow truck nearly hit a New Richland Fire Department truck which was headed to the aforementioned accident with injuries on County Road 30.

Around 11:00 a.m. the stolen tow truck was used to ram a United Parcel Service (UPS) truck. The UPS truck was hit four times from behind and forced off the road near the small town of Matawan. About fifteen minutes later, Minnesota State Patrol (MSP) trooper Brad Smith spotted the tow truck abandoned in a wildlife management area a few miles away from the UPS truck. This area is near where Blue Earth, Watonwan, and Faribault Counties meet. Within minutes a third vehicle, a green 1993 Ford Tempo, was reported stolen from a residence in the City of Minnesota Lake.

At 11:00 a.m. Trooper Smith pulled in behind the stolen Ford Tempo and began his pursuit northbound on Highway 22. Smith was joined by two Blue Earth County sheriff deputies. The officers observed the Tempo swerving into oncoming traffic and forcing at least two vehicles into the ditch to avoid being hit. The Tempo was passing cars on the shoulder of the road and was driving at speeds to 100 miles per hour An attempt to bump the Tempo using the Pursuit Intervention Technique (PIT) maneuver pushed the Tempo into the ditch. However, Miller returned to the road. Attempts to deploy stop sticks to deflate the tires failed as Miller swerved into the ditch at eighty miles per hour to avoid them.

Besides Trooper Smith, Troopers Chad Mills, and Gabriel Cornish joined the chase of the Tempo. Twenty-seven-year-old Mills, a seven-year veteran of the MSP, had begun his shift at the Mankato office at 6:00 a.m. He had been listening to the radio transmissions regarding the crash near New Richmond and the reported stolen vehicles. Mills left his office and started "working my way down Highway 22 just in case they (other troopers) needed help." He was monitoring transmissions and watching for the reported stolen vehicles. He heard that the tow truck had been recovered and another car (the Ford Tempo) was stolen. As he was proceeding south, he clocked a vehicle matching the description of the Tempo going 107 miles per hour in the northbound lane of Highway 22. Mills turned around and began his pursuit with emergency lights and siren.

Mills saw the Tempo on the tapered shoulder of the road and believed that the driver "was losing it" as he was passing a vehicle on the right. He saw the Tempo pull alongside a red Lincoln town car and swerve into it. The Tempo had slowed down to about sixty miles per hour at that time. The Tempo hit the Lincoln, but the driver of the Lincoln was able to maintain control and slowed down. Mills saw that Miller was going into the southbound lanes as he was speeding north. It appeared as if he were trying to cause a head-on crash, but cars were avoiding him by going into the ditch.

Mills was able to catch up to Miller. He was directly behind him and decided to implement the PIT maneuver. As Mills came up behind the Tempo to get in position for the PIT, Mills saw Miller look in his rear-view mirror. Miller then "locked up his brakes" causing Mills to hit the back of the Tempo. Mills increased his speed and was able to get up to the left side of the Tempo. Mills turned his squad into the Tempo. Miller spun out to Mills' left as Mills went into the ditch. Believing Miller may have stopped due to damage of the Tempo, Mills exited his squad and ran up on the road. Mills saw the Tempo run into a Blue County deputy's squad. The Tempo then proceeded north on Highway 22. Mills returned to his squad. Mills got back on Highway 22 in pursuit with the emergency lights and siren operating. Miller continued running vehicles off the road and sideswiping them.

Mills later told investigators that Miller would go about one hundred miles per hour and then slow down to near the speed limit. Mills passed another Blue Earth squad and was the first vehicle behind Miller. Mills decided he should attempt the PIT maneuver again. Miller saw him coming and cut him off. They both went down into the ditch. Miller actually drove through a person's yard and then back onto Highway 22. Mills radioed ahead for someone to try the stop sticks again.

They proceeded north on Highway 22 and law enforcement was able to

get stop sticks placed. Mills recalled a semi-tractor and numerous other vehicles ahead of Miller. Miller slowed down, but went on the right shoulder
avoiding the stop sticks again. Mills followed.

Mills was able to catch up to Miller and used the PIT again. After he hit
Miller's car, Mills was able to run into the rear tire on the passenger side.
Miller's car stopped. The Blue Earth County squad assisting in the chase
and previously behind Mills pulled in front of the Tempo. It appeared to
Mills that Miller was "messing with the gears or something." Miller "floored"
the Tempo causing it to hit the side of the deputy's driver's door. The Tempo
stopped and Mills exited his squad with gun drawn. Mills did not believe
that the Tempo was still mobile. Mills told investigators that Miller turned
and looked at him. Miller then put the car in reverse. He accelerated toward
Mills.

Mills fired his .40-caliber Beretta five times into the rear window of the
Tempo in the direction of the driver's seat. The Tempo spun out and Miller
appeared to Mills to "go just kind of limp." Troopers Smith and Cornish
came over a hill and upon the scene where Mills and the deputy had stopped
Miller. It first appeared to them that the two squads had Miller boxed in.
They both told investigators that they saw the Tempo backing up toward
Mills. Cornish believed that Mills had been run over as he disappeared. The
Tempo was coasting at a slow speed toward them in the southbound lane.
Smith placed his squad in a position to stop it from moving. Cornish pulled
up along the side of the Tempo and saw Miller in the driver's seat.

Smith and Cornish exited their vehicles with guns drawn and shouted,
"Show me your hands. Show me your hands." Cornish also yelled, "Watch
for cross-fire." The windows of the Tempo were up and Miller was not responding. Smith took an axe from his squad and shouted that he was going
to break out the passenger window. Cornish could see through the driver's
window that Miller was leaning to his right and "kind of blinking." Cornish
did not believe Miller was comprehending the troopers' demands. He was
not certain if Miller was reaching for something in the front seat or just ig-

noring them. Smith smashed out the passenger window. The deputy came up and used his stun gun. There was no reaction from Miller. Cornish took his axe and smashed out the driver's window. The stun gun was then used again.

Cornish saw Miller react to the second shot from the stun gun. Cornish opened the door and started to pull Miller from the car. Miller had a strong grip on the steering wheel. Trooper Smith and the deputy tried assisting, but without success. Cornish twice yelled, "Let go of the steering wheel." Cornish then took the axe handle and hit Miller in the forearms. They eventually were able to pull him from the car. As they were trying to handcuff him, Mills came running up shouting that he had shot Miller. After he was handcuffed, a trooper pulled back his shirt and saw blood. Cornish radioed that shots had been fired. He also requested to start Mayo 1 (helicopter ambulance rescue from Mayo Clinic) and a local ambulance. Miller was pronounced dead upon arrival at a nearby Mankato hospital.

Miller had a lengthy criminal record. He was convicted in 1984 for the murder of twenty-three-year-old Edward Smith. Court records reveal that Smith was killed because Miller and his two partners thought Smith was going to alert authorities of their burglary plans. Miller was the one who fired a shotgun into Smith's head near a lake in Cass County, Minnesota. While in prison, Miller was involved in a drug trafficking operation. Three individuals were murdered in Minneapolis relating to that operation. Rodney's brother Gary Miller was convicted of those murders. Rodney was charged with racketeering in the drug operation in 1993. He was convicted and received an additional fifteen years. However, the Minnesota Court of Appeals ruled the case was not prosecuted soon enough, and he was released in 1994.

Miller was not out very long. In September 1995, Miller and an accomplice robbed a liquor store in North Branch, Minnesota. Miller had a sawed-off shotgun and took one thousand dollars in cash. He was charged with aggravated robbery. While out on bond, he and the same female accomplice robbed a bar in LeSueur, Minnesota. Miller had a semiautomatic pistol on this occasion and departed with over four thousand dollars in cash from the till and the pull-tabs cash drawer. He received a 120-month sentence. He was eventually released from prison to a halfway house under supervised release on July 29, 2004.

Gary Miller, after hearing of his brother's death, attempted to escape from Stillwater Prison. He was caught hiding in the prison's workshop area. He received additional time for his attempted escape. He was transferred to Minnesota's maximum-security prison at Oak Park Heights, and no release date has been scheduled.

Ron Arneson, the Blue Earth County Attorney, declined prosecution of Mills on March 10, 2005.

VII

It appears that stealing a car can result in being shot by law enforcement even though those involved are not armed. A screwdriver can be mistaken as a handgun from a distance. This was the situation just after noon on Wednesday November 15, 1989.

Three young Asian boys decided to steal a car in South Saint Paul, Minnesota. The owner discovered that her vehicle was missing when coming out of a dance studio. She had parked her car just before 10:00 a.m. As the police were taking her theft report, the officer informed her that police had located it and were following it at that moment.

At 12:31 p.m. a Rosemount police officer spotted a vehicle matching the description of the stolen car a few miles south of where it was reported stolen. The officer was able to catch up to the car and verify the license plate as that of the stolen car. The officer activated his emergency lights in order to stop the car. The vehicle would not stop and began to flee in excess of the posted speed limits. The Rosemount officer was joined by a Dakota County Sheriff's Office squad in pursuit of the vehicle. Radio transmissions were broadcast to all law enforcement agencies in the area of the chase.

The car turned eastbound on 110th Street in the City of Inver Grove Heights. The stolen car swerved off the road into a cornfield. All three suspects fled the car on foot into nearby woods. Inver Grove Heights officer Kenneth Murphy, a fifty-four-year-old with twenty-four years' experience, and two Rosemount officers arrived on the other side of the woods to attempt to intercept the suspects. The two Rosemount officers exited their vehicles and took cover behind a large tree. Murphy exited his squad at 12:38 p.m. with his .12-gauge shotgun and took a position behind a hay wagon near the house and barn of John Maher. Murphy only knew that the suspects were occupants of a stolen vehicle and had no additional information. He had his hand-held radio with him and was alerted by other officers that two of the suspects were headed in his direction.

Murphy spotted the two young boys, who were later identified as thirteen-year-old Thai Yang and thirteen-year-old Ba See Lor, about thirty yards away near a row of five-foot high raspberry bushes. Murphy yelled to the boys to stop as he identified himself as a police officer. Lor ran out of his sight. Yang turned toward him and Murphy saw an object in his hand. Murphy backed away behind the wagon. Murphy saw Yang raise his hand and holding what Murphy believed to be a weapon. Fearing for his life, Murphy aimed at Yang and fired one round from his shotgun. Murphy did not see Lor who was standing ten to twelve feet away from Yang.

Murphy ran up to the area where Yang fell. As he was running to Yang, he saw another officer pointing his gun at a spot beyond the area where Murphy had last seen Yang. When Murphy got closer, he saw something between the raspberry bushes. He found Lor lying on his back and ordered him to come out; but he responded, "I can't." He directed Lor to keep his hands where he could see them. He opened Lor's jacket and asked him where he hurt. He said that the pain was in his back.

Other officers and medical personnel arrived. Murphy walked back to Yang. He observed a screwdriver about eight to ten inches in length on the ground between the two boys. A different officer found another screwdriver about the same length partly under Yang's body. Another tool used to break auto ignitions was found nearby. The other boy, a fourteen-year-old Hmong, was caught a few minutes after the shooting.

The round that Murphy fired consisted of nine metal 00 buck—each slightly smaller than a pea. An autopsy by the Ramsey County Medical Examiner's Office determined that only one pellet struck Yang. The pellet hit him in the back of his left shoulder. The pellet entered his chest severing his aorta. One pellet hit Lor in the back just left of his spinal column and traveled up to the neck area. Another pellet hit him in the buttocks and entered his abdominal area causing bleeding that resulted in his death. Three other pellets only penetrated Lor's jacket.

The backgrounds of the two boys received much attention. It was determined that Lor was sent to Boys Totem Town, a residential juvenile correction facility, for what family members described as stealing a car. He was to be at the facility until February, 1990, but somehow he was absent. Yang was described as a fairly good student at his junior high school. Yang had missed school on Tuesday and Wednesday. This was unusual for him. School officials, not knowing about the shooting, went to Yang's residence on Wednesday to determine why he had been absent.

There was an outcry from the Hmong community leaders. Yang's father, through an interpreter, claimed, "I think he (Murphy) shot because he hates Hmong. He knows that he will not face capital punishment. He used the gun to shoot the boys like he was shooting an animal." Yang's father came close to claiming that Murphy lied about seeing the screwdriver. The Minnesota Asian Advocacy Coalition and other groups called for removing the investigator from Dakota County. A special prosecutor and a grand jury including Asians were demanded. Representatives from the Minneapolis and Saint Paul National Center for the Advancement of Colored People (NAACP) joined in the call.

Two attorneys from the Minnesota Attorney General's Office were named as special prosecutors to represent Dakota County in the grand jury proceedings. Dakota County Attorney Backstrom requested them to "avoid any appearance whatsoever that this matter will not be fairly investigated and prosecuted fairly and impartially." A Dakota County grand jury deliberated less than one hour and decided on December 8, 1989, not to indict Murphy for the deaths of the two boys. The FBI investigated the shooting as a civil rights matter and sent their report to the United States Department of Justice's Civil Rights Division. The matter was not pursued by the government.

The families of the two boys filed a civil suit in United States District Court in 1990, and a trial was scheduled for September 1991. The lawsuit alleged that the shooting was influenced by race and violated the boy's civil rights under Minnesota and federal law. In addition, the suit said that the city was negligent in failing to adequately train Murphy in the use of deadly force and supervise him properly. Nkajlo Vangh, board chairman of the Leo Family Community of Minnesota, Incorporated, a Hmong support group based in Saint Paul, claimed, "This killing will go down as the worst thing to happen to the Hmong in this community." He added, "The killing has created a lot of fear of authority here. Ninety per cent of the Hmong in the community do not believe the officer's story."

The case was settled on November 19, 1993, almost four years to the day of the shooting. The families of the two boys received two hundred thousand dollars. The money was paid by the League of Minnesota Cities Insurance Trust, which insures the City of Inver Grove Heights.

VIII

The next chase involves nineteen-year-old Christopher Hirsch and his nineteen-year-old friend Adam Hotkiewicz. According to Hirsch's roommate, Melissa Devaney (*Saint Paul Pioneer Press*, April 22, 1996), the two men were drinking at their apartment in Chisago City, about thirty-five miles north of Saint Paul with friends on Friday afternoon April 19, 1996. The two men said they were leaving to drive to a nearby lake. They left, but quickly returned and obtained some tools. Hirsch told her they were having alternator problems and could not get the car started. Devaney heard squealing tires and minutes later saw police come into the apartment building. Apparently, Hirsch and Hotkiewicz had decided to steal a neighbor's 1989 GMC pickup truck.

Around 12:35 a.m. on Saturday April 20 a Department of Natural Resources officer at the Carlos Avery Wildlife Management Area noticed a suspicious vehicle in the area. The wildlife area is located a few miles from where the pickup was stolen. When the conservation officer approached the pickup, the driver (Hirsch) took off toward Interstate 35 and a chase of one hour and fifteen minutes began. The chase was initially conducted by conservation officers. However, city officers from nearby Forest Lake and a county deputy joined in the chase. Ten different agencies eventually became involved in the chase. The Minnesota State Patrol (MSP) took over as the lead agency in the pursuit when it reached Ramsey County.

Around 1:00 a.m., twenty-seven-year-old MSP trooper Curt Karges, a six-year veteran of the patrol, had joined other troopers for coffee in Bloomington, a southern suburb of the Twin Cities. The troopers were monitoring the chase of the pickup that was many miles north of their location. Karges later told investigators that he recalled hearing sirens in the background every time one of the troopers used a radio indicating the location and status of the chase. After finishing their coffee break, Karges and the other officers left to patrol their assigned areas.

Karges began proceeding eastbound on Interstate 494. (It should be noted that I-494 and I-694 makes a loop completely around the Twin Cities metro area. I-494 is the southern one-half loop and I-694 is the northern half. Interstate 35 splits north of the Twin Cities into I-35E and travels through Saint Paul and I-35W winds through Minneapolis. The two merge together again many miles south in Dakota County). Karges could hear that the chase was now on I-35E proceeding south. His lieutenant, who was ahead of him, radioed that he was getting low on gas. Karges continued on I-35E and then turned northbound on I-494. He was monitoring the radio transmissions and was aware that the chase was coming toward him from the north.

Karges exited and got into position to re-enter I-494 if the chase continued toward him. Sure enough, the chase kept coming, and he joined with lights and siren activated. He assumed the number two position behind trooper Mike LeDoux. Karges radioed that he would call (radio) the chase direction and location. Karges noticed that the pickup was swerving all over the road. Hirsch would swerve at vehicles to get them to move over. When a squad tried to get close, he would slam on his brakes. Hirsch would swerve across all of the lanes of the freeway to stay ahead of the pursuing officers. Karges recalled that he thought Hirsch was going to hit a South Saint Paul squad that came onto I-494, but he turned away at the last second.

There was a MSP helicopter following the chase from the air. The troopers were informed that the pickup had hit Washington County Sheriff's Office and City of Forest Lake squads. The chase continued around the Twin Cities westbound through construction zones at speeds of ninety to one hundred miles per hour. They continued into the MSP West District out of Karges' assigned territory. Karges relinquished his position as second to Trooper Jones of that district and became the third in line. Trooper Dennis Vandergriff became the lead car about the same time. The chase continued west and then north on I-494. They then turned east on I-694. Had they not turned east, I-494 would have become I-94 toward St. Cloud. They continued east on I-694 through Hennepin and Anoka Counties into Ramsey County again.

The stolen pickup was spraying some type of fluid that was coating the windshields of the troopers' squads, making it difficult to keep them clean. Vandergriff backed off the lead because of the spray, and LeDoux assumed the lead. Even Karges at number three was getting the spray on his windshield. They continued east on I-694 and south again toward I-94 where it changes to I-494. This time Hirsch decided to go west on I-94 toward Saint Paul. There is an area near downtown Saint Paul known as "spaghetti junction" because of the sharp curves. This is also where there are exits and entrances to both north- and south-bound I-35E. When Kirsch got to this area, a Saint Paul police squad on I-94 came alongside of the pickup. The pickup and Saint Paul squad exited to I-35E north. The Saint Paul police squad was able to get in front of the pickup and box it in between the trooper squads.

At this point Lt. Jay Swanson, who had re-joined the chase after getting fuel, told his units to make physical contact with the pickup if it slowed down enough. The Saint Paul squad was able to keep the speed of the pickup slow enough for trooper LeDoux to make contact with the pickup. The pickup started to spin in a clockwise manner at the Maryland Avenue exit of I-35E. Karges continued toward the pickup as it appeared to him that it was going to keep driving ahead. He was able to hit the right front wheel of the pickup. All the vehicles stopped. It was now 1:50 a.m.

Karges told a Bureau of Criminal Apprehension (BCA) investigator when interviewed at 5:50 that morning that he could see the driver (Hirsch) with his hand out in front of him as if giving up. Hotkiewicz, in the passenger seat, had his right hand raised; but Karges could not see his left hand. Karges had his handgun in his right hand and then switched it to his left. As he was reaching to open the passenger door, he saw Hotkiewicz's left arm come over his jacket. Karges saw a flash that he thought was a gun. Karges started backing up and fired one round from his .40-caliber pistol. Karges kept backing up and then "something started going black from the side like I thought I'd been shot ...." Karges added, "I thought he was going to kill me when his arm came up. I thought that I was going to get shot." It was determined that Hotkiewicz did not have a weapon and died instantly from one shot in the forehead. Investigators believed he was holding a screwdriver which was used to steal the pickup.

Karges was again interviewed at a later date by the BCA. Karges said, "I still remember saying to him (Hotkiewicz) and yelling to him that, that, put your hands up, and um, it was his left hand that came, looked like it came up, and towards me, I saw a, what looked like a flash of a gun barrel, and, and I fired my weapon."

This case was presented to a Ramsey County grand jury on May 27, 1997. No indictment was returned against Karges. The grand jury was able to see four different videotapes from cameras in the troopers' squads of the chase and shooting.

Hirsch pled guilty to theft of a motor vehicle and fleeing police officers. Hirsch had been previously arrested in 1994 for auto theft. Hirsch made the news again in January, 2001, when he allegedly fired a gun at a fast food restaurant manager in Saint Paul who told him and a friend to stop urinating on the side of the restaurant. No one was hurt. He received a sixty-month sentence for that offense.

In September, 2000, the State of Minnesota paid $375,000 to the family of Hotkiewicz.

Chapter Five

Just Shoot Me
aka Suicide by Cop

I

A routine traffic stop can immediately turn into a deadly situation. Around 7:00 p.m. on Wednesday, April 13, 1994, a Minneapolis squad car saw a vehicle with a broken taillight. The emergency lights of the squad were activated as the squad pulled in behind the car. As the police squad was catching up to the car, the car pulled over and stopped. Before police could get to the car, a man walked up and entered through the front passenger door. Twenty-four-year-old officer David Pleoger exited the passenger side of the squad and approached the passenger side. The man got out of the car and began to walk away. Pleoger shouted, "Sir. Stop, I need to talk to you." The individual, later identified as twenty-three-year-old Steven Cole, fled. Pleoger pursued and continued to call for Cole to stop. As he was chasing Cole, he observed him digging in the area of his waistband in the front of his pants. Pleoger was about ten to fifteen feet from Cole when Cole stopped and faced Pleoger with a knife in each hand.

Pleoger drew his 9-mm handgun and ordered Cole to drop the knives.

Cole said, "I can't do that." Cole began running again and Pleoger followed. Cole stopped several times and turned toward Pleoger. Each time, he raised the knives and made slashing motions back and forth in the air. Cole ran to the area of 31st Street and Grand Avenue. Cole stopped. He had possibly seen another squad converging on the scene and blocking his escape route. Cole began pacing back and forth with the knives poised in a threatening manner. At least ten officers arrived on the scene. Cole continued saying that he could not put down the knives. It was a standoff.

Officers were pleading with him to put them down and told him that they would get him some help. He continued to say that he could not put the knives down. He told the police to "go ahead and kill me." He constantly ran short distances back and forth. He appeared agitated. Officers backed away from him and took positions of safety behind squad cars.

Officers told Cole that an ambulance was coming to the scene and they would take him to the hospital. Cole complained that he did not want to go to jail or the hospital and the officers should just leave. They responded that they could not just leave. They added that no harm would come to him if he would put the knives down. He said he wanted the officers to shoot him as he was going to die anyway.

Supervisors on the scene told the officers near the street not to chase him if he ran to the alley as he had officers located there. The supervisors also authorized the use of deadly force if Cole ran toward them.

Officer Pleoger and thirty-two-year-old officer Curtis Graff were the closest to Cole behind cover of their squad. For another ten minutes or so, Cole made several short charges toward the officers. However, he never left the grassy area across the sidewalk toward the officers. Efforts continued to have him put the knives down. Pleoger later told investigators that he did not feel entirely safe with Cole on the grassy area—just "more comfortable."

Someone from the crowd which had gathered shouted, "Steve, drop the knives; I will get you some help."

Cole yelled back, "No, I'm going to be dead soon." Cole kept shouting, "You'll have to kill me. I'm going to die soon, kill me now."

Cole then became more agitated and was physically shaking. Cole then angrily screamed, "Fuck this!" and began to walk quickly and deliberately toward Graff. Cole came to the curb as the officers were shouting at him. Pleoger felt that Graff's life was in danger and shot at Cole. Graff related that he heard, "Fuck you," and saw Cole coming toward him across the sidewalk. Fearing for his life, he fired his .45-caliber handgun. Cole fell to the sidewalk about ten feet from the officers. Officer Richard Koats ran to where Cole had fallen and removed the knives from Cole's reach. An ambulance immediately took Cole to Hennepin County Medical Center. He died during surgery about ninety minutes after being taken from the scene.

A computer specialist who lived in an apartment next to the shooting scene told police investigators that he heard police yelling at a man to drop his knives. He watched the shooting take place. He said, "They gave him a chance. They had no choice but to defend themselves. No telling what he was going to do. I don't know if it was drugs or what."

One of the sergeants at the scene recognized Cole. He recalled an incident with him on November 15, 1992. On that occasion, Cole had shot his roommate in the head with a pellet gun. During that incident, Cole held officers at bay with a knife. After forty-eight minutes of negotiations with Cole in his apartment, he gave up. Several knives and a machete were taken from the apartment.

After this shooting, police interviewed a friend and discovered that Cole had AIDS and was not expected to live. The friend said that Cole was drinking Colt 45 beer and smoking marijuana earlier that day. Cole was also on prescription medication for treatment of AIDS. He told numerous friends that he wanted to die and if he ever had contact with police he would force them to shoot him. Friends also said that he had a "knife fetish" since early childhood.

An autopsy determined that Cole died from multiple gunshot wounds to the abdomen. A Hennepin County grand jury returned a no bill regarding Graff and Pleoger on August 23, 1994.

II

This next incident began with a call to Anoka Police Department 911 on Sunday, June 12, 1994, at 8:20 p.m. The call is as follows:

911: Police and fire

Female Caller: Yes, I have ah…a person here who's trying to take her own life

911: Trying to do what?

Caller: Trying to take her life

911: Okay.

Caller: She's got a knife…

911: Okay.

Caller: I can't get it away

911: What's your address?

Caller: (Address given)

911: Has she been drinking?

Caller: Yes. (Gives person's name as Wilma Brown) Wilma is going after her arms.

The conversation continues, and the 911 operator tells the caller to set the phone down and get out of the house. The officer arrives and recorded on the 911 call is an operator saying to another operator, "Do you hear (inaudible) yelling?" Then you can hear an officer say, "Put down the knife. Put the knife down… Put the knife down Wilma… put it down." Then one shot is heard immediately followed by two rapid shots. The 911 operator then said, "I think that they shot her."

Ed Egly, a thirty-eight-year-old Anoka Police Department officer with almost eleven years' experience, and Officer Mike Antiqua arrived at the house. They only knew that an adult female was in the house saying that she wanted to die. They knew her name was Wilma. After calling for everyone to get out of the house, Egly went to the front door of the house. Antiqua was to Egly's right side, but Egly took up most of the area of the doorway.

Egly shone his flashlight into the house and saw Wilma Brown, a forty-three-year-old female American Indian, standing with a large knife a few feet into the house. Egly told Brown that he would get her to a doctor. Antiqua also called to her to put the knife down. Brown made a slashing motion to her right leg and three slashing motions to her throat. She started toward the front door, making more slashing motions to her throat. Egly brought his weapon up and pointed it at her. Brown hesitated momentarily and then continued walking rapidly toward Egly and Antiqua at the door. Egly shouted at her to put the knife down.

Egly, based on Brown's refusal to obey his commands and the immediate threat to himself and officer Antiqua, fired three times at her with his Beretta 9-mm handgun. Brown slumped to the floor and dropped the knife. Antiqua was not in a position to fire his weapon. After securing the knife, Egly began rendering first aid to Brown. Paramedics responded. After an assessment of her condition, the paramedics announced that she was dead.

An Anoka County grand jury cleared Egly of charges.

III

This incident began with a telephone call from a concerned parent. At 8:30 p.m. on July 21, 1995, a Washington County Sheriff's Office (WCSO) deputy responded to the call and interviewed the parents of Charles Edward Lesnau, known as Charlie to his friends and family. Seventeen-year-old Lesnau had been fired from a job at a local drug store. He was apparently upset about the firing, and his whereabouts were unknown to his parents. They were concerned and believed him to be suicidal. They believed he would be driving his 1986 black Chevrolet Camaro. The deputy immediately contacted his dispatcher and had all the information regarding Lesnau entered into the National Crime Information Center (NCIC). Unfortunately, the deputy was involved in a car accident and did not return to work until 3:00 p.m.

on July 24.

When the deputy returned to work on July 24, he had a message from Mrs. Lesnau. He contacted her about 7:00 p.m. She told the deputy she learned that Lesnau had been at his girlfriend's home in Saint Paul on July 23. Lesnau apparently told his girlfriend that he was upset and wanted to kill himself. His girlfriend was frightened by his behavior and called the Saint Paul police. Lesnau left her home prior to Saint Paul police arriving.

Lesnau's mother further related to the deputy that he was sleeping in his car at freeway rest stops in the metropolitan area. It was very apparent to the deputy that she was upset and concerned about her son. The deputy related this updated information to the dispatcher.

Unbeknownst to the deputy taking the report, his own WCSO had contact with Lesnau just after midnight on July 21. A deputy on routine patrol had observed a Camaro behind a service garage among numerous automobiles. It appeared as though a person was asleep in the car. After making a safety check of the car, he woke the sole occupant. It was Lesnau, and he gave the deputy a Minnesota driver's license. While moving items in his console to get his driver's license, the deputy observed a knife with an approximate five-inch blade in a black sheath.

The deputy took the knife when he went back to his squad to check for warrants or driving violations. Lesnau was not wanted, nor did he have any driving violations. When questioned further by the deputy, Lesnau related that he had had a disagreement with his parents. He was resting and then was going to drive to Eau Claire, Wisconsin, approximately two hours away, to stay with his grandmother. The deputy informed him that he could sleep at that location and expected him to be gone in the morning. He wished him luck with his parents and returned to his normal patrol duties. The deputy came back around 3:00 a.m. and observed Lesnau sleeping in the car. No incident report was written at that time. The only record was the radio transmission checking for warrants and driving violations.

The next known whereabouts of Lesnau was on Sunday, July 23. Lesnau had taken a girl from Saint Paul to the prom earlier in the spring. He had been calling her even though she had a steady boyfriend. He called her numerous times before eventually arriving at her residence between 12:30 and 1:00 a.m. on July 24. Lesnau was unwilling to go into her house, so they talked for about ten minutes on the front porch. He told her that he wanted to get something from his car for his parents and requested that she give it to them. When he went to his car, she told her parents to call the police as he appeared to her to be very depressed and possibly suicidal.

When he returned, she convinced him to come into the house. Her mother came downstairs to see Lesnau. He appeared frightened and returned to his car. The girl followed him to his car. He told her he would be punished by God if he continued to live. Lesnau told her God had a sick sense of humor. He labeled himself as a "drug addict" and "thief." He told her he was the fault for all of his problems and was going to go to jail for stealing four thousand dollars from his employer. He also told her he was going to commit suicide with a single gunshot to his head. He wanted her to put a white rose on his grave.

When the girl's mother called the police, she told them she was uncertain if she wanted police or a crisis intervention person. The dispatcher told her a uniformed officer should come to evaluate the situation. She told the dispatcher she would call back.

The girl's mother also called Lesnau's mother. The girl's mother then went out to talk to Lesnau. He told her he was a terrible person. He said he was a criminal who had stolen four thousand dollars from his employer. He kept telling her, "I am a criminal." She told him she had talked to his mother. His mother wanted him to know that he was not in trouble and they wanted him to come home. His mother also wanted him to know that no one was mad at him and friends were at his house who would "stick by him." Lesnau told the girl's mother words to the effect, "No, I deserve this, I am a terrible person. I don't feel that I can stay here. I have to go." The girl ran to the house just prior to the end of her mother's conversation with Lesnau and called

911. Police responded just after Lesnau had left the area.

A review of Saint Paul police records revealed a call was dispatched to the girl's residence at 12:39 a.m. on July 24. No report was made by the responding officers as the transmission to dispatch "gone on arrival."

Thirty-seven-year-old WCSO Deputy Lonnie Van Klei came on his tour of duty at 11:00 p.m. on July 24. He was assigned as a marked patrol squad to a specific area of the county. He was in uniform and carrying his personally owned .45-caliber semiautomatic Sig Sauer handgun. Around 3:35 a.m. on July 25, Van Klei's attention was drawn to a Chevrolet Camaro that was making a U-turn in the middle of the highway in the downtown business district of Hugo. He was curious due to the time of the night and the possibility that it was involved in criminal activity. Van Klei also made a U-turn and accelerated to catch up. He was able to get the license number and attempted to get information regarding the vehicle on his mobile data terminal (MDT). The Camaro made another U-turn, and this made Van Klei believe that the driver was trying to avoid him.

Van Klei activated his red lights and turned to follow the Camaro. The car accelerated and made a left-hand turn onto a county highway. He felt he had a fleeing felon. He notified the dispatcher that he was in pursuit with lights activated. As he was chasing the car up to speeds of seventy to eighty miles per hour, he learned there was a "hit" from NCIC for the person in the car as a runaway. Because he was busy driving, he was unable to key up the MDT to review the response.

The fleeing vehicle was unable to negotiate a right ninety-degree turn on the main street in downtown Centerville. Van Klei saw the Camaro crash into a power pole. He turned off the siren and shone the squad's spotlight on the car. He had parked to the driver's side and slightly to the rear of the Camaro. Lesnau sat in the driver's seat looking straight ahead. Van Klei could not see any injury to Lesnau. Van Klei exited the squad and used the opened driver's door as cover. He then saw Lesnau's eyes glance toward him. Van Klei felt that Lesnau was acting strange. He thought Lesnau might be injured or under the influence of drugs. He then moved toward the car to check on Lesnau.

Van Klei approached the Camaro by walking around the rear of his squad. He continuously asked Lesnau if he was okay as he approached. When he got up to the driver's door, he leaned forward to look into the car. Lesnau was looking straight ahead with his hands down to his side. He again asked Lesnau if he was okay. At this point Lesnau made a violent lunge out of the window with a very large knife as if to slash or stab Van Klei. The knife actually brushed his left arm; but he was not cut. Van Klei immediately backed away.

Lesnau opened the door and stepped out of his vehicle. Van Klei drew his .45-caliber handgun. Lesnau was standing next to his car and said, "Go ahead, shoot me, shoot me, kill me…" He then made a pointing gesture to his chest and hollered, "Shoot me here." He began waving the knife over his head and stood in the open space between the two cars. Van Klei attempted to calm Lesnau down. He told him that there were more officers on the way. Lesnau continued to shout, "Shoot me."

Van Klei said that Lesnau "jockeyed for position" and moved toward Van Klei. Van Klei continued to retreat. Lesnau told the deputy that he was going to have to kill him. Lesnau's actions made no sense to Van Klei. Van Klei told investigators later that Lesnau began "coming hard, running and picking up speed." The deputy continued to retreat toward the front of his squad and beyond. Van Klei said it was like Lesnau was "going to make a full tackle." Lesnau was also making a growling type cry as he was progressing toward Van Klei. Van Klei had no choice. He had to shoot Lesnau as he was moving back. Lesnau fell to the ground. Van Klei took cover to behind a nearby dumpster to protect himself.

A nearby neighbor was awakened by the accident and went outside to discover Lesnau with a knife challenging Van Klei to "shoot me." This neighbor told investigators that Van Klei "just kept backing up. The kid just kept coming at him. It was like talking to a wall. He (Van Klei) didn't want to shoot him. He was looking pretty sick. He looked like he was going to faint."

Another neighbor said, "The kid obviously wanted to die; that's the impression I got. I feel so sorry for the cop."

Crime scene investigators determined that Van Klei fired three rounds. One shot hit Lesnau in the chest and one to the right side of his head. The weapon that Lesnau used had an overall length of almost seventeen inches with a polished chrome blade of twelve inches.

Investigators were also given a note that Lesnau had given to the girl in Saint Paul while at her house. The note, written on a Burger King napkin, was addressed to "mom and dad" and signed "Charlie." The note could be described as a suicide note and started, "Obviously, you now what happened by now." Also in the note was, "I'm sorry. No one can be held accountable for my actions except me from now on." It is sad that a young boy with so much ahead of him felt so hopeless that he felt he had no choice but to cause police to end his life.

IV

Forty-one-year-old Robert Allen Peterson had been experiencing some personal difficulties. He had problems during his marriage and now with his significant other. To add to his troubles, he abused alcohol and drugs. Everyone close to him said his use of methamphetamine was his biggest problem. He was hospitalized for a drug overdose on May 2, 2005. He was released on May 6. His wife feared him because of his drug usage. She had an Order for Protection issued against him by a local court. They had only been married for a few months when he started using methamphetamine. She stated that his entire behavior changed within six months of his drug use. He became involved with another female and binged on drugs. He told his girlfriend that he heard voices in his head. He apparently owed money for drugs. In addition to his drug use, he borrowed almost five thousand dollars to sustain his gambling habit.

The Order for Protection was to be served on May 18, 2005. His wife believed he was hiding on their property; so she called the Isanti County

Sheriff's Office to search for him. A deputy, along with family members, began searching the rural premises. The deputy went into a pole barn. There was a closed door to a partitioned shop area. He attempted to open the door, but found it locked. He tried kicking it once. He then heard a shot ring out from inside the shop area. He heard some moaning sounds followed by two additional shots. The deputy retreated and requested additional officers.

Twenty-eight-year-old Deputy Justin Wood of the adjacent Chisago County Sheriff's Office was one of many officers responding. By the time Wood arrived, there were ten to twelve officers in assigned locations around the pole barn. Wood contacted the command sergeant at the scene to get his assignment. The only type of negotiation occurring at that time was officers shouting from behind a utility shed toward the pole barn. Wood took his position by a tree and listened to officers yelling to Peterson. They were asking him to give up and come out of the pole barn without his gun. Wood was informed that there were three shots before his arrival, and he heard five more shots from the pole barn after his arrival. About every twenty-five minutes or so, Peterson would fire a round.

People who knew Peterson told officers that he was probably using a .22-caliber handgun. There were three officers positioned just east of the pole barn behind a utility shed. Wood heard them shout, "He's pointing the gun at us" as they fled for cover. The only area not be covered, due to a large slough running next to it, was on the west side of the barn. Officers were also taking cover behind police squads positioned by a nearby utility shed.

Wood was on the scene for over forty-five minutes before he actually saw Peterson. Wood related that the reason he had not seen Peterson earlier was due to a towel or blanket covering the window to the shop area. When Peterson removed the cover, Wood was able to see a handgun in Peterson's right hand as he paced back and forth. He relayed this information to other officers via his radio.

Peterson was screaming obscenities. Peterson would come to the window and pat his chest shouting, "You're going to have to kill me…let's get it over with." When not in sight, Wood could hear him shout, "I'm gonna make you shoot me."

The sergeant trying to negotiate would cal back, "I don't want to shoot you; let's try to work this out."

Deputy Wood had loaded his shotgun with 00 buck when he left his squad. After being there for three to four hours, he decided the first round to be fired should be a rifled slug. This decision was made because he estimated his distance to the pole barn to be about thirty-five yards. If Peterson exited and rushed him, the first round could possibly bring him down. If he continued rushing him, the 00 buck pattern would be larger and possibly stop him.

Wood could see what appeared to be blood on Peterson's white shirt in the area of his shoulder. Wood had seen Peterson break out the window with his gun and was not sure if the blood was caused by the glass or from an earlier shot. Peterson would kick the tin of the barn causing loud bangs. He also would come to the window and wave his middle finger and shout, "You're gonna have to kill me."

Suddenly, Peterson fired a shot and exited through an overhead door. Peterson put the gun to his head. Officers caled for Peterson to put the gun down. He started to go back toward the barn. He stopped and turned back toward the officers and pointed the gun at them. He moved quickly from those officers and turned toward Wood. Peterson then pointed his handgun directly at Wood. Fearing for his life, Wood fired one shot from his Remington 870 .12-gauge. He saw Peterson fall. Other officers began approaching Peterson yelling, "Drop the weapon!" The officers secured the handgun. EMS personnel, who had been on standby at the scene, began administering first aid.

The post-shooting investigation determined that Peterson's weapon was a Smith and Wesson Model 41 .22-caliber pistol. A suicide note was located in the residence on the property. He described himself as "a piece of shit." The note also stated that he was "checking out" and "going home to be with my grandpa." He indicated in the note that he heard voices in his head and that "drugs could make them go away."

An autopsy revealed that Peterson had the presence of methamphetamine, amphetamine, cannabinoids, THC, tricyclic anti-depressants, propoxyhene and opiates in his system at the time of his death.

This shooting is different as it did not go to a grand jury. Isanti County Attorney Jeffrey R. Edblad wrote on July 15, 2005, that "the acting of Deputy Wood using deadly force against Robert Peterson was authorized and justifiable under Minnesota law. Further, it appears that this tragic situation was brought on by Robert Peterson acting in a manner consistent with that of an individual who has chosen to end his life." Edblad added, "Robert Peterson had made the decision to use law enforcement as the mechanism to end his life on May 18, 2005."

V

Officers from the Brooklyn Park Police Department were dispatched to a residence in their city, a northwestern suburb of Minneapolis, at 4:55 a.m. on Sunday, April 4, 1993. A forty-four-year-old woman reported to 911 that her son had stabbed himself in the chest in the kitchen of the house. She ran upstairs to make the 911 call. She was not sure where he was in the house.

Steve Pearson, a thirty-three-year-old officer with twelve years' experience, and Steve Palmquist, a twenty-eight-year-old officer with five years' experience, responded to the call. The mother saw the officers arrive. She let them in the house. She told the officers that her son had probably gone to the basement. When asked if her son, later identified as twenty-eight-year-old John M. Bertelsen, had been drinking, she responded "a lot." She also added that he had used a steak knife to stab himself in the chest.

The officers quickly checked the areas other than the basement to make sure he was not hiding. After further discussion with his mother, it was determined that he had indeed probably gone to the basement. The officers then directed their attention to the basement door located in the kitchen. They could see that the door was slightly ajar. The "working space" for them was very tight. Officer Palmquist took a position of cover with his handgun drawn, and Pearson opened the door. There was a stairway leading to the basement. The basement was dark, and it did not appear that any lights were on. Both officers called to Bertelsen.

Within a few seconds, Bertelsen appeared at the bottom of the steps. They could see from light in the kitchen that he had a knife with a black handle in his right hand. Both officers shouted at him to put the knife down and come upstairs to talk to them. Bertelsen immediately replied, "No." He then took the knife, still in his right hand, and began to cut his throat with "determined and aggressive" strokes. It was obvious to the officers that he wanted to harm himself. He was bleeding severely from his neck area. It appeared that he had serious cuts. The officers again asked him to put the knife down.

Bertelsen then disappeared from their sight. They next heard some very loud bangs. The officer did not know what caused the bangs. They thought the bangs were possibly gunshots. They officers feared that bullets could be coming through the kitchen floor where they were standing.

They called out to Bertelsen. He appeared at the bottom of the stairs again. They pleaded with him to put the knife down. Bertelsen shouted back to them, "No…what are you going to do…shoot me?" Pearson yelled back that they were there to help him, not to hurt him. Bertelsen seemed enraged, and his eyes were wide open. He then put the knife in a raised and combative posture toward the officers.

Bertelsen then began charging up the stairs. Palmquist, who was on Pearson's right and closest to the wall, continued to call for Bertelsen to put the knife down. Bertelsen continued charging up the stairs in an "attack position." Bertelsen quickly neared the top of the stairs. It was obvious to both officers that he was not going to stop and fully intended to stab one or both of the officers. Feeling they were in immediate danger, both officers fired their Smith and Wesson 9-mm handguns. Bertelsen's momentum carried him through the top of the doorway, and he fell onto the kitchen floor.

Palmquist disarmed Bertelsen. Pearson immediately radioed the situation. He requested paramedics and additional officers. Palmquist stayed with Bertelsen. Pearson went upstairs to check on Bertelsen's mother. He returned to the kitchen after determining she was okay. He then went to the basement to determine if there were any weapons. After clearing the basement, he returned to Bertelson's mother. She informed Pearson that her son had hepatitis. Pearson immediately returned to the kitchen to inform the other officers and medical personnel of his hepatitis. Bertelsen was taken to North Memorial Medical Center where he later expired.

Both officers were cleared by a Hennepin County grand jury in May 1993.

VI

This shooting was a tragic event for everyone involved. It can be described as an emotionally disturbed person, domestic situation or suicide by cop. East Grand Forks Police received a 911 call just before 6:00 p.m. on Wednesday, May 5, 1999, that two elderly people had been stabbed. One was able to flee the house and was at a local gas station. Officers Brian Cheney, Curtis Graff, and Brian Solem responded from the police department.

Cheney, a twenty-three-year-old officer with one year's experience, was the first to arrive at the location. He pulled into the parking lot of Orton's Gas Station. A young male and female motioned Cheney to the southwest corner of the building. An elderly male was getting out of a car. Cheney could see that he had a large spot of blood above the left side of his waist. The man, later identified as eighty-year-old Ardell Hangsleban, kept saying, "My wife, my wife, my pickup." He had a set of keys to his pickup in his hands. Cheney called for fire and rescue. He applied pressure to the wound.

The two people who were with Ardell told Cheney that someone had taken Hangsleban's wife to the hospital. They related that she appeared to have been stabbed numerous times. When Cheney asked Hangsleban where he lived, he pointed toward Rhinehart Drive and 6th Street Southeast and said, "Right over there." Cheney thought he was pointing at a former police officer's home and knew it was not the correct house.

Fire and rescue arrived and began administering medical treatment. Cheney continued to ask Hangsleban for details. Just prior to being placed into the rescue vehicle, he told Cheney that his son was the person who stabbed him and his wife. Cheney could hear Graff and Solem talking to other witnesses in the background while he was talking to Hangsleban. After the rescue vehicle left, Graff and Solem told him that the address was 545 Rhinehart Drive and that Brian Hangsleban was the son.

Someone at the scene told officers that Brian had left in his pickup, but he returned to the house. Officer Solem informed Cheney and Graff that he had prior contacts with Brian. Solem said Brian had mental problems and could become very violent. He had been in the psychiatric ward in Thief River Falls, Minnesota, numerous times. His parents also had restraining orders against Brian in the past.

The three officers proceeded to the Hangsleban house. Graff pulled his squad on the north side of the house, and Cheney parked his on the opposite side at an angle to use as cover. Cheney and Graff took their .12-gauge shotgun in the event they had to use deadly force. Officer Solem called the dispatcher and asked for the phone number to the Hangsleban house.

Additional officers were arriving to assist. Numerous people started to gather and watch what the police were doing. Crowd control was beginning to be a problem. Graff also called and requested an additional ambulance to be on standby.

A few minutes later, Graff radioed that he could see movement through a window in the house. All of a sudden officers began hearing Solem talking on the telephone. He was holding his radio key down as he was talking to Brian on his cell phone. The officer's could hear Solem's side of the conversation, but they were unable to hear Brian's responses. Cheney heard Solem say, "Come out. Come outside. Don't bring the knife. Leave the knife. We don't want to hurt you. We don't want anyone else hurt. Leave the knife inside. Come out without the knife."

Cheney had another officer take his position in front of the house. He ran around to back of the house where Solem was located. Solem was on the phone with Hangsleban and was saying, "Brian, come out, your parents aren't dead. They're at the hospital." Solem was obviously trying to encourage Brian to surrender and leave the knife inside. Solem closed his cell phone and told Cheney, "This guy told me that he is gonna take one of us with him." He added, "He's gonna come out fighting."

Cheney returned to the front of the house. He told Graff what Solem had said about the situation. They also discussed what to do if Hangsleban came out. It was decided that Brian could not leave in his pickup. They would shoot out the tires if he tried to leave in it. They knew he had already stabbed two people, and he would not be allowed to leave. They also knew he had used his knife against his parents and had threatened to use it against police. A detective at the scene drove his unmarked vehicle into the driveway of the residence to block an escape.

Solem was replaced in the backyard. He came out to the area where Cheney, Graff and other officers were located. Solem continued to talk to Hangsleban on his cell. The officers could hear Solem say, "Just come out. Yes, you will be arrested, but we are not going to hurt you. We're not gonna shoot you if you come out without the knife. Don't do anything to threaten us." Similar dialogue went on for sometime. Cheney told investigators later that his legs were beginning to hurt from being crouched down behind his squad. Cheney stood up and placed his shotgun over the roof of the car.

Solem then shouted, "He's coming out." Cheney saw the side door open and a white male (Hangsleban) come out. Cheney could only see his head because the pickup in the driveway blocked his view. Cheney moved away from his squad and crossed the driveway in order to get a better view of Brian. He saw a large butcher-type knife in his right hand.

Hangsleban walked toward Cheney. Cheney yelled, "Drop the knife" three times. Hangsleban continued walking toward Cheney. Cheney backed up to his original position by his squad. Cheney could also hear other officers calling for him to drop the knife. Cheney heard Graff come up almost next to him. Graff was shouting for him to drop the knife, too. Cheney backed to the curb.

Hangsleban then turned to toward Graff. He was holding the knife at shoulder height with the tip pointing at Graff. Brian took a step at Graff, and Cheney fired his shotgun at him. He ejected the spent cartridge and racked in another round. He saw Hangsleban fall to the street. Another officer ran up to Hangsleban and ordered him to drop the knife as it was still in his right hand. That officer stepped on Brian's wrist and kicked the knife away. Paramedics who were on the scene rushed to render aid.

As soon as Hangsleban went down, Cheney heard Graff say, "I shot." It surprised Cheney. Cheney told Graff, "I shot." Their shots were simultaneous. Cheney then made the weapon safe by ejecting the live round. He and Graff then placed their shotguns on the ground. Cheney was driven back to the police department. Cheney told investigators he was surprised that Graff fired his weapon. Cheney said he concentrated on squeezing the trigger of his weapon and felt the recoil. He had not heard Graff's weapon discharge.

Graff, a thirty-seven-year-old officer with eleven years' experience, was also at the police department when the call came in. He and Solem left in Graff's squad. When he arrived at Orton's Gas Station, a very hysterical woman told him there had been a stabbing and two people were hurt by their son. She pointed at a white house with a beige pickup in the driveway and said, "There's the truck." Another witness said that he (the son) had tried to leave. Graff told the two officers also there that he was going to "sit on the house" and not to allow anyone to leave.

Graff related the same information as Cheney until Hangsleban came out of the house. Graff said he saw him approaching three officers to his right. Hangsleban was watching those officers as Graff started to approach him. It appeared as though he was concentrating so much on those three officers that he did not see Graff. Graff was able to get fairly close to him. He wanted to make sure Hangsleban did not get to the street and injure a bystander or take one as a hostage.

Graff was able to come up to about ten to twelve feet from Hangsleban before he turned and saw him. Hangsleban stopped and turned slowly toward Graff. Graff took two steps back. Hangsleban, who previously had the tip of the knife pointed in the air, lowered the blade and pointed it directly at Graff. Graff told investigators later that he was shouting, "Drop the knife" so loud that his throat hurt. Graff had his shotgun at his shoulder ready to fire. Hangsleban took one step toward Graff, and Graff fired once.

Graff saw Hangsleban falling to the street. He immediately put his weapon on safe and announced, "I shot." Cheney immediately said that he had also fired. Graff, just like Cheney, had not heard the other shot. After other officers' secured Hangsleban and the knife, Graff told Cheney, "Let's put our guns down."

Other officers said they should go into the house to determine if anyone else was hurt inside. Graff told Cheney they should not go in the house. They had used deadly force and should remain outside. After other officers did a quick search of the house, a deputy took Graff back to the police department.

Hangsleban was dead at the scene. Both officers had fired 00 buck. His mother, "Dell" Hangsleban, died from her stab wounds. His father was in serious condition, but did recover. Brian Hangsleban had a history of problems. He never had any employment history. He lived off and on with his parents. He had been released from the Northwest Regional Correction Center in Crookston, Minnesota, for drunk driving the day before the incident. He had been in jail twice in 1994 for contempt of court. In 1991, he went to jail for assaulting his mother. During that incident, a passerby saw him assaulting her and called police. He pled guilty to terroristic threats. He had the reputation of having a volatile temper.

The entire shooting by the officers was photographed by Eric Hylden of the *Grand Forks Herald*. He arrived during the incident. Four of his photographs were on the front page of the paper the following day. The photographs showed Hangsleban threatening Graff with the knife, walking toward him, Graff firing his weapon and Hangsleban slumping to the street. The photos matched the statements given by the officers.

Reactions to the photographs were very negative. Letters to the editor of the paper were laced with comments as follows: (1) totally tasteless, (2) outraged, (3) extremely distasteful, (4) should be ashamed, (5) insensitive, (6) absolutely horrified, and (7) totally unnecessary. Only two of the letters to the editor were positive. One claimed that the photos showed "reality" and "the *Herald* did its job and did it well" (*Grand Forks Herald,* Letters to the Editor, May 9, 1999).

VII

Just after midnight on March 2, 1994, Minneapolis Police Department officers responded to a domestic dispute at an apartment on the northeast side of Minneapolis. Donald LaPoint, a thirty-two-year-old Native American who had a history of domestic abuse and suicide attempts, was there to greet the officers.

The history leading up to this event is significant. LaPoint, his longtime companion and her two children, moved into the apartment during the summer of 1993. Neighbors said there were several disputes between the two. Neighbors heard LaPoint threaten her numerous times. LaPoint threatened suicide many times. He had a scar across his throat from one of the attempts with a knife. A neighbor heard screams from the apartment on March 2. She went to the door and asked LaPoint's female friend if she wanted to file charges. She requested that the woman call police.

When officers arrived, LaPoint was located in the kitchen. He was slashing and cutting his arms with a knife. The two officers were standing in a small hallway to the kitchen. They were trying to talk him into dropping the knife. Witness interviewed later stated that the officers spent three to five minutes trying to convince him to cooperate.

LaPoint kept telling the officers that they would have to shoot him before he would surrender. LaPoint finally charged the officers. Twenty-nine-year-old Officer Mark Osland had no room to retreat as LaPoint charged. He fired four shots from his 9-mm handgun. The officer standing behind Osland had his weapon drawn and ready to fire. However, he decided not to fire due to the positioning of Osland and LaPoint.

Chief of Police John Laux was quoted in the media following the shooting saying "It was apparent this person wanted to die and it seems it was the police department chosen to effect that death."

Osland was cleared by a Hennepin County grand jury in April, 1993.

VIII

When a person attempts suicide once, the chances are that person will try again. In 1987, forty-three-year-old Dennis Seiz put a gun to his head and threatened suicide. Seiz, who was a police officer at the University of Minnesota, was off duty at the time. He led officers on a fourteen-mile chase from Saint Paul to Burnsville, Minnesota. Once stopped, he sat in his car for nearly three hours before giving himself up to a Dakota County sheriff's deputy who was acquainted with him. He pled guilty to careless driving. He was sentenced to one year probation, a $220 fine and ordered to complete a counseling program. His personal situation did not improve, and he filed for bankruptcy in 1990.

At 1:40 p.m. on Sunday, December 13, 1992, Seiz's wife went to the Eagan Police Department. She claimed Seiz was going to commit suicide by exploding a fuel oil and fertilizer mix located in their home. Police responded and made several attempts over the next few hours to contact Seiz. They were unable to speak to him. Later that afternoon, Siez's attorney called police. He had spoken to Seiz and "he (the attorney) thought everything was all right." The attorney said he believed that Seiz was sleeping and did not hear the police. The attorney also told the police that he would be coming to Eagan to see if he could assist them.

Chief of Police Patrick Geagan directed his officers to leave Seiz's property. The attorney arrived at the police department around 6:00 p.m. Shortly after his arrival, Seiz called 911 and reported that he had set fire to the house. He said, "The fire is lit; you know were it's at. The fire alarm just went off. Remember, I am armed and dangerous. Good-bye." A neighbor also called 911 to report smoke coming from the Seiz residence.

Police responded to the Seiz home again. The SWAT team from Eagan set up a perimeter outside of the house to observe activity in the house. Members of the team included thirty-two-year-old Jim Theilen, twenty-five-year-old Dan Mason, and thirty-two-year-old Brad Jurgens. Seiz was seen inside the house. He was observed firing his shotgun inside and outside of house five or six times. He came out onto his deck and police yelled to him to put his shotgun down. Seiz responded, "Kill me, kill me." Officers kept shouting for him to drop the gun, but he continued to ignore them.

Seiz fired a shot toward the backyard where officers were located. An officer saw the flash from the gun and heard pellets pass over his head. Seiz yelled at the officer, "Go ahead, shoot me, I'm a big target."

Seiz then came down the steps from the deck into the backyard. He knelt down in the yard and continued to shout at the officers to shoot him. They again called for him to put the gun down. He turned the shotgun toward the officers and fired. An officer fired back but did not hit him. Seiz dropped the shotgun and reached for a handgun in his waist. All of the officers then fired at him. The shooting, according to the police transmissions, occurred at 6:26 p.m. Seiz was rushed to a local medical center where he was pronounced dead at 8:22 p.m. The three officers firing at Seiz had a total of nineteen years as officers. They had trained together numerous times for such an incident.

A search of Seiz and the residence (the fire was extinguished) determined that Seiz had a police scanner, .44-caliber magnum revolver, shotgun, and night vision equipment.

This case was referred to a Dakota County grand jury and a no bill was returned in January 1993.

IX

Minneapolis is a city where there are 911 calls daily regarding shots being fired in a neighborhood. Usually, when the police arrive the people responsible are gone. You do not expect something like that in a small town like Wadena (population 4195) located in rural north central Minnesota. However, this is exactly what happened around 12:45 a.m. on Tuesday, December 9, 2003.

Officers Resech and Kimber responded and interviewed the complainant who claimed to have heard three gunshots. They checked with additional neighbors who heard the shots, but they were unable to locate exactly where the shots had originated. They suspected a certain address where the shots might have been fired. However, no one responded at the residence. They cleared the scene.

Resech and Timber returned to the area later to see if they could locate anyone suspicious in the area. The officers located a blue car in the alley of the suspected address. The officers interviewed two witnesses and determined that a person had fled on foot from the car and was in possession of a 9-mm handgun. Resech called Sgt. Thomas Crawford for assistance. The officers were attempting to locate the suspect with the 9-mm when the original complainant called again. She and her husband were watching out a window of their residence and saw a suspicious person. She said the unknown man was hiding behind a wood/junk pile in the alley behind their house near the corner of a neighbor's garage.

Forty-five-year-old Sergeant Crawford had worked his normal shift of noon to 8:00 p.m. the previous day. A dispatcher called and informed him that two officers he supervised were requesting assistance regarding shots being fired. Crawford was told it appeared that the individual had been located. The two officers did not want to approach the suspect at that time.

Crawford called Resech on the squad cell phone. Resech told Crawford that the suspect was possibly located and was armed with a 9-mm handgun. Resech also related that the suspect had been in some type of altercation in the neighborhood earlier in the evening. He had fired multiple shots either in the air or on the ground. A crime had occurred as the person had fired a weapon within city limits. Resech added that he did not have the suspect under surveillance, but he was getting information relayed from a neighbor to the dispatcher.

Crawford, who lived in rural Wadena, got dressed and drove directly to the scene. He was to meet the two officers who said they would be parked in an alley not far from where they believed the suspect was hiding. When he arrived, he saw Resech and Timber walking north in the alley. Crawford could see their flashlights were pointing on a pile of firewood, lattice, and garbage cans near the alley in the backyard of a residence. Crawford then saw an individual crouched behind the pile. The person was wearing a plaid jacket similar to the one Resech had described to him. Crawford did not have a flashlight, but he could see the man by the illumination of the streetlight.

Crawford ordered the man to stand and show his hands. The person did not comply. Resech then called for him to stand and show his hands. He also announced that he was a police officer. Crawford was near a pine tree and did not have visual contact with Resech and Timber, but he could see their flashlights. Crawford had drawn his .45-caliber Glock. He could not see if the other officers had their weapons drawn.

After several commands to show his hands, the man lifted his right hand up near shoulder height holding a weapon. Resech ordered him numerous times to drop the gun. The person did not comply and took a couple of steps backwards. The man then turned the gun barrel toward his own chest and started walking backwards. The man, who was later identified as forty-three-year-old Kenneth F. Lessley, then turned and faced Crawford. Crawford shouted twice, "Police officer. Drop your weapon." Lessley then placed the gun to his right temple and walked slowly away. Momentarily, he stopped.

Crawford yelled again, "I'm a police officer; drop your weapon." Lessley took the weapon from his temple and pointed it at Crawford. Crawford fired. Lessley fell on his back. The gun went out of his hand into a snow bank next to him. Crawford ran up and secured the gun. Resech and Timber then moved in to assist. An ambulance was called. Resech and Timber started to administer first aid. Chief of Police Bruce Uselman arrived and took over the scene. Crawford gave Lessley's 9-mm handgun to Resech. Crawford initially told the investigators that he did not recognize the person he shot.

Lessley died following surgery in Fargo, North Dakota, that morning at 11:00 a.m. He had been shot once in the chest. His blood alcohol was .17.

Later, Crawford told investigators that after he learned Lessley's identity, he recalled knowing the name. During the summer of 2003, Wadena police received a teletype from California requesting assistance locating Lessley. California authorities had a felony warrant for him. They were also attempting to serve an Order for Protection against him. Crawford said that Wadena police tried to locate him at a residence in Wadena but were unable to locate him. There was an active warrant in California at the time of his death for assaulting his ex-wife.

Located in the vehicle that Lessley had been driving was correspondence believed to have been written by him. There was an envelope addressed to his ex-wife in California. The letter indicated that Lessley was suicidal and did not want to live any longer. He said he was depressed. He wanted to say goodbye to her and their children. The letter also contained information that he had previously attempted suicide.

Wadena County Attorney Jon Eden declined prosecution of Crawford on January 21, 2004, saying that the shooting was justified.

X

An extremely difficult situation for any officer is to respond to a parent who has concerns that a son or daughter is armed and threatening suicide. Twenty-four-year-old Scott A. Omodt had threatened suicide around Christmas of 1995. His handgun was taken during that situation, and he was placed in a state mental health facility.

Sometime after his release in the late afternoon on June 9, 1996, his father called a local police department to report that his son was again suicidal. Subsequently, an officer spoke to Omodt's father. His father said he had received a call from his former wife, the mother of Scott, saying that Scott was drinking again. He had a gun and was threatening to kill himself. Omodt's father was concerned as he did not know where Scott lived nor did he have a phone number for him. He gave police the description of Scott's vehicle. He had met his son on the road about one hour before the phone call from his wife. Scott made no mention of suicide and did not appear to be intoxicated at that time.

Omodt's father was very concerned that no uniform officers approach Scott. Scott was apparently upset with law enforcement for placing him in a mental health facility after their last contact with him. He believed that police confronting him would cause Scott to kill himself. Fortunately, this situation was resolved by a sheriff's deputy meeting Scott with his mother and father. Scott was convinced to go to a mental health facility again. An empty .45-caliber gun was located in his vehicle.

Omodt spent two days in a detoxification center in Rochester. He was released around 7:00 p.m. on June 11, 1996. His father drove him back to his residence where he had stored Scott's pickup while in detox. Scott left him around 7:30 p.m. Scott had the same .45-caliber handgun previously with him during the June 9 encounter. He claimed he wanted to return it to his brother who owned it.

Around midnight Scott called his mother and told her he wanted to say goodbye to his brother, sister, father and her. He told her, "I love you, Mom, but I can't take it anymore." He told her he did not want to go through detox and be away from family. She tried to determine his whereabouts; but he told that he did not want her to know because she would call the police.

Officer Andy Ochs began his law enforcement career in October, 1995, after completing his bachelor's degree and skills training. He reported for work at Rushford Police Department on June 11, 1996, for his normal 7:00 p.m. to 3:00 a.m. shift. Shortly after midnight, Ochs responded to a dispatcher's call to contact Omodt's mother who resided in Rushford. She said that Scott was threatening to commit suicide and a gun was involved.

When he arrived at the residence, Scott's mother was on the phone talking to Scott. Her husband came to the house and also talked to Ochs. His parents believed Scott was possibly at his brother's farm. Law enforcement went to the farm to locate Scott. He was not there. His workplace was also checked. Ochs remained at the house while other officers checked on his whereabouts. Scott talked on and off with his mother for approximately an hour and a half. He asked her numerous times if she had called police. Ochs left around 2:00 a.m. for a few minutes. He returned shortly to see if there was any new information regarding Scott's whereabouts.

Ochs eventually began patrolling the area to see if he could locate Omodt. He soon observed the red Toyota pickup belonging to him. Ochs began following him, but he did not activate his emergency lights or siren. After following him for a short time, Ochs stopped on the bridge and watched the pickup go toward his mother's residence. Ochs had dispatch call the mother's residence to determine if he had arrived. He had not.

Ochs then noticed Omodt's pickup coming toward him where he was parked on the bridge. Omodt stopped about 75 to 100 yards away. Ochs flashed his bright lights and overhead flashers. Omodt flashed back with his bright lights. He then started toward Ochs. Ochs decided to get off the bridge. He had to go across the curb, over a sidewalk and onto a grassy area to keep from getting hit by Omodt.

Ochs then made a U-turn to see where Omodt had gone. After some maneuvers on local streets, Ochs pulled over to the side of the street. Momentarily, Omodt pulled directly in front of him. He reached down to the floor like he was picking up something. Ochs exited the vehicle and pulled his weapon. Ochs shouted at Scott at least three times to show his hands. Omodt keep looking at Ochs and reaching down to the floor. Omodt gave Ochs a hand gesture like "bring it on." Omodt then put his pickup in gear and rapidly departed. Ochs drove to a higher location on the local dike in order to observe a larger area. He turned his lights off and stood outside of his car. He saw Fillmore County Deputy Jack O'Donnell drive up near Omodt's pickup.

Ochs got back in his squad and went to assist O'Donnell. As Ochs got closer, he saw O'Donnell get out of his squad. Omodt pulled up next to O'Donnell's vehicle. Ochs could not see what was happening, but momentarily Omodt drove off. O'Donnell got back in his squad before Ochs could talk to him. At the same time, Ochs noticed Rushford Chief of Police Sam Stensgard drive up next to him and got into the squad. Stensgard, forty-year-old and chief of the department for four years, had been called by the dispatcher around 3:30 a.m. The dispatcher had informed him that Ochs was having problems with a suicidal person. He immediately got dressed to assist.

Ochs only drove a few feet when he noticed Omodt's backup lights. The pickup was coming at them in reverse. Ochs immediately pulled over to the parking lane on the street. Omodt continued in reverse and hit the squad's left front fender. He then drove away from them. Omodt drove up onto the dike and off into an area of riprap-type rocks. Omodt started to slide and possibly overcompensated, causing himself to get stuck.

Ochs and Stensgard both exited the squad with guns drawn. Omodt dove into the passenger area of the pickup. Ochs yelled, "Let's see your hands, Scott. Scott, I want to see your hands." Ochs could hear Omodt shouting something, but he could not make out what he was saying. Ochs then saw a dark-colored weapon in Omodt's hand pointed out the rear sliding window of the pickup. Ochs and Stensgard called for him to put the weapon down.

Within seconds, Stensgard shouted to Ochs that they needed more light. Ochs took his flashlight from his belt and turned it on. Omodt looked directly at Ochs. Ochs felt as though he became a clear target for Omodt, so he turned the flashlight off. He then ran back to his squad and turned on his "take-down" lights to provide more visibility.

Momentarily, Omodt exited from the passenger door. Omodt was holding the gun with both hands outstretched and pointing it at Stensgard while walking toward him. Omodt then went into a crouch-type position over the box of the pickup. Ochs heard Omodt call to Stensgard, "I'm going to kill you." Ochs did not see a muzzle blast from Omodt and assumed it was Stensgard who shot. Ochs then fired two shots into the rear quarter panel of the pickup. He saw Omodt fall to the ground.

Both officers approached Omodt. A large handgun was next to his body. Omodt was not moving. Stensgard directed Ochs to handcuff him and radio for an ambulance. Omodt did not say anything, nor were any questions asked.

Momentarily, a person later identified as Omodt's father, came running up to them and said, "Did you get him? I've been dealing with this for two years."

It was determined by the responding medical personnel that Omodt was dead at the scene. A .45-caliber Ruger revolver with five live rounds was next to Omodt. Crime scene investigators recovered three spent cartridges from Ochs and two from Stensgard.

Evidence was presented to a Fillmore County grand jury on July 1 and 2. A no bill was returned regarding charges against Ochs and Stensgard.

XI

This shooting started with a 911 call at 9:51 p.m. on March 29, 2001:

911: Police and Fire. Hello? Can I help you?

Male caller: Yes, I'm looking for, ah, Fridley.

911: Yes, this is the dispatcher for Fridley Police and Fire. What can I do to help you?

Caller: We're at [address] and someone is outside throwing stuff at the building.

911: What are they throwing?

Caller: We have no idea what they are throwing. The caller describes that the person has an Order for Protection against him and then says, "He, he just broke into the (apartment) building."

911: Okay, what is your first name?

Caller: Just a second, I gotta go down there.

Female caller: Hello. [The female called describes that there is an Order for Protection against the husband of the woman in apartment 3. She told the 911 operator that the man was leaving in his car and gave a license number.]

Twenty-eight-year-old Fridley Police Officer Jason Cardinal was working in a marked squad when he received the original call of a man throwing items at a building. He received further information regarding the Order for Protection and that the person was leaving in a car with the license provided. As he was responding to the address, he observed a car matching the description. He pulled in behind the car. However, the license was not exactly the same. Due to the time of the night, close proximity to the address and light volume of traffic, Cardinal believed it to be the suspect vehicle and decided to stop it.

When the car turned south on University Avenue, Cardinal followed it and activated his emergency lights. He could see the driver, later identified as thirty-three-year-old Timothy Golden, look in his rear-view mirror and accelerate. Golden was in the right lane, and Cardinal moved partially into the left lane to turn on his Opticon to clear traffic. (Opticon is a remote program that officers use in their vehicles to change the traffic lights to green and give them the right-of way). Golden suddenly slowed down and cut right in front of Cardinal. Cardinal interpreted this to be an aggressive move toward his squad. Golden then made an illegal U-turn against a red light and went north on University Avenue. Cardinal continued with his lights and siren activated.

Dispatch advised Cardinal at this time that Golden was known to carry weapons, particularly shotguns. At this point, Cardinal requested dispatch contact his sergeant to determine if he should continue the chase. Cardinal could see another Fridley squad was facing south at the intersection of University and 57th Avenue. That squad was occupied by thirty-three-year-old officer Thomas Swanson. Golden drove over a median at the intersection and traveled eastbound on 57th Avenue. Cardinal followed only a short distance when Golden's Chevrolet Caprice suddenly stopped on the front side of the building where the 911 call originated. Because of Golden's sudden stop, Cardinal stopped closer than he wanted. He later described the distance to Golden's car as approximately twenty-one feet.

Cardinal stated to investigators that numerous thoughts were going through his head: (1) there was an Order for Protection, (2) he was known to have weapons, (3) did he leave a scene of a burglary, and (4) did he actually live at the apartment? Cardinal radioed that they were stopped. Cardinal and Golden both exited their vehicles. Cardinal saw Golden immediately put a gun in his right hand and place it to his temple. It appeared to be a small black gun. Cardinal yelled for Golden to "drop the gun" numerous times. They were about two car lengths apart at that time.

Golden did not obey any of Cardinal's demands. He simply turned and walked away as he lowered the gun to his waist. Golden went to the front of his car, casually walking away from him. By this time, Officer Swanson had arrived and was standing to Cardinal's left.

Golden started shouting something that Cardinal did not understand. Cardinal was continuously calling for Golden to drop his weapon. Cardinal was not certain if Golden heard him as he was not reacting to any of the demands. Golden then turned back toward Cardinal and Swanson. At the same time, Golden "racked the slide" and started to raise the gun toward them.

Cardinal fired his .40-caliber pistol three times and saw Golden fall to the street. He heard Swanson firing his weapon. Cardinal immediately radioed that shots had been fired and the "subject was down." He also requested an ambulance and supervisor. Cardinal estimated that it only took about thirty seconds after the cars stopped for the shooting to occur.

Officer Swanson told post-shooting investigators that he responded to the call in his squad. He first saw Golden's Caprice with Cardinal following him north toward 57th Avenue. He saw the Caprice "jump a median" at 57th Avenue and proceed on 57th Place. Swanson followed the Caprice and Cardinal's squad. Both vehicles stopped by an apartment building. Swanson pulled up to the left of Cardinal's squad. Cardinal was out of his car shouting at the driver of the Caprice, who was also out of his vehicle, to "drop the gun." Cardinal turned his emergency lights and siren off, but Cardinal's stayed on.

Swanson also called to Golden to put down his gun. Golden ignored all of the commands and just started walking away. The gun was down at his side as he walked away. Golden was about fifteen feet away when he turned and started back toward them. Swanson said that he shouted twice, "Sir, drop the gun, get down on the ground." Golden began to raise the handgun up from his side. Fearing for his life, Swanson, who was in a crouched position behind his door, fired his .40-caliber pistol twice. He recalled that he heard Cardinal fire just prior to his shooting.

Another officer arrived immediately after the shooting. That officer and Cardinal approached Golden. They also looked into the Caprice to make sure it was not occupied. Golden was not moving. A small .25-caliber semi-automatic pistol was on the ground by his knee.

Ironically, Cardinal had just completed training nine days before at the firearms range. There was a training scenario of a suicidal armed man. It involved a traffic stop with the person exiting the car with a gun to his head. During the training, Cardinal yelled, "Drop the gun," numerous times. The training ended with the man dropping the gun and surrendering. Cardinal related to investigators, "He [Golden] didn't drop the gun like we commanded and he started to raise it on me."

An autopsy determined that Golden died from a gunshot wound to the head. It was also determined that Golden had "acute methamphetamine intoxification" at the time of his death. In his pockets were several lighters and an improvised smoking device. His blood alcohol was negative.

An Anoka County grand jury returned a no bill regarding the shooting. Officer Swanson left law enforcement later to join a established family business. Cardinal remains on the department.

XII

There are those who want to die and use law enforcement to assist them in their endeavor. Such was the case in New Hope, a first-ring suburb of Minneapolis, on Wednesday, April 13, 2004.

Fifty-year-old Ron Adamson had been arrested for burglarizing his ex-wife's house and violating her restraining order against him. Neighbors related that Adamson had been a good neighbor. However, he had become withdrawn the past year and half as he was going through a divorce. People around him believed that he had drug and alcohol problems.

Adamson had spent Thursday, April 8, until the morning of Tuesday, April 13, in jail before posting bail. He had been in jail for theft. He stole his ex-wife's passport, cash, checks, and other items. She reported the theft. He waited until she was home and returned the items. He had previously been arrested in January for a similar incident at the house. He claimed he was intoxicated during both of the events.

David Friskney, a thirty-seven-year-old New Hope officer with twelve years' experience, was working the 7:00 a.m. to 5:00 p.m. shift on April 13. He was informed at roll call that Adamson had attempted to purchase a shotgun, but he had been denied. Adamson was well known to Friskney, as Adamson's ex-wife only lived a few houses away on the same block from Friskney. There was much discussion regarding Adamson' escalation of harassment against his wife and different attempts to purchase a weapon. Extra patrol was requested for the area. That was Friskney's area of patrol.

Friskney received a radio call at 10:43 a.m. that there was an "open 911" call at 3404 Ensign. At first, he believed this to be the ex-wife's house. When he arrived on the street, he realized that it was the house where Adamson was illegally staying. Friskney was cautious due to the recent information regarding Adamson. He waited for backup. Officer Pete Stanley arrived, and

they proceeded to the residence. Friskney, who had been to the house before, checked the perimeter. Everything appeared to be closed and the shades
were drawn. There was no way to see into the house. Dispatch then advised
that the 911 call was still "open."

The front door was locked. They shouted, "Police," numerous times.
They radioed their captain and he advised them to kick in the door to check
for an attempted or successful suicide. The door was forced open. Initially
the officers retreated to cover in the yard behind trees. They called, "Police,
Ronald come out." When no activity was noted, they entered the house.

They determined that no one was in the front room. They continued
to shout that they were they police and called out his name. They entered
the kitchen area and no one was there. They secured the door to the basement and agreed it would be the last area to check after "clearing" the upstairs. They continued down the hallway toward what appeared to be
bedrooms. At the end of the hallway, one door was open. Friskney peaked
around the corner and saw someone lying in the dimly lighted room.

The person, later determined to be Adamson, was lying on his stomach
with his arms and hands out of sight under his body. His head was closest to
the hallway, and he appeared to lying partially on the floor next to the bed.
Friskney saw a red substance, possibly blood, in a pool by the body in left
thigh and knee area. The lighting was poor in the bedroom. However,
Friskney's eyes had adjusted, and he could see fairly well. Officer Stanley had
a flashlight attached to his weapon and shone it toward Adamson. Friskney
yelled to see his hands as he felt that Adamson had used a weapon to cause
his injuries. Officer Stanley also shouted. Adamson remained motionless.

Just as Friskney decided to go farther into the room to determine if
Adamson was alive, Adamson started making a loud growling or snorting
sound. Friskney started to back out of the room as Adamson was rapidly
getting up. Adamson arose and came at him in one motion. Adamson was
advancing on Friskney faster than Friskney was backing up. Friskney had
his gun pointed at Adamson. Adamson was lunging and charging as he con-

tinued growling. Fearing for his life, Friskney fired his .45-caliber Sig Sauer. Both officers backed down the hallway into the kitchen area to take cover. They could not see Adamson but could hear what sounded like labored breathing. They called for him to come out and show his hands. There was no response. Friskney radioed that shots had been fired. He requested an ambulance and body bunker. Officers began to arriving within a few minutes, but no one had a body bunker. Responding officers from nearby Plymouth had a body bunker. That officer had body bunker and stun gun training. Friskney and the Plymouth officer went down the hallway. Adamson was not moving. He was handcuffed. Friskney saw an ejected shell casing from his weapon in the hallway. His captain arrived and directed him to leave the scene.

Officer Stanley's account of the incident to investigators was essentially the same as Friskney's statement of the events. Stanley saw blood on Adamson's left hand. Stanley believed that Adamson was only about five feet from Friskney when he fired his gun.

The medical examiner came to the scene and pronounced Adamson dead. There were four superficial stab wounds to his chest. There were an additional six stab wounds to his throat area. Blood stained his left arm from wrist to elbow. There was a bullet wound to the left side of his forehead.

Hennepin County Sheriff's Office processed the crime scene. Two spent .45 casings were found: one in the hallway and the other in the bedroom. A small notebook with a handwritten note was sitting on a small stool in the bedroom. The note indicated that his wife was out to get him and she had turned her back on him. A filet knife with blood on the blade and grip was found in the bedroom. A sheath for the knife was on the floor in the bedroom. There was a large amount of blood on the floor. There was a handwritten note in the kitchen bequeathing his boat, snowmobile, trailer, and truck to his children.

A Hennepin County grand jury returned a no bill in May 2004 regarding the shooting.

Chapter Six

Trouble at Home
aka Domestic Situations

Calvin Sam, a forty-nine-year-old American Indian, and his wife had marital difficulties. They moved into a south Minneapolis neighborhood in the late 1980s. When they separated sometime in March 1993, he moved out of the house. His wife obtained a restraining order as Calvin had abused her in the past. His wife lived in the house with their seven-year-old son and two teenage daughters. Upon returning from a weekend trip, she and the children discovered that the house had been forcibly entered. They went to a friend's house to stay and called police.

On Monday, April 4, 1994, Susan Sam reported to Minneapolis Police that she had checked the house and determined that her Winchester 30/30 rifle and .22-caliber rifle had been stolen. She was certain Calvin had been the one to break into the house because, in addition to the guns, his jewelry was gone and some of his clothing had been taken. Calvin left a note saying he had chased two unknown males from the house and boarded up the broken back door. She told police she had been the victim of domestic assault and that Sam had pleaded guilty on two different occasions to the assaults. He had also previously threatened her with a shotgun. When he received the divorce papers on March 17, 1994, he asked her who would get custody of their son when she died. She interpreted that comment as a threat. She added that he was on probation for a previous domestic assault.

On Friday, April 8, one of the daughters stopped by to get mail and saw a man in the house with a gun. Police were called around 3:00 p.m. Susan met officers at the house. Officer Tammy Diedrich, a thirty-one-year-old officer, informed Susan that they had checked the exterior of the house before her arrival and everything seemed secure. Susan informed her and thirty-year-old officer Joel Kimmerle that she was getting a divorce from Calvin Sam and had obtained an Order for Protection on Tuesday. However, Calvin had been avoiding being served. She told them she had changed locks and, to her knowledge, Calvin did not have a key. She also informed the responding officers about the missing weapons and asked them to accompany her into the house.

Susan unlocked the front door, and the three of them entered the house. The officers checked the main floor and the second floor and found no one. The door to the basement in the kitchen was open. Susan remained in the kitchen area while the officers went to the basement. Suzan told investigators that following the incident the next thing she heard was officer Diedrich saying, "Minneapolis Police. Get out of there." Instantaneously, she heard Diedrich shout, "Oh my God, he has a gun." She heard shots, and Diedrich yelled, "Mrs. Sam, get out of the house. He's got a gun." Susan ran to the living room and hid in the closet.

Diedrich related to investigators that after clearing the upper two floors she and Kimmerle went to the basement. As she went around the water heater, she noticed an opened door leading to a room. She saw an ashtray with cigarette butts and a brown paper sack. As she approached the door, she observed a male (Sam) holding a "long gun" just inside the doorway. She shouted, "Gun, gun, gun, he's got a gun." Sam stepped into the doorway and pointed the gun at her as she was backing up to the water heater for cover. Then she heard Kimmerle firing at Sam.

Diedrich then fired her 9-mm handgun at Sam. The area became very smoky, and she lost sight of Sam. She felt a warm, wet feeling on her right hand and arm and believed she may have been shot. She quickly determined that she had not been shot, but the water heater had been hit and she was getting wet from the warm water leaking. She and Kimmerle exited the basement. As they were going up the stairs, she heard Kimmerle called on his radio that there was an "emergency."

Kimmerle gave investigators the same description of events leading up to the shooting. He said that when he heard Diedrich yelling about the gun, he saw Sam standing in the doorway pointing a long gun at waist level toward Diedrich. He then fired his 9-mm pistol numerous times at Sam. After exiting the house with Susan, he set up at the front door, with Diedrich at the back, in the event Sam was alive and tried to escape.

Additional officers responded to the shooting and entered the house. They discovered Sam dead in a corner of the basement. Numerous 9-mm spent casings were found in the area. There were two bullet holes in the water heater and one in the furnace. Three empty beer cans and two full cans were found in a paper sack. Another sack contained a package of hot dogs and a partially consumed package of salami. There was also a loaf of bread in the area. The stolen 30/30 rifle was found next to Sam. and the stolen and loaded Marlin .22 was against the wall in the room where he had been. The cocking lever on the thirty/thirty was in the down position, perpendicular to the stock, with a live round in the feeding chamber. Also recovered were the divorce papers.

The autopsy reveled that there was one fatal shot to Sam's stomach. The cause of death was blood loss due to exsanguination. In the pocket of his shirt was a note apparently written by Sam. The note read in part, "I'm sorry about all of this. Please forgive me …."

A Hennepin County grand jury returned a no bill on August 23, 1994.

II

A radio call went out near midnight on Friday, January 16, 1987, to Minneapolis police officers that a woman had called and requested that the police respond to her residence because her boyfriend, fifty-four-year-old Hosie Walton, had a gun. Two officers, thirty-eight-year-old Bruce Johnson and thirty-year-old Steve Day responded. They spoke to Walton's girlfriend, Ruth Coleman. The officers walked up a flight of stairs to the bedroom where she said Walton was located while Coleman stayed downstairs.

Johnson and Day found Walton in the bedroom on the bed partially covered by blankets. The officers stayed by the doorway and ordered Walton to raise his hands so they could see them. The order was given twice with no response from Walton. He only looked at them with an unresponsive stare. He was told a third time to raise his hands. At that point, Walton brought his arm around and aimed a loaded .45-caliber handgun at them. The officers both fired at Walton. One round hit him in the head, killing him instantly.

Investigation determined that Walton had pled guilty to third-degree murder in 1968 and had served three years. Family members claimed he was never in any trouble after his release from prison. Apparently, he felt that being in possession of a weapon as a convicted felon was not a problem. Family members also told police that Coleman had taken the gun away from Walton earlier in the evening, but Walton convinced her to give it back to him so he could keep it near the bed. Walton had purchased the weapon a few weeks earlier because he suspected someone was trying to break into their house.

Unfortunately, Coleman told the media that the officers overreacted to the situation. Although she was downstairs, she claimed that she did not hear the officers tell Walton to put the gun down. She was quoted in the paper, "I heard no words. Nobody spoke nothing. They killed him in cold blood" (Minneapolis *Tribune*, 1/18/87, p.1B).

The officers were cleared in February, 1987, by a Hennepin County grand jury.

III

We all read about domestic situations where a husband, former husband or boyfriend becomes irate and kills his spouse or girlfriend. Often, these situations result in a murder/suicide. This incident is unique, as the first person killed was the wife's father.

On Wednesday, June 2, 2004, officers Bob Braumgartner and Erin Nordum from the St. Louis Park Police Department responded to a harassment complaint at 1:13 a.m. in the 7300 block of Minnetonka Boulevard. Shannon Hubbell reported that her soon to be ex-husband, Todd Hubbell, had driven by the house several times. He still had his key for her car parked in the driveway and would activate the alarm by opening the truck. She would have to go out and deactivate it. She told the officers that Hubbell had been calling her at work and leaving harassing messages on her answering machine. She added that he was probably drunk and would be driving his older white Ford Explorer. As they were taking the complaint, she suddenly cried, "There he is."

Both officers jumped into their separate squad cars and attempted to follow the Explorer. They were attempting a traffic stop by activating their emergency lights and siren. Hubbell would not stop. The speed limit was thirty miles per hour, and Hubbell was driving around fifty miles per hour They followed him to the city limits of the adjacent City of Hopkins. According to departmental policy, they terminated the chase and notified Hopkins police where they had last seen the vehicle.

Shortly thereafter, they were advised via radio that Hubbell was back at Shannon's parents' home. Dispatch could hear screaming and yelling in the background during the 911 call. The two officers began responding to the location. Just prior to arriving, the dispatcher advised them that shots had been fired.

Officers Braumgartner and Nordum arrived at the residence. Nordum parked his vehicle in a safe position. He put his spotlight on the Explorer which was in the driveway. Braumgartner then observed whom he believed to be Hubbell walking from the house to his vehicle. Braumgartner, with his weapon drawn, ordered Hubbell numerous time to put his hands up and get on the ground. Nordum was shouting the same orders. They could see no visible weapons in his possession.

Hubbell jumped into his Explorer and was attempting to leave. Braumgartner ran up to the vehicle and smashed out the driver's window. He was attempting to unlock the door as Hubbell continued backing down the driveway. Braumgartner became entangled in the seatbelt and was being pulled down the driveway. Braumgartner struck Hubbell several times in the head and shoulder trying to stop him. Eventually, Braumgartner was able to break free. Hubbell fled west in his vehicle. Nordum came from the house and confirmed that there had been a shooting and the victim was in the house. Braumgartner went to his vehicle and began his pursuit.

Hubbell led officers from St. Louis Park and Golden Valley on a five-mile chase. Speeds reached as high as eighty miles per hour. Officers involved in the chase were aware that Hubbell had shot his father-in-law. Officers set out spike strips, and Hubbell swerved to avoid them. Eventually, he came to the T intersection of Laurel and Louisiana. He went over the curb into a grassy area and appeared to be stuck. Squads attempted to box him in. Hubbell's tires were spinning as he was trying to get back on the paved road.

Siar Nadem, a twenty-six-year-old St. Louis Park officer who was working the 5:00 p.m. to 3:00 a.m. shift, had been dispatched to the very first call by Shannon Hubbell around midnight. He was handling another call when Braumgartner and Nordum went to the second call at 1:13 a.m. He heard radio traffic regarding the first chase which had been terminated. He then heard about the shooting on his radio and came toward the residence. He saw Hubbell on Minnetonka Boulevard and was able to get in directly behind him. At one point, he saw Hubbell slam on his brakes as if he was going to stop the car and flee on foot. Hubbell opened the passenger door and pushed his dog out to the street. Nadem said later that he felt Hubbell did this because he was going to kill himself or shoot it out with police and did not want his dog to be injured. Nadem continued as the lead vehicle. He saw Hubbell avoid spike strips and go over the curb into the grassy area at Laurel and Louisiana.

Nadem exited his vehicle and pointed his weapon at Hubbell. He saw Officer David Smith to his left. He heard gunshots and then saw Hubbell's vehicle drive directly where Smith was standing. Hubbell's vehicle ran into Smith's squad. Nadem heard more shots and believed that Hubbell was firing at Smith. Nadem came around Smith's squad and saw Hubbell in his vehicle. It appeared that Hubbell was moving his weapon toward him. Nadem fired his .45-caliber Glock at Hubbell from about six to eight feet. He saw Hubbell slump to the passenger side of his Explorer. He then felt a sharp pain in his right leg. Nadem had been hit by gunfire. He was taken to a nearby hospital. He was treated and subsequently returned to duty.

Forty-three-year-old St. Louis Park Officer David Smith was also working the 5:00 p.m. to 3:00 a.m. shift. He was on another call when he heard sirens during the first chase of Hubbell. When he finished his call, he decided to go toward Minnetonka Boulevard where the chase began.

Smith next heard a radio transmission that shots had been fired and a person had been hit. He was aware that Officer Braumgartner was in pursuit of a vehicle. Smith joined the chase. Nadem was the lead squad, followed by Braumgartner. Smith was listening to the direction of the chase and decided to stop and wait in the event Hubbell doubled back. Sure enough, Hubbell doubled back. Smith saw Nadem in pursuit, and Smith was able to pull in behind him and ahead of Braumgartner. Smith also saw Hubbell throw the dog out.

As previously described, Hubbell went off the road and was spinning his tires and kicking up dirt. Hubbell was not going anywhere, so Smith pulled up to the left of Nadem's squad and jumped out of his vehicle in case Hubbell decided to flee on foot. Smith's spotlight was on Hubbell's Explorer. He drew his Beretta 9-mm pistol. Hubbell's vehicle started to get some traction and return to the pavement. Smith decided to shoot at the tires. Hubbell straightened out his vehicle and began heading directly at Smith. He was accelerating. Smith jumped back into his squad.

Hubbell crashed directly into Smith's driver's door, breaking out the window. Smith sat up after the collision and saw Hubbell still behind the steering wheel. Smith again fired at Hubbell from inside his car. Hubbell leaned to the right in his vehicle. All Smith could see was Hubbell's left shoulder and head. Smith exited the passenger side of his squad. Smith was able to get in a better position to see Hubbell. He saw that Hubbell had a head wound and was bleeding.

Smith and Golden Valley Officer Dean Kettner approached the Explorer and opened the passenger door. There was a 9-mm IMI Desert Eagle pistol beneath Hubbell's hand on the floor. Kettner secured the weapon. A Minnesota State Trooper and Braumgartner removed Hubbell from the vehicle and began administering first aid.

Kettner, a forty-nine-year-old officer from Golden Valley, had joined in the chase of Hubbell upon hearing it on his radio. He came to the same T intersection. Kettner was there with the three St. Louis Park squads. Kettner believed Hubbell was stuck, as his tires were spinning in the grass. Momentarily, Hubbell was able to get traction and back on the pavement. It appeared that the Explorer was coming directly at Kettner, but it suddenly turned and hit Smith's squad. Kettner exited his vehicle and immediately heard gunshots. He believed Smith was exchanging gunfire with Hubbell. Kettner then fired three shots from his .40-caliber Glock at Hubbell's vehicle. He then saw Smith approach the passenger's side of Hubbell's Explorer. Kettner came up behind Smith. When they opened the door, he saw a weapon on the floor. He secured it. There was another magazine to the weapon on the passenger-side floor.

An autopsy determined that Hubbell had been hit by three rounds. One was to the neck, one to the bridge of his nose and one to the left side of his chest. The medical examiner said that any of the wounds would have been fatal. Hubbell's blood alcohol was .24. Richard Atkins, the sixty-one-year-old father-in-law of Hubbell, was shot eight times. Seven of the .22-caliber rounds remained in his body. According to the medical examiner, three shots to the chest were most likely the cause of his death. His blood alcohol was negative. Crime scene technicians recovered numerous fired casings from both shooting sites. Fired casings from a Ruger .22-caliber rifle and 30/30-caliber Marlin were found in addition to the ones from the officers' weapons.

A Hennepin County grand jury returned a no bill on December 9, 2004.

IV

Thirty-nine-year-old Robert Stewart was released from the Marshall County jail in rural northern Minnesota around noon on Friday, May 3, 1985. Stewart had been incarcerated at the jail related to some violent acts which had occurred at his residence in mid-April. His release had certain conditions: (1) stay away from his residence in Kittson County, (2) not use alcohol, and (3) stay away from his wife, Sandra Stewart. Divorce papers had been served on Stewart. They had been married for twenty years.

Robert had been a jockey during the first ten years of their marriage. However, injuries plagued him and he had to leave the profession. He put all of his savings into a farm and unfortunately lost the farm. Drinking was used to help his physical and emotional pain. To add to his problems, in the late 1970s he was in a car accident in which a woman was killed. He was convicted of the traffic death and served thirty days in jail. He also received a fine and served five years' probation which ended in October, 1984. He became violent toward Sandra in December, 1984. She moved out of the house and lived with others in an attempt to stay away from Robert. He had destroyed many things belonging to Sandra in the house. He cut and pulled apart much of her jewelry. In addition, he cut her clothing. Sandra ceased talking to him after April 3.

While in custody, Stewart was given a court-ordered psychological evaluation. He admitted during his interview with the psychologist that he had a history of chemical dependency. He also admitted destroying Sandra's jewelry and other items. He said he was angry and was doing "anything to hurt her." He also said he still loved his wife and did not like the idea of a divorce.

The psychologist stated that, "Mr. Stewart is *not* mentally ill...." He added that Robert resorted to aggressive and hostile behavior which was "further complicated by Robert's addiction to alcohol." He also believed that when Robert was under the influence of alcohol his behavior was "unpredictable." Lastly, the psychologist reported, "I believe that Mr. Stewart's wife, Sandy, is presently in danger, and will continue to be in danger as long as Mr. Stewart remains in the immediate or nearby vicinity and that sufficient steps should be taken to ensure her physical safety."

On the afternoon of May 3, Sandra called the Kittson County Sheriff's Office and requested assistance. She wanted a deputy to accompany her to her house in order to remove personal property. She stated she was fearful of Robert. Sheriff Overland directed Deputies Craig Spilde and Roger Thompson to assist Sandra. Spilde went to the residence and determined that Robert was not there. Just prior to 7:00 p.m., Spilde and Thompson met Sandra and went to her house to get her property. Student intern Jon Ness was with Thompson. In addition, two Minnesota state troopers were in the area. While in her house, her sister-in-law called and informed her that Robert was probably in the area as his pickup truck stored at their residence while he was in jail was gone. Also, there was a deer rifle missing from the gun cabinet at her house.

Sandra took some property from her house and placed it in her Ford Pinto. A red and white pickup came driving up her driveway from the main road. Sandra said that it was Robert's. He drove almost to the house. When he saw the three law enforcement vehicles, he stopped and started driving backwards down to the road. Spilde and Thompson got in their squads. Spilde had been told by the sheriff of the conditions of the court order, and they were going to arrest him for breaking the court order by being on the property.

Spilde was driving forward and Stewart was backing up. Spilde could see Stewart waving a rifle out of the window as he was backing up. Spilde also saw the two state trooper squads pull up to the end of the driveway, blocking Stewart's exit to the road. The troopers had been called while assistance was given to Sandra. Spilde radioed to them that Stewart had a rifle. Robert stopped the pickup and exited carrying the rifle. Spilde saw something white in color in one of Stewart's hand blow away in the wind. It was later found to be the Styrofoam from an empty cartridge box. Stewart started walking away from the deputies. Initially, Spilde and Thompson got behind their squads: Spilde with a .12-gauge shotgun and Thompson with his revolver.

Stewart began walking directly at them on the driveway. He then cut off into a field but was still walking at a slight angle toward them. Both deputies continued to call for him to put down the weapon. Stewart was swearing at the two deputies. He told them that he did not want to go to prison and he was going to kill them. One of the troopers even used his PA system on his squad to try to get him to drop the rifle.

They were shouting at him to put the weapon down and give up. He would turn and point the rifle at them and then quickly turn and walk away again. He dropped the rifle once, and Spilde and Thompson discussed making a dash to him and retrieving the rifle. As soon as they moved toward him, he would pick it up again. It should be noted that the ground in the field where they were following him was very sandy, and a person could not move very rapidly. Stewart would drop shells on the ground and then pick them up. Spilde and Thompson returned to their squads and drove ahead of Stewart to prevent him from getting to a wooded area where he could hide from them.

Stewart then turned and again came directly at them. This time, however, he yelled at Thompson that he was going to kill him. He said, "Roger, you fucker, I'm going to kill you." From about twenty-five feet, Stewart raised the rifle at Thompson. Spilde, who was near Thompson, fired one shot from his shotgun which was loaded with no. 4 buckshot. The shot splintered the rifle stock and also hit Stewart. The officers ran to him and secured the weapon. Stewart had been hit in the upper thigh of his right leg. The femoral artery was severed. The officers performed immediate first aid, but he died at 7:34 p.m., soon after an ambulance arrived.

Stewart was carrying a .35-caliber Marlin rifle. In his pickup was an empty box of .35-caliber cartridges, his divorce papers and the court order signed that day. A half-empty liter bottle of vodka fell out of the pickup when the door was opened. There was also a half can of 7-Up.

No charges were filed against Spilde.

V

Jealously is a terrible thing. It is especially bad when it leads to the death of the jealous person. This was the case on Wednesday, April 28, 1993. Forty-year-old Lorraine Butcher had dated Dale Johns in the past, but she had broken off the relationship. Apparently, he would not hear of that.

Butcher and her current male friend, Clyde McDonald, were relaxing in her Minneapolis apartment around 4:00 p.m. Suddenly, there was kicking at the apartment door. After two big bangs, the door flew open. McDonald left the bedroom where the two had been and rushed to the hallway. He began fighting with Johns. Johns hit McDonald on his forehead with something. He was dazed and staggered backwards. McDonald saw what he believed to be a scissors in Johns' hand. McDonald ran down the stairs away from Johns. McDonald, when interviewed later by investigators, said that Johns told him he was going to kill him.

Butcher initially went out to the hall but ran back into the apartment and called 911. When she returned to the hall, Johns grabbed her and took her into the bedroom. She later told investigators that Johns had blood on him when they went into the bedroom. Johns threw her on the bed. He had scissors in his hand and asked if she had "been" with McDonald. She said that she had not "been" with him. Johns said that McDonald did not have any clothes on. She told him that he did have shorts on and she was washing his other clothes. He let her up, and she ran out to the hall again.

She fell on the floor, and Johns jumped on her. He had taken the scissors apart in the apartment and had half with him. He told her, "The boys (police) are coming, the boys are coming." Johns had not hurt her yet. The scissors were at her throat, but he had not cut her. While holding her down, he asked her if she loved him. She told investigators, "I swore that I loved him." She also told him that "she would do anything for him." Momentarily, police came into the hall. Johns got up and started running toward them.

The two Minneapolis officers arrived. They were forty-five-year-old David Berkeley and fifty-year-old Jeffrey Drew. The two had almost fifty years' experience between them. They noticed a young American Indian lady with a baby just outside the entrance of the apartment building. They asked her if she had a key. She did and unlocked the door to let them in. They walked to the top of the stairs. Berkeley was about two steps behind Drew. Berkeley saw an Indian male on top of an Indian female at the far end of the hallway. Berkeley could see that she was on her back and he was "holding a shiny object in one of his hands." He and Officer Drew proceeded down the hall toward them. Drew cried, "Drop it."

Berkeley heard the male say, "Don't come any closer or I'm going to kill her."

Both officers took about two more steps toward them. Johns jumped up and started running at them shouting, "I'm going to kill you."

Drew yelled, "Drop it" at least two times. Berkeley had his gun out, but did not fire it as Drew was in front of him. In addition, he could not see exactly where the female was located. Berkeley told investigators he feared that he or Drew was going to be stabbed.

Drew's statement was very similar to that of Berkeley. He added that he radioed another Minneapolis squad responding to the same 911 call to go around to the back of the apartment and come in that way. He remembered seeing a man with his left arm around the woman's neck and what he believed to be a knife in a raised threatening manner above the woman. Drew said that he shouted for the man, "Drop it."

Johns yelled at Drew, "Get away from here or I'm gonna kill her."

Johns got up and started running at them with the weapon over his head. Johns was about eight to ten feet from Drew when Drew fired his .38 revolver twice. Johns collapsed and fell backwards. Drew went up and kicked the weapon away from him. Drew then checked on Butcher as he had seen blood on her blouse. She told him she was okay. He called for emergency medical personnel.

Johns died from two gunshot wounds to the left chest area. The woman who let the officers into the apartment building told investigators that she heard the officers shouting, "Drop it," at least two times before she heard gunshots.

No charges were filed against Drew.

VI

The St. Louis County Sheriff's Office (SLCSO) received a telephone call from Rachel Stavenger just after 4:00 p.m. on Thursday, March 4, 1999. She said that her forty-three-year-old brother David Sanders had been drinking and was acting violently. She requested that the SLCSO respond to the residence. Sanders had a long history with the SLCSO, and there was a standing order that an officer should not have contact with him unless backup was present.

Lt. Charles Burns, a forty-nine-year-old deputy with twenty-four years' experience, had finished for the day at 4:00 p.m. He was en route home when he heard a radio transmission that an assault had occurred on Allavus Road. He called on his cell phone for directions as he was uncertain of the exact location. He told dispatch that he would respond to the location. He was told that Sanders' sister would be at the end of the driveway to meet him.

When Burns arrived, Stavenger was sitting in her pickup at the end of the driveway. She told him Sanders was in the house acting crazy and that he had told her he was going to "rip up the house." Burns inquired about the red mark on her right cheek and temple area. She told Burns that Sanders had grabbed her in the lapel area of her jacket. Sanders began shaking her and also hit her in the lip. Her lip was noticeably swollen. Three other deputies arrived. Investigator Stephen Skogman arrived. Also arriving were Deputies Jodi Kangas and Laurance Cuffe. Skogman told the deputies about his previous contacts with Sanders and his propensity to become violent. Skogman said that Sanders had made previous threats toward law enforcement.

Burns tried calling the number he had for Sanders. He got a message which he assumed was from the phone company saying that the number was blocked. He radioed dispatch and asked that they try calling. Dispatch radioed back that the line was busy. Burns made the decision that the squads would all go up the long driveway to the house and block it to prevent Sanders from leaving. Stavenger had told Burns that a pickup in the driveway was probably not operating and not to worry about it. Burns put on his ballistic vest and grabbed his .12-gauge shotgun from his vehicle. Deputy Kangas proceeded up the long driveway first, and Burns got in Deputy Cuffe's squad as the passenger. They proceeded up the driveway to the residence. Burns radioed to Kangas to pull all the way up to a dump truck with a snowplow to help provide cover. Deputy Cuffe stopped immediately behind her squad.

Burns got out of the squad and left the door open so he could have access to the radio and cell phone. He directed Skogman to go to the south side of the house to observe any activity. Other SLCSO squads arrived and parked at the entrance to the driveway. Kangas, Burns and Cuffe were watching the house from the north side of the house and could also see a door that exited to the west. Burns activated the PA system on the car and asked Sanders to come to the door in order to talk to him. He did not get any response.

Burns decided to call out the SLCSO SWAT team in the event they might be needed. Burns continued to call on the squad PA and continued getting no response. Deputy Cuffe was a member of the SWAT team and left to get his equipment. Burns directed Kangas to move a little farther north to watch some of the west side of the house. Burns moved over to the left front fender of the dump truck.

Burns saw a dog on the east side of the house. He assumed Sanders let the dog out as he had not seen the dog when they drove up. Kangas told him she could see Sanders looking out the window which was the farthest west on the north side. Burns continued watching the dog, and it appeared to become more attentive at times toward the door on the east side of the house as if someone was trying to call it. Burns thought he heard someone whistle twice. Through a window Burns was able to see Sanders go toward the door. The third or fourth time he saw Sanders, he saw a rifle in his left hand.

At one point when Burns used the PA system, Sanders responded by telling Burns that it was his property and for Burns and everyone to "get the fuck out of there." Burns replied that he needed to talk to him about the fight with his sister. Sanders replied, "What sister?"

When Burns said, "The one that left here a short time ago," Sanders said, "Fuck you. Get out of here. This is my property." One time he shouted, "Who are you?" Burns told him that he was from the sheriff's office.

Burns did not see Sanders exit the house, but Sanders came around the northeast corner of the house. Sanders was carrying a long-barreled rifle with a scope in his right hand. He held the rifle in a horizontal position but not pointing it at Burns. Sanders walked over to the truck which Burns believed was not operable and started to open the door. Burns yelled for him to put the rifle down.

Sanders said, "Fuck you. I'm leaving and I'm going to shoot you." Burns held up his badge with his left hand as Sanders had put the rifle across the top rail of the box of the pickup. Burns could see that his right hand was behind the receiver in the area of the trigger. His left hand was on the front stock. The weapon was pointing away from Burns but in a ready position.

Sanders said, "I'm leaving."

Burns told him, "You know you can't leave. I have to talk to you." Sanders told him that he was leaving. Burns told him he could not leave as the road was blocked. Sanders started walking toward Burns with the rifle. Burns called for him to put it down. Sanders kept walking at Burns. Burns fired one round from his shotgun. Sanders stopped momentarily and appeared to look at his left chest area. Burns then heard the discharge of another weapon. Burns then fired again. Sanders fell to the ground.

Burns, along with Kangas, approached Sanders. He could hear the other squads coming up the driveway. He also observed blood coming from a wound in Sanders' left chest and neck area. Burns told one of the arriving deputies to call for an ambulance. He and another deputy could not locate a pulse or any sign of life. He was certain that Sanders was dead. Burns estimated that he was about forty yards away from Sanders when he fired the shotgun.

Deputy Jodi Kangas, a twenty-nine-year-old with six years' experience, told investigators basically the same information as had Burns. After she pulled up to the dump truck with the snowplow, she removed her M-16, .223-caliber rifle and went to the back of her squad and used the trunk for cover. She listened to Burns on the PA trying to get Sanders to come out.

Kangas heard Sanders shout, "Get the fuck off my property. I'm going to shoot you." She then saw Sanders go to a window and break it. She also could see him pacing back and forth in the house near the front door. She then lost sight of him. Momentarily, she heard Burns say that Sanders was coming around the corner of the house. She saw that he had a long-barreled weapon in his right hand. He started coming directly toward where she and Burns were located. Burns repeatedly yelled for him to stop and put the gun down. Sanders said, "Fuck you. I'm gonna shoot you. Get off my land." His weapon came up and pointed at them. She heard Burns fire, and she then fired once. She heard Burns shoot again. They walked toward him together, and Burns was shouting, "Don't move." She recalled that Burns either picked up or kicked the rifle away from Sanders.

Kangas related to the investigators that Sanders, in her opinion, appeared to be "cocky." She thought he was acting like "you ain't gonna mess with me." She said he was walking toward them "at a steady pace" and looked "very confident" and "obviously upset."

A St. Louis County grand jury failed to return an indictment against the officers. Kangas later married and left the Sheriff's Office.

VII

On, October 29, 1991, twenty-four-year-old Theodore Bobo surrendered to police after a fifty-minute standoff which began when he put a gun to his girlfriend's head and threatened to kill her. Bobo later claimed that the gun was not loaded and was broken. Bobo was charged with assault, disorderly conduct, carrying a pistol without a permit and obstructing the legal process. He pled guilty to assault and possession of a firearm. He was sentenced to spend thirty-five days of a 395-day sentence in the Hennepin County Workhouse. After serving his sentence for this offense, he decided to do it all over again—after only three days of freedom. This time he decided to use a knife rather than a handgun.

This event began around 12:35 p.m. on Sunday, February 9, 1992. Bobo's girlfriend, Nikki Howard, was asleep in the living room of her apartment with her new boyfriend. Nikki, who had three children by Bobo, left him because of previous incidents. Her sister, her boyfriend and their baby were also in the bedroom of the apartment. Bobo began banging on the door. Nikki said that it was Ted (Bobo) and not to open the door. Bobo gained entry by kicking the door. Nikki's sister fled to summon police. When she returned, everyone but Bobo and Nikki were in the hall outside the apartment. Bobo had taken her into the bedroom and shut the door.

Prior to taking her in the bedroom, Bobo began punching Nikki in the head and choking her. He also dragged her into the kitchen and took a knife from the sink. He pushed a dresser against the bedroom door. Nikki scooted to the wall and covered herself with a comforter. Bobo told her, "You know you are gonna die and I'm going to die with you, cuz I'm not going to jail alive."

Minneapolis Officers Gary Manty and David Ulberg were informed by a security guard at the apartment that a black male had kicked in the door of apartment D-307. The guard also informed the first arriving officers that two individuals were inside the bedroom and that the male had a knife. Bobo was trying to pull the comforter off Nikki and was punching her when the police began pushing the door open. When they entered the bedroom, Bobo was leaning up against the headboard with Nikki between his legs. He had his left forearm in a choking manner under her chin and a knife in his right hand at her throat.

Bobo was requested to drop the knife. He refused and replied with words to the effect of, "Go ahead and shoot me…I'm not going to drop the knife." Officer Manty called dispatch on his portable that there was a hostage situation and added that there was a standoff between the officers and the suspect.

While waiting for backup and a supervisor, Manty continued to try to reason with Bobo and get him to drop the knife. Bobo moved around on the bed and used Nikki as a shield in front of him. Manty continued his pleas. Officers Mike Hentges and Colin Koski arrived and stayed back in the living room area, while Ulberg stayed in the doorway. Sgt. Charles Dodge arrived. Bobo claimed that he only wanted to be alone with Nikki to talk to her. Dodge told Bobo he could talk to her all he wanted if he gave up the knife.

Just as it appeared that Bobo was loosening his grip on the handle, he suddenly started choking Nikki, and she started screaming. All of the officers—Ulberg, Koski, Hentges, and Sergeant Dodge—came into the bedroom. The officers continued to tell Bobo to drop the knife. At that point, Bobo put the knife in his left hand, took a cigarette out of his pocket with his right hand and lit it with both hands in front of Nikki. One of the officers went into the kitchen and brought a bowl for Bobo to use as an ashtray.

Bobo kept talking into Nikki's ear. She was not responding, but continued to cry. The officers could tell that Bobo was also crying. Bobo finished his cigarette and put it into the ashtray that was balancing on his thigh. He moved it aside and put the knife back in his right hand. The officers had been talking to Bobo for almost forty minutes.

His attitude changed abruptly. Bobo brought his right arm up and punched Nikki in the face. After being struck, Nikki curled up tighter and this resulted in her head being lower than Bobo's chest. He raised the knife up as if to stab her. Fearing that he was going to stab Nikki, Dodge, Ulberg, Koski and Hentges all fired. A total of eight shots were fired.

Paramedics, who were standing by in the hallway, responded immediately after Nikki, unharmed by the gunshots, was removed from the bedroom. Bobo was checked by the paramedics, and it was determined that he was dead. The knife which Bobo had was broken into two pieces by one of the shots.

An autopsy determined that Bobo had two wounds to his right hand and five additional wounds to the upper chest area. Ironically, during the autopsy, a .22-caliber bullet was recovered from a previous shooting where Bobo had been the victim. Minneapolis criminal records showed that there had been four separate assaults by Bobo on Nikki in 1990 and 1991.

A Hennepin County grand jury returned a no bill on April 4, 1992. On May 12, 2007, Bobo and Nikki Edward's son Deaunteze were convicted of a fatal drive-by shooting. The nineteen-year-old was sentenced to thirty years.

VIII

Shari Lynner was the estranged wife of thirty-eight-year-old Shane Lynner. Shari lived in Rosemount, a southern suburb of the Twin Cities. A Dakota County judge issued a no contact order in June, 2002. Shari had cited several occasions when Shane had hit her in the face, pulled her hair and threatened to kill her. He violated the order in July and was jailed in August. He was released from jail on September 23. As in many cases like this one, a piece of paper telling someone to stay away does not have much effect.

Shane's thirteen-year-old stepdaughter was not living at her mother's trailer. She had moved to a nearby neighbor's home approximately two weeks earlier because Social Services felt that she was in danger being with her mother. She related that Shane had been abusive toward her. If Shane came to Shari's house while she was there, Social Services would become involved again. Shane had once grabbed the girl and thrown her onto clothes dryer. She had numerous bruises from that assault. He also assaulted Shari on that occasion. Another time he grabbed Shari by the neck and told her daughter that her mother was a drug dealer. While holding Shari by the neck, he kept yelling for her to show her daughter the drugs she used. He made her search her mother's purse for drugs. None were found.

On Wednesday October 2, 2002, about 8:00 p.m. a man came running to the trailer where the stepdaughter was living. He shouted for her to "Call the police, Shane is down there beating on your mother." She called 911. She identified herself and gave her mother's address and stated that her stepfather was beating on her. The girl ran to another house where four friends were located. She got into a car and the five drove down to her mother's house. Two officers in one vehicle arrived at the same time. She went to open the door for them, but it was locked. The officers kicked the door open. She saw the officers go to the back bedroom where her mother and Shane were. One officer kicked that door open. She saw Shane with a softball bat. One officer yelled, "Put down your weapon." She saw Shane swinging the bat and saying, "No." She then heard two gunshots and ran out of the house.

Rosemount Police Investigator William O'Donnell was at police headquarters talking to Sgt. Jewell Ericson when the 911 dispatch call of an assault came across the radio. O'Donnell was off-duty and was not carrying his weapon. When O'Donnell heard the address of the assault, he recognized it immediately, as he had been there previously. He felt that it was Shane assaulting Shari, and he also knew Shari's daughter. O'Donnell had talked to the social worker assigned to Shari and her daughter. This person believed the situation was so volatile that it would end up a murder/suicide situation. O'Donnell had previously seen Shari with a black eye.

When they arrived at the trailer, Shari's daughter was there with some friends. Ericson pushed the door in and ran to the back of the trailer as he could hear some noise there. O'Donnell ran around the trailer to see if Shane was trying to get out a window. He was not, so he went into the trailer and saw Ericson at the door of the bedroom. He heard Ericson say, "Shane, put the weapon down. I've got a gun."

Because he had no weapon, O'Donnell ran out of the trailer to get the rifle from the squad. He also knew there was a less lethal shotgun in the truck. When he got outside near the squad, he heard at least two shots. He opened the door to the squad to get on the radio. He heard Ericson call on his portable that there was a "man down" and he needed an ambulance.

O'Donnell ran back into the trailer and saw Ericson standing with Shane lying on the floor with blood around him. O'Donnell checked Shane for a pulse and found none. He then grabbed Ericson's flashlight to check on Shari. He found her lying against the bed. She said that Shane had beaten her on her back, arms and head. He could see bruising on her ear and cheek. Other officers and an ambulance soon arrived.

Sgt. Jewel Ericson, a forty-year-old officer with seventeen years' experience with Rosemount police, came to work his shift at 6:30 p.m. that day. Around 8:00 p.m. he was talking to Investigator O'Donnell when the assault call came in. O'Donnell recognized the address and told him about the problems there. He related that after arriving and getting in the locked trailer, he saw Shane with a softball bat in his hands near the back of the trailer. He shouted for him to put the bat down, but he entered the bedroom slamming the door shut.

Ericson tried to open the door. When he did get the door pushed opened, Shane was behind the door and the wall. Shane was able to get out from behind the door. He swung the bat at Ericson, and Ericson felt the breeze of the bat go by his head. Ericson stepped back and Shane slammed the door. Ericson was able to push the door and get in the room again. This time Shane hit him on the hand with the bat. Ericson backed up, and the door slammed again.

Ericson drew his weapon and yelled to Shane that he had his weapon out. He commanded him to come out. The door opened and Shane shouted, "Here I come." Shane started running and screaming at Ericson with the bat in the air. Ericson continued backing up the hallway. He felt that he was going to be hit again, so he fired his .40-caliber pistol at him. Ericson kept firing as he backed all the way to the kitchen counter. Shane fell at his feet. He called on his radio for an ambulance and assistance. He heard Shari crying and ran back to check on her. She said that she was in pain but was okay. He went back to check on Shane and was soon joined by O'Donnell. Paramedics arrived and declared Shane dead at the scene. Shari Lynner was taken to Regions Hospital in Saint Paul for injuries she sustained. She recovered with no permanent problems.

The man who had been staying with Shari told investigators that he was there "kind of for protection" in case Shane came by. He was in the bathroom when he heard Shane's voice and Shari scream. He jumped out of the window and ran to where Shari's daughter was staying. He told her to call the police. He said that he "used to be a friend" of Shane, but he no longer associated with him because of his violent tendencies when he was doing cocaine.

Court records revealed that Shane Lynner had a criminal record in Dakota County which included criminal sexual conduct and assault. Shari was not the first person he had abused. In 1993, another woman obtained an order for protection after Lynner broke into her home while she was sleeping. He repeatedly hit her in the face and threatened to kill her. Rosemount Police had been to the Lynner address twenty-two times in 2002. Eight of the calls were for domestic abuse or violation of protective orders.

The case was investigated was the Dakota County Sheriff's Office and the Minnesota Bureau of Criminal Investigation. On November 1, 2002, a Dakota County grand jury returned a no bill.

IX

As many officers know, the worst event can begin with a routine 911 call. This is what happened at 2:04 a.m. on Saturday, July 13, 1991, in Brainerd, a small town in central Minnesota. The call came in as "I need some help." The 911 operator asked about her problem. Natalie Peterson replied, "I, I need some help with my husband. Come and get him. He's gone nuts on us." She also related that her husband was well-known to law enforcement in the area. She added, "He's drunker than you know what. He's got about eight knives on him, sharp ones." She said, "He's getting ready to get in my car and drive away." She gave the description her car and added, "Bring backup because he's drunk." She was told to stay on the phone, but she terminated the call. Officers were dispatched to the residence. Another call came in a few minutes later saying that Peterson had driven into a car parked in the driveway. That call was terminated quickly as she stated that she was going to check on the damage.

Law enforcement in the Brainerd area was very familiar with Barry G. Peterson. He had minor problems. In August, 1987, he threw rocks at a passing car and broke the windshield. He was questioned by a Crow Wing County deputy about the incident and admitted to the rock throwing. He was charged with third-degree criminal damage to property—a misdemeanor. He claimed he was drunk at the time.

In December, 1987, Peterson's then girlfriend Natalie (later wife) called the Brainerd Police Department to report that he was attempting suicide. He had all the natural gas in their trailer turned on. She and their seventeen-month-old baby were also in the trailer. When two officers arrived, they observed Barry with his nose to the burner area of the stove inhaling gas coming out of the burners. There was a strong odor of natural gas in the trailer. When the officers approached him, he turned quickly and offensively as if ready to fight. The officers tried to calm him down as they waited for two additional officers. As soon as the other two officers arrived, Peterson started fighting. He was subdued and handcuffed. During the struggle, Peterson stomped on one officer's foot and ripped another officer's badge from his shirt. One officer's watch was broken and they all indicated that their lungs hurt from the gas. Peterson's legs had to be tied to stop him from kicking at the officers and trying to break out the window in the back of the squad. After taking him into custody, Natalie told the officers that he had been drinking all day and was depressed. She had gone to a friend's house and when she returned fifteen minutes later, he had broken things in the living room and kitchen. He was inhaling gas, and that caused her to call police.

Peterson was transported to the Brainerd Hospital and admitted for a seventy-two-hour hold. Peterson settled down at the hospital and questioned police why he was there. When informed that he had attempted suicide, Peterson denied it and stated, "That is your opinion versus my opinion." Peterson admitted to the police sergeant that he had been in the Chemical Dependency Unit on two other occasions.

Peterson's contact with law enforcement continued. On December 14, 1987, he was listed as a missing person. He was quickly located. In May 1989, he was again placed on a seventy-two-hour hold and charged with driving while under the influence (DUI) of alcohol. He was again arrested for DUI in May, 1990. This was the third alcohol-related offense in five years, and his license was revoked in June 1990.

Late on July 12, 1991, a Brainerd police officer was on routine patrol in downtown Brainerd. He turned down a street and observed two individuals standing in the middle of the street. The two appeared to be getting ready to fight, as one had the other by the shirt. He stopped and identified the person who had grabbed the other man's shirt as Barry Peterson. Peterson appeared very intoxicated and agitated. The officer broke up the incident and allowed the two to walk their separate ways. At approximately 2:00 a.m. that same officer was dispatched to assist the Crow Wing County Sheriff's Office at Peterson's residence.

Brainerd Officer Tom Pfingsten, a thirty-three-year-old with five years' experience, parked his squad at the end of the driveway and waited for other officers to arrive. Eventually three additional officers and deputies from Brainerd police and Crow Wing County arrived at the Peterson residence. When the others arrived, Pfingsten walked up the driveway toward the house. He observed a blue vehicle running with lights on and backed up against a tree. It did not appear that it could move. There was a female (Natalie) yelling at the driver. As Pfingsten approached, he heard Natalie tell the driver (Barry) to put the knife down. Pfingsten drew his .357-caliber revolver when he heard the knife comment.

Pfingsten instructed Peterson to get out of the car. He was able to see the knife in Peterson's right hand when he exited the car. Pfingsten backed away and shouted at Peterson several times to drop the knife. Peterson walked to Pfingsten's right as if to circle him. Peterson looked directly at Pfingsten and said, "What are you going to do?" Another deputy at the scene described Peterson as having a "cold stare in his eye."

Pfingsten continued to tell Peterson to drop the knife. One of the sheriff's deputies recalled Pfingsten requesting Peterson to drop the knife. He recalled Peterson saying, "What will you do if I don't," at least three times. Pfingsten saw that Brainerd officer Brad Paulson also had his weapon out. Peterson was only about seven to eight feet away from the two officers. According to Pfingsten, Peterson "squared off" and continued to move toward him. Fearing for his life, Pfingsten fired twice. Peterson immediately fell to the ground. Paulson told investigators that Peterson made "a deliberate step toward Officer Pfingsten." The officers began administering first aid and called for an ambulance.

When Natalie was interviewed after the shooting, she claimed that officers did not tell Barry to drop the knife. She said they only told him "to take it easy." Natalie also said that "He (Barry) really didn't know who he was talking to … he was just going 'come on let's party.'" She was also upset that the officers would not let her perform CPR and made her go into the house while they were performing first aid.

An autopsy determined that Peterson died from two gunshot wounds to the left shoulder area. Two recovered rounds from the body were from Pfingsten's .357-caliber revolver.

William Klumpp, Assistant Attorney General, Criminal Division, Saint Paul, Minnesota, handled the grand jury testimony for the Crow Wing County attorney's officer. The grand jury returned a no bill on August 7, 1991. Officer Pfingsten left the Brainerd Police Department and remains a licensed peace officer with the Minnesota Department of Natural Resources.

X

Just before midnight on Saturday, December 28, 2002, Saint Paul Police dispatch received a telephone call from Pam Dochniak stating that her son, twenty-two-year-old Walter Dochniak, was threatening her with a rifle at their home in Saint Paul. The initial call from the dispatcher to responding squads was that Dochniak had a weapon and that he was loading it. The weapon was described as an AK-47. When officers arrived, a white car sped away. The officers radioed a description of the car to other squads.

Shawn Shanley, a twenty-nine-year-old Saint Paul officer, and his partner saw a white vehicle similar to the one described and began following it. It was determined to be a Toyota Corolla. The car stopped for a red light about three blocks from the Dochniak residence at University and Marion Avenues. Shanley radioed the license number to other squads and informed them that they were going to stop the car. Shanley also reported that the passenger was moving around and appeared to be reaching for something under the front seat. Shanley activated his emergency lights, and the Toyota stopped on southbound Marion Street. The passenger still appeared to be reaching under the seat.

Shanley had Officer Darren Johnson retrieve the squad's .12-gauge shotgun for him. Shanley chambered a round. He exited and used the squad as cover while Johnson gave verbal commands to the occupants. Additional officers, thirty-one-year-old Cort Baumgart and twenty-six-year-old Ann Anderson, arrived at the scene. Johnson, using the PA system of the squad, directed the driver and passenger to exit the vehicle. The driver, later identified as a friend of Dochniak, complied with the demands. The driver appeared agitated and was yelling at the passenger as he exited the car. Dochniak, who was the passenger, appeared to be talking on a cell phone and continued reaching reach under the seat.

Dochniak was not responding to any of the verbal commands over the PA. Shanley was shouting when Johnson was not using the PA. Dochniak opened the passenger door. He exited the car and began turning toward Shanley and the other officers. When he turned, Dochniak pointed a black handgun at the officers. Fearing for his safety and other officers, Shanley fired his shotgun four times.

Officers Baumgart and Anderson related basically the same story to investigating officers. Both said that when they arrived Johnson was giving verbal commands over the PA system. The driver complied and came back to other officers at the scene out of their sight. Dochniak exited the vehicle and came around with a handgun pointed at them. Bramgart fired one shot from his .12-gauge shotgun, and Anderson fired once from her .40-caliber pistol.

Dochniak did not immediately go to the ground. A canine officer at the scene released his dog. The dog took him to the ground. Dochniak was fighting with the dog. When Baumgart saw the weapon was out of Dochniak's reach, he ran forward and handcuffed him. The weapon was a Ruger P89 9-mm pistol.

Witnesses, other than police, are always good to have at the scene—especially when they substantiate the officers' statements. A car with three adults and two children was sitting at the drive-through of a McDonalds and saw the shooting. The three adults were interviewed separately and provided essentially the same narrative of the shooting. They all reported hearing the officers giving orders to people in a small white car. They saw the driver exit and go back to the police who were giving the orders. They saw the passenger exit with "something black in his hand." The witnesses thought that it looked like a gun. They said the person pointed it at the police and the police began shooting.

Dochniak was transported to Regions Hospital where he was pronounced dead at 3:00 a.m. the following day. An autopsy determined that he had been hit by buckshot in the upper right chest area. He also had non-penetrating dog bites.

Investigation determined that Dochniak had been convicted of credit card fraud in 1999 and had served six months in prison because he had violated the conditions of his probation regarding that conviction. The reason for his behavior on that day was never determined. A Ramsey County grand jury cleared the officers regarding the shooting.

XI

Young officers are told over and over that there is no routine assignment. Two sheriff's deputies from Chippewa County, Montevideo, Minnesota, discovered that to be true just after midnight on June 22, 1989. On June 21 the sheriff's office received a restraining order from the county court to be served on forty-three-year-old Dennis Ostenson. The restraining order was filed by Ostenson's former wife Sandra Berends. The restraining order alleged that Ostenson sexually abused his three-year-old daughter and, further, that he had made threats against Sandra's life, as well as against her present husband. An attempt to serve the order was made by Deputy Joe Linneman during the evening of June 21. However, Ostenson was not at home. Deputy Linneman told Ostenson's 83-year-old mother to have him contact the sheriff's office.

Around 11:00 p.m. the dispatcher at the Montevideo Police Department received a call from a person identifying himself as Dennis Ostenson. He said he was home and the police could contact him there. Ostenson made some vague threats to the dispatcher. However, they were not specific as to whom they were directed. The dispatcher radioed Deputies Linneman and Kelly Aalfs regarding the call. The dispatcher also requested that one of them call the dispatch center for further information. The two deputies returned to the office, and Aalfs called the dispatcher. The dispatcher told Aalfs that Ostenson sounded intoxicated and made threats to kill someone, but the exact identity of the person was not clear. Aalfs called the Ostenson residence and spoke to Ostenson's eighteen-year-old son Danny. Danny informed Aalfs that his father was not there and seemed concerned that there might be trouble. Aalfs called Montevideo Officer Weber and told him that he was concerned for Sandra and her new husband's safety. He requested Weber to keep their residence in Montevideo under surveillance.

Aalfs and Linneman were in a Chippewa County marked squad with Linneman driving. They decided to go by Berends' residence. Ostenson was not seen in the area. They then decided to go to Ostenson's house. They saw a vehicle pulling into the Ostenson driveway. Linneman pulled in front of the house and exited the squad. Aalfs started to open the passenger door to get out. He saw a person he recognized as Ostenson getting out of the vehicle that had pulled into the driveway. Ostenson was coming toward the squad at a rapid pace. Aalfs did not see a weapon until Ostenson was about twenty feet from the squad. Ostenson was holding what was later determined to be a Taurus .357-caliber revolver in both hands. It was pointed directly at Aalfs. Ostenson was saying something to Aalfs, but he could not understand any of it.

Aalfs made the decision not to draw his weapon as he felt that might escalate the situation. Ostenson continued to come toward the squad and positioned himself just inside the opened squad door. The weapon was about six inches from Aalfs' face. Aalfs leaned back as far as he could against an armrest in the middle of the front seat. Aalfs said that Ostenson had a "wild look" in his eyes, and he felt that Ostenson was going pull the trigger. He could hear Deputy Linneman and another person (Danny Ostenson) yelling to "Put the gun down" and "not to do it." Aalfs decided to kick at the gun. The kick forced the gun up and to the right. Ostenson started to bring the gun back down at Aalfs. Aalfs pulled his 9-mm pistol. He fired one shot at Ostenson. He saw him stagger back about twenty feet and fall to the ground. Aalfs exited the squad and saw the .357-caliber revolver about halfway between the squad and where Ostenson lay. Aalfs picked up the revolver and put it in his gun belt. Danny Ostenson appeared extremely upset and had to be restrained. Ostenson's mother came out of the house and began shouting at the deputies. Linneman radioed the dispatcher that shots had been fired and requested assistance and an ambulance. Aalfs and Linneman attempted to maintain order until other officers and the ambulance arrived. Aalfs gave the .357-caliber revolver to Officer Jim Bowen from the Montevideo Police Department. The hammer of the gun was cocked when Aalfs picked it up, and there were also six live rounds in it.

Thirty-five-year-old Deputy Linneman told investigators that he had known Ostenson about two years. He recalled taking a motor vehicle accident report from him. He said that he discovered the restraining order when he came to work at 6:00 p.m. that evening and tried unsuccessfully to serve it around 7:00 p.m. at Ostenson's house. He only found his mother at home.

Deputy Linneman's statement was the same as Aalfs' up to the time of pulling in front of the Ostenson house. After parking the squad, he exited and came around to the left rear of the car. He saw Ostenson walking quickly toward the squad. He initially thought that he had a gun in his hands. However, he was not certain until he was about ten feet from the passenger door where Aalfs was sitting. He yelled, "Drop the weapon."

He heard another individual (Danny) shout, "Dad, don't do it." The passenger door was open, but Aalfs remained in the car. Ostenson was yelling something at Aalfs. He could see that the hammer of the gun was cocked and that he had both hands on the grip. He was afraid to fire at Ostenson as he thought the impact of being shot would cause him to pull the trigger and possibly kill Aalfs.

Seeming only like a split second, Linneman saw Aalfs kick at Ostenson's weapon. This caused Ostenson to pull the weapon up to his right. Linneman then fired his 9-mm pistol "three or four times." He recalled hearing Aalfs fire one shot. Ostenson staggered back into his yard and collapsed. Linneman saw Aalfs get out of the car and pick up the gun Ostenson dropped.

An autopsy determined that Ostenson had been hit four times. One shot went in his left forearm and one to the back of his right hand exiting out the palm. The third shot hit him in the left area of the stomach, and the fourth went into the lower right area of his back.

A Chippewa County grand jury cleared the deputies.

XII

Who would ever believe that a man sixty-five-year-old currently in hospice would be shot by police, but that is exactly what happened during the early morning hours of December 13, 1999, in Duluth, Minnesota. At 2:34 a.m. Duluth Officer Daniel Fogarty cleared a call at St. Mary's Hospital in Duluth. When he returned to his squad, he checked his CAD (Computer Aided Dispatch). For those unfamiliar with CAD, it is the same as receiving a mobile email—no actual voice. There was a "check on the welfare" message for him. At almost the same time, he received a call on his normal radio with the same message as the CAD.

Apparently there were two calls from the residence at 2837 Hutchinson Road. The CAD information said that a male had called stating that his wife was not giving him his correct medication. There was also mention of hospice involvement. It also stated that 911 had spoken with the man's wife and she seemed much more rational. He responded to the address.

It took him approximately five to seven minutes to get to 2800 Hutchinson Road. The driveway was illuminated. Fogerty pulled his squad into the driveway toward the back of the house. As he exited his vehicle, he noticed two sets of car tracks in the snow as if someone had recently left the residence. About the same time, Fogerty noticed a female in the kitchen window. It appeared as though she was standing over a sink. Fogerty walked on the deck to the back door which was off the kitchen area.

As Fogerty opened the screen door, the woman, later identified as 57-year-old Sherry Herold, opened the inside door. They went into the area that Fogerty described as a kitchen/dining area. He questioned her about the circumstances of the calls. She stated that she was having a problem with her husband's medications and that hospice was involved in his care. She told Fogerty that her husband had taken a knife after her earlier that evening.

About that same time, Donald Herold came from somewhere to Fogerty's left and was standing by the stove. Donald had a knife in his right hand. The butt of the knife was by his thumb and index finger, with the blade pointing down. Fogerty and Sherry were standing in the area of the sink at that time talking. Fogerty told investigators later that Herold, "Didn't say a word, I mean…he's standing there with a knife." Fogerty gave him verbal commands to, "Drop the knife, drop the knife."

Momentarily, Herold brought the knife up and was grabbing at his wife. Fogerty took his Smith and Wesson .40-caliber handgun from his holster. As Herold brought it down at his wife, Fogerty fired one shot. Fogerty said, "I was expecting something to happen, it didn't." Herold's arm came up again like he was going to stab at his wife. Fogerty fired again.

Herold fell to the floor, and his wife moved away to the kitchen table. Fogerty immediately called on his radio that a shot had been fired. He also called for a supervisor and Gold Cross ambulance. He moved the knife away to make the situation safe. He next checked for a pulse. Then realizing that he had not clarified who had been shot, he radioed again that the suspect was the person shot.

Sherry Herold started screaming and shouting just as another Duluth officer arrived. Sherry wanted to call her daughter. Fogerty tried to calm her down. She was told as soon as a supervisor arrived she would be able to call family members. Paramedics and a supervisor arrived. Fogerty returned to police headquarters and gave his weapon to a supervisor. He then went to the hospital to furnish blood and urine samples. Fogerty told investigators, "I guess you know, I just, I feel sorry for that woman. I didn't, you know go there to intentionally hurt anyone. I was there to help you know."

Herold had retired from the Minnesota National Guard in Duluth in 1989. His behavior that night was completely out of character because of his cancer and medication. Sherry had given him the correct medications and dosage, but he became confused and agitated.

On February 9, 2000, the St. Louis County Attorney ruled that the shooting was justified and no charges were filed.

XIII

Whether the city is small or large, rural or urban, the chance that law enforcement will get involved in a domestic situation is always high. This was the situation on Wednesday, January 9, 1985, in the City of Sauk Rapids in Benton County. Shortly after 10:00 p.m. that night a neighbor of Susan Richards called the police to report that a man with a knife was threatening Richards.

Apparently a neighbor of Richards was working in his garage when he heard screaming. The neighbor and some of his friends who were in the garage with him went out to the alley and saw Richard's son standing by a tree wearing only his pajamas. It was very cold, so the men brought the boy into the garage. Soon after, twenty-four-year-old Michael J. Rahrlien, who was the live-in boyfriend of Susan Richards, came out of Richards' house looking for the boy. He was only wearing shorts and appeared to have been drinking.

Following a confrontation with the men in the garage, Richards' son returned to the house with Rahrlien. Two of the men walked out of the garage toward Richards' house. They saw a woman (Richards) huddled outside the house. The woman screamed to the men that "He is going to get a knife."

The men retreated and made the initial call to 911. Other neighbors also heard the screaming and called 911.

Twenty-three-year-old Patrol Officer Douglas Brinkman, Capt. Art Daniels and Officer James McMahon responded to the scene. When they arrived, Rahrlien met them at the back door of the house. They attempted to enter to talk to Sherry and her son. Rahrlien began waving the knife in a slashing manner in the air and threatened to kill the officers. He then threatened to kill Sherry and her son. Rahrlien backed far enough into the house to allow the officers a chance to grab Sherry and her son. As they were attempting to get them out of the house, Rahrlien moved directly toward Richards with the knife in his hand. It appeared that he was going to stab her. Officer Brinkman fired two rounds from his .357-caliber revolver. Rahrlien was struck in the right chest area by one round, and the other grazed him.

Rahrlien was immediately transported to a nearby St. Cloud hospital. He was pronounced dead in the emergency room at 11:30 p.m. Richards and her son where also transported to the hospital. She was treated for several knife wounds and released. Her son was not stabbed. However, he was treated for a bruise on his head and released. No officers were injured.

A Benton County grand jury returned a no bill against Brinkman.

XIV

Around 9:50 p.m. on Saturday, June 3, 2000, the police department in the eastern Twin Cities suburb of Woodbury received a call from Tami Parks stating that her husband was drunk and arguing with her. Police officers responded, and subsequent events resulted in the death of Perry Parks.

Woodbury Officer Michael Pomeroy, thirty-nine years old and a twelve-year veteran of the department, was at police headquarters when he heard the radio call of a domestic situation at 2704 Horseshoe Lane. He heard Officer Jeff Gottstein being dispatched to the call. Pomeroy also responded to assist Gottstein. He actually arrived about twenty to thirty seconds before

Gottstein. Pomeroy, just before his arrival, saw on his CAD screen in his squad that the call was a "domestic/father is DK'd" meaning that the father is drunk.

When Pomeroy arrived, he saw a white male, 250 pounds, six-foot-two to six-foot-three and possibly in his early forties pacing back and forth on the sidewalk in front of the house. Pomeroy got out of his squad and approached the individual, later identified as Perry Parks. Pomeroy asked Parks words to the effect of how everything was going. He was trying to make conversation to determine if he was involved or just a bystander. Parks responded that everything was fine and invited Pomeroy inside the house. Pomeroy asked Parks if his wife was home, and he said that she was in the house. Gottstein was just getting out his squad at that time. Parks appeared calm and was not combative.

The three of them walked up to the front door. Parks stopped and told the officers to go in first. Pomeroy told Parks that it was his house and he should go first. As they were entering, Parks shut the door and called to his wife. Tami came around a corner and walked toward them as they proceeded from the front door into a kitchen/dining area. Those two rooms opened up into a larger area like a family or living room. They went to the kitchen area. It was a typical kitchen with sink and countertop. There was an island that divided the kitchen from the dining area.

Instead of walking to the dining room table, Parks walked to an area near the kitchen counter. Pomeroy saw two large steak knives lying on the counter. Pomeroy walked around and positioned himself between Parks and the knives. Parks chuckled to Pomeroy and said something to the effect that Pomeroy had seen the knives. Parks leaned up against the counter, and Tami was standing in the dining room almost to the family/living room. Officer Gottstein was standing where the hallway came into the kitchen area. Parks was holding a large glass like a beer mug but it appeared to have ice and water in it. Parks was waving with the mug in his hand as he talked.

Pomeroy asked Parks to move from where he was standing so they could sit down at the table and talk about why they were there. Parks said he was not going to move and said, "This is my damn house. I'll do whatever I damn well please." He had previously been calm but now was speaking loudly with anger in his tone. Pomeroy said they should come around away from the counter and sit down. Parks started to walk toward the area of the counter where the knives were. Pomeroy stepped between Parks and the knives. Pomeroy raised his left hand with a gesture to stop and verbally told him to stop.

Parks continued to come toward Pomeroy until he made contact with Pomeroy's hand. Pomeroy pushed him back and told him to stop. Parks went back against the counter. He immediately came back and started to swing at Pomeroy. Parks, who was somewhat off balance, grabbed Pomeroy and knocked him to the floor. Pomeroy stated that when he landed on the floor, he was actually in a sitting position—not on his back. Officer Gottstein came over and grabbed Parks.

The three of them were struggling. The officers called for Parks to stop and get on the floor. They continued pushing and wrestling. Parks did not appear to be slowing his efforts against the officers. All three fell to the floor. Gottstein was on the bottom, with Parks on top of him and Pomeroy on top of Parks. Pomeroy was trying to pull Parks off Gottstein as he was able to get into a semi-standing position over Parks. Gottstein shouted, "Stop or we're going to spray you." Parks continued and Gottstein was able to spray pepper spray into Parks' face.

The pepper spray had no effect on Parks. Gottstein continued demands for Parks to stop. Gottstein sprayed him another two or three times. He missed Parks and sprayed directly into Pomeroy's face.

Gottstein was still on the bottom and Pomeroy asked him, "Jeff, can you get out of there?" He responded that he could not get loose. Pomeroy got on the radio and told the dispatcher they needed help and were involved in a fight. As Pomeroy called dispatch he heard Gottstein yell, "Let go of my gun. Don't take my gun."

Pomeroy put his radio away and tried to force Parks to the floor. Pomeroy saw Gottstein's hand on his gun and Parks' hand on top of Gottstein's hand. The gun was in the holster, but the holster was unsnapped and the gun partially withdrawn from it. Gottstein was pushing down on the gun to keep it in the holster, and at the same time Parks was pulling up on it. Pomeroy tried to help Gottstein keep the gun secure and was able to push it all of the way back into the holster but could not get it snapped.

Parks then grabbed Gottstein's wrist and started to grab the gun with his other hand. Pomeroy tried to stick his finger in Parks' eye. That did not work. Pomeroy reached for his nightstick and could not find it. Pomeroy pulled his pistol. Pomeroy, who is left-handed, poked the pistol into Parks' right side ribcage below his arm. Pomeroy told Parks to let go or he would shoot. Parks did not respond. Pomeroy moved back and pulled the trigger. The weapon did not fire. He shouted again that he was going to shoot. Pomeroy heard Tami yell, "Don't make them shoot you." Pomeroy slapped the magazine and pulled the trigger. Again it did not fire. Pomeroy again slapped the magazine, and this time he also worked the slide. He saw a round eject. He shouted again to Parks that he was going to shoot.

Pomeroy, who was now standing, fired his weapon. He hit Parks in the upper right chest area. Parks looked at Pomeroy and said, "You fucker!" He appeared to be moving his foot under him as if attempting to stand. Pomeroy told him to get down on the floor. Gottstein was rolling away from Parks at this time. Pomeroy was not sure if he had hit Parks with the shot. He then stepped forward and kicked Parks in the sternum. Parks fell over backwards.

Gottstein then grabbed Parks. Pomeroy holstered his weapon, and they put Parks face down on the floor. As they got one handcuff on his left arm, they rolled him over slightly to get his right arm from under him. Pomeroy noticed blood on Parks. His right wrist was handcuffed, and he stopped struggling. Pomeroy noticed a large pool of blood on the floor. Pomeroy, who is also a paramedic, ran to his squad to get his medical equipment and render medical aid. Parks died from the wound.

A Washington County grand jury returned a no bill on September 12, 2000. On October 24, 2000, a four-million-dollar civil lawsuit was filed against the city and the officers. The suit sought one million dollars from the city and three million dollars from the officers. The case was subsequently dismissed in U. S. District Court without any award.

Deceased hostage taker.
(Chapter 2, Case IV)
Minnesota BCA photo

Weapon with all rounds fired used to
challenge officers in suicide by cop.
(Chapter 2, Case VII)
Hennepin County Sheriff's Office photo

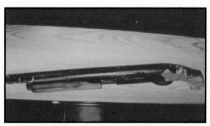

Sawed-off shotgun
used by deceased.
(Chapter 7, Case I)
Ramsey County Sheriff's Office photo

Bank robber's getaway vehicle.
(Chapter 4, Case IV)
Minnesota BCA photo

Hennepin County
deputy shooting at
bank robber.
(Chapter 1, Case I)
Bank surveillance
photo/Minneapolis FBI

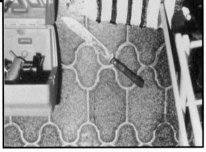

Knife used by
person charging police.
(Chapter 5, Case II)
Anoka County Sheriff's Office photo

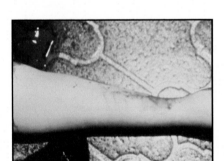

Hesitation wounds on
arm of person charging
police in suicide by cop.
(Chapter 5, Case II
Anoka County Sheriff's Office photo

Deceased assailant who
threatened officers with weapon.
(Chapter 6, Case VI)
Minnesota BCA photo

Assailant charging police with knife.
(Chapter 5, Case VI)
Permission of *Grand Forks Herald*, Photographer Eric Hylden

Knife used by person to stab himself and then charge police.
(Chapter 9, Case III)
Minnesota BCA, photographer Jim Boyer

Photo of steel gun port
in deceased's home.
(Chapter 2, Case V)
Minnesota BCA photo

Reenactment of officer
shooting from hood of car when
assailant came at him with knife.
(Chapter 9, Case III)
Minnesota BCA, photographer Jim Boyer)

Replica weapon used by deceased.
(Chapter 11, Case V)
Minnesota BCA, photographer Janet Nelson

.38 revolver used by bank robber.
(Chapter 1, Case III)
Courtesy of Chief Deputy David Bellows, Dakota
County Sheriff's Office

Shooting scene of bank robber.
(Chapter 1, Case III)
Courtesy of Chief Deputy David Bellows, DCSO

Bank robbery loot in
front seat of stolen vehicle.
(Chapter 1, Case III)
Courtesy of Chief Deputy David Bellows, DCSO

Bank robber's rented getaway SUV.
(Chapter 1, Case IV)
Photo courtesy of Erik Amundson,
Edina Police Department

Edina Police squad shot
by bank robber with .223 rifle.
(Chapter 1, Case IV)
Photo courtesy of Erik Amundson,
Edina Police Department

Deceased bank robber.
(Chapter 1, Case IV)
Photo courtesy of Erik Amundson,
Police Department

Bank robber's .223 rifle.
(Chapter 1, Case IV)
Photo courtesy of Erik Amundson,
Edina Police Department

**Minneapolis Police
squad shot by assailants.**
(Chapter 8, Case VI)
Minnesota BCA photo

Deceased fugitive.
(Chapter 8, Case X)
Hennepin County Sheriff's Office photo

**Shooting scene at
end of high speed chase.**
(Chapter 4, Case VI)
Minnesota BCA photo

**Aerial photo of assailant's SUV crash-
ing into driver's door of police squad.**
(Chapter 6, Case III)
Hennepin County Sheriff's Office photo

Shotgun used by assailant.
(Chapter 2, Case V)
Minnesota BCA photo

Chapter Seven

You're Breaking the Law
aka He Has a Gun—Shots Fired

I

On Friday, January 22, 1994, twenty-year-old Shawn Mettler caught a ride to the metro area of Ramsey County to visit a friend in the City of North Saint Paul. Prior to the incident which ultimately took his life, he offered to sell his friend a sawed-off shotgun. Mettler told the friend that he had sawed off the shotgun. His friend told him he did not even want to see the shotgun and supposedly told him, "The only thing a sawed-off shotgun is good for is getting you killed." Truer words were never spoken.

Mettler had been to visit his friend before and said he came to watch his friend's band practice and "hang out for awhile." They also played cards and drank some alcohol. Around midnight, Mettler called someone in his hometown north of the Twin Cities attempting to get a ride back home. Apparently, he could not convince anyone to make the eighty-mile round trip at that hour of the night. Mettler decided to get a ride from his friend's younger brother who was taking his girlfriend home. Mettler was dropped off at a gas station just off the freeway. He claimed he could walk to another friend's apartment about one-half mile away. Just before 1:00 a.m., not far

from where he was left, a lady on the ground floor of her apartment building in the City of Little Canada was talking on the telephone to a friend. She
heard a gunshot outside. The woman immediately turned off her lights and
moved away from the window. She called 911, and officers from the Ramsey County Sheriff's Office responded. Little Canada has no municipal police department. She reported to the deputies that the shot was "very loud"
and she could tell that it was "very close."

Ramsey County Deputies Thomas Haltiner and Edward Whitledge responded to the call. Whitledge also had his canine partner with him. After
they interviewed the lady, they searched the area on foot. They wanted to
look closer in the area slightly away from the apartment building. There
were large buildings which had single-car garage units for the occupants of
the apartment. The garage building had overhead doors on each side of the
building so cars faced each other when driven into the stalls. Whitledge's
canine remained in his squad as they searched the area.

While the deputies were searching one row of the garage stalls, Deputy
Haltiner saw a person in another row enter a stall about fifty feet away. In a
deposition at a later date, Haltiner said he noticed the person was carrying
a "long gun" in his left hand. Haltiner notified Whitledge of what he had
seen. They both walked to the row of stalls were Haltiner had last seen the
man. As they passed Whitledge's squad, canine Bud was removed to assist.

The deputies noticed that one garage door in the row was unlocked and
pulled open a few inches on the bottom. They raised the door further and
saw a Dodge Stealth parked inside with the front of the vehicle pointing toward the far end of the approximately twenty-foot stall. Standing at the
opening of the garage, the deputies identified themselves and requested that
the person exit. They did not receive a response, so Whitledge announced
that he would send his canine into the stall. Again, there was no response.
Whitledge then directed Bud to inspect the stall. Bud did as ordered, and as
he approached the far end of the stall at the front of the Dodge he began to
growl.

Mettler was apparently crouched down or prone at the front of the Dodge. When Bud growled, Mettler fired one shot from his shotgun at him. It was obvious that Bud was probably hit and was injured by the shot. Both deputies fired all of their rounds in their 9-mm pistols at Mettler. A total of thirty-two rounds were fired, with fifteen of them striking him. Mettler yelled out, "You can stop now—I'm dead."

After the shooting, both deputies said that Mettler fired at them and they return fired. However, the investigation determined that Mettler only fired the one shot that killed the dog. Mettler's shotgun was found laying on the garage floor under his body. The spent shell from the shot that killed Bud was still in the chamber and live shells were loaded in the shotgun's magazine. The shooting review board found that the deputies were justified in returning fire after Mettler shot Bud and cleared them of any wrongdoing

Unfortunately, the initial investigation of the shooting encountered some difficulties. Questions came up regarding the trajectory and ballistic analysis. They were not conducted until litigation began two years later. Other questions arose. It could not be determined who shot the fatal shots or where each deputy's rounds struck. It also could not be determined if the deputies were inside or outside the garage when they started shooting or how long the shooting lasted. (The best estimate is that it lasted less than ten seconds.) The investigation at the scene failed to record the location of the ejected shell casings after the shooting, nor were the bullet holes in the wall of the garage charted.

Over two years later, on April 2, 1996, Marsha Mettler, Shawn's mother, filed suit in Federal Court against Ramsey County, Sheriff Patricia Moen, and the two deputies for violation under 42 U.S.C §§ 1983 and 1985. The suit had four counts. Count I alleged that the two deputies violated Shawn's Constitutional rights by using excessive force resulting in his death. Count II alleged Ramsey County violated his rights by training the deputies negligently and showing deliberate indifference to the deputies' custom, pattern, or practice of using excessive force. Count III alleged that Sheriff Moen had supervisory liability for failing to correct the Sheriff Office's pattern of using excessive force. Count IV alleged that all of the defendants had conspired to violate Shawn's constitutional rights by permitting or encouraging the use of excessive force, conducting an inadequate investigation, and concealing evidence of wrongdoing.

All parties stipulated to the dismissal of Count III. The defendants moved for summary judgment of the remaining counts. The District Court granted judgment to Counts II and IV. However, the District Court denied summary judgment on Count I despite the argument that because the deputies were police officers qualified immunity protected them from liability on Ms. Mettler's Section 1983 claim. The deputies filed an interlocutory appeal of the District Court's denial of their motion for summary judgment on Count I on qualified immunity grounds. The District Court then made its order granting summary judgment on Count II and all defendants on Count IV. Ms. Mettler cross-appealed that decision.

The lawsuit was subsequently dismissed in January 1999—five years after the shooting occurred. When the District Court ruled that the *Mettler* case could go to trial on one issue—the deputies' use of excessive force—the matter was appealed to the Eighth Circuit Court of Appeals. The Federal Appeals Court dismissed the lawsuit brought by Ms. Mettler. The Court held that the deputies were immune from liability for returning fire and hitting Mettler fourteen times. After the dismissal, the Ramsey County Attorney said, "The decision recognizes that police officers have to make tough decisions when confronted with life threatening decisions, and recognizes that the courts are reluctant and should be reluctant to second guess those decisions."

II

Minneapolis Police responded to "a crazy man with a gun" at 3:50 a.m. on Wednesday, August 12, 1981. The night began with a twenty-four-year-old lady going to a local tavern where she met a man. Shortly after midnight, the two decided to leave the bar with a twelve-pack of beer and go to her residence. The man, later identified as fifty-one-year-old Melvin Johnson, asked the lady to have sex. She agreed and twenty dollars was established as the price. Her apartment was a mess, with no furniture in most of the rooms. There was a mattress on the floor of the front bedroom. They moved the mattress and a blanket to the back porch. They proceeded to kiss and re-move some clothing. The woman told police that Johnson "passed out" be-fore they had sex. She decided to go to a friend's house and watch television.

After about two hours, she decided to return to her apartment. On the way there, she saw her twenty-six-year-old brother. He walked with her to her apartment. As she began walking up the stairs to her apartment, John-son opened the rear door and stepped out onto the landing. He shouted at her, "You fucking bitch—you took every nickel—you didn't leave me with a penny." He pointed a handgun at her and threatened to shoot her. She and her brother ran from the apartment to call police. Ironically, she went to the residence of Donald LaPoint, who was later shot and killed by Min-neapolis Police in 1994, to call the police. LaPoint did not let her in, but he did call 911.

When Officer David Niebur arrived, the woman came running toward his squad. She appeared to be frantic and told Niebur, "There is a crazy man in my house with a gun and my three kids are in there." Other offi-cers arrived. Niebur tried to enter the apartment from the front door and found it locked. He went around to the back and was joined by two addi-tional officers.

There was a wooden staircase to a landing at the top of the stairs. Niebur had his .357-caliber revolver in his right hand and a flashlight in his left. He had taken only one step up the stairs when Johnson bolted out the back door. Niebur observed Johnson holding a long-barreled handgun above his head in his right hand and a beer bottle in his left hand. Niebur yelled, "Po-lice, drop the gun." Johnson leveled the gun toward Niebur. Niebur fired twice. Officer Mike Carey was standing below the landing and fired his revolver six times. Carey said that everything appeared to happen in slow motion and that he could see the trail of the bullets like tracer bullets as they went from his gun to the landing.

Johnson's .22-caliber Colt New Frontier Buntline revolver was examined following the shooting. The weapon had misfired. It appeared that a shell had been struck by the firing pin, but the gun failed to fire.

Both of these officers were cleared in the shooting and advanced within the ranks of the Minneapolis Police Department and later became police chiefs in jurisdictions outside Minnesota.

III

A few minutes past midnight on December 27, 1992, chaos and terror shook the walls of the Turtle Shell Club just outside the Red Lake Indian Reservation located about ten miles northeast of the Bemidji, Minnesota. Forty-two-year-old Delwyn Dudley, a lieutenant with the Red Lake Bureau of Indian Affairs Police Department on the Reservation, walked into the bar and went directly to his estranged wife. She was there with two friends listening to a county western band. The two began arguing. A thirty-eight-year-old man from another table stood up—either out of curiosity or to intervene. Dudley pulled a 9-mm handgun from his belt and shot the man. Dudley walked out of the bar. People recognized him as he had been kicked out of the bar earlier around 9:30 p.m.

The wounded man was getting attention from patrons, and police had been called. Dudley then re-entered the bar with an AR-15 assault rifle. It was later determined that this weapon was missing from the Red Lake Police Department. He began firing the AR-15, and people started scattering. Some of the thirty patrons ran to hide in a big walk-in cooler. Some were trapped away from the exit. Others escaped out the kitchen and fled into the nearby woods. One witness, who was hiding behind a large speaker, heard Dudley walk up by him and shout, "Get up, get the hell out." The witness realized that Dudley was talking to a woman hiding behind an overturned table. Dudley turned the weapon to the male witness and pointed it at his head.

The man quickly asked, "Can I go too?"

Dudley responded, "You, get the hell out." The man and two women walked out of the bar.

Beltrami County Deputy Steve Kovacic was on routine patrol at approximately 12:51 a.m. when he received a dispatch call to respond to the Turtle Shell Club. It was reported that a man had a gun and shots were being fired. While en route, the thirty-six-year-old deputy was again notified by dispatch that shots could be heard over the telephone during the 911 call. A description of the gunman was broadcast to all of the responding deputies as an Indian male, six foot, 230 pounds, short black hair, maroon sweatshirt and blue jeans.

Deputy Kovacic arrived and parked on the lower one-third of the back driveway of the club. He turned off his lights and was waiting for backup officers as ordered by the sheriff. Kovacic, fearing for his safety, went to his trunk and put on a second bullet-proof vest. He also got his shotgun and binoculars. He then moved to a location approximately 75 to 100 feet from his squad. While scanning the area of the club with his binoculars, he saw a man in a white sweatshirt crawling on his hands and knees. The man fell two or three times while crawling. The man eventually made it to the front of the club and fell prone on the ground. It was obvious to Kovacic that the man was seriously hurt. However, not knowing where the gunman was and on orders from the sheriff to wait for backup, he maintained his position.

Kovacic then observed another male with short black/gray hair wearing a maroon sweatshirt with gold lettering on the front of it walking around the bar as if following the tracks of the man who came crawling out of the club. The man matched the description given by the dispatcher of the gunman. It appeared to Kovacic that he had an M-16 or AR-15 assault weapon in his right hand. Kovacic was too far away at that point to effectively use his .12-gauge shotgun. He saw the man walk into the parking lot out of his sight. He then heard several shots from the area where the man went. The gunman then walked back into his sight and tossed the assault rifle on the hood of a vehicle. It appeared to Kovacic that the man now had a long-barreled handgun in his right hand. The man then walked up to the man in the white sweatshirt on the ground.

Kovacic was approximately 150 yards away, observing the two individuals through his binoculars. The man in the white sweatshirt, later identified as forty-year-old Darrell Lussier, moved up to a kneeling position. It looked like the two were talking. Lussier at one time had his hands up in a pleading type gesture with the palms stretched upward. Dudley pointed his weapon at Lussier several times in a threatening manner. Ultimately, within seconds, Dudley turned away and immediately turned back and grabbed Lussier's hair. Dudley then pointed the gun at the front of Lussier's head. Kovacic heard a "pop" and Lussier fell to the ground. Kovacic notified dispatch about what had occurred.

Dudley went into the parking lot and walked out of his sight. He appeared to be giving most of his attention to the woods on the south side of the club. Unbeknownst to Kovacic, several club patrons and Beltrami deputies were located among the trees in the area.

Kovacic watched Dudley walk to a two-tone Ford pickup. Dudley entered the pickup and started coming in the direction where Kovacic was located. Kovacic decided to act. He ran to an area about ten feet off the road. He shouldered his shotgun in full view of the pickup's headlights and yelled, "Halt! Sheriff." He heard the engine rev, and tires were spinning. Kovacic fired his shotgun at the tires and once into driver's window. The pickup crashed into some trees. Kovacic threw down the shotgun and ran to the pickup as he saw the backup lights go on. Kovacic, as safely as he could, ran up to the driver's side and fired numerous times where he thought the gunman would be sitting. Kovacic opened the door and saw Dudley lying across the seat. He was able to grab Dudley's visible left hand. He put a handcuff on that hand and then was also able to secure the right hand to handcuff it. He then shouted for assistance from the other deputies in the area. He pulled Dudley from the pickup and began checking for vital signs. Dudley was dead.

Located in the pickup were a .12-gauge shotgun, 9-mm handgun and the AR-15. Kovacic was cleared as the shooting was ruled as justified. Kovacic left the sheriff's office and is now teaching criminal justice courses for students majoring in law enforcement.

IV

A call to Faribault Police Department 11:30 p.m. on Tuesday, January 18, 1983, reported a man with a gun. Lois Lambert called police and said her husband was in their garage with a shotgun and had fired it twice. One shot was outside the garage, and the other one was through the roof. She later claimed that she asked the 911 operator for two officers who knew her husband as she felt they could persuade him to come out of the garage. The two officers she requested where not on duty at that time. Lois said her husband was upset about something. However, it was never determined what the source of his anger was.

When officers arrived, they looked through the garage window and saw an armed man. Officer Robert Basel entered the garage. Russell Lambert grabbed the shotgun and began advancing toward Basel. Basel called to him to stop and drop the shotgun. When he failed to respond to the commands, Basel shot him with his police-issued .12-gauge shotgun. Lambert died from the shot to his chest.

Sadly, this incident played out in the local newspaper. The managing editor of the local newspaper wrote an editorial entitled, "The patrolman did the logical thing." The editorial opinion stated that, "He (Basel) fired in self-defense." Other citizens wrote letters claiming that Basel had other options. One letter to the editor was from the decedent's wife. She wrote in her letter that she had "a ringside seat to the shooting." She claimed it "was like watching two clowns with guns at a circus." She added, "Our fearless police officer thought he was Wyatt Earp." She ended her letter, "If our police officers aren't any smarter than to enter a building where a man is inside with a gun, by himself, then I think we have one sick police force" (editorial page, *Faribault Daily News*, Faribault, Minnesota, January 26, 1983).

Police must respond to situations involving individuals who may have circumstances in their lives about which no one, let alone the responding officer, has any knowledge. Apparently, Lois Lambert had concerns the night before the shooting. Russell had taken his shotgun downtown, and she called two of his friends at a local bar to check on him. The friends said he was in good spirits and was able to drive. Another friend said Russell claimed to have been stopped by a Faribault officer other than Basel. Lambert told that friend earlier the night of the shooting that he was going to shoot out the officer's tires.

It should be noted that Basel did not enter the garage alone, as another officer was with him. Basel was cleared of any wrongdoing in the shooting. He subsequently left the Faribault Police Department for employment with a larger department in Minnesota.

V

Some shooting incidents begin with an event which no one could imagine would lead to a police shooting. This shooting occurred because of a typical event during winter in Minnesota—a snowstorm. Thirty-eight-year-old Mark Beaupre, a fifteen-year veteran of the Minneapolis Police Department, was working a "snow emergency" detail on Saturday, January 22, 2005. A snow emergency occurs when the city believes that the snowfall is deep enough to have snowplows clear the streets. This means that persons with cars on the odd side of the street must have their cars off the street on the odd date of the calendar and the even side the following day. A "snow emergency" remains in effect for two days following a storm. Police will go down streets ticketing cars parked on the street and request tow trucks come to remove them.

About 3:20 a.m. that morning, Beaupre was working the detail on the north side of Minneapolis. He observed two individuals walking westbound on 26th Street. One of the individuals appeared to be carrying a long weapon, possibly a shotgun. Beaupre was eastbound at the time. He immediately turned the vehicle around and exited the vehicle with his .45-caliber weapon drawn. He momentarily lost sight of the two when he turned the vehicle, but soon spotted the two again. Beaupre focused on the man with the shotgun. He saw the man, later identified as twenty-seven-year-old Dana Blue, aka David Dickenson, attempting to walk up a small hill in the yard at 2549 Upton Avenue North. He was stumbling and losing his balance. Beaupre yelled, "Police, freeze." Blue dropped his shotgun.

Almost immediately, the other individual began firing at him. That person, later identified as twenty-one-year-old Benjamin DeCoteau, shot twice at Beaupre as he moved to the rear of the police vehicle for cover. Beaupre could see the muzzle flash and heard the report of the weapon. Beaupre fired back while seeking cover.

DeCoteau continued to fire and Beaupre also returned fire. Beaupre believed that he hit DeCoteau as he had been standing in the middle of the yard and next he was lying on his right side still shooting. DeCoteau then stopped shooting. Beaupre looked back where he last saw Blue. Blue was lying on his back with his hands straight up in the air as if to show that he was unarmed. He could see the shotgun about five feet from him in the snow.

Beaupre saw that DeCoteau was attempting a magazine change of his weapon. DeCoteau had the weapon and magazine directly in front of his face. Beaupre feared he was possibly wearing body armor and would start shooting again after the magazine change. Beaupre aimed at his head and fired twice. He saw DeCoteau's head snap back and the weapon fall into the snow. Beaupre then radioed the dispatcher of, "shots fired." He advised he was okay and that an ambulance was needed for the suspect.

Officer Bonnie Edwards, a canine officer, arrived to assist Beaupre. They could see the weapon alongside DeCoteau and also that he was not moving. Blue was still on his back with his arms extended in view. Two additional officers arrived and removed Blue from the yard where he had fallen. Edwards, with cover being provided by Beaupre, sent her dog to DeCoteau. The dog grabbed DeCoteau's pant leg and pulled him about two to three feet away from the gun. Beaupre rushed to DeCoteau and placed handcuffs on him. He then secured a Browning 9-mm pistol and two magazines that were in the snow.

Beaupre went back to his police van and discovered that the driver's window and back window had been shot during the shooting. Beaupre told investigators later that Blue complied with his first order to drop the weapon. However, DeCoteau never did. Neither Blue nor DeCoteau ever said anything during the incident. Beaupre stressed that he was initially focused on Blue carrying the shotgun and did not know that DeCoteau had a weapon. Beaupre said, "He (DeCoteau) had every opportunity to leave the scene without incident."

The Minneapolis Police crime scene team responded to the shooting, as did medical personnel. It was determined that DeCoteau was dead at the scene. Following his removal by the Medical Examiner's Office, the crime scene team completed their processing. The temperature was fourteen degrees above zero with a wind chill factor of three below. The wind was blowing eighteen miles per hour and was causing some drifting as a result of the seven inches of snow earlier (the reason for the "snow emergency"). In addition to the two windows being shot, there was a bullet hole in the van driver's side door. A live bullet for DeCoteau's weapon was found under his body. Crime scene investigators requested the street department to bring blowtorches to melt the snow. Five discharged 9-mm cartridges were found near where DeCoteau had been. They were later matched to his weapon. There were nine discharged cartridges from Beaupre's H & K .45-caliber handgun near his vehicle, one was actually located on top of the van.

An autopsy revealed that DeCoteau died of multiple gunshot wounds. There were at least three wounds which were potentially fatal.

There was considerable media coverage of this incident as DeCoteau was Native American and Beaupre was Caucasian. Some "community activists" questioned the use of deadly force. One important factor quelled the outcry: Dana Blue told police that DeCoteau had vowed to shoot a police officer. No one will ever know why he picked that day to attempt to do so. A Hennepin County grand jury returned a no bill on April 14, 2005.

VI

Around 6:15 p.m. on Wednesday, November 11, 1996, officers of the Saint Paul Police Department responded to a call on the city's eastside that a male, later identified as thirty-nine-year-old Robert Benson, was threatening to harm relatives and himself. Police arrived. However, Benson had already left the house. Witnesses said that Benson had been drinking and fired three rounds from a handgun. He also placed the gun to his head and pulled the trigger several times. The witnesses said Benson talked about how he wanted to die like his father. The female witness furnished his description and his possible destination on East Cass Avenue. Approximately fifteen minutes later, police received a call that a person matching his description had pointed a gun at a man in a telephone booth and pulled the trigger. The gun clicked, but it did not fire.

Officers David Sohm, Julie Harris, Rob Thomasser, Tom Perzichilli, and Vince Martin arrived in the area the area of East Case Avenue. Sohm, Thomasser and Perzichilli gained access to the apartment building where they had information that he might be going. They heard a television in the apartment. However, after repeated knocking, they were unable to get anyone to answer the door. At the same time they were knocking at the door, a radio call came from Officer Tim Bradley indicating that he was in the alley behind the apartment building and had confronted Benson. He added "man with a gun." The three officers could hear him shouting, "Drop the gun."

Sohm, Thomasser and Perzichilli exited the back door of the building. They immediately saw Benson with a gun in his right hand pointed at Bradley.

Bradley was at the corner of the building more or less pinned down. Bradley continued to shout commands at Benson. None of the three officers who exited had any cover. Officers Harris and Martin also joined the other officers in the alley. All of the officers were yelling for Benson to "drop the gun." Benson took a step in the direction of Sohm and Perzichilli at the same time moving his weapon in a sweeping motion at them.

Sohm, along with Perzichilli, Harris, and Martin, felt an immediate threat that one or more of them were in danger of being fired upon. All four of the officers then fired at Benson until he fell to the ground. The four officers firing at Benson were all using .40-caliber Glock pistols.

Sohm, Perzichilli, and Martin slowly approached Benson, who still had the weapon in his right hand. Officer Martin kicked the weapon from his hand. Benson was handcuffed and searched for any additional weapons. Benson kept shouting to the officers, "I just want to die, I just want to die, just let me die." Other officers at the scene thought he said, "Let me die, I wanna die, leave me alone."

A man from a window of the apartment yelled out to the police, "I saw everything. You guys didn't do anything wrong." That person gave a full statement to the police. He told them he was not a friend of Benson's and did not know why he was at the apartment.

A female witness in the apartment also gave a statement to police. She heard the officers giving orders and then heard many shots. She thought the man had said, "I wanna die like this."

Investigation by Saint Paul homicide officers found that Benson had an extensive criminal record. He had been in reform school as a youth and had five convictions for burglary. He also had four drunk driving convictions. Unfortunately, three chemical dependency treatments were not successful, and Benson continued to have problems resisting alcohol and drugs. In 1992, Benson was sentenced to nineteen months in prison for displaying a firearm in public. His statement to police when arrested for the firearm charge was that he was "blind drunk."

An autopsy determined that Benson died from multiple gunshot wounds. A Ramsey County grand jury returned a no bill on November 20, 1996.

VII

Minneapolis police officers responded to the burglary of a drugstore on the 4100 block of Bloomington Avenue in south Minneapolis around 3:00 a.m. on Monday, April 2, 2001. A passerby had observed a person break into the business and the person flee southbound on foot from the store. Several squads were responding.

Officers Tim Costello and Brandy Steberg had been one of the first squads to arrive and reported they had seen the suspect running. They lost sight of the suspect about a block away. A perimeter was established, and a canine was requested to track the suspect. After some time, it became apparent the suspect had probably left the area prior to the perimeter being set.

Costello was with canine officer Bonnie Edwards during the search. Steberg was sitting in the driver's seat of Squad 313 with Officer Jason King securing the perimeter at the intersection of East 43rd Street and 11th Avenue South. As Costello approached the intersection on foot, he heard several shots coming from the area just north of them. He aired this information via his portable radio. Almost immediately, dispatch aired that a caller had reported gunshots in the area of 38th Street East and Chicago Avenue South not far from their location.

Steberg immediately heard a vehicle traveling at a high rate of speed from the area where it was reported that shots had been fired. The vehicle went through the stop sign at 43rd Street without stopping and made a wide turn into the oncoming traffic lane. The vehicle continued at speeds in excess of the posted limit. King activated his lights and began to pursue the vehicle, a dark green Jeep Cherokee 4X4, to get it to stop. Steberg could see that the passenger was continually making motions into the rear seat of the Jeep as if he was trying to reach for something. The Jeep eventually stopped, and Steberg exited the squad.

Officers Paul Kaiser and Jason Okerberg were in Squad 331 working the perimeter one block away from King and Steberg. Kaiser, who had his window down, had also heard the shots. They saw Squad 313 going westbound in front of their squad on 43rd Street. They made the decision to follow them as backup.

The Jeep was heading west on 43rd Street with Squad 313 directly behind it. The emergency lights of Squad 313 were activated. The Jeep turned north on Park Avenue, and Squad 313 was attempting to make a traffic stop of the vehicle.

Kaiser and Okerberg activated the lights and siren of their squad as they came off 43rd Street onto Park Avenue. Okerberg turned the spotlight of the squad on the rear window of the Jeep. The Jeep was moving slowly. However, it was not coming to a complete stop. Okerberg was able to observe the driver and a passenger directly behind the driver in the back seat. He could not see any other occupants in the Jeep due to the tint of the windows.

The Jeep kept creeping forward several times, stopping and then proceeding forward again. Kaiser stopped his squad, and Okerberg jumped out and proceeded toward the Jeep with his weapon drawn. Okerberg stated he observed a male in the passenger seat behind the driver wearing a dark jacket with a white and darker-colored logo on the back of the jacket. Okerberg then noticed what he believed to be a shotgun or rifle come up from the backseat in the hands of the man. The barrel was pointed toward Squad 313 which was directly behind the Jeep. Okerberg called out, "He's got a gun inside the car." Okerberg took cover by the door of the squad and shouted at Kaiser who was crouched behind the driver's door of the squad that the Jeep was going to "take off." About two or three seconds later, Steberg yelled, "Gun." Steberg told investigators that he saw the passenger pull up a long-barreled gun from the seat or floor. He saw the man point it in the air and "rack the pump."

The Jeep sped away north on Park Avenue with Squad 313 in pursuit. Okerberg and Kaiser jumped back in their squad also in pursuit. Kaiser was driving and watching the intersections for red lights and traffic in the area. Okerberg was directing him at intersections. Okerberg had tried to call out the chase, but Steberg in Squad 313 said that he would as they were directly behind the Jeep. The Jeep and Squad 313 were about one to two blocks ahead of them. Steberg proceeded to call out the direction of the chase.

While in pursuit, King and Steberg observed the Jeep go through a red light at 42nd and Portland Avenue, forcing a car to slam on the brakes to avoid a collision. Steberg was able to see the rear passenger door open. The passenger leaned out and pointed the weapon, later determined to be a shotgun, toward their squad. It appeared that he was unable to brace himself and was thrown back into the Jeep as it went around a corner. The passenger again opened the door and was pointing the shotgun in their direction again but did not fire at them.

King and Steberg followed the Jeep into the alley behind the Bruegger's Bagel Store. The passenger, later identified as twenty-seven-year-old Demitreus Sesler of Minneapolis, jumped out of the rear seat with a shotgun. Steberg exited his squad with his weapon. He saw that Sesler was holding the shotgun by the pistol grip in his right hand. Sesler started running north to the rear of the Bruegger's Bagel parking lot. Steberg heard King shout that Sesler was running toward him. Steberg then saw Sesler coming at him with the shotgun pointing at him. Steberg, about fifteen feet from Sesler, brought up his 9-mm weapon and fired once at Sesler. It appeared that Sesler was hit as he jerked. However, he made no attempt to drop the weapon.

King, who was still driving, drove into the alley behind the bagel store in an attempt to parallel Sesler. He stopped the squad and fired his 9-mm once through the open passenger window. Steberg was able to see that Sesler jerked again and stumble as if hit by the shot. Again, Sesler did not drop the shotgun and continued across the parking lot. Steberg pursued him and yelled for him to stop. He then saw Sesler stumble to the ground directly behind a fence.

Steberg approached Sesler while King was exiting the squad to assist. Steberg continued to shout at Sesler to drop his weapon as he came around the corner of the fence to confront him. Sesler was on all fours when Steberg came around the corner. He looked directly at Steberg. He was only about three or four feet away and started to bring the shotgun up toward Steberg. Steberg fired his weapon several times at Sesler. King did not fire, as Steberg was in his line of fire. Steberg removed the shotgun from Sesler's reach, and King handcuffed him. Steberg called for rescue, ambulance and a supervisor. Both officers looked nearby for the Jeep as it drove away after Sesler exited. When it was not located in the immediate area, they returned to the shooting scene. They were placed in separate sergeants' squads.

Kaiser and Okerberg were able to see the vehicles ahead of them go across the Interstate 35W overpass into the area of the Fifth Precinct on 42nd Street. The vehicles then turned south on Nicollet Avenue and then west on 46th Street. They decided to parallel the chase on 45th Street. They went about one block when they heard Steberg yell over the radio "shots fired." Steberg added that the suspect had been shot and rescue along with an ambulance Code 3 was requested. They turned back and could see the vehicles at 46th and Nicollet near and Bruegger's Bagel Store and Amoco Station. Okerberg saw Steberg on the north side of the Bruegger's Bagel by the alley. There was a handcuffed male lying in the snow and a shotgun about ten feet near him. Okerberg then assisted in securing the crime scene and with crowd control.

The driver of the Jeep sped away after the shooting and was not located. The Jeep was found abandoned about six blocks away. A canine came to the area to track the person who left from the Jeep. The canine went directly to the same address as listed on the registration. Officers determined the registered owner of the car and went to the address. A twenty-four-year-old woman told officers that her boyfriend Demitreus Sesler usually took her Jeep to work around 3:15 a.m. while she slept. She added that Demitreus usually gave his brother Everett Sesler a ride to work about the same time. No one was located at the house other than the girlfriend and her infant child. Investigation determined that the shotgun next to Sesler was used to shoot the windows out of a barbershop on East 38th Street. A green shotgun shell found near the barbershop and one from the abandoned Jeep had been fired from the shotgun. Apparently, the shots fired at the barbershop were the ones the officers heard while searching for the person who broke into the drugstore. It should be noted that the .12-gauge shotgun found next to Sesler was a SPAS-12 with a folding stock. SPAS stands for Special Purpose Assault Shotgun. It is an expensive, high-quality weapon designed for police or military use. It also has a black polymer pump action, high magazine capacity and black non-reflective finish—not exactly the weapon one would expect to find on the street.

Two juveniles were later arrested for the burglary of the drugstore that prompted the initial call to police.

On December 14, 2001, a Hennepin County grand jury returned a no bill that cleared King and Steberg in the shooting.

VIII

Any police officer knows that a "shots fired" call at a bar is going to be trouble. This was the call out to the Saint Paul Police Department around 8:36 p.m. on Wednesday, September 18, 1990. It was reported that shots had been fired at the Spot Bar, 480 South Victoria. Two officers immediately responded.

Officer Michael Hinzman, a thirty-seven-year-old officer and veteran of eleven years, was the first to arrive. He was only two blocks away when dispatch told him the man had fled the area after firing the shots. Hinzman asked if the name of the person was known. The dispatcher did not have a name, but she gave Hinzman and the other squads responding the description of a white male, long dark hair and scruffy looking.

Hinzman ran into road construction at the Victoria intersection. He had to turn into the parking lot of the Spot Bar. Just prior to his arrival, the dispatcher received another call that the shooter was hiding in a bush at 428

South Victoria. He took his canine from the car. A large white male that Hinzman believed was a bar employee told him the person with the gun had left the bar and nothing happened in the bar. The shooting had occurred just outside of the bar. When asked where he had gone, the man pointed north on Victoria and said "that way."

Dispatch called again and said the suspect was hiding behind a telephone pole at 428 South Victoria. Hinzman was not certain where 428 was located as there were no homes facing Victoria for him to check numbers. He began walking north on Victoria, checking each telephone pole as he progressed on the street.

Hinzman saw the glow of a cigarette by a telephone pole between James and Palace Streets. He shouted, "Police, hold it right there." The man, later identified as twenty-seven-year-old Fred Weed, turned and started to run westbound. Weed then fell off an embankment about three feet high where the street construction had been dug. Weed fell into the mud but immediately got up and ran into an alley between the two streets. Hinzman ran after Weed and again yelled for him to stop. As Hinzman arrived at the alley, he saw Weed turn, going south into a yard about two or three houses down the alley. He released his dog and ordered him to pursue.

Hinzman was able to see Weed enter a yard by opening a gate to a chain-link fence, latching the gate behind him. Hinzman opened the gate, and his dog was able to pursue Weed again. Weed went out another gate in the yard, latching it just as the dog arrived at the gate. His dog stopped and began barking at Weed. Weed backed up about ten feet and brought up an object in a two-handed grip toward the dog. Hinzman could tell by the outline that it appeared to be a handgun. Hinzman took out his 9-mm handgun and pointed it at Weed. He shouted for him to drop the gun. Weed turned the gun toward him. Hinzman fired his gun twice. Weed fell to the ground and moaned, "I give up."

Almost immediately after the shots, Officer James Fischer came around the corner and approached Weed. Hinzman checked the area and found a

High Standard .22-caliber semiautomatic weapon lying on the ground a few feet from Weed. The slide was back and a cartridge was sideways in the chamber.

Officer Fischer later told investigators that he arrived about thirty seconds behind Hinzman and saw Hinzman about one-half block ahead of him. He was running to catch up to him and his canine. He was not able to see Hinzman. However, he heard him yell something and then heard two shots in rapid succession. Fischer then came around the corner and saw Hinzman standing with his gun, pointing at Weed who was on the ground. Fischer radioed for an ambulance, supervisor, and the crime scene team. Arriving paramedics pronounced Weed dead at the scene.

Crime scene investigators found an empty box of .22-caliber ammunition outside 428 South Victoria. Near the telephone pole where Hinzman first saw Weed were two spent .22-caliber cartridges and one live cartridge within a few inches of each other. Another live .22-caliber round was found about twenty-four feet from the pole in the middle of Victoria. When Weed was searched after the shooting, a small .25-caliber pistol was also found on him.

Additional investigation determined that Weed was ejected from the Spot Bar after arguing with a woman. He returned about twenty minutes later and fired about three or four shots. It was unknown if he was firing at someone or something.

Weed had an extensive record. He was only sixteen when he was shot by a Roseville, Minnesota, police officer following a pharmacy robbery in October, 1979. Police had responded to an alarm at the pharmacy and confronted Weed. Weed and another young man came out shooting. Weed was hit twice during that shooting. He was a suspect in ten drugstore robberies at that time. He pleaded guilty to robbing that pharmacy twice and was sentenced to twenty years in the state prison system in 1980. Additional records revealed he was arrested in 1983 for an assault. In August, 1990, he was cited for criminal damage to property after breaking the window out of a local business.

Hinzman was cleared by a Ramsey County grand jury.

IX

This next incident occurred on Saturday, December 1, 1990. The aftermath of this shooting has never gone away. What happened that night has been debated by certain community activists for years. The call which went out to Minneapolis Police after midnight was that a large fight was occurring at a party on the north side of town near 15th and Girard Avenue North. Officers Rick Altonen and Dan May were just clearing a disturbance call nearby and were en route when additional information came in that shots had been fired at the location.

What is known for sure is that there was a large party taking place just one-half block west of Girard Avenue at 1311 15th Avenue North. That house faced north next to the alley, with a vacant lot across the alley to the east. South of the vacant lot on Girard were single-family residences at 1423 and 1419 Girard Avenue. Individuals at the party gave conflicting stories as to who was attending the party. The number of those attending varied from forty to seventy-five. Apparently one dollar would get you in the door and then you had to buy drinks once inside. One person who had just returned from California said she did not know who lived at the house, but added, "It was a lot of Disciples." With this many people and alcohol something was certain to happen.

A neighbor across the street from 1311 15th told police that she was watching television around 10:30 or 11:00 p.m. on Friday night when she heard what she believed to be two gunshots. She reported it to 911. Around midnight she heard some loud shouting like someone arguing. She dialed 911 and waited for someone to answer. While waiting, she continued looking out her window and saw two black "teenagers" (a male and female) walk to a car in front of her house. The male unlocked the truck and removed what she believed to be a pistol. She described the weapon as a "western cowboy style gun." The male walked back across the street with the female following close behind. She described the male as fifteen to eighteen years old, wearing a baseball cap and dark clothing. The female was possibly fourteen to sixteen, wearing all white with black shoes. She saw the male start at a "small trot" toward a crowd of people outside the house across from her. She saw the male shoot into the crowd four times. She asked the 911 operator who had just answered if she had heard the last shot over the phone.

The woman then told the 911 operator, "That's all right, the police are here now." The operator asked her again how many shots had been fired and she responded, "Four." She then saw a white police officer get out of his car and walk to the sidewalk. The officer immediately returned to his car, and she saw him take out a shotgun. She then lost sight of him as many people were outside and other police cars were arriving. She recalled one police officer yelling at the crowd, "Don't block the street so the ambulance can get by." She stated she then heard one "big boom." She saw two other black males whom she had not seen before get into the car where the gun was taken and drive away. (It was later determined that the car had been reported stolen before the incident.)

What was taking place at the party? Donnie, a seventeen-year-old from Saint Paul later related that he and some friends, all belonging to the Vice Lords, went to the party. He and his friends felt uncomfortable there. Some people were asking him and his friends who they were and what were they doing there. One person asked his friend Deon, "Are you from the big Oh U?" He said that this question meant was his friend "an unknown Vice Lord." He and his friends walked outside.

He said that a "crowd" was following them so he turned around and said, "What's up?"

Someone responded with, "Nothin, just keep walking" and there "would be no trouble." He said he heard gunshots and started running with his friends. As they were running, his friend Paul told him he had been shot. Donnie said four or five of his friends and Paul flagged down a cab to get Paul to the hospital. Donnie went to another friend's house to get a ride to Hennepin County Medical Center (HCMC). Donnie said he had been to the house previously four or five times for parties and recognized many of the people there. Donnie told police he recognized six Disciples there and that he knew some names. One of them was Tycel Nelson and added that he had known him for about four years.

Minneapolis police went to Illinois on December 15 to interview Fred, a twenty-nine-year-old witness. He related a similar story as that told by Donnie. When Deon went to pay his money to get into the party, someone inside the party told the doorman that Deon had slapped him earlier in downtown Minneapolis. Fred said he told his friends that they should leave because it was a Disciples party and "wasn't no Vice Lords allowed." Fred said that people started coming outside. One person "with a forty ounce in his hand" was "steady talking to Deon." (A "forty ounce" is a bottle of Old English malt liquor.) Fred saw a group of individuals by a garage in the alley. He saw someone hand a pistol to a person whom he knew as Tycel Nelson. He told the others, "Let's go, I just seen a pistol." Tycel started pointing and firing the gun. Fred said he saw the first muzzle flash. He heard two shots and started running. He then heard two more shots.

Fred said he ran to the house where he was staying. He went to bed. About 10:00 a.m. that Saturday morning he saw a "news flash" that Tycel Nelson had been shot and killed, but he did not know who had shot him. He left Minneapolis on Sunday and returned to Illinois. Fred told police he knew that Tycel fired at least one shot as he saw him do it before he turned and ran. Fred also told police he saw Nelson with a gun in June and July, 1989. He said he was with a friend by "the high rise" when Nelson displayed what looked to him like a .32-caliber pistol.

Minneapolis police also interviewed Paul, the sixteen-year-old who had been shot, at HCMC. He stated he was at 1311 15th Avenue North standing outside. He said two black males were fighting over a girl and he tried to break it up. He heard two shots and then a third. The third shot hit him in the abdomen. He felt a burning sensation in his side and began running south to Plymouth Avenue. He flagged down a taxi and determined for sure that he had been shot. He was taken to HCMC. He claimed to have heard eight shots but later changed his story to not seeing a weapon or who shot it.

Eighteen-year-old Deon was also interviewed at HCMC by Minneapolis Police. He first told police he was not at the party and was walking down the street when he heard gunshots. He was hit in the arm and ran away. The interviewing officer told Deon that he had interviewed Paul, and he had a different story. Deon then changed his statement. Deon admitted he was at the party when an argument began outside. He was not certain what was being said, and then he heard gunshots. He was hit in the left arm in the biceps area. He claimed that he saw no one with a weapon, nor did he know who shot him. He ran with Paul and took a taxi to HCMC for medical attention. Deon stated he knew Tycel Nelson was a member of the Disciples.

A fourteen-year-old witness in a house near 1311 was interviewed and told police he was looking out a window and saw police chasing someone through the alley. He said the man was holding a weapon straight in the air. He heard a policeman say, "Stop," and then heard a shot. The boy said the person running did not stop, but the policeman stopped and then fired. He stated he did not hear any shots before he saw the events he described.

The seventy-six-year-old occupant of 1423 Girard told police he was on his front porch having a cigarette around midnight when he heard several shots from the rear of his house by the alley. He believed about seven or eight shots were fired. He then saw a white policeman come running around from 15th Avenue southbound. He had a shotgun in his hands. The officer ran to the front south side of the house next to him at 1419 Girard. He believes the officer said, "There he goes," and shouted something else. He then saw the officer fire the shotgun once toward the west. He heard no other shots fired. He saw approximately three black females and about ten black males run east on 15th Avenue away from Girard. Numerous police then arrived.

Officers Rick Altonen and Dan May arrived at 1311 15th Avenue North just after midnight. Altonen parked just west of the address. May observed several people running from the side of the house. May took the shotgun from the boot in the front seat and exited. He saw a black male in dark clothing standing near the rear of the house holding a long-barreled handgun down to his side in his right hand. May could see clearly from the moonlight, house lights and brightness from the snow cover reflecting from the moonlight. When the person holding the gun saw May, he ran southeast to the back of 1311. May radioed the information and ran around to the east side of 1311. He lost sight of the person. Individuals at the rear of the house pointed toward Girard Avenue and said, "He has a gun."

May ran around to the west side of the 1400 block of Girard and stood at the corner of 1419 facing the west. He then saw the same individual with the gun again at the rear of the house. He could plainly see that the man had a long-barreled gun in his right hand. The individual hesitated briefly and then turned in May's direction. As the individual raised his gun, May yelled, "Drop." The person did not respond. May brought his shotgun up to his shoulder and fired once. He racked another round. May radioed that he had fired his weapon. He took a position on the west side of the house, not knowing if the suspect was hit or might be waiting for him at the rear of the house.

May heard screaming form the direction of 1311 and saw Altonen running from the rear of 1419 to 1311. May followed and saw a large crowd around someone who was lying on the ground. Officers were already performing first aid on the person on the ground. May told Altonen he believed this was the person he had shot. May did not see a gun in his hand at this time. May told Altonen and Sgt. Tom McKenzie of the situation regarding his firing his shotgun. The three of them backtracked following the blood trail to the rear area of 1419. They found a black leather hat on the ground in the area where the person was standing when May fired. They searched further in the area and found a handgun on the ground partially covered by snow. May and Sergeant McKenzie requested that someone stay next to the weapon while the two of them searched for the ejected .12-caliber shotgun shell that May had fired. The shotgun shell was found, and another officer stood by it until the crime scene team arrived and secured it as evidence.

The crime scene team recovered an Iver-Johnson Trailsman Model .22-caliber revolver. The weapon was an eight-shot weapon with a six-inch barrel. There were two fired rounds and six live rounds in the weapon. The owner of the weapon was never determined. The weapon had never been listed in any Minneapolis Police records as being inventoried, pawned or sold in Minneapolis. Records of firearms transfers going back to 1968 were checked with negative results. The .12-gauge shell found was determined to have been fired in May's shotgun. Also recovered was a black leather hat with a Nike emblem.

The police had difficulty keeping bystanders away from Nelson while medical aid was being performed. There were fights in the crowd behind them. Individuals were crying and shouting obscenities at the police. A perimeter had to be established to keep the crowd back. Fourteen people came to North Memorial Hospital where Nelson had been transported. One person tried to get into the room where doctors were attending to him. They were yelling and screaming at police and hospital security. After order was restored, individuals walked by the officers saying "it was on" and "paybacks would be coming."

Initial media releases by the chief of police at the time said that Nelson was shot in the chest. An autopsy determined that he was hit in the right side of his back. The media and the community activists made a big issue that no fingerprints were found on the recovered .22-caliber handgun found at the scene. One African-American minister called an African-American Minneapolis Police Inspector and the shooting investigators "liars." Speakers at meetings claimed there was no justice for black people in the State of Minnesota and that Minnesota is too racist. In one meeting about neighborhood violence, a "disturbance" broke out bringing the meeting to a halt. At Nelson's gravesite, some youths placed carnations tinged in blue on the coffin. Blue is the color of the Disciples. Marches were organized and the crowd chanted, "Hey, hey, ho, ho, police brutality's got to go," and, "If we don't get no justice, they don't get no peace." Signs were being carried which said, "Police Officer Dan May, Public Enemy," and "Prosecute Police Officer Dan May."

One interesting part in the police file regarding the Nelson shooting was a report by Officer Greg Kossan. In August, 1990, Kossan interviewed Nelson at the Hennepin County Boys Home regarding taking him on the Minnesota Boundary Waters Canoe Outreach Program. Nelson was supposedly in the home for selling narcotics. Nelson agreed to go on the trip from August 22 to 28. While on the trip, Nelson explained that his tattoos meant he was a member of the Disciples. He told officers he had used a gun to shoot rival Vice Lords.

Sometime after returning from the trip, Officer Kossan was dispatched to James and Plymouth on the north side of Minneapolis to check on people supposedly gambling. Kossan saw Nelson run away from the area where he was dispatched. Nelson was stopped and told to leave the area. About one and one-half hours later Kossan and his partner were dispatched to the same location about "a black man dealing drugs." Two people, one of whom was Nelson, were at the intersection. The person fitting the description of the person selling drugs was seen riding away on a bicycle. Nelson told the officers the person on the bicycle was his brother. Nelson was patted down and placed in Kossan's squad. Nelson had over five hundred dollars on his person. Kossan took Nelson home and told him to stay away from Plymouth Avenue. Just before Thanksgiving Kossan saw Nelson and gave him photographs taken during the Boundary Waters trip. On Thanksgiving Day, Kosan saw Nelson walking on the street. He stopped and Nelson told him that he was en route to his girlfriend's house.

A Hennepin County grand jury did not indict May for the shooting. The Nelson family subsequently received $250,000 from the City of Minneapolis regarding the shooting.

On July 13, 1991, violence erupted in downtown Minneapolis at the

Skyway Theater on Hennepin Avenue during the opening of the movie *Boyz N the Hood*. Six people were injured. In a Minneapolis *Star Tribune* article about the gunfire by Ken Duchschere on July 14, 1991, Duchschere wrote, "In an ironic twist, a critically injured boy received medical attention from Officer Dan May that may have saved his life. In December, May, a white policeman, shot and killed a black youth, Tycel Nelson, who May said pointed a gun at him." (Now that really added a lot to the article about the movie opening and the people getting shot!)

This story never seems to go away. May was awarded a Medal of Valor in January 2006 by an independent committee regarding the Nelson shooting. Ron Edwards, a member of the Police Community Relations Council, who spoke on behalf of the Nelson family, wrote a letter to Minneapolis Mayor Rybak and Chief of Police McManus saying they should start the healing process by asking Dan May, now a sergeant in the Canine Unit, to return his medal. The media reported that May did return the medal.

Chapter Eight

One of Our Own
aka Officers Killed or Assaulted

I

One never knows when a situation can suddenly turn tragic. Just when it appears an emotionally disturbed individual is cooperating and docile, things can erupt into chaos. Officers from the Saint Paul Police Department received a radio call at 10:44 p.m. on Monday, September 2, 2002, to respond to a domestic dispute at the Evergreen Apartments. The problem was between a mother and her nineteen-year-old son, William Hayek. The call indicated that Hayek was six-foot-eight and weighed three hundred pounds. It was also transmitted that he was in possession of a sword.

The initial call to police was to the adjacent suburb of Maplewood. The caller identified herself as the aunt of Hayek and stated that her sister was concerned about William's behavior. The call was transferred to a Saint Paul police operator, and Margaret Hayek was subsequently contacted. She believed William was having a nervous breakdown. She told the operator that William had his sword out and was sitting in a chair saying that the police were following him. Margaret indicated she was scared and would try to leave. The operator told her to leave the phone line open. As she was leaving, the police operator could hear a male voice ask her where she was going. A door then closed, and she told the operator that she was in the hallway. She then told the operator that the police had arrived.

Officers Matt Toronto and Mark Nelson were the first to arrive. Margaret Hayek met them at the security door and let them into the apartment building. They questioned her regarding William's behavior and asked if he had suicidal tendencies. She said that he had in the past, but he had not displayed any that day. She told the officers that William thought the devil was in her and the cops were after him. William was in a chair reading a Bible when she left the apartment. She added that he was not taking any medications. She gave them a key in the event he had locked the door.

As Nelson and Toronto walked up to the third floor, they saw out a window in the staircase that another squad had arrived. They decided to wait for the additional officers. The officers and Margaret came up to the floor. The door was unlocked, and Officer Toronto opened it. They were not able to open it completely as something was behind it. They were able to see Hayek sitting in a chair with a large sword in his hands. The butt end was on his lap with the blade sticking straight up. It appeared to be an inch to two inches wide and three to four feet long.

They started a conversation with him and asked him to put the sword down. He told them no, that he could not do so because he was doing "his job." He said he had to protect himself because the devil was in his mother. They continued to try to talk him into putting the sword down. They kept telling him that they were the good guys and were there to help him.

The officers discussed between themselves that they would shut the door if he came at them with the sword. About that same time, Hayek started a discussion about another person. He said there was a man who was mean to him and trying to poison him. He took one hand off the sword and threw a pill bottle and toiletry items at the officers. Hayek said the pills were probably poisoned. They began talking about the Bible and how the officers wanted to help. Officer Toronto asked him to put the sword down and come out and talk to them. Hayek suddenly said, "Okay," and threw down the sword. He walked out of the apartment, but the door did not shut all the way.

Toronto asked him to put his hands on his head. Hayek complied, and Toronto "patted him down." Toronto put one handcuff on and was bringing his hands around to his back when he noticed Officer Jay Thompson and his canine partner coming up the stairs. Hayek spun away from Toronto while pushing him into the corner of the hallway.

Thompson told investigators that he and his canine partner went up the stairs and listened while Toronto was talking to Hayek from the hallway near the stairs. He and the dog were quiet and out of sight. Thompson saw Hayek walk out of the apartment and Toronto put one handcuff on him. Hayek then suddenly began fighting and trying to get back into the apartment. Thompson released his dog. The dog grabbed Hayek by the leg, but the dog had little effect on him and was dragged inside the apartment. Thompson entered the apartment and tackled Hayek in an attempt to try to prevent Hayek from reaching the sword. He was unsuccessful.

Hayek got to the sword and raised it over it his head. Hayek swung the sword down, but he missed Thompson. His hands and arms struck Thompson as he was backing up. Thompson fell to the floor. Thompson was face down and began to crawl to the door. Thompson was then stabbed in the back of his right arm. Thompson then heard handgun shots from the doorway. He then felt another stab to his right leg just above his knee. He then heard a shotgun discharge. Thompson recalled getting out of the apartment and Officer John Linssen putting pressure on his leg to stop the bleeding. He then passed out.

Twenty-six-year-old Officer Mark Nelson brought his shotgun up to the apartment. After Hayek broke away from Toronto, Nelson saw Hayek stab Thompson. He heard officers near him firing their handguns. The shots seemed to have no effect on Hayek. Nelson fired his .12-gauge shotgun and saw Hayek fall.

Officer John Linssen was patrolling on the east side of Saint Paul when he heard the call regarding Hayek. He arrived just after Thompson and his dog. He was with Thompson while they listened to Toronto and Nelson talking to Hayek. He heard a handcuff ratcheting and then the sound of a struggle. Thompson then called for the other officers to move and told his dog to "get 'em."

Linssen then moved up to the door of the apartment where he could see Hayek and the dog in the apartment. Thompson was just entering the apartment. The door partially closed and someone pushed it open. Linssen saw Thompson on the floor, and Hayek was stabbing him with a large sword. Linssen believed Hayek was killing Thompson, so he removed his .40-caliber Glock and began firing at him. Hayek eventually went down. Linssen helped Thompson out and applied first aid. He saw a large laceration on his right thigh and under his right arm. Both wounds were bleeding profusely.

Officer Pete Crum was in the hallway like Linssen. He also went to the door of the apartment when Hayek ran back inside. He saw Hayek stab Thompson with the sword and also fired his .40-caliber Glock at Hayek. Twelve total rounds were fired by Linssen and Crum. Nelson fired his shotgun four times. Hayek was dead at the scene.

An autopsy determined the cause of death to be multiple gunshot wounds. A Ramsey County grand jury returned a no bill on October 30, 2002.

Thompson remained in the hospital for ten days as the stab wound to the leg nicked an artery and he almost bled to death. The situation was much more serious than originally thought to be. He recovered and has returned to duty.

II

Saint Paul Police received a teletype from nearby Washington County at 1:00 p.m. on July 18, 1985, that a warrant had been issued for the arrest of twenty-one-year-old Eric C. Schmieg on July 11 for failure to appear in court. Bond was recommended at one hundred thousand dollars. He had been arrested on May 11 in the City of Cottage Grove for two counts of assault and one count of a felon in possession of a firearm. He had been released on bond and had failed to appear on July 11. About 2:15 p.m. Saint Paul Police received a call regarding a domestic dispute and were told that Schmieg was the person involved. Officers Richard Horman and Dennis Able went to 1177 Dale Street in separate squads in response to the call. They were made aware of Schmieg's violent past and the possibility of his being violent.

Horman parked his squad and began walking up to the house. He saw Schmieg exit a side door and begin running. A foot chase began. Both stopped momentarily. Horman pulled his weapon and yelled, "Freeze." Schmieg ran to Maryland Avenue a short distance away. Schmieg forced his way into a pickup truck driven by a citizen. Another squad blocked the pickup after traveling only one-half block. Schmieg exited the pickup and again fled on foot. He entered a house on Maryland Avenue. He called a friend for help and then immediately left that house. He then forced his way into a house on Maywood Street another short distance away. In that house were a thirteen-year-old boy and an infant. Three additional officers, Sergeant Weisman and Officers Harden and Richard Schmidt had arrived at this time.

Schmidt entered the back door of the house with Horman just behind him. Horman went to the front door and let Able into the house. They began searching for Schmieg and Schmidt in the house. Unbeknownst to them, Schmidt had gone into the bedroom where Schmieg was holding the thirteen-year-old boy. He let him go, and Schmidt attempted to take him into custody. The two of them began struggling. Able and Horman heard Schmidt shout, "He's got my gun." Able and Horman ran into the bedroom, and Schmidt was up against the wall half sitting on a vanity. Schmieg had Schmidt's .38-caliber revolver in his right hand pointed to the floor. Horman jumped on his back and grabbed his right arm. They went to the floor. Able joined in and grabbed Schmieg's arm. The struggle continued into the hallway and the weapon went off. Able yelled, "He shot my foot" as he backed away.

Horman continued fighting with Schmieg as they went into the bathroom. Schmidt joined in the struggle after Able was hit. Schmieg broke lose and pointed the gun at Schmidt who had been knocked into the bathtub. Horman jumped at him again and was fighting Schmieg. They were wrestling for the gun. Schmieg actually had the gun pointed at Horman's head at one time. By this time Schmidt was able to get up and also grab at his arm and gun. Another shot went off and Horman was hit in his protective vest, but the bullet ricocheted into his left arm severing an artery. Schmidt gained full control of the gun and shot Schmieg twice in the chest.

Ambulances arrived and the three wounded men were taken to the hospital. Schmieg was pronounced dead at 3:08 p.m. Schmidt, who was fifty-seven at the time of the shooting, retired after thirty-six years on the department in 1991. Able returned to duty and retired in 2000 after twenty-nine years. Horman recovered. He was granted a medical retirement in 1998. This incident shows how a strong desire not to be taken into custody gave three officers all they could handle.

A Ramsey County grand jury cleared the officers.

III

Most officers can relate to this next situation. Work is relatively quiet and there is a chance to sit and do the necessary paperwork at the end of the shift. Suddenly, the sound of squealing tires became a life-or-death situation. Minneapolis Police Officer Don Heitland was sitting in his squad about 1:00 a.m. on Friday, November 6, 1987, working on his log sheet. He heard tires squealing. He looked up and saw a car pulling into the Burger King parking lot on Franklin Avenue at a high rate of speed. The driver backed up and then squealed his tires again back to his original spot. Heitland was a short distance away and pulled into the parking lot as thirty-five-year-old Kerry Howk was getting out of his car. Heitland tried calling on his radio, but there was too much radio traffic for him to get through.

As Howk was walking toward the entrance, Heitland exited his squad and shouted to Howk, "Come over here." Howk did so, and they met between the two vehicles. Heitland asked for his driver's license. Howk mumbled something that Heitland did not understand. The next thing Heitland knew Howk punched him in the left side of his face. Heitland went to his knees and got back up and began struggling with Howk. He was hit twice more in the face. When Heitland cleared his head, Howk was standing over him pointing his own gun at him. Howk again said something he did not understand and started shooting at Heitland.

Two fellow Minneapolis officers were leaving the Third Precinct building at 1:00 a.m. The veteran officers, David Peterson and Mike Sundstrom, had forty years' experience between the two of them. Peterson started down Lake Street to see if he could see any suspicious activity. He saw a marked Minneapolis Chevrolet Suburban canine unit in the parking lot of the Burger King. He saw what appeared to be a stocky white male (Howk) near the vehicle. Peterson pulled into the lot and saw Howk run up to someone lying prone in the lot. The person on the pavement looked like he was an officer. Howk ran up and kicked the person (Heitland) in the head. Peterson then saw something shiny in Howk's hand. Howk then pointed it at the person and fired. Peterson saw a flash and heard the report of the shots.

Peterson stopped, opened his driver's door as cover, and drew his revolver. Howk was standing near the rear of his own pickup truck. He turned and pointed his weapon at Peterson and, unbelievably, yelled, "Freeze, asshole." Peterson began firing at Howk and called for Sundstrom to "get the shotgun out." Howk fired at Peterson and apparently hit the driver's window, as Peterson was stuck on the left side of his head with particles of flying glass. Believing he was hit, Peterson went to the ground for cover.

Sundstrom, riding with Peterson as the passenger, saw exactly what Peterson had seen up to the shots being fired at Heitland. Sundstrom opened his door to use as cover. He removed the shotgun from the rack, holding it and putting a shell into the chamber. Howk pointed his gun at the two of them and began firing. Sundstrom recalled Peterson firing as he returned fire with the .12-gauge shotgun. Bullets from Howk were hitting their squad. While Sundstrom was shooting, he saw Heitland get up and go to his squad. Heitland removed his shotgun and fired once at Howk. The shooting stopped.

Peterson shouted, "Is the suspect down?"

Heitland replied, "Yes." Peterson ran up to him and kicked the gun away from his right hand. He checked for a pulse and found none.

Investigation determined that Sundstrom fired five shots from the shotgun. Peterson fired two rounds and Heitland the one round from his shotgun. Howk fired all six rounds from Heitland's revolver. Heitland was treated and had eight stitches in the back of his head and two on his left thumb. The left side of his head was bruised. Peterson's squad had the right headlight and the driver's door window shot out and the lower right side of the windshield hit by Howk's rounds.

The autopsy of Howk revealed fourteen individual projectiles hitting him in the upper portion of his chest and shoulder. Three rounds had entered his heart. Howk had a blood alcohol of .16 and cocaine in his system. There were numerous needle marks on the inner portion of both arms. He also had almost $1,100 in cash, marijuana, beer, and food stamps in his vehicle.

A Hennepin County grand jury returned a no bill against the three officers on November 17, 1987.

IV

Many fatal shootings by law enforcement begin with a 911 call from a concerned citizen. A call at 8:00 p.m. on Wednesday December 2, 1992, had that unfortunate outcome. A lady fled from a Minneapolis apartment building near downtown by Loring Park and sat on the steps of the building. She was sitting crying as a concerned citizen went to talk to her. The woman went back into the building. A few minutes later she came back out. However, this time she had a bloody lip. The citizen went back to her and this time the woman requested that she call 911.

A few minutes later a person later identified as thirty-year-old Earnest Dean-El came out of the building. Dean-El was the boyfriend of the woman with the bloody lip. He appeared calm to the citizen, but he did smell of alcohol. He said something about the police coming and that he wanted to go to detox. The citizen saw a large knife in his back pocket and told him that he should get rid of it before police arrived. He again said he wanted to go to detox. Dean-El walked back toward the building. His girlfriend who had been hiding in nearby bushes told the citizen that no one had ever hit her before.

Jeff York, a twenty-seven-year-old Minneapolis officer, arrived with his partner Cheryl Alguire. The 911 caller first came to York's window and explained the situation. Citizens and victims approach police cars all the time to express concerns. As she was telling the officers the situation, the victim girlfriend came up. The victim of the assault told the officers she had come home from work and found Dean-El there drinking. They had a disagreement about her purchasing money orders. Dean-El hit her twice in the lip with his fist. Her lip was bleeding. She said she left the apartment and hid until they arrived. York was in the driver's seat of the squad as she was telling him the story. The girlfriend then told York that Dean-El was walking toward them, approaching from the rear passenger side of the squad. Dean-El came around the front of the squad. York got out of the squad and told Dean-El to stop. Dean-El continued moving rapidly toward York. The girlfriend told investigators later that the next thing she recalled was Dean-El raising his arm and coming down with it at York. She saw York stepping back grabbing his neck and announcing, "I've been stabbed in the neck!" The female officer in the passenger side got out of the squad and yelled at Dean-El to, "Hold it. Hold it." She then heard two shots and Dean-El collapsed to the street in front of the driver's side of the car.

Officer Alguire related a similar synopsis of the events. She said when the girlfriend indicated that Dean-El was approaching, she and York started to get out of the squad. Alguire saw a knife in Dean-El's back pocket as he went toward the front of the squad. She shouted at him to stop, but he continued around the front and go toward York. She called to York that the man had a knife. Unfortunately, he was moving fast and was almost next to York. She saw him stab York twice in the upper neck area, and York staggered back saying that he had been stabbed. Alguire pointed her gun at Dean-El and told him to drop the knife. She could see York holding his neck and removing his gun from his holster. Dean-El turned toward York and extended his arm and knife over his shoulder. He took one step toward York, and York fired two rounds. Dean-El fell back, and the knife flew out of his hand. Alguire stated that she did not fire as the girlfriend was in her line of fire.

York gave the same description of the events except he told Dean-El to put his hands on the hood of the squad when he approached him. Dean-El told him, "Yea, I'll put my hands on the hood, mother fucker." Dean-El charged him, and York turned sideways. He then felt two separate stabs to the right side of his lower neck area. He said that he backed up a few feet and pulled out his weapon. He fired twice, and Dean-El fell to the street. He was about seven feet from him when he fired.

An autopsy determined that Dean-El died from two gunshot wounds to the left side of his chest. York was hospitalized from the two stab wounds. The attending physician said that if either stab had been millimeters to either side, York would have died. As it was, the wounds severed nerves to the right cheek and ear. He returned to work and is now a Sergeant with the department.

York was cleared by a Hennepin County grand jury.

V

An officer can be criticized for being overly cautious and making a citizen upset. On the other hand, an officer can to too lax, and it could cost him or her life. This incident resulted in an officer doing everything right, and he was still shot. When he returned fired, he did kill the suspect.

Two friends arrived at the Overtime Bar on Pierce Butler Road in Saint Paul around 11:30 p.m. on Wednesday, June 24, 1987. One of the two, who does not drink any alcohol, told investigators later that when they arrived he and his friend saw two men arguing in the parking lot. One of the men lifted his shirt, exposing a gun tucked into the small of his back, and stated, "Do you want a piece of this?" The witness said that he and his friend followed the man into the bar. His friend, who had previously been a bouncer at the bar, told the present bouncer that the man, later identified as twenty-seven-year-old Scott Winder, had a gun in his possession. This witness said he saw the bouncer and owner of the bar take Winder back to the office of the bar. He saw Winder exit the bar and return several times over the course of the next hour or so. Winder was consuming drinks and dancing.

About 1:00 a.m., this witness saw a police officer drive up outside the bar. He and his friend went outside and told the officer about the man with the gun. His friend knew the officer and called him "Geno."

Eugene Polyak, a twenty-eight-year-old Saint Paul officer, was told at roll call for his shift that an individual called "Freeze" had a warrant outstanding and that he frequented the Overtime Bar. Polyak left roll call and was occupied on a call until about 12:40 a.m. He decided to go to the Overtime Bar and check to see if "Freeze" was there. When he arrived, a person who he knew had been a bouncer contacted him outside the bar. The man told him there was "a wacko inside the bar with a gun."

At the same time, the current bouncer at the bar came out and asked them to move away from the door as it was near closing time and people were trying to leave. The bouncer told Polyak that there had been a man who was carrying a gun in his waistband, and the man told him and the owner that he was a police officer. He refused to show them his badge. They told him he had to put his gun out in his car in the parking lot. He said the man did so. The bouncer said he saw the man go to his car and then return to the bar. Polyak requested to have the man pointed out to him.

They went into the bar and the bouncer Winder was pointed out to Polyak. Winder was sitting at the bar. Polyak walked up behind Winder and ran his around his waist. He felt no weapon. Polyak asked him if he was a police officer. Winder replied, "No." He asked Winder to move away from the bar area and he complied. Polyak asked him if he had a gun on him and he again said, "No." Winder told him that he had a "squirt gun earlier," but the bouncer made him put it in his car. Polyak stated the man was "very, very polite" and did not appear to be intoxicated.

Polyak then asked Winder if he would mind going out to the parking lot and showing him the squirt gun. Winder responded, "Not at all." Polyak pointed to the front door and Winder led the way. As Polyak passed the bouncer by the door, the bouncer said, "I think that he has something in his belt." By this time Winder was already outside the door and walking quickly away.

It appeared to Polyak that Winder was going to start running so he called for him to stop. Winder took a few more steps, and it looked to Polyak like he was reaching into his groin area with both hands. Winder's back was still to Polyak. As a precaution, Polyak drew his .38-caliber revolver from his holster. As he was drawing, Winder turned around and Polyak saw a muzzle flash. He immediately felt a "nick" in his upper right chest area. He was not sure if he had been shot. He saw another two or three muzzles flashes before he began firing at Winder. Polyak was not sure how many times he had fired when he was hit in the right hand, causing him to drop his weapon. It was determined later that each of them had fired six rounds.

Winder took two or three steps away from Polyak and then fell to the ground. Polyak bent down to retrieve his revolver. He saw the former bouncer run up to Winder and begin kicking him. Polyak ran up to them and told the bouncer to "leave the guy alone" as he could see Winder's gun on the ground out of his reach. After he picked up Winder's gun, Polyak radioed that shots had been fired. Numerous squads arrived. It was determined that Winder was dead at the scene from a shot to the chest.

Polyak heard a woman screaming. It was determined that a man with her had been behind Polyak and was shot in the lower leg. He was bleeding and in pain. He later told investigators that he was standing outside and heard "firecrackers." He next felt a pain in his lower leg. He told police he had not been drinking very much. However, when blood was drawn at the hospital during his procedure to repair the wound, his blood alcohol was .29.

The former bouncer told investigators he was certain that Winder fired first as "I never took my eyes off the guy." He said Winder "was standing his ground and firing at the officer." He also stated that he ran back into the bar during the exchange of the shots. One round from Winder was determined to have hit the front door.

Records at the Saint Paul Police Department showed that Polyak had arrested Winder in September 1985 for fighting and in December 1985 for driving while intoxicated. A deputy from the Ramsey County Sheriff's Office had been assaulted by Winder in 1982. The deputy had seventeen stitches in his mouth area after the assault. The report regarding that incident revealed that Winder told the deputy, "I'm sorry that I had to do that; last time the Saint Paul police arrested me, they beat the shit out of me."

A relative of Winder's wife told police that the police acted properly and that Winder "hated cops." He claimed they always beat him when they arrested him. That relative also claimed that Winder pulled his guns on others in the few months before his fatal shooting.

Polyak only had a large bruise on his chest thanks to his protective vest. He recovered from the wound to his right thumb and returned to duty. A Ramsey County grand jury returned a no bill on September 2, 1987.

VI

It all started on Minneapolis' north side around 8:10 p.m. on Sunday, July 29, 2001. The call to Minneapolis 911 was that shots were being fired from a moving vehicle. Responding officers spotted the car, a turquoise Pontiac Grand Am with the occupants shooting out of it. They began chasing it. A witness said she was with her five children in Folwell Park when she saw the

Pontiac go by at a high rate of speed with four police cars chasing it. She heard "boom, boom, boom" and saw a gunman hanging out of the car firing at police and adding that, "There was dust rising up everywhere."

The Pontiac crashed in an alley behind a house in the 3700 block of Girard Avenue North. At the end of the chase, Officer John Ochs and his partner saw fifteen-year-old Abdullah Simmons running from the passenger side of the car toward the street. The officers approached the driver's side of the car and saw a handgun in the car. Simmons turned and started running back toward them. Ochs shot, and Simmons fell to the ground grasping his chest. The officers ran to him and handcuffed him. When they turned him over searching for additional weapons, they saw he was wounded in the chest. They were attempting to administer first aid and called for an ambulance. However, more gunfire was reported. The ambulance personnel and firemen could not enter as the crime scene was not safe and under control. By the time the shooting stopped and paramedics got to Simmons, he was dead. The time was 8:30 p.m.

The other occupants of the car bailed out of the car and ran into a nearby house while firing at the police. Officer Ryan Rivers was hit by gunfire from the house. He was pulled to safety, and it was determined that he sustained a shot to the leg that broke his femur.

Officers, and later SWAT members, set up their perimeter. There was not a phone in the residence. Negotiators had to use a bullhorn to communicate with those in the house. The negotiator called on the bullhorn, "We know you are in there...We need to talk...We need to talk now...Come out with your hands up." Eventually a light went on inside just before 10:00 p.m. A few minutes later, two men walked out with their hands up. SWAT members searched the house. Another suspect was found hiding under the porch. The three arrested were ages twenty-seven, twenty, and eighteen.

Investigation determined that Simmons was riding in the car with twenty-seven-year-old Antwan D. Thomas. A citizen witness saw Simmons in the fleeing car with Thomas. Thomas was charged with attempted murder of a police officer and eight additional charges. The twenty-year-old was charged as an accomplice after the fact. The police squad driven by Ochs had bullet fragments in the grill and windshield.

Unfortunately, Simmons' family members used the media to question the use of force by police. They questioned the police account of the shooting and wanted proof that he was more than an innocent bystander in the shooting. Subsequently, following a thorough investigation by the Minneapolis Police and Hennepin County Sheriff's Office, it was acknowledged by the family that they knew Antwan Thomas, a convicted felon.

A 200-page report released in January 2002 of interviews of witnesses, police, and relatives showed that Simmons met Thomas in the late afternoon that day. Thomas initially said he and "Shorty" (Simmons) were not involved in the chase. Thomas, who entered a guilty plea to assault, told investigators he was not sure of all the events that day due to his consumption of alcohol and drugs. Thomas is presently incarcerated at Stillwater State Prison with an anticipated discharge date in 2015. The handgun found by Simmons was a .22-caliber Ruger with a laser site. It was not loaded. Investigation also found that Simmons' fingerprints were found inside the Pontiac on a box of .22-caliber cartridges. Casings in the car matched the gun next to Simmons.

A Hennepin County grand jury returned a no bill on January 2, 2002. Officer Ryan had surgery on his broken leg. He returned to duty and later transferred to the University of Minnesota Police Department where he is now a sergeant in the K-9 Unit.

VII

Will a stun gun effectively stop a person? This next incident shows that it is not always the answer. Jason Christensen, a thirty-two-year-old Olmsted County sheriff's deputy, was working his assigned territory as the deputy in the City of Stewartville, Minnesota, on May 22, 2003, from 6:00 a.m. to 6:00 p.m. He was in a fully marked squad car and B uniform ,which is brown cargo pants and short-sleeved uniform shirt with patches and badge.

Christensen was very familiar with the area and about a month before had responded to a domestic at 604 8th Avenue Northeast. The resident, forty-three-year-old Calvin Barrett, had threatened his estranged wife with a baseball bat. Christensen was not the first deputy to respond. When he arrived, it was determined that Barrett had run into the residence and locked the door upon seeing the deputy. The wife was outside and not injured. A supervisor told the deputies not to forcefully enter the residence. A warrant was issued for Barrett, and all of the deputies who worked the area were told to be on the alert for him.

Christensen checked on May 21 to see if the warrant was still active. It was. Christensen drove by during the morning of May 22 and did not see him or any activity. The address is a building with two apartments upstairs and two downstairs, with a common stairway. The apartment had a back entrance and a garage for each of the units.

After lunch, Christensen went back to the area. He saw that the garage door was up and a dark-colored Ford Ranger was backed up to the apartment building. He was not certain of the apartment number, but he knew it was the lower north side of the building. He saw a male loading or unloading from the apartment to the Ranger. The male did not match the photo of Barrett. The person was larger and did not wear glasses. Christensen left the area and continued on routine patrol.

Christensen drove by again later and observed a white van backed up to the same apartment. He called on his radio to again verify that the warrant was active. He was told that it was a misdemeanor level warrant for contempt of court and not for second degree assault as Christensen thought. He parked in front and went around to the back of the building. He notified dispatch of his location and intention to arrest Barrett.

When he went around to the back, he saw a man getting ready to go into the apartment through a doorway. He said to the man, "Hey, is Calvin home?"

The person responded, "Yeah, he is." Christensen followed the man into the residence.

The man blurted out, "Calvin, the police are here." He heard Barrett respond with an expletive, definitely not hello. Christensen asked if he was Barrett, and he responded, "Yep."

Christensen told him he was with the sheriff's office and, "I have some bad news sir, I have a warrant for your arrest. You are under arrest."

At that very moment the phone rang and Barrett answered it. Christensen let him talk on the phone, but told him he was going to have to follow him around the house while he was talking on the cordless phone. Barrett did not respond. He was pacing back and forth, and it sounded to Christensen like he was talking to a creditor of some kind. He commented to the caller that his wife had mailed a payment. Christensen told Barrett to get off the phone as he was not going to keep following him around. The man who let him in and another man were taking boxes out of the apartment. Christensen told them to stay outside by their vehicle.

Christensen told Barrett to terminate the call as they needed to leave. Barrett made no acknowledgement to Christensen. He was using profanity and said "fucking wife." Christensen then told him to get off the phone or he would hang it up for him and physically remove him from the apartment. Barrett nodded. He had his back up against the fully opened patio door. Recalling how the previous deputy had been locked out, Christensen was positioned so he could see outside to the two men and be close to Barrett. One man came in and asked to look for the keys to the van.

Barrett, still on the phone, asked if he could get his jacket. Christensen followed him into another room while he continued to talk on the phone. He put his jacket on and Christensen said, "Calvin, wrap it up."

Barrett told the person on the phone, "They're here. I got something to do. I gotta go." He then said, "Fine, Good-bye." He then grabbed the patio door and shut it as he took off running. Christensen opened the door and began chasing him. As they were going across the street, he radioed dispatch and told them that he was in a foot chase.

Christensen twice shouted at him, "Don't make me taz you." Across the street there was a short chain-link fence. Barrett hit it and fell down. Christensen took his Taser M26 from his belt and fired it into Barrett's back. Both probes stuck. Barrett was on the other side of the fence and went beyond the twenty-one-foot range of the Taser. Christensen opened the gate to continue his chase while he expelled the old Taser cartridge and snapped in a new one.

Christensen continued the chase and was gaining on him. They reached a split-rail fence and Barrett fell. The Taser was fired again. The probes went into Barrett's chest. Christensen yelled for him to roll over on his stomach. The Taser was having no effect. Christensen was considering his options: use a chemical spray or use his collapsible baton. Not wanting the spray to affect himself, he decided upon the baton. He struck Barrett once in the leg between the buttock and knee. He then saw something that he described as "a flash of bright steel." He recognized it as a gun.

Christensen immediately moved away to get a safe separation. He heard what he said sound like a cap gun. He then felt a "blunt force" hitting him over his left kidney area. Christensen related later, "I felt like I was getting hit by a bat or punched really hard. I knew it was my armor because it was dull blunt trauma sensation." He then felt pressure in his left hip area. He was hit again. The second shot dropped him to his knees. He took his .40-caliber Glock from his holster and fired at Barrett. He told investigators that he did not recall dropping the Taser or baton.

Barrett got up and moved around the corner of a deck. This deck was only off the ground about twenty-four inches, not a second-story deck. The ground dropped off down and away from it. Christensen continued shooting though the deck where he believed Barrett was. Christensen climbed the two stairs to the deck. He saw Barrett again with the pistol in his hand. He fired again at him. Barrett went down. The weapon fell from Barrett's hand, but his hand was still near it. Christensen moved to the edge of the deck and then realized that he was hit. He had to use the railing of the deck to hold himself up. He shouted, "Move away from the gun. Move your hand away from the gun or I'm going to shoot you again." Barrett moved his hand away and never moved again.

Christensen radioed dispatch that there had been a shooting and the suspect was down, he had been hit and medical attention was needed immediately. He did not recall getting any response on the radio. He then took out his cell phone and called 911. He told them his Olmsted County identification number and the same information regarding the shooting. Christensen saw a man and woman on a second-story deck across from where he was. He shouted that he was a deputy and for them to call 911. They went back inside, but the woman came out and asked him if he needed anything. He requested that she bring him a towel. She came over to him and applied pressure on his hip. Blood was still pooling under his foot. He then pulled over a lawn chair on the deck and sat on it to put more pressure on the wound. He recalled yelling back to Barrett, "Don't fucking move or I'm going to shoot you." He called on the radio again that he needed medical attention and to launch Mayo 1 (the emergency helicopter).

Christensen saw Deputy Sgt. Kevin Torgerson coming down the street in an unmarked vehicle. He radioed him his location and to stop. Torgerson came running to him. He quickly explained what had occurred and told Torgerson to secure Barrett's weapon. He stood back up and provided cover for Torgerson while he secured the gun and handcuffed Barrett. He saw that Barrett was bleeding from the upper portion of his body.

Christensen next recalled someone who said that he worked for Gold Cross ambulance service take him out of the chair and put him on the deck elevating his foot. He was still watching Barrett and saw him move. He took out his weapon again and pointed it at Barrett. Torgerson told him everything was okay and to holster his weapon. He then recalled someone he knew from Stewartville Fire and Rescue putting an oxygen mask on him and telling him that he was doing okay. He also recalled seeing a Minnesota

State Trooper and officers from the Rochester Police Department. He was removed from the scene and transported to Rochester for medical attention. He would later tell investigators that the weapon used by Barrett must have been in his jacket that he put on in the apartment.

Barrett had been evicted from the apartment and had to be out by May 31. His landlord told police his eviction was because the police had been called too many times and it disturbed the other tenants. Barrett's wife of eighteen years was divorcing him and asking for full legal and physical custody of their five children, ages six to fifteen. Barrett had been convicted in September 2001 for the gross misdemeanor of driving while impaired and had served thirty days in jail. In December 2000 he was sentenced to 120 days in jail/home detention for being in possession of a firearm and driving while impaired. He had been recently cited on April 29, 2003, with four misdemeanors including fifth-degree domestic assault and harassing phone calls. His wife was the victim in both charges. He was also charged on May 6 with two counts of driving after revocation.

Barrett died during surgery at Rochester's St. Mary's Hospital. A .32-caliber revolver was recovered at the scene next to him. An autopsy determined that he had alcohol and cocaine in his system when he died. The cocaine had not been metabolized, and the coroner believed that he had consumed it shortly before his death. His blood alcohol was not high enough to be considered legally intoxicated while driving. It was opined that the alcohol and cocaine were more than likely the reason the Taser had no effect on him.

An Olmsted County grand jury cleared Christensen. He recovered from his wounds and returned to duty. He made the news again regarding a head-on crash on July 29, 2003. The accident occurred on a highway about thirty miles north of Rochester. He was the lone survivor of the crash that killed three others, one being his fiancée. The driver of the other vehicle was proceeding northbound in the southbound lane.

Christensen was given the Minnesota "Officer of the Year" award for

2003 by the Minnesota Peace Officers Association. He has since left law enforcement.

VIII

Mentally ill individuals are very unpredictable. Around 10:00 p.m. on August 25, 1993, citizens in the small northern town of Moose Lake began calling the police complaining that shots were being fired from the residence of Arthur Polcyn. The police were very familiar with the address as they had prior contacts with forty-two-year-old Donald Polcyn who lived at the residence with his father. Donald was mentally ill and required prescribed medication. Moose Lake officers responded to the location and determined that Donald was the person firing the gun. He had been seen by neighbors in the yard indiscriminately firing a handgun. It was also determined that his seventy-five-year-old father was in the house. The police were concerned for Arthur's safety. A perimeter was established by Pine County Sheriff's Office deputies, Carlton County deputies, Minnesota State Patrol, a Minnesota Conservation officer, City of Scanlon Police, and Moose Lake officers.

A command post was set up east of the house, and telephone contact was made with Donald. Efforts were being made to convince him to come out of the house. The neighborhood was alerted, and residents of nearby houses were told of the possible danger of gunfire. They were told they should leave or go to their basements for protection in the event of gunfire. Assistance was requested from the nearby SWAT team for St. Louis County.

One of the officers there was thirty-eight-year-old Conservation Officer Grant Coyour. He had received a radio call for assistance from Carlton County about the shots being fired. He was with Minnesota Trooper Bruce Lang when they arrived around 10:15 p.m. Coyour was familiar with the area of the Polcyn residence as there was a snowmobile trail behind the residence which had previously been a Soo Line Railroad grade. After being briefed of the situation, Coyour was instructed by Sheriff David Seboe to take three officers and secure the south perimeter. He could see Donald and his father moving around inside. When telephone contact was made, Donald could be heard shouting into the phone and acting upset. He and the others there were able to see in a window with a view of the entire length of the house from north to south. Donald could be seen carrying what appeared to be a four-inch blue steel revolver.

Coyour went to east side of the house and met with Carlton County Deputy Ervin Clemons. Moose Lake Chief Bruce Manty, Clemons and Coyour went to the area of the opened window to continue watching the events inside. Donald and Arthur were in the living room. About 1:00 a.m. officers could see Arthur walking toward the back door on the east side of the house. The three officers positioned themselves near the door to take him to safety in the event he exited.

They went to the door, and Arthur came out. Coyour grabbed him by his right shoulder and pulled him toward the three of them. Arthur shouted, "It's me, God damn it." Coyour covered his mouth, and Deputy Clemons told him to be quiet and asked where Donald was. Arthur told them that he was lying down in the living room. He told them that Donald had only one gun and that he would go back in the house and get him. Clemons told him he would not be allowed to back in and that he was going to safety with them.

Suddenly, the outside light above the back door came on, and Donald came out. Coyour grabbed Donald's right shoulder to pull him down. Donald pulled away and his right arm came up with his revolver firing. The muzzle flash blinded Coyour, and he felt the discharge across his right arm. Coyour dropped to his knees and pulled his Glock 9-mm pistol and fired twice. Coyour then saw additional muzzle flashes coming from the left side of his face. Donald fell backwards and his .357-caliber revolver fell near his right knee. Coyour grabbed the gun and threw it out of his reach. Clemons was grabbing his own leg and said that he had been shot. Other officers came to the area and began to administer first aid to Clemons and Donald. Ambulances were called in as they had been on standby.

Manty, the fifty-year-old Chief of Moose Lake, related the same version of the shooting. He added that the three of them were actually trying to keep Arthur from going back inside his house to get Donald. They were about three feet from the door when Donald came out. He saw Coyour trying to take Donald down to the ground, but he broke loose and came up firing. Manty saw Clemons immediately spin around and fall on his back. He drew his 9-mm weapon and began to fire at Donald. After Coyour tossed Donald's gun aside, Manty picked it up and placed it in his gun belt. Manty said that the ambulance crew was there within a minute, and Donald was declared dead at the scene. Clemons was carried away on a stretcher.

A trained crisis negotiator, Osten Berg, had talked to Donald twice during the incident. During the first call, Donald told him that "There's people out in the yard sneakin' around with guns with silencers and I got them." He also told Berg that he got them and that they were in the morgue. Berg tried to convince him to come out so they could go to the morgue and identify them. Donald told him that he thought Berg was "trying to trick him" to come out. Berg had previous contacts with Donald. In June 1992, Donald had been outside firing a weapon. He was taken into custody and committed for a mental examination. Two .22-caliber rifles and a 9-mm handgun were removed from the residence.

Donald spoke very little during the second call and basically told Berg that he was done talking to him. Arthur answered and talked during the third call. Donald could be heard ranting and raving in the background. It seemed that Arthur was trying to get Donald to come out. Donald could be heard yelling, "They're going to throw me in jail… there's agents out there." Berg told Arthur to call 911 if they were coming out. Thereafter, repeated calls went unanswered. Plans were being made to put a "throw phone" through the window when the shooting occurred.

Arthur Polcyn was interviewed after the shooting. He said they moved to Moose Lake in 1980, and his wife died in 1988. He told investigators he had problems with Donald as he was mentally ill and had been diagnosed as paranoid schizophrenic. Donald had taken a gun outside and fired "a couple of shots" that night. Arthur thought that the neighbors reported it to the police. Donald told him that "somethin's after me." Arthur tried to get him to take his medicine, but Donald told him that "they make me look like a zombie." When Donald lay down on the couch, he thought he could go out and talk to the police. He said two or three officers grabbed him and "cuffed his mouth." He said Donald came out in a few seconds and "as soon as he seen the policemen, bang, bang, he was shooting." Arthur related he was sorry for the "poor policeman." He said a social worker tried to get Donald to take his medication, but he would slam the phone down on him. Arthur added, "He was six-foot-four; I couldn't control him."

Deputy Clemons was taken to Mercy Hospital in Moose Lake. He was pronounced dead at 2:13 a.m. The shot fired by Donald had entered his upper left hip and traveled downward and exited by his right hip severing his femoral artery. He was forty-seven-years-old and had been with the department for twenty-three years.

Polcyn died from gunshot wounds to the upper body. His .357-caliber Smith and Wesson revolver had four live rounds remaining in it. There were approximately twenty officers at the command post and perimeter.

Coyour also had prior contacts with Donald. On July 4, 1989, Donald had called him and said he killed his father and the remains were in his freezer. Berg talked him into surrendering on that occasion, and he was placed on a seventy-two-hour hold. Coyour was involved with him in January 1992, and he was again committed.

No charges were filed by the Carlton County prosecutor regarding the shooting.

Unfortunately, on July 11, 1999, Coyour, along with a civilian observer, was killed in an airplane accident while conducting aerial moose telemetry in northern Minnesota. He was forty-three at the time of his death and had been with the Department of Natural Resources as a Conservation Officer for twenty-two years.

IX

National Night Out should not be celebrated with an officer being shot and a SWAT member killing the assailant. However, that is exactly what happened in the ninety-degree heat in Chaska, a southwestern suburb of the Twin Cities, on Tuesday, August 7, 2001. Chaska police were dispatched at 6:16 p.m. to the five-hundred-unit Brandondale Mobile Home Park to investigate a suicidal man at Lot Seven. Thomas "T. J." Opalinski's present wife had called the police to report that he had talked to her and threatened to shoot himself. She added that he had access to two shotguns. Uniform officers arrived at the park and began to form a perimeter for the safety of other residents in the area. Sergeants Ben Anderson and Joe Carlson, both in full uniform, were two of the officers.

Houses nearby had been cleared of occupants for safety reasons. Anderson was across the street waiting for a negotiator to call Opalinski to see if he would come out. A woman came by with a small child and wanted to know what was happening. He tried to explain that she needed to leave the area until things were secure. She was being difficult about leaving and demanded more information. Just then, Sergeant Carlson informed him that someone was coming out of Lot Seven. Anderson left the lady and began walking to a tree for cover with his 9-mm MP5. A white male, later identified as Opalinski, came walking toward Anderson and made eye contact. Anderson identified who he was and requested that he show his hands and get on the ground. Opalinski immediately began using profanity that included "fucking pigs." He turned around and began running back to the mobile home. Anderson again asked him to stop. Opalinski turned back to Anderson and said, "You wanna fucking play, we'll fucking play." (It should be noted that the mobile home park is hilly, and there are garages built into the side of the hills with the trailers above, giving the appearance of a home with a tuck-under garage). Anderson moved to the cover of a large pickup by the front passenger wheel. He could hear glass breaking in the home and then saw the big front window of the trailer home being broken. Anderson was kneeling on his left knee when he heard shots. Unfortunately, he was not protected by the wheel and his knee was hit and "exploded" simultaneously with the shots. Carlson dragged him away from the truck and he was eventually taken to an ambulance by other officers. Anderson said he never saw a weapon. Emergency personnel and law enforcement from the area immediately responded.

Just after the incident began, Opalinski called his ex-wife, whom he had divorced in 1997, and asked to speak to their daughter. He was told she was outside playing. Opalinski said to the mother, "Tell her I love her." His ex-wife was alarmed by his quiet nature so she went out and got their daughter. They tried calling him, but there was no answer. She dialed again around about 6:45 p.m. and handed the phone to her daughter. She heard her say, "Hi, daddy," and later, "Me too."

She gave the phone to her mother and said, "He wants to talk to you." He was upset that his daughter had called. His ex-wife asked him why he was so mad at her. He told her that he was not angry with her but with everyone else. He said he had thirty-four years of built up anger and that he was "tired." Before ending the call he said, "As soon as this bottle of Jack Daniel's is gone, I'm gone." He also talked about moving out of the state and said that he would not be picking up his daughter for the weekend. She said the daughter was expecting to see him, and he responded, "Yeah, sure." She did not get the feeling he was going to take his life.

His brother-in-law called during the incident. He told officers later that he questioned him about what was going on. Opalinski acknowledged what was happening and said, "It's all fucking true." He said something about "doing it" and that he only had thirty seconds to talk. The brother-in-law tried to calm him down, but Opalinski hung up.

Negotiators made contact with Opalinski. He admitted during conversation with the negotiator that he was the person responsible for shooting Anderson. He kept expressing his desire to die and saying that he would take as many officers with him as he could. Sniper observers reported they could see him in the mobile home and had seen him fire five or six rounds through the ceiling of his trailer.

Deputy William Vendel of the Scott County Sheriff's Office had responded to the scene. He was a member of the SWAT team and a sniper. The thirty-eight-year-old had his issued Remington 700 .308-caliber rifle with him. He set up in the bathroom across the street from Opalinski's home. He and his observer watched Opalinski come to the window and shouted for the officers to shoot him. They were able to see him take shots out the window toward empty cars. They also could see that he had taken off his shirt and could see a shotgun or silver type long weapon in his possession. On one occasion they saw him on the telephone screaming, "I need a pack of cigarettes, get me a pack of cigarettes or I'm going to start shooting people."

Around 9:15 p.m., about forty-five minutes after Vendel had arrived, a Ford Ranger occupied by a female driver with small children drove past the barricaded road to the trailer park. She was driving down the street toward Lot Seven. Opalinski leaned out of the window and began shooting at it. The woman in the Ranger stopped. That information was relayed, and the command post gave approval to use deadly force against Opalinski. Vendel fired once, killing Opalinski. He fell back and the weapon dropped out the window.

A Carver County grand jury returned a no bill in September, 2001.

Sergeant Anderson was hospitalized for the injury to his knee and recovered. He returned to the police department and presently has the title of Executive Officer. Would the incident have ended differently had the pickup truck been stopped at the perimeter and not allowed to enter? One will never know. This does prove how every assignment during such an incident is important.

X

Minneapolis Officers Jeremy Hulke and James Boyd were working on the city's north side around 1:30 a.m. on Wednesday, May 7, 2003, when they observed two vehicles which appeared to be drag racing. A 1993 Cadillac DeVille and 2000 Ford Explorer were going between sixty and seventy miles per hour on Broadway Avenue. The vehicles were stopped. The owner of the Cadillac was a passenger in the car, with her friend driving. The person in the Explorer was not the registered owner and had no driver's license. He presented the officers with a YMCA card in the name of Frank Phillips. Immediately red flags went up because one does not present such identity when a driver's license is requested.

Officers Sean McGinty and Mark Bohnsack were in the area and stopped to see if the other officers needed any assistance. The Explorer was parked near the curb about five car lengths ahead of the Cadillac. There was concern that the person in the Explorer was not being truthful regarding his true identity. Bohnsack was looking for a suspect in a shooting incident who had been driving a similar Explorer. He believed he would recognize the person if he saw him. Bohnsack decided to walk up to the passenger side of the vehicle to see if he was the suspect.

Officer Boyd went up to the driver's side door. Bohnsack saw that the passenger window was completely down. Bohnsack heard Boyd tell the driver to exit the vehicle. The driver told Boyd that he was not getting out. Bohnsack knew that the person was not his shooting suspect. However, the man appeared nervous and moving his hands back and forth from his lap to the steering wheel.

Bohnsack believed he was concealing something from them. The driver, later identified as thirty-one-year-old Eric Netters, was not aware of Bohnsack, as he was giving his attention to Boyd. Bohnsack reached in the open window and opened the door latch. He removed his chemical spray as he opened the door, leaned forward and told Netters to get out of the vehicle or he would spray him. Netters looked at Bohnsack and without any hesitation put the Explorer in gear and started to go forward. Bohnsack jumped into the passenger seat and slammed the door shut so he would not fall out.

Boyd yelled for Netters to stop. The next thing Bohnsack saw was Boyd being thrown from the driver's side door. He described Netters as moving the Explorer side-to-side and crossing the oncoming lane of traffic. Bohnsack kept shouting for Netters to stop, but he stared ahead without any acknowledgement of his commands to stop. They were going about thirty miles per hour, and the engine sounded like it was racing. Bohnsack reached over and put the vehicle in park while yelling for him to stop. They were in the eastbound lane traveling west.

The transmission was making a clicking sound, but it did not stop the vehicle. It appeared as if the vehicle was in neutral because the engine was racing and they were not accelerating. Netters pushed Bohnsack's hand off the gear shift lever located on the steering column and put it back in gear. They sped off again—still in the wrong lane of traffic. Bohnsack continued trying to put the car in park, but Netters kept knocking his hand away. He tried quick bursts of the chemical spray, but Netters would turn his head away. He was careful with the spray as he did not want to be affected by the spray in such close proximity.

Bohnsack feared he was going to get hurt as the vehicle was going approximately sixty miles per hour and he was not wearing a seatbelt. Bohnsack took his weapon out and pointed it at Netters. He shouted, "Stop the car or I'll shoot." Netters looked directly at him and reached for the gun. Bohnsack fired his Beretta 9-mm twice. Netters slumped forward. Bohnsack grabbed the steering wheel and tried to shift it into park. He again heard the clicking sound from the transmission. It was slowing down somewhat. The oncoming traffic light was green. He moved over into the driver's seat as much as he could and used the brake to stop it. He felt what he believed to be warm blood on his leg and upper arm as he was stopping the vehicle. The Explorer was still racing as Netters had his foot on the accelerator. He exited via the passenger' door. His weapon and chemical spray fell out to the pavement. He secured them and ran around and turned the racing engine off. McGinty arrived and told him to sit in his squad. McGinty called for an ambulance.

Officer Boyd related that when he went to the driver of the Explorer and asked him why he was driving so fast, he said, "Well, the guy behind me was bumping me." He was asked if he knew the driver of the other car and he said, "Well, no, well, yes I do." Boyd asked him for his driver's license and was given a YMCA card with a photo and name Frank Phillips. There was no date of birth on it, and Boyd was not satisfied that the picture was that of the driver. He said he had a driver's license at home and gave a birth date to Boyd. He seemed disinterested and wanted to eat his White Castle meal.

Boyd went back to his vehicle to run the information furnished. His partner was interviewing the driver of the other vehicle who was in the back of the squad. After a short period, the information regarding the driver of the Explorer came back "not on file." Because of this information, he told his partner that he wanted to bring the man back to question him further. It was at this time that McGinty and Bohnsack came up to their squad and told him that the driver might be a suspect in another matter.

Boyd then went up to the Explorer and told the driver (Netters) that the information given by him could not be verified. Boyd requested him to come back to the squad. Netters became agitated and claimed he had done nothing wrong and that Boyd should follow him to his house to get further identification. He kept insisting that, "I haven't done anything wrong," when asked to get out of the car. Boyd told him he needed to start telling the truth. Suddenly, Netters reached for the gearshift lever. As he threw it in gear and hit the accelerator, Boyd said he "was shocked" to see Bohnsack in the passenger's seat. Boyd said he thought to himself that he could not let him leave with Bohnsack. Boyd was hanging onto the opened window of the Explorer and "my left foot was running alongside." The next thing that he recalled was "flying onto West Broadway" and seeing his gun spinning across the street.

Boyd was not sure when he took his pistol out of this holster. When he retrieved it from the street, his hand was hurting so bad he could not snap the holster. He saw McGinty's squad chasing the Explorer with lights and siren. He walked to the north side of the street and saw another squad coming. It was Officer Hulke. He got in and they proceeded to Penn and West Broadway where the Explorer had stopped. Boyd jumped out to greet Bohnsack who was walking toward him. Boyd asked, "Are you okay, Mark?"

Bohnsack replied, "I shot, Jim. He's dead. I can't talk to you."

Officer Hulke said that he was just letting the driver of the Cadillac out of the squad when he heard the Explorer leaving at a high rate of speed. He saw Boyd "dangling" from the driver's side door. He saw the car swerving back and forth. He then saw Boyd "tumble away and hit the pavement." He jumped into his squad and noticed that the other squad was already in pursuit. He stopped and picked up Boyd who appeared "to be in pain and stunned."

McGinty said he was in his squad watching Hulke let the driver out of his squad. Bohnsack had gone up to the Explorer with Boyd to identify the driver. He looked up and saw the Explorer leave with Boyd hanging on. He saw him fall away and roll on the street. He shouted for Bohnsack and got no response. He decided to chase the Explorer and went past Boyd who was in the middle of the street. He caught up to the Explorer as it stopped just past Penn and West Broadway. He exited his vehicle and pointed his weapon at the passenger door that was opening. He started to yell for the person to stop and saw that it was Bohnsack. Bohnsack told him that he was okay, but that "he's [the driver] dead." McGinty checked for vitals on the driver and could find none. He told Hulke who had arrived to tape off the scene and notified the shift supervisor.

The owner of the Cadillac had an interesting story. She and a friend had stopped at White Castle for food around 2:00 a.m. After going through the drive-up, her friend stopped to talk to a guy only known to her as the "Devil's Advocate" in a green Explorer. When her friend came back to the car, he said he wanted to go to the residence of the "Devil's Advocate" to look at a couple of cars. They started following him and were speeding when a Minneapolis squad pulled the Explorer over. Her friend pulled alongside the

Explorer to wave good-bye, but the officer told him to pull over too. One officer took her friend back to the squad. Another squad also arrived.

She related that she sitting there not paying attention when she heard a loud "screech." She looked up and saw the Explorer leaving and one officer "go flying off the vehicle." She saw one of the squads put on emergency lights and siren to chase the Explorer. She then heard two shots and "flashes of fire" from the Explorer. She heard the officer who went flying from the Explorer say to his partner that his arm hurt. She and her friend, who was just getting into her car when the chase began, drove up to where the Explorer stopped. She could see "Devil's Advocate" slumped over the steering wheel. She assumed he was dead.

Responding medical personnel determined that Netters was dead at the scene. Boyd was taken to Hennepin County Medical Center. He had a broken right wrist and thumb. He had various small abrasions and bruises on his arms and legs. He mended and returned to duty.

The reason Netters was uncooperative was that he was a wanted fugitive. He had been convicted in June 2000 for possession of crack cocaine. He was on intensive supervised release in July 2001 when he failed a drug test. His whereabouts was unknown until his death. Police found marijuana and one-fourth ounce of cocaine in the Explorer. The autopsy determined that he died from a gunshot wound to the upper neck and one to the right cheek. Beneath a scar on the left side of his neck was another bullet. His mother told investigators that he had been shot as a youth in Detroit and the doctor did not remove it at that time.

A Hennepin County grand jury cleared Bohnsack on September 4, 2003.

XI

How many times does a police officer see someone driving erratically and say, "I probably have another drunk driver." This was exactly the case around 1:00 a.m. on Wednesday, October 22, 1997.

Hennepin County is quite a large area where Minneapolis and many other densely populated suburbs are located. The extreme northwest area of the county is more sparsely populated, and there are more lakes and woods. Forty-four-year-old Hennepin County Deputy Gary Johnson was on patrol in that area when he saw a vehicle that piqued his attention with some erratic driving. When Johnson ran the license, he discovered that the plates did not match the vehicle. He turned on his flashing lights. The vehicle driver, thirty-year-old Gerald T. Lehn, initially stopped just after entering Interstate 94. However, when Johnson went to approach the vehicle, he sped away.

Johnson followed the vehicle with lights and siren in an attempt to get him to stop again. They were proceeding on I-94 westbound from Rogers toward Wright County. Lehn exited the freeway in Wright County and went south on roads unfamiliar to Johnson. Johnson notified his dispatcher that the chase was in another county and for the transmissions to be on the statewide frequency. Wright County deputies heard the transmissions, but they were unable to catch up to the chase because of the speed they were going and the constant changes of direction.

The twenty-mile chase continued on paved and dirt roads until Lehn crashed his car. He jumped out and started running. Johnson lost sight of him. Not knowing if he was armed or why he ran, Johnson began walking with his flashlight in one hand and gun in the other. Johnson was scanning with his flashlight. He found Lehn with his jacket pulled up over his head, tucked down underneath some brush next to a tree. Johnson shouted for him to put his hands up and come to him. Lehn yelled, "Fuck you," and took off running again.

Johnson caught up to him and cut him off. Johnson reached out with his left hand to grab his shoulder when Lehn leaped toward him and the struggle began. Lehn actually had Johnson in a "partial-headlock." Johnson was able to hit him with a blow to the head with his flashlight. The first hit did not affect him, but the second one caused Lehn to back up for a second. Lehn then leaped at him again and this time grabbed the barrel of Johnson's gun in his right hand.

Johnson told investigators later that he was afraid he was going to have his gun taken away from him and be shot with it. He said all kinds of things were going through his mind about why the person was doing it and why did he not stop after being hit with the flashlight. Johnson continued "barreling" his shoulder try to push Lehn away. He was not having any success getting him away. Johnson, fearing for his life and believing that the gun was pointing at Lehn's stomach, pulled the trigger once. It seemed to have no effect on Lehn. Johnson said he pulled the trigger again, but this time it did not fire. He was not sure if Lehn was holding the barrel too tight or what happened. He pushed some more and they broke free. Johnson fired again. Lehn stopped fighting and said, "I'm hurt."

Johnson told him to sit and he would get help. He went to call on his portable radio, but it was not where it was supposed to be. His glasses were knocked off and the flashlight was about four or five feet away. It was still on so he retrieved it and found his glasses and radio. He called for help and an ambulance. They were so far away and into the woods that it took approximately fifteen minutes for rescuers to arrive. Johnson was performing first aid when the first deputy came on the scene.

Lehn was flown to Hennepin County Medical Center and underwent surgery to save his life. He never regained consciousness and died around 2:00 p.m. later that day. What Johnson did not know that night was that Lehn had been arrested for drunken driving and six other offenses in April 1990. He pleaded guilty to two of the charges and was sentenced to ten days in the workhouse. He also was sentenced to probation. He violated his probation in May 1991, when he was arrested again for drunk driving. He was arrested for another traffic offense in July 1991. Another unknown to Johnson was that Lehn had told authorities he would never be taken alive again. Many say this, but few do what he did.

Johnson had minor injuries that included an abrasion to the left side of his nose, a bloody nose, a one-inch cut to the left side of his chin, contusions to both sides of his neck, abrasions to his left hand, and abrasions and contusions to both lower legs. None of the injuries were life-threatening and he was able to return to duty following the required administrative days off following a shooting.

On December 9, 1997, a Hennepin County grand jury returned a no bill regarding the shooting. Johnson later received the sheriff's office highest award—the Medal of Honor.

XII

Whether dispatched to a home or business, no call is ever routine. An employee of the American Inn motel in Blackduck, a town of about seven hundred located in Beltrami County in northern Minnesota, called 911 at 5:05 a.m. on July 30, 2001, to report that a guest was acting strangely and appeared agitated.

As background, Mark Patch and his mother had checked into the motel under his name around 9:30 p.m. the night before the shooting by his mother. She paid cash. They were upset because there was no room on the second floor away from the lobby. Patch had a backpack and some cigarettes, and his mother had no luggage. After going to the room for a few minutes, they both came and again asked for a different room. They were told that none was available. They then asked if other members of the family would be allowed to swim in the pool. Mark seemed to be most dissatisfied with the room and asked for the money back. They told him no because he had already been in the room.

Patch and his mother left in a pickup with Mark driving. His mother returned a little later with a younger woman and small child. They went to the room and then came down to swim. The clerk noticed Mark driving around the parking lot and in and out of the lot. He did not come into the motel. The male clerk was being relieved by a female, and he did not leave until the woman's husband and son arrived. Patch had not returned, and he thought the swimmers were still in the pool when he left.

Forty-seven-year-old Beltrami County Deputy Greg Winskowski and

Blackduck Chief of Police Matthew Grossell, who had been chief only since July 1, responded to the call. The 911 caller thought the person was possibly drunk and his name was given as Mark Patch. Winskowski recognized the Patch name because he'd had contacts with members of the family on several occasions. He requested the dispatcher to check for any warrants or issues of which he should be aware. He was advised that there was a "no drink" notice regarding Mark. Winskowski knew that such a notice is court ordered. This means that an officer who has contact with an individual under such an order and smells alcohol can take the person directly to jail. Patch's order also included a controlled substance order. Just prior to their arrival at the motel, they were advised that Patch had a "wrench." The wrench was not described further, but Winskowski said later that he imagined a large pipe wrench.

The officers were met by a male who stated he was the son of the female desk clerk. Winskowski recognized him as a member of the Blackduck Ambulance Service. He told the officers his mother was concerned about statements Patch had been making. He was asked if Patch smelled of alcohol. He said, "No," but added that he thought Patch was on some type of controlled substance. The man said Patch told him he knew the location of an intern for a senator who had been killed and buried. The man thought maybe Patch was someone who was not taking his proper medications.

They entered the motel, and Winskowski immediately recognized Patch sitting on a couch near the wall by a fireplace in the room that was the lobby/continental breakfast area. Winskowski said, "Hey Mark, what's shaking?" Patch did not respond. Winskowski walked between Patch and a big coffee table and sat about two feet from him. He asked, "What's happening?" At the same time he reached and took a wrench sitting directly in front of them on the coffee table. Winskowski noticed that next to Patch was a metal fireplace poker stick with a hook used to roll logs. He reached back and secured the poker. Grossell walked to the left side of Patch and remained standing.

Patch then attempted to stand up and said, "I'm gonna kill my family."

He was not completely standing and leaned back at an angle. His hands went down toward his belt, and he pulled up his shirt. The brown handle of a gun was visible. Winskowski stood up and went to his right to distance himself while pulling his weapon. At the same time, Chief Grossell jumped toward Patch and grabbed for his arms. As the two were wrestling, two shots rang out. Grossell was still struggling with Patch and making groaning sounds. Patch was actually on top of Grossell, and it appeared to Winskowski that they were fighting over the weapon. Patch was starting to stand above Grossell with his arms extending as if to pull the weapon loose. Knowing that Grossell had been shot and concerned about his ability to hold on to the weapon, Winskowski fired his weapon at Patch from a distance of about ten to twelve feet. Patch was hit in the head and fell on Grossell.

Grossell told Winskowski that he still had hold of Patch's weapon, a .38-caliber Colt revolver. Winskowski was able to secure the gun and placed it on the fireplace mantel. He also saw a paring knife with a four-inch blade in Patch's back pocket. He retrieved it and threw it aside on the floor. He then pushed Patch off Grossell. Grossell started to stand and complained that his arm hurt. Winskowski had been an EMT for seventeen years and could tell that Grossell was bleeding and going into shock. He grabbed a cushion from the couch and had him lie down. His radio was not working so he called 911 from the front counter. Beltrami Deputy Cross arrived and saw that Patch was not moving. He stood by while Winskowski went to his squad to retrieve his medical supplies to work on Grossell.

Chief Grossell related that he was out on foot checking on a call he had received at 4:45 a.m. that morning when he received the call regarding Patch. Winskowski came, and they went to the motel together. He said they were just making small talk with Patch when he stood up and started talking about people killing or trying to kill his family. At that same time Patch pulled out a revolver. Grossell tried to grab Patch's arm, and at that moment a shot went past the right side of his head and ear. Immediately, he felt ringing in his ear. He grabbed the cylinder of the revolver to keep it from rotating. He heard another shot, and his right arm was not responding to him. He saw a hole in his arm. He then wrestled Patch to the couch and was turning the gun away from himself. He heard another shot and felt blood all over his face, and Patch collapsed. He held onto the revolver until Winskowski pulled it away.

In the file of the Minnesota Bureau of Criminal Investigation which conducted the shooting investigation was a memorandum from the FBI. It indicated that on November 22, 1999, a person identifying herself as Mark Patch's mother said that Mark was on his way to the FBI office in Bemidji. She said he was unstable and was not taking his medication for his psychological condition and was delusional. He did arrive and wanted to be placed in the Witness Protection Program because the Mafia in Chicago was seeking him to kill him. He claimed to have worked in a Mafia-run "chop shop." He said the Mafia did a background on him costing ten thousand dollars and that he owed them seventy-five thousand dollars. He said the Mafia had planted video cameras in his house because they were concerned that he was an informant for the FBI. He admitted he had recently been in the hospital for anxiety and was given a prescription, but he did not want to take it. He said he was living with a girlfriend, but she was contacted and said he was living with his mother. She added that his mental state was deteriorating.

Patch was dead at the scene. A Colt six-shot .38-caliber revolver was recovered from Patch with three live and three spent cartridges in the chamber. He had twenty-one live rounds in his right jacket pocket and twenty-two in his left jacket pocket. Winskowski had fired two rounds from his 9-mm pistol. The wrench at the scene was possibly the jack handle from his pickup. One of Winskowski's rounds was recovered from the carpet in the room and the other one from Patch during autopsy. The autopsy also revealed that Patch had methamphetamine in his system. It is interesting to note that there was a video camera in the lobby area. Patch was seen in and out of camera view at 4:50 a.m. The clerk and her son were seen at 4:58. Chief Grossell and Deputy Winskowski arrived and walked through the lobby to the area where Patch was last seen walking at 5:04:06. The clerk's son is seen reacting to shots being fired at 5:04:26. At 5:04:51 Winskowski approached the front desk and grabbed the phone. The female clerk takes the phone and calls 911 at 5:05:51. Winskowski is talking on the phone at 5:05:02. Deputy Cross arrives and walks through the lobby at 5:06:09. Winskowski is seen going out to get his EMT bag and returning with it at 5:07:56. The ambulance arrived at 5:17:44 a.m.

The Beltrami County attorney declined prosecution of Winskowski on October 29, 2001, claiming it was a justifiable homicide. Grossell was hospitalized and returned to duty. He is now a deputy with the Clearwater County Sheriff's Office and assigned to a drug task force.

XIII

Law enforcement responds to a wide variety of calls. Loud music is one that usually has officers telling the occupants of the residence to turn the music down and they comply. The Bee Gees are famous for the song "Staying Alive." It is a great song, but not if it is so loud that it keeps neighbors awake at 2:25 a.m. Who would think that this would result in an officer being shot and the owner of the house where the music originated ending up dead. This is exactly what happened on Tuesday, May 13, 2003, in suburban Anoka County.

The person renting one-half of a duplex owned by twenty-nine-year-old Erik D. Nylen was hearing music from Nylen' residence that was unbearably loud. Unfortunately, Nylen was his landlord. What do you do? There had never been a problem previously, and he wanted to be courteous, so the renter decided to call the police and let them handle the situation. The caller was not sure if Nylen was passed out or what had happened but was requesting that the music be turned down.

Anoka County Deputy Samantha Cruze received the loud music call. The twenty-two-year-old deputy had been on the job for five months and was on her second night patrolling alone. She was familiar with the area as she had been a Community Service Officer for years at Anoka County. She was working the 7:00 p.m. to 3:30 a.m. shift. Deputy Dustin Reichert also heard the call to Cruze and advised that he would respond as a backup. The thirty-one-year-old Reichert had been a deputy for over six years. Cruze arrived at the location at 2:31:09 a.m. and Reichert a few seconds later. She told investigators that as she approached the address with her windows down she could not hear the music. When Reichert arrived, he told her he could not hear the music.

They saw a female walking from the house where the complaint had originated. She was bringing the trash down the driveway to the street. She told the deputies that the music had been loud and was concerned that her three-year-old daughter was sleeping and did not want her to awaken. Cruze told her, "I don't hear anything now, but we'll go up and talk to him."

There was no record of any previous calls to the residence. They walked in front of a Lincoln car in the driveway toward the front door. Cruze was in front with Reichert following. As they approached, the windows were open and they could hear music by the Bee Gees playing. It was not loud or disturbing. Cruze could see a faint light in the house and peaked into the window to see if she could see anyone. No one was seen. Cruze walked up two of the steps to the landing of the door. There was a storm door and a brown wooden front door. Both were closed. She rang the doorbell twice. Reichert, who was on the ground level by the window, told her that it appeared a light was on in the kitchen. Cruze had to crouch down to see in the window.

Cruze could see an opening from the living room into the kitchen. She could see a white male in his 20s wearing a dark shirt and shorts. She saw a black gun in his hand. It was down to his side. She shouted, "Dustin, he has a gun." They both removed their weapons from their holsters. Cruze could see that the man, later identified as Nylen, take a step toward the front door. She left the landing of the door, and they both squeezed tight against the house by the window. Cruze, thinking that maybe he was not sure who they were, called, "Sheriff's Office. Drop the gun." Cruze recalled that both she and Reichert yelled it numerous times. Nylen was out of their sight, but he should have been able to hear them through the open window.

They could see the screen door opening. They continued to shout commands. Cruze stayed tight against the house and moved back toward the corner of the house. Reichert ran toward the Lincoln in the driveway for cover. Momentarily, shots rang out and Cruze saw a "flash" by the screen door. She was not sure who fired first as she also saw "white lines" from his weapon. She knew that Reichert had been hit by fire as she heard him scream "very, very, very loud." She heard no sound from the direction of Nylen. She saw Reichert fall to the ground by the Lincoln. She then saw that the screen door was closed. She called dispatch advising that shots had been fired and they needed an ambulance. She also furnished the description of Nylen.

Cruze then took cover behind a red car in the driveway. She yelled to Reichert that she was not hit and asked, "Dustin, are you okay?" She wanted him to know that she was not hit and was watching for Nylen as well as letting him know that help was on the way. Backup and emergency vehicles arrived quickly.

Reichert related the same scenario as Cruze. He told investigators that as they approached the house he told Cruze, "It's your call." They made light of the music playing. After Cruze rang the doorbell, he saw Nylen with the gun and before he could say anything Cruze shouted something about a "gun." He drew his Beretta 9-mm pistol as he retreated toward the Lincoln in the driveway. He could see Nylen opening the inside door and yelled, "Sheriff's Office. Drop the gun." He also heard Cruze shouting basically the same command. He saw the screen door open. Unbelievably, when interviewed later he described Nylen and the weapon's size and shape exactly. The gun in Nylen's hand came up toward Reichert. Reichert said, "I was looking straight down the barrel of a gun." He fired twice at Nylen as he was going for cover. Reichert then heard "two pops" and immediately felt "two jolts on my body." He knew that he had been hit, but he also knew that he had hit Nylen as he could see that he reacted and backed into the house. He heard Cruze radio the situation to dispatch.

The first shot hit Reichert's right arm, and his weapon flew out of his hand. The second shot hit him in the pelvis. He attempted to crawl for cover, but his arm "just flopped." He knew it was broken. He searched for his gun but could not find it. He made another attempt to pull himself to the Lincoln. He described the pain as intense and that he did not have the energy to move. He said, "So I just put pressure on my pelvis area and lay playing dead. Literally played dead." He heard Cruze yell for him twice, but he did not respond. He did not want the person to come out and "execute me or what." Emergency medical personnel arrived and Reichert was removed from the scene to the hospital.

A 911 operator received a call at 2:33:15 a.m. with the caller stating, "Ah, 2110 140th Lane NW. I've been shot."

The operator responded, "Okay, what's going on there? Hello?" (Loud music was heard in the background.) "Hello? Have you been shot?"For one minute and twenty-two seconds only loud music could be heard and no verbal response. Attempts to contact Nylen inside the residence were unsuccessful. The Anoka County SWAT team eventually made entry into the residence a few hours after the shooting. Nylen was found in the kitchen area at the top of the basement stairs in a prone position. A portable phone was next to his left shoulder. Based upon the blood trail in the house, crime scene investigators believed that Nylen went to the basement and obtained his portable phone. He then came to the top of the stairs and collapsed. He was dead at the scene.

An autopsy determined that Nylen was shot in the right chest. He died from exsanguination. His blood screen revealed the presence of benzodiazepines (prescription drug such as Librium, Valium, Xanax, and Ativan). Blood alcohol was negative.

Deputy Reichert was hospitalized for his wounds and returned to limited duty followed by full duty. He had further complications and subsequently received a medical retirement. Deputy Cruze married a police officer from a local police department and is a full-time mother of twins.

An Anoka County grand jury returned a no bill on July 1, 2003.

XIV

This shooting event began with an armed robbery and the shooting death of a police officer before one of the armed robbers was subsequently killed.

Thomas Kantor, age twenty-six, Brian Ederhoff, age twenty-six, and Kenneth Roering, age nineteen, decided to get together around 3:00 p.m. on Monday, January 29, 1996, to have a few beers. The next few hours created chaos for many families. At 9:02 p.m. three armed robbers entered Freeway Liquors in Albany, Minnesota. The robbers wore masks and Playtex gloves. They tied up the store cashier and made off with two cases of beer, a bottle of rum and $372. An alarm was activated and an excellent description of a stolen pickup used in the robbery was immediately given out to law enforcement.

At 9:14 p.m. twenty-five-year-old St. Joseph Police Officer Brian Klinefelter, who was scheduled to end his shift at 9:00 p.m., radioed that he had the pickup stopped on a county road and there was no visible license plate. As Klinefelter approached the vehicle with his weapon drawn, Kantor fired six rounds from his Beretta .380-caliber semiautomatic weapon. Two struck Klinefelter in his ballistic vest and two shots fatally hit him in the neck and waist. A sheriff's deputy responded to the location where Klinefelter reported he had stopped the pickup and found the officer on the pavement. He was pronounced dead at a St. Cloud hospital at 10:14 p.m.

After Klinefelter was shot, St. Cloud police spotted the pickup in a residential neighborhood in that city. By the time they caught up to it, all of the occupants had fled into the freezing night. The temperature was ten degrees below zero.

About 9:30 p.m. Lillian Klawitter, age 86, heard a knock at her patio door. She then heard noises in her garage. When she started to open the kitchen door, Kantor pushed the door open and knocked her to the floor. He demanded her car keys. She told him that it was not her car and only being stored there. She saw a gun tucked into his pants. When he could not find the keys in the kitchen area, he returned to the garage. She immediately locked the door behind him. Kantor ran out of her garage and went next door to the residence of Doug and Connie Thomsen, both age forty-three. There was knocking at the door and Connie went to see who it was. Kantor walked in with his gun drawn. He told Doug that he was going to come with him. Kantor gave him ten seconds to put his boots on. They went to the garage and Kantor got in the back seat. He told Thomsen to start driving. Connie called police to report the kidnapping.

Thomsen began driving as instructed and actually drove by many police cars. Thomsen's car was not handling very good as the roads were icy and the tires were often spinning. Kantor was upset and accused Thomsen of "messing" with him. Kantor told Thomsen he would shoot him if the police spotted him. He told Thomsen to drive carefully so as not to attract attention. They went about seven miles north of St. Cloud when Kantor told him to stop and ordered him to get in the trunk. There were three eighty-pound sacks of salt in the trunk that had to be removed before Thomsen could get in. Thomsen had only a sweatshirt, jeans and boots in the subzero weather. Kantor drove around for a few minutes. Thomsen could tell that he would speed up and then slow down. He assumed they were on rural roads. Kantor had said something about getting a different vehicle. Thomsen said he feared that Kantor would "dump his car" in a remote area and leave him to freeze to death.

Thirty-one year-old Nancy Wiggin of the Benton County Sheriff's Office began her assigned shift at 3:30 p.m. that day. She was aware Klinefelter had been shot and that law enforcement was looking for an older model white pickup truck with three occupants. She was directed to sit stationary at an intersection and watch for the pickup. She was sitting at the intersection when a radio message was broadcast that the pickup had been abandoned and a hostage was taken in his vehicle, a 1994 Ford Thunderbird. The color and license was given.

Wiggin saw what she believed to be the suspect vehicle going south at one of the cross streets of her assigned intersection. It was about one-half mile away, so she started to catch up to it without lights or siren to verify if it was the vehicle. She was able to get close enough to get a partial license plate and believed it to be the one they were seeking. As she was getting on the radio to report the car and her location, the Thunderbird pulled over and stopped. She had not activated lights or siren to have him pull over. She then turned on her light bar.

Kantor got out of the car and started walking toward her. Wiggin started getting out of her squad and noticed that Kantor had a gun in his hand. She was too far out of the car to use her radio so she tried her lapel microphone. She was in an area where the radio did not work. She crouched behind her opened door and shouted at Kantor to "Stop! Drop the weapon." Kantor began walking toward the squad with the gun to his side. When he got to the rear of the Thunderbird, he brought it up to his right temple.

Kantor refused to put the gun down and continued walking toward her. As he approached her, she moved back to the rear of her squad. He kept coming and she backed away to keep the car between her and Kantor. She continued backing up until she was just about back to her original spot by her open driver's door. She was now on the opposite side of the hood of the car across from him. She could clearly see him from the lights of the squad. She had been giving commands for him to drop the gun and now saw the gun pointed at her. She fired her Smith and Wesson .45-caliber pistol once, and Kantor fell to the pavement. She approached him and kicked the gun away from him. She then returned to the squad and called in what had just occurred. That call was at 10:02 p.m.

Sauk Rapids Police Officer Brian Novak was the first to arrive. Wiggins yelled at him to call for an ambulance. She could tell that Kantor was shot in the chest, but he still had a pulse. She then heard banging from the truck of the Thunderbird. She took cover and waited for other officers to arrive. They provided cover as she approached the trunk. She shouted to determine if anyone was in the trunk. She heard someone answer. She asked,

"Who are you?" and the response was "the owner." After checking the interior of the car, the key was used to open the truck and a happy Thomsen raised his hands.

Ederhoff and Roering were arrested at 10:13 p.m. hiding under a deck not far from where Kantor abducted Thomsen. Besides Kantor's .380-caliber pistol, two other weapons were recovered. One was a .30-caliber Chinese Norinco pistol, and the other was a .45 double-barreled FMJ .45-caliber derringer. The .380-caliber pistol was the weapon used to shoot Klinefelter. Ederhoof and Roering were later convicted of their part in the robbery and murder of Klinefelter and remain in Minnesota prisons. The anticipated released date for both is early 2009.

Klinefelter was the 178th Minnesota officer to die in the line of duty. On Friday, February 2, 1996, in minus-thirty degree weather, over two thousand friends, relatives, and law-enforcement officers attended his funeral. Kantor's funeral was the same day with two hundred attending.

Wiggin was cleared in the shooting. She has since left law enforcement.

XV

This shooting involves the death of the first female officer from Minneapolis. Around 7:00 p.m. on August 1, 2002, a 911 operator received a call from Cassandra Williams that her aunt, sixty-year-old Martha Donald, was threatening her and other residents at 1424 East 22nd Street with a gun. Donald's description and other pertinent information were given.

Officers Tammy Friestleben and Mark Madich went to talk to Williams. She initially told officers that Donald had been waving a gun but later told them that she never pulled out a weapon to show. She said that Donald had a heavy build and was wearing very tight clothing that showed the outline of the gun in her waistband. Williams said that Donald was heading to her home address of Horn Terrace at 15 West 31st Street, apartment 104. This building mainly housed senior citizens.

Officer Melissa Schmidt heard the radio transmissions regarding Donald and proceeded to Horn Terrace. Schmidt, a thirty-five-year-old officer, was trained to interact with people in crisis and was assigned to patrol the public housing units in Minneapolis. She also had worked with the deaf and hearing impaired for over two years in a program to help them understand how to protect themselves. The residents there knew and welcomed her.

Officers Sean McGinty and Michael Sanden located Donald's vehicle in the parking lot of Horn Terrace. They were informed that Donald was inside with Officer Schmidt. They went inside to meet with Schmidt. She showed them live .38-caliber rounds that she had removed from Donald's purse. Donald said Cassandra Williams had put the bullets in her purse to get her in trouble. All four of them left the building to go to Donald's Cadillac. She gave them permission to search the car. No weapon was found. Donald informed the officers that she urgently had to go to the bathroom inside the building. Schmidt told McGinty and Sanden to leave as Madich and Friestleben were almost there and could assist her.

Schmidt allowed Donald to enter the handicap stall of the two-stall restroom on the first floor of the building. When Friestleben arrived, she went to the restroom to check on the status. The door to the stall was being held partly open by Schmidt. Donald wanted to know who had joined them. Schmidt told her that it was another female officer. Donald tried to close the stall door. Schmidt, according to Friestleben's statement to investigators, told her, "Don't shut that door; we're used to watching people in the bathroom." Friestleben could only see Donald's feet beneath the walls of the stall.

Friestleben asked Schmidt if she had found a gun. Schmidt told her that they had searched the car and purse but had only found bullets in her purse. Schmidt then said, "Before I forget, let me give you these." Schmidt handed her the bullets found in Donald's purse. She left the restroom to show Madich the bullets. Madich indicated there had to be a gun somewhere if she had the bullets. Madich went back out to look in the car, but he could only look through the windows as it was locked.

Friestleben went back into the restroom. Schmidt told Donald to "hurry up." Donald asked to close the door. Schmidt again told her that the officers had to leave it open. Donald said, "I'm a sixty-year-old woman. You are going to have to give me more time." There was no confrontation, and neither raised their voices. Friestleben went back out to tell Madich that it would be a few more minutes and went immediately back in the room.

As she came back, she noticed that Donald was again trying to close the door. Schmidt said, "What are you doing?"

Donald said, "I'm wiping do-do off my shoes." Schmidt said, "We don't care if there is do-do on your shoes. You need to hurry up." Friestleben saw Donald rustling around with her hands on the floor. Schmidt rushed into the stall yelling "show me your hands." Friestleben then saw Donald sitting on the stool holding a black revolver with wooden grips in her right hand. Both officers began backing up, but did not have room to go anywhere.

Friestleben saw Donald grab Schmidt by the shirt and pull her toward her. She then saw a bright muzzle flash and the sound of a gun firing as she fell back. She thought she had been shot. She heard additional shots.

Officer Madich was in the adjoining men's restroom when he heard the shots. He raced immediately to the door of the women's restroom and notified dispatch that shots had been fired. He requested assistance. Madich went into the restroom and saw Friestleben on the floor by the sinks. They both then entered the stall and saw Schmidt holding her lower abdomen with her hand and holding cover on Donald with her gun in her right. Donald was seated on the toilet. She had been shot and her arms were hanging by her side. Madich covered Donald as Friestleben assisted Schmidt out of the stall. Schmidt sat on the floor waiting for the ambulance. Schmidt and Donald were taken by ambulance to Hennepin County Medical Center. Both went to surgery, but neither of them survived the night. The cause of death of both of them was a gunshot wound.

Investigation by the Hennepin County Sheriff's Office determined that Donald fired two rounds from her .38-caliber Taurus revolver. It was also determined that the weapon had purchased by Donald in Illinois in 1990.

It is not known for certain, but it is believed that Donald had the weapon located deep in her crotch or buttock area. There was fecal matter on the weapon. Schmidt fired her 9-mm pistol five times. Schmidt's wound entered just under her protective vest in her lower right abdominal area. The bullet traveled in an upward direction from left to right. Donald's blood alcohol was .24.

Friestleben did not fire her weapon. She had powder burns and stippling across her cheek. Had Donald's first shot been two inches to the left, Friestleben would not have been alive to give an account of the shooting. It is not known if Schmidt searched Donald.

Donald was raised in Chicago by an aunt after she lost both of her parents by the age of twelve. She moved to the Twin Cities after retiring from the City of Chicago where she had worked in a clerical position and as a truck driver from 1972 to 1992. She lived in the southern suburb of Rosemount in 1993. Police records in Rosemount showed thirty-four documented contacts with her that included medical calls and domestic disputes. She spent four days in the Dakota County jail after being convicted of drunk driving in 1996. The Minnesota State Trooper wrote in his report that she was "very belligerent, yelling and cursing" at him. She filed two civil court cases regarding that arrest, claiming to be a victim. Both cases were dismissed. She was also arrested for disorderly conduct in September 1999. She was found guilty.

Melissa Schmidt was born and raised in Wisconsin. She was a starter on her basketball team for four years. She was the most valuable player for three years and still holds her school record for the most points scored. She went to a technical college and graduated with a police science degree in 1987. After working for two small Wisconsin law enforcement agencies, she entered the Marine Corps. Upon completion of four years in the Marines she joined the Minneapolis Police Department in March 1996.

Rumors in the community had Schmidt being killed by "friendly fire." Ballistic examination confirmed that Schmidt was killed by a .38-caliber round. Friestleben had not fired her weapon, and it was not a .38-caliber. It was determined by the Hennepin County Attorney's Office that the matter not be presented to a grand jury as both had died in the incident.

XVI

This is the last of the 110 fatal shootings in my twenty-five years of research. Even though no officer was killed, it was one of the more violent. It appears that citizens are becoming much more aggressive with knives and guns toward officers and causing more injuries. Monday, August 1, 2005, was the second anniversary of the shooting death of Minneapolis officer Melissa Schmidt. A message had been sent across squad computers reminding the officers of the anniversary and for everyone to be safe.

At 8:17 a.m., a citizen driving down Lyndale Avenue on the near south side of Minneapolis called 911 on his cell phone saying that he had just seen a man pushing a screaming lady inside a check cashing business. The caller called back and said that he parked to observe what was happening. He heard the woman scream, "Get out." He could see that the man had dragged the woman into a corner of the store. He told 911 that he would let them know if the man left the business. He saw a police squad approaching him in his rear-view mirror. The squad did not have lights or siren activated. The officer parked the squad just out of sight of the building, and the caller saw the officer exit with his shotgun.

The caller watched the officer crouch down near the corner of the building. The caller went to the officer, identified himself and told him what he had seen. The officer told the caller to get behind his squad. The witness said that the guy was in the store then "bolts out the front door and starts taking off north toward Franklin Avenue and around the corner." He saw other officers responding and heard gunshots. He did not see what had happened. He went to the business and saw the woman who had been abducted standing in the doorway. He asked her if she was okay. She appeared to be visibly shaken and traumatized. She asked him to call police.

Minneapolis Officer Charles Herzog, a forty-eight-year-old veteran of the department, was working his normal 6:30 a.m. to 4:30 p.m. shift. He was investigating a burglary when he heard a radio dispatch of a robbery of a business in progress. The original call was given to Officer Jason Walters who was working a single-person squad. Herzog told dispatch to put the burglary call in "pending" and he would respond also. When Herzog came to the area, he saw Walters to the front and side of the business. He radioed him and said he would go around to the back and check for a rear exit.

Herzog parked away from the street so that the offender would not see him. He went around to the back side of the building. There were several entrances to the building to check. He heard shouting and turned to see Walters running north on Lyndale. He saw the suspect running west on Franklin Avenue from Lyndale. Herzog joined in the chase after the suspect. Herzog saw another marked squad driving west on Franklin at a high rate of speed. The squad pulled in front of the suspect, cutting him off. The suspect, later identified as forty-seven-year-old Ricky Redin, turned and began running back toward him at an angle. Herzog got closer and pulled his weapon. He told the Redin to stop, but he kept running. Redin stumbled and fell to the ground. Herzog holstered his weapon and ran to him as he was trying to get up. Herzog fell on him. Herzog knocked him on his back and pinned his outstretched arms down with his knees as he straddled his torso. Herzog was attempting to gain control of his left hand when he heard someone yell, "He's got a knife. He's got a knife." He could not see the person shouting, but he thought it sounded like Officer Jesse Garcia.

Herzog was starting to push himself up when he heard another male voice from behind him shout, "Shoot him, shoot him." He did not recognize the voice, but at the same time he felt something on his left arm and saw the barrel of a shotgun pointed at the suspect. As Herzog was pushing off Redin, he heard the blast of a shotgun and felt something on his left arm. The suspect moved about one and one-half feet as it appeared the shotgun blast hit him in the chest.

Herzog continued to stand up and then, for the first time, saw something silver in Redin's right hand. He was swinging both of his arms. Herzog realized it was a knife. Redin was trying to get up, and Herzog heard another shotgun blast. Herzog removed his handgun and saw the knife on the pavement about twelve feet from Redin, who was not moving. He then heard Walters say something about being stabbed and bleeding. Walters went down to the pavement. Immediately he saw Garcia and another Minneapolis officer attending to Walters. Herzog walked backed to Redin and saw that a Minneapolis motorcycle officer (he could tell by the helmet) was pointing his handgun at the suspect. Herzog the felt something warm on his left thigh and realized that he was bleeding. He then saw blood running on his boot and knew that he had been stabbed. He was attended to by numerous officers at the scene. The two officers were next to each other on the pavement when the ambulance arrived. Walters was transported first and another ambulance took Herzog. Herzog did not fire his weapon.

Officer Jason Walters related that he was in his squad when he got the call of a robbery in progress. He went to the area of the business and took his .12-gauge shotgun as he exited the car. He requested a call to the business and was told there was no answer. A person approached him and told him he was the 911 caller and had not seen anyone exit the building. Herzog arrived and said he would go the back of the building. Walters then moved up closer and peered into the business. A man (Redin) quickly ran out of the door north on Lyndale. He called for him to stop and radioed his status. He began chasing Redin and saw Herzog join him in the chase.

Walters caught up to Redin as he attempted to cut through some bushes and shrubs in front of an apartment on Franklin Avenue. Walters stopped and pointed his shotgun at Redin. He ordered him to the ground or he would shoot. Redin told him something to the effect of "Shoot me" or "Do it." Redin had his hands extended to his sides as if he were waiting for Walters to shoot him. Walters did not see a weapon. With his hands still on the shotgun, Walters used it to try to knock him to the ground. The blow did not affect him and merely glanced off his left shoulder. He started to run past Walters, and Walters swung the shotgun, hitting Redin in the back. He stumbled as he was trying to maintain his balance and fell in the middle of Franklin Avenue. Walters ran to him. Redin was sitting on the ground. Walters straddled him and was attempting to control him until another officer could assist him. Walters saw a knife in Redin's hand.

Walters was stabbed in the back of his right thigh, but he was not aware of it. He moved away from Redin. When he turned back around, he saw Herzog on top of him. Someone shouted that Redin had a knife, and he saw Herzog get stabbed in his left thigh area. Walters ran up to the two of them struggling. He placed the barrel of the shotgun on Redin's chest and pulled the trigger.

Redin curled up into a fetal position and rolled to his right side. Walters advanced to handcuff him. As he got closer, Redin quickly turned and started getting up. Redin looked directly at Walters and still had his knife in his right hand. Walters fired again and saw Redin fall directly on his back. After shooting his second round, he backed up and tripped over a police motorcycle. He looked toward Redin and saw a uniformed officer firing a handgun toward him. Walters used his portable radio to call for an ambulance.

Officer Garcia and other officers tended to him. While waiting for the ambulances to arrive, Walters recalled being at the scene of Melissa Schmidt's shooting two years before. He recalled comforting her and telling her that everything would be okay. He did not believe that her wound was life threatening. She died during surgery. He had doubts about his own survival because of his loss of blood. He told Garcia not to let him "bleed out and die on the street."

The last officer involved in this shooting was thirty-three-year-old John Engle. He was riding his department motorcycle to an area west of the robbery call. He heard the call. However, he did not initially respond. He was stopped at a red light when he heard that a chase was in progress. He changed direction to assist. When Engle approached the area, he saw a Minneapolis officer (Herzog) knock Redin to the street. As he got closer, it appeared that Redin was in a fist fight with Herzog as he could see his arms swinging. He saw Herzog roll away from Redin and could see that he had a black and silver knife in his right hand. He then saw Walters fire his shotgun in close proximity of Redin's chest. Engle came to a stop on his motorcycle and saw Redin trying to get up again after being shot once. He pushed his cycle away. As he dismounted, he pulled his .45-caliber Sig Sauer handgun and fired five shots at Redin's chest. While he was firing, Walters fired once again. Redin was down and not moving. He looked and saw Walters' right hand and arm was covered with blood. Walters radioed that shots had been fired and ambulances were needed.

It was all over by 8:23 a.m. Redin lay dead on Franklin Avenue and two officers were taken to the hospital with severe stab wounds. Although unknown at the time, Redin was a fugitive from Anoka County. Redin had pleaded guilty in January 2005 to sexually molesting the four-year-old daughter of a woman he knew. He had spent one year in jail before a plea agreement was negotiated. He was released with a variety of conditions pending his scheduled sentence of April 1, 2005. Redin failed to appear for a court ordered psychological evaluation and sentencing. A warrant was issued. Efforts to locate him had been unsuccessful. Between 1991 and 1997 he had been convicted of criminal sexual conduct and several drunken driving offenses. In the early 1980s he had two felony sexually related charges and one of fleeing a police officer. In December 2003, he served less than a year on a drug conviction.

Officers looked in the area for a vehicle or accomplice. They found nothing until August 3. A stolen Harley Davidson motorcycle was recovered near the scene in a parking lot. A key fitting the motorcycle had been found in Redin's pocket during autopsy. Investigation determined that the motorcycle was stolen from someone who knew Redin's girlfriend. The owner suspected Redin when it was stolen on July 14.

The female victim at a check-cashing business saw Redin (he was a stranger to her) loitering in front of the store when she came to open at 8:00 a.m. She waited for him to walk away before she started to open the door. He rushed in behind her as she entered. He called her by name and told her to use the code to enter the inside door. She was having problems entering the code. Redin became angry and demanded to know what she was doing wrong. He said, "I thought the code was 36-36-36." It was the code, but she was going to enter another code that would cause a silent alarm to be activated. Redin then hit her, causing her to fall to the floor. He pulled out a knife and showed it to her. He told her he had just seen the police. He grabbed her cell phone and keys. He ran out the door. She did not see him again, nor did she witness the shooting. It never was determined how he knew her name or the code to the store.

Walters and Herzog recovered from their wounds and returned to duty. Engle and Walters were cleared by a Hennepin County grand jury.

XVII

Around 7:40 p.m. on Tuesday, May 12, 1998, Saint Paul Police Department dispatch received a call of an assault in a residence on the city's near east side. The caller related that an Asian male wearing a white shirt and black pants had stabbed a person.

Brad Schultz, a thirty-three-year-old canine officer, was the first officer to arrive at the residence. Medics and fire personnel had arrived and were entering the house just as Schultz pulled up. There were numerous individuals, including a female victim, in the living room when Schultz entered. As he entered, he noticed a person matching the description given over the radio by dispatch hurrying towards the kitchen. A fireman told Schultz that the individual was acting nervous and left upon seeing him.

Schultz went into the kitchen and did not see anyone. He noticed that the security chain on the back door was swinging back and forth. Schultz removed his .40 caliber handgun from his holster and ran out into the backyard. He had a flashlight in his other hand as he ran to the alley. He saw the Asian male, later identified as thirty-year-old Teng Xiong, standing by a gray four-door automobile. Schultz called for Xiong not to move. Xiong looked directly at Schultz and quickly jumped into the driver's seat of the car.

Schultz believed that Xiong locked the door so he hit the window with his flashlight. The window did not immediately break. He then tried the door and it opened. Unfortunately, Xiong had started the car and was trying to put it in gear. Schultz hit Xiong in the face with the flashlight in an attempt to distract him so he could pull him from the car.

Xiong put the car in reverse and accelerated quickly. Schultz was caught between the door and the side of the car. Schultz was dragged backward and slammed into a garage door across the alley. He was pinned between the vehicle and the garage door. The car began to accelerate again and Schultz believed that his life was in jeopardy. He reached up and fired his weapon into the side window of the car. The car continued forward at a high rate of speed, striking another garage in the alley.

Schultz was able to break free after shooting his weapon. He notified dispatch that he had been run over and shots had been fired. Schultz moved behind a garage for cover until other officers arrived. When it appeared safe, medics approached the car where it appeared Xiong was slumped over the steering wheel. Schultz was transported to a nearby hospital with injuries to his arm and legs.

Xiong was also rushed to the hospital with a gunshot wound to his head. He died the following day. Xiong had a suspended driver's license and was on probation for a narcotics arrest in Hennepin County when the shooting occurred. His wife, the initial assault victim prompting the call to 911, was treated and recovered from a knife wound. Schultz was treated for his injuries and eventually returned to work. He subsequently left Saint Paul Police to become an enforcement officer with the Minnesota Department of Natural Resources.

A Ramsey County grand jury returned a no bill on July 15, 1998.

Chapter Nine

I'm Okay, You're Okay
aka Emotionally
Disturbed Individuals

I

Emotionally disturbed individuals are a serious problem in any city. The public and media have all kinds of solutions for the police, but are the solutions always practical? Unfortunately, police in Saint Paul had to use deadly force regarding such a person on Saturday, September 22, 1990, only four days after another fatal shooting by Saint Paul police.

This particular incident began shortly after 4:00 p.m. from a call to police that thirty-four-year-old James Ludwig had been living behind a fast food restaurant for several days and was talking "crazy stuff about Vietnam." The caller was concerned about the safety of his children and other children in the area.

Officer Denise Hossalla was the first to arrive. In an area next to the restaurant was a motorcycle partially covered with a black tarp. Hossalla drove across the curb in her semi-marked squad. Ludwig took several steps toward her. She got out of her vehicle and began walking toward where he was. She immediately noticed words written in the dirt near his "living area."

First written in the dirt so anyone approaching him could see was "+ your choice." Following that was "RB" and "constitution." The last was the outline of a stop sign and the word "stop" inside the outline. Hossalla stopped at the beginning of the writing and saw that the tarp over the motorcycle was also fastened to a tree, offering shelter for someone sitting under it. There was also a tin cup and an open twelve-pack of beer.

Hossalla asked Ludwig if this was his temporary residence. Ludwig responded that it was his "domain." Ludwig emphasized the word "domain" clearly and precisely. He invited Hossalla to come in and sit down. Ludwig was approximately six feet tall, two hundred pounds, with brown hair and a full beard. He had a blue cloth tied around his head and was wearing mirrored sunglasses. He wore a blue poncho over a brown leather jacket, blue jeans, shoes and leather gloves. He began chattering about nothing relating to why the police were there. She told him people were concerned about him as the weather was beginning to get colder. He told her that was the reason he built the tarp over a tree. He asked her if she wanted to see his identification. He pulled off his right glove, dropped it to the ground and reached inside his poncho.

Officer Richard Munoz pulled up to the scene in his marked squad. Ludwig became excited and began saying over and over that he was not going to have two cops in his domain. Ludwig told him to stop as he was close enough to him. Hossalla asked to see his identification. He pulled a Minnesota driver's license from his wallet and went toward Munoz as if he were going to hand it to him. Ludwig then made an aggressive sidestep, similar to a martial arts move, toward Munoz. Both officers jumped back from him. Ludwig then handed the license to Munoz.

Ludwig put his right hand under the poncho, and Munoz asked him to keep them out where they could see them. Ludwig said, "No." Both officers requested him to show his right hand. He told them he did not have to do anything they asked. He started backing up into the nearby Phalen Center parking lot. It appeared as though he had a strong grip on something. Suddenly, he stopped and took a step toward Munoz. Hossalla then sprayed a chemical agent at Ludwig. It had no effect.

Ludwig continued walking backward toward the Phalen Tennis Club at the Center. He was constantly looking around in a rapid fashion. Two marked squads arrived and parked in the Phalen Center parking lot. Fifty-one year-old Charles Anderson and thirty-three-year-old Joe Strong were the arriving officers. Ludwig then pulled out a fixed-blade hunting knife. He took a crouched position, with the knife in his right hand. Hossalla and Munoz drew their weapons and called for Ludwig to put the knife down. He told them he did not have to and they could not take it from him. He continued backing up. Other officer arriving on scene attempted to convince him to drop the knife. They had him surrounded on three sides. Ludwig took his only means of escape by running into some nearby woods.

The officers pursued Ludwig to the top of a hill on a nearby street. He stopped and told the officers that he was tired, but he still maintained his defensive fighting stance holding the knife. The officers had him surrounded at this point.

Hossalla continued to call Ludwig by his first name and requested him to put the knife down. He responded that the police would have to kill him. A chemical agent was again sprayed at him. Again, it had no effect, and he turned the knife over, holding the tip between his thumb and index finger. He brought his arm back as if he intended to throw it at the officers. He was asked to put the knife down and said, "I don't have to; it's legal." He appeared "hyped up" and was looking around rapidly. Hossalla noticed several adults and children about fifty yards away. Ludwig looked at them and started to sprint in their direction.

Sergeant Anderson ran after him and continued to call for him to drop the knife. Anderson felt that Ludwig was quickly getting too close to the bystanders. When he saw he had no one in his line of fire, he fired his 9-mm handgun. At the same time Strong, standing next to Anderson, fired his .12-gauge shotgun once. Ludwig fell to the ground. Hossalla called for an ambulance. When paramedics arrived and examined him, they pronounced him deceased.

The investigation following the shooting determined that Ludwig was a paranoid schizophrenic. This diagnosis was determined sometime after he was in a serious vehicle accident at age nineteen. Ludwig had been previously hospitalized for his mental illness. He had been arrested by Saint Paul police in 1976 for aggravated assault and in 1977 for possession of a disabling chemical.

Sergeant Anderson and Officer Strong were cleared by a Ramsey County grand jury. Ludwig's mother filed a lawsuit in1993 against the officers and the City of Saint Paul. Subsequently, on July 26, 1995, the city approved a payment of seventy-five thousand as a settlement to Merilyn Ludwig.

II

On Saturday, October 12, 1991, at approximately 3:00 a.m., thirty-five year-old Theresa Lindquist committed a robbery at the Colonial Amoco Station at 9001 Lyndale Avenue in the City of Bloomington. She had gone into the station while the sole employee, Tom Ortenblad, was outside "reading the pumps." When he completed his outside tasks, he came back inside and offered her a free cup of coffee. She did not move, so Ortenblad went from the cashier's area to the coffeemaker. He poured a cup of coffee for each of them. He went behind the counter and exchanged small talk. He suddenly noticed that Lindquist was holding a paper bag in her left hand. She had a grasp on the bag as if there were a gun contained in the paper bag and was pointing it at him. She announced, "This is a stick-up, give me all your money." Ortenblad did not believe her and told her that she was on video. He asked her if she really had a gun. She said, "Yes, do you want me to show it to you?" She pointed it again, and Ortenblad distinctly believed that the object appeared to be a gun with the paper bag twisted around its outline. As he felt his life was in jeopardy, he removed the paper money from the till in one pile and gave it to her.

Lindquist folded it with one hand and put it in her pants pocket. There was $263 in denominations of twenty, five, and one. He asked her if he could close the glass opening to the cashier's area. She said that was okay. He closed it and called 911 to report the robbery. She remained in front of him pointing the bag at him. He gave a perfect description of her as she stood there until he completed the call. She then turned and exited, running away in an easterly direction.

About that same time, an off-duty Saint Paul police officer who had grown up in the area saw Lindquist running. He thought it was strange for someone to run toward a commercial area at that time of night. He pulled over to look around, and Bloomington officer Edward Hanson drove up. Hanson had responded to the scene fifty-five seconds after the robbery call went out. The Saint Paul officer told him what he had seen.

Other responding officers joined Hanson and began searching for Lindquist on foot. Hanson observed her running behind Twin City Auto Body located on 90th Street. She slowed to a walk, and Hanson was able to approach her. He called for her to stop. She turned toward him, and he saw her grasping what appeared to be a paper bag in one hand. He identified himself as the "police" and told her to "halt." Officer Phil DeGia pulled up along the east side of the auto body building in an effort to cut off one avenue of escape. Lindquist did not see him, as she had her back to him. Based upon the 911 call and observing the bag in her hand, both officers believed she had a gun. DeGia initially contemplated tackling her, as she was giving her attention to Hanson, but she suddenly became aware of his presence and turned in his direction, pointing the bag at him. He also gave verbal commands to her.

Sgt. Leonard Anderson, a forty-three-year-old officer with twenty years' experience, arrived and took a position on the west side of the building. He was using a metal dumpster as cover while he tried communicating with Lindquist. All three officers were armed and pointing their weapons at her while trying to convince her to put the bag down. DeGia and Hanson had pistols, and Anderson had a .12-gauge shotgun. Radio logs clearly indicate that the standoff existed prior to 3:13:48 a.m. and beyond 3:15:20 a.m. Sergeant Anderson called for an ambulance, Code 3, at 3:15:45 a.m.

At some point only moments before 3:15:45 a.m., Lindquist broke the standoff by charging toward Sergeant Anderson. Her approach, with her arms erect and pointing the bag at him, made Anderson feel that he was unable to remain safely behind the dumpster. Anderson fired at Lindquist when she was only ten feet away from his position. DeGia discharged his weapon at her as he felt she was going to shoot Anderson. Three other officers at the scene heard the shots and described them as being almost simultaneous, with some saying they were not sure if one or two shots had been fired. Officer Hanson did not fire his weapon due to possible crossfire.

Lindquist did not have a weapon. She had a hair brush in the bag. Unfortunately, Lindquist had some mental illness concerns and possibly used police to assist her in a suicide. No one was able to determine the reason for her behavior that night. A Hennepin County grand jury returned a no bill on January 28, 1992.

III

This shooting has to be one of the strangest ones reported here. It began with a call to St. Cloud police on Tuesday, May 11, 1999, around 7:45 p.m. The caller stated that an individual was acting suspiciously at 608 Raymond in that city. The caller lived at 612 Raymond and said her neighbor was covered in blood and acting strangely. She said her neighbor Kevin had come over to her house with blood all over his hands. He was carrying a Bible and said he had just sacrificed his dog to God. He turned and walked back to his house.

The call went out to Squads 41 and 42 to check on the welfare of a person. Officer Jason Hanson, a newly hired officer in training, his training Officer Kevin Kutzman and Officer Tom Schlieman responded about the same time. Schlieman spoke to the caller. She gave the same information she had given to the dispatcher. She also added that Kevin wanted to baptize one of her children in blood. She said he was acting "really weird." She saw that Kevin had gone inside the north entrance to his house and had probably gone to the upstairs apartment where he stayed.

Schlieman proceeded to 608 Raymond to the door on the north side. Kutzman and Hanson were standing outside the house. There were two vehicles on the north side of the house. One was a smaller blue car and the other a Jeep Cherokee. Schlieman walked by them to get to the door. Kutzman and Hanson came to where Schlieman was standing on the top step at the door. Kutzman stated he found blood on the ground. Schlieman noticed there were bloody handprints on the door and pointed them out to the other two officers.

The neighbor said Kevin lived upstairs, so Schlieman opened the storm door, left to right outwards. He opened the door with his left hand, as he had taken his Glock .40-caliber handgun out of his holster. He held the weapon down his right leg as he did not know what to expect with all of the blood present. He could see stairs going up and assumed there would be a door at the top of the stairs which would go to Kevin's apartment.

Kutzman and Hanson moved to Schlieman's left side. Schlieman held the door open with his right shoulder and shouted, "Kevin."

He heard a response of, "Yeah." Schlieman called back that he was with the police department and wanted him to come down to him so they could talk. Kevin said he would come down. Kevin came into Schlieman's view, and he could see he had what looked like dried blood on both of his hands which were hanging down to the side of his legs. His hands were completely covered, and because it was becoming dusk it made them look very dark. The man, later identified as thirty-three-year-old Kevin Hartung, began coming down the steps. Hartung came down four or five steps when Schlieman noticed something sticking out of his chest. As Hartung got closer, Schlieman recognized it as the handle of a large folding knife. It was sticking straight out of his chest through his shirt in the area of his heart. There was blood around the knife on the shirt.

Schlieman immediately called for an ambulance on his portable microphone on his shoulder. He believed Hartung was bleeding and that the knife in the wound was helping to stop some of the flow. Schlieman called out to Hartung to sit on a step. Hartung did sit down and was far enough away to be at eye level with Schlieman, who was standing. Schlieman told him, "Whatever you do, don't pull the knife out of your chest." Hartung then reached out and grabbed the knife handle with both hands. He pulled the knife out. Schlieman saw that it was about a four- to six-inch blade. It appeared to be sharp and was covered with blood. Schlieman said, "It was like it isn't real."

Schlieman started to back up and said, "Kevin, put the knife down."

Hartung said, "Okay," and placed the knife on the steps between his feet. Schlieman asked him to back up a couple of steps as he wanted to secure the knife. Just as Schlieman was going to get the knife, Hartung said, "I don't think so" and reached down and grabbed it. He stood up and came running down the stairs yelling and screaming like "ahhhh." The knife was over his head, and he was making slashing motions at Schlieman.

Schlieman backed off the steps and ran into Kutzman. Kutzman backed away and went east along the side of the house. Hanson, who was in front of Kutzman, did the same. When Schlieman came off the steps, he went to the west along the Jeep in the driveway. Schlieman kept backing up, and Hartung came at him, continuing to make slashing motions. He was still screaming some kind of "war cry."

Schlieman backed up into the car that was in the driveway. He hit the front bumper with the back of his legs. He ended up tripping and falling flat on his back on the top of the hood of the car. Hartung continued screaming and coming at him. Schlieman described Hartung having "a look in his eye, he was, like a madman, and he was coming at me, he had an angry look." It appeared Hartung was about to reach him as he had "nowhere to go." He raised his Glock and fired once. That shot caused Hartung to "flinch." It seemed like Hartung pulled away for a split second but then continued shouting and coming at him. Schlieman fired four more rounds. Hartung went down to the ground on the right side of the car, and Schlieman rolled off to the left. Schlieman believed his first shot fired at Hartung was from about eight feet away and the last one about four feet. Schlieman told investigators he could not fire when he first exited the house as Kutzman would have been in a crossfire.

All three officers went around to where Hartung lay face down on the ground. He was moving slightly. They could not find the knife. Schlieman told Kutzman to cover him while he handcuffed Hartung. Schlieman holstered his weapon and went to handcuff him. Kutzman called, "Look out Tom, he's got the knife in his hand." Schlieman saw the knife in his right hand near the side of his head. Schlieman "squatted" down on top of his neck, grabbed his wrist and shook it. The knife fell to the ground, and he proceeded to handcuff him behind his back. Hartung was removed from the scene by ambulance and later died at a local hospital.

This was another case not decided by a grand jury. Stearns County Attorney Mike Jessee said the shooting was justified and Schlieman's use of deadly force was "reasonable and necessary." Jessee also said, "The evidence was so conclusive that a grand jury wasn't needed to make that determination."

IV

This is a sad case, and it changed the training of Minneapolis police officers handling such situations. This started with a call to 911 at 10:39 p.m. on Monday, June 12, 2000. The caller, apartment manager Harvey Baughman, told 911 that a woman in the building, a Jewish historian, was mentally ill "every once in a while." He asked for a mental health crisis team. However, he was told there was no team available and police would be sent. (Powell, J. [2000, June 15] *Star Tribune*, page B1).

The woman, forty-nine-year-old Barbara Schneider, had been bothering neighbors for a few days because they heard her shouting about the end of the world and terrorists and babbling nonsense. Seven years before this event, in 1993, Schneider had been involved in a similar incident. Police were not called on that occasion. The manager of her apartment called her brother in Massachusetts, who, in turn, called two social workers. When the social workers arrived, she had a butcher knife in her hand. She was talked out of hurting herself and was stabilized with medication.

Schneider had been diagnosed with bipolar disorder. She had mood swings that went from elation to depression. Apparently, Schneider, who grew up in the affluent Boston suburb of Belmont, came to Minneapolis after she received a master's degree from the University of Michigan. Her mental illness, which first surfaced in college, caused many problems in her career. Rather than excelling in her chosen field of library science, she usually had clerical positions far below her intellectual ability.

Officer Jeffrey Parker and his partner John Hawes were the first officers to arrive. They were met by a woman at 3129 Holmes Avenue South. She told them it was more than a music complaint because the music had stopped and only loud static was coming from an open window in Schneider's apartment across the alley. The woman told police that Schneider had previously been in the window yelling, screaming, and waving her hands. She had also been playing loud religious music.

Parker and Hawes were able to enter the apartment building via an unlocked rear door that faced the alley. They eventually ascended to the third floor. As they arrived on the floor, a woman came out of apartment 303 and pointed to 304. She told the officers the address was 3120 Hennepin Avenue, as the officers had responded to the complainant on Holmes Avenue. The officers wanted to be sure that any other officers came to the correct location.

Officer Parker checked the door to apartment 304 and found that he was able to turn the knob. He knocked on the door and called out, "Police." There was no response. He slowly opened the door and looked into the apartment. As the door was opening, he observed a middle-aged woman (Schneider) standing approximately eight feet in front of him. She began screaming something about Satan and then brought out in her right hand what appeared to be a large serrated knife with a black handle. She extended the knife over her head and screamed. She then said laughingly, "I see they sent the Satan squad tonight."

A neighbor later told investigators that she heard, "Get out. Leave me alone, Satan squad."

Parker backed away, pulling the door partially closed, and told Hawes that she had a knife. Hawes shouted for him to close the door. He pulled it shut and held on to the knob with both hands; he knew the door was not locked. Schneider was trying to pull it open from the other side. She continued screaming about Satan and was banging on the door.

Parker continued holding the door as they kicked at the door several times trying to get her away from the other side. Despite the attempts by the officers, Schneider was holding the door so it was moving only two to three inches. Officer Hawes grabbed Parker's chemical spray and sprayed a steady stream through a one-inch gap in an attempt to get her away from the door. They could hear her coughing from the other side. The door of apartment 305 across the hall opened. A woman asked the officers if they needed more chemical spray; she had a small container in her right hand. They told her no and asked her to go back into her apartment.

Approximately one minute later, Squad 510 arrived with Officers Sarah Saarela and Geoffrey Johnson. Parker could not hear Schneider behind the door, so he opened it a few inches. He saw there was a short hallway directly in front of them, and Schneider could not be seen. About ten feet in front of them was a closed door. Saarela said she saw movement under it. A bathroom was to the immediate left and the kitchen to the right. Behind the kitchen area appeared to be the living room. All of those areas were cleared by the officers.

They officers believed that Schneider had to be in the room, probably a bedroom, with the closed door. Squad 524, with Officers William Palmer and Bob Illetschko, also arrived. Parker told the other five officers to back out to the hallway to the entrance of the apartment. He said he would go back in and try to kick the door open. He said that if he opened it, he would run back to the entrance.

He was able to kick the door open. He ran back to the entrance and took a position on the left side of the door behind Saarela and Hawes. Schneider was about three feet inside the bedroom, still holding the knife. She had some sort of covering over her nose and mouth, apparently reacting to the chemical spray. She was still shouting about their being Satan's officers.

All six officers had their weapons drawn and watched as Schneider waved the knife over her head. The officers continued to order her to put down the knife. Parker was in a crouched position, with Saarela and Hawes just ahead of him. On the right side of the entry were Palmer, Illetschko, and Johnson. Schneider came rapidly toward the door. When Schneider was about four to five feet from the door, Saarela and Palmer fired their 9-mm handguns at her a total of five times. The other officers did not fire due to the confined space and possibility of hitting another officer.

Dispatch was immediately notified of "shots fired" by an officer, and an ambulance, Code 3, was requested. The officers began rendering first aid and did so until medical responders arrived. Schneider was pronounced dead at Hennepin County Medical Center. An autopsy determined that she had been struck by four possible fatal shots.

When crime scene investigators searched Schneider's apartment, they found items indicative of someone with a mental illness. There were writings on the walls over the doors reading "AIDS, SNOOKER-KING, TOUGH KID." There were numerous books scattered on the floor, and the bed was unmade. Some of the book titles were: *Facing Evil, The Adult Children of Alcoholics Syndrome, Diet and Nutrition, Why Me? Why Anyone?, Children Who Hate,* and *Death in Life.* On top of her coffee pot where the water is poured was the word "PLASMA." On the bottom of her left foot in red ink was written "stuckroblastic, anemia."

A Hennepin County Grand Jury returned a no bill in February 2001. A lawsuit was filed by her brother James Schneider in June, 2003, claiming that the officers used excessive force and that the Minneapolis Police Department had not developed policies for dealing with people in mental health crisis. The lawsuit was dismissed with no award being given. Officer Saarela left the department. Palmer is a still on the department and has been trained as a member of the Crisis Intervention Team, as have many other Minneapolis officers, to assist officers responding to those having mental health issues.

V

This shooting had a history that began two months prior to the actual event. On January 22, 2002, Detective Dan Kirby of the Hennepin County Sheriff's Office was reviewing reports from the Hennepin County Government Center's private security office. This was one of his many assignments. A report caught his eye about a possible terrorist threat that had occurred on January 21 at 9:06 a.m. An unknown person came to the guard desk and placed a pink envelope containing a letter on the desk. On the outside of the envelope written in red ink were the words, "The last decision came from God." Security officer Owen Rice started opening the letter when he noticed the person leaving. Rice followed him and saw him get into a minivan. He requested the man to exit the vehicle. Instead, the man accelerated and departed. Rice obtained the license number. He returned to his post and called the Minneapolis police. The letter was on red paper with black ink. Written on the letter was:

> God, God, God, God, God, God, Angry, Angry, Angry, Angry, Angry, America, America, America, America, Dream, Dream, Dream, Dream, Christyn, Christyn, Christyn, Christyn, All, All, All, All, Evry, Evry, Evry, Evry, Were, Were, Were, Were, Untold, Untold, Untold, They, They, They, They, Dead, Dead, Dead, Dead, Lake, Lake, Lake, Lake, Soil, Soil, Soil, Soil, Friday 25, time 3:15 a.m.

A check of the license determined that the vehicle was registered to Abu Kassim Jeilani with a date of birth of January 1, 1974, and who was living in Minneapolis. A photo spread was shown to Rice, and he identified Abu as the person leaving the letter.

On January 23, Detective Kirby and Minneapolis Police Sgt. Mark Lenzen contacted the residents at the address on the registration. A female answered the door and said Abu was there. She pointed at him and made a circular motion with her finger around her head and pointed at Abu. The officers assumed this meant that he had mental problems. Abu indicated he was willing to talk to the officers. However, he told them he had a slight language barrier. He said his brother could assist. A short time later a person arrived saying he was Alawi Kassim Jeilani, Abu's brother. Alawi told them he felt his brother was suffering from mental illness, and he was trying to get him committed to the Hennepin County Medical Center's Crisis Unit. The interview determined that Abu had left the letter and it was not meant to be threatening, nor did he want to hurt anyone. He claimed it was a message from God, and he was only the messenger. He added that God was angry with Christians and Americans. Abu consented to a search of his vehicle and house. No firearms or other possible weapons were found. Alawi seemed concerned about his brother's mental condition, and the officers gave him some options to pursue. The matter was closed.

The next contact with Abu was around 4:00 p.m. on Sunday, March 10, 2002. Sgt. Todd Gross was driving his marked squad on Franklin Avenue of the south side of Minneapolis. He was stopped at a stoplight when a black male (Abu) came up to the passenger side of his squad with what appeared to him to be a stick in his hand. Abu then came around to the driver's side. Gross then realized that Abu was holding a machete and a crowbar. The man said something which Gross interpreted to be, "Come get me." The window was only partly down and then Abu swung the machete at the squad. Abu started walking westbound in the middle of Franklin Avenue. Gross called for more units and the Crisis Intervention Team (CIT).

Twenty-seven-year-old Hien Dinh responded to the call by Gross. He drove by Abu, who was making slashing motions with the machete. Dinh made eye contact with Abu and Abu pointed the machete at him. Dinh then heard Gross (Abu over his PA system) ordering Abu to drop the weapons.

Officer Jim Jensen of CIT arrived and tried communicating with Abu. When that was unsuccessful, he fired his stun gun. Abu fell to the ground and dropped both weapons. Dinh began exiting his vehicle to run over and secure the weapons, but Abu immediately got up and grabbed them. Dinh watched Jensen pull the trigger of the stun gun again and could hear the electronic current, but it did not affect Abu. Abu then ran toward Officer Mike McCarthy. He backed away with his gun drawn. Abu eventually turned and walked to the intersection of Chicago and Franklin Avenue.

Numerous officers arrived, and the stun gun was again used by Officers Jensen and Vickie Karnik. Dinh recalled Abu saying, "I don't care" and something about it did nothing to him. In addition to Jensen and Karnik, Officers Joel Kimmerle, Justin Marten, and McCarthy were in the immediate area. Other officers were on the perimeter keeping pedestrians away.

Dinh ordered Abu to drop his weapons several times. Abu looked directly at Dinh and began walking toward his squad. Dinh was halfway out of his car, using the passenger door as cover. Abu approached so quickly that Dinh jumped back into the passenger side of his car. Immediately after closing the door, Abu struck the hood of the car with the machete and raised it like he was going to strike the windshield. Dinh pointed his weapon at Abu and ordered him to back up. Abu stepped back and Dinh exited his squad.

After Dinh exited, Abu quickly came toward him, making slashing motions with the machete above his head. Dinh felt that Abu was going to throw the machete at him so he back-pedaled to the rear of the squad. Abu made a grunting noise as he raised the machete and struck the trunk of the car. He then made a grunting sound and raised the machete to shoulder level. There was no cover, so when Abu took a step toward him Dinh fired his 9-mm pistol twice. Dinh later told investigators, "I thought the subject (Abu) was going to chop my head off." Dinh heard other shots being fired. Abu fell to the street. Another officer told Dinh to grab the weapons as he would provide cover. Dinh grabbed both of them and put them in his squad. Kimmerle handcuffed Abu, and Gross requested emergency medical personnel.

James Jensen, a thirty-six-year-old officer with thirteen years at Minneapolis, responded as a member of CIT trained to deal with those in crisis. When Jensen asked him if there was a problem he could help him with, Abu responded in a foreign language unknown to him. Abu was waving the machete. Feeling that he was not able to communicate with Abu, who was approaching bystanders, Jensen used his stun gun to immobilize him. Abu fell, but got right up. Jensen deployed another five-second shock with the gun.

Abu began running away as the prongs from the stun gun pulled away or broke. Jensen reloaded another cartridge and threw the spent one into the middle of Franklin Avenue. Jensen thought to himself that he had to retrieve the cartridge because policy said they had to be inventoried. He fired a second shot from the stun gun, but it had no effect as one prong failed to hit. Jensen received a shock because the five seconds had not passed. He reloaded. Jensen caught up to Abu at an area where other officers were pointing their handguns at him. Jensen fired the stun gun. Both prongs hit him in the upper torso and again had no effect. Jensen was out of cartridges so he drew his .45-caliber pistol.

About this same time, thirty-five-year-old Vicki Karnik, also a trained CIT member, came alongside of Jensen. She fired her stun gun with no effect. She reloaded and fired another. Again, no effect. Abu yelled, "They ain't working."

Jensen moved around behind Dinh's squad. He saw Abu take a deep breath and suddenly raise the machete over his head. He struck down on Dinh's rear trunk area. He then appeared to shift his weight as if preparing to come at Jensen. Jensen fired his weapon.

Vicki Karnik gave basically the same statement of events as Jensen. She came to the area because she was a CIT member and had been radioed to do so. After using her only two stun gun cartridges, she drew her 9-mm pistol. After Abu struck Dinh's squad, she believed he was going to fatally injure one or more officers. She made the decision to fire.

Joel Kimmerle stated that he observed the stun guns being fired with no effect. He recalled Abu saying, "It ain't working." After Abu struck Dinh's squad, he saw him take two steps toward other officers with the machete above his head. He then fired his 9-mm at him.

Officer Michael McCarthy was also at the scene. When Abu came toward the other officers, he also fired his 9-mm pistol. Justin Merten was the partner of Dinh. He had exited the squad prior to Dinh. He was also in the immediate area when Abu came at officers. He fired his 9-mm weapon once.

A total of thirteen spent casings were recovered by the Hennepin County Crime lab. Six of the twelve officers at the scene fired their weapons. All of the officers heard the comments about the stun gun not having any effect on Abu.

Interestingly, an employee of a nearby hardware store saw Abu's photo in the paper after the shooting and called police. Abu had been in the store around noon that day looking for a machete. He said it was to be used to cut goats and turkeys for a restaurant business. Around 3:00 p.m. he came back and purchased the machete (also called an acorn knife) and a crow bar. He said that it was to "cut meat."

When the female clerk commented that it was a "big knife for meat," he said, "Well, it's big meat." He mentioned something about goats. She said he understood English and what she was asking. The manager of the store told him it had to be wrapped because he did not want people to see him walking down the street with such a purchase visible. The manager also said he could understand English and did not recall him having an extreme accent.

The autopsy revealed twelve gunshot wounds to Abu's body, including his arm and neck. Both .45-caliber and 9-mm rounds were recovered. One round hit a major artery. There were stun gun marks observed on the body.

The Somali Justice Advocacy Center in Minneapolis called for the removal of the police chief and an independent investigation because the sheriff's office was biased. There were others interviewed who claimed Abu was killed because he was a black male.

On June 2, 2002, a Hennepin County grand jury cleared all six officers and the chief was not removed.

VI

As usual, a call to 911 gets the police involved. At 8:20 p.m. on Friday, September 27, 2002, a caller to Saint Paul 911 said, "I have a brother who is just next door … he has a long history of, of, psychiatric problems." The caller continued by saying, "And right now he's just been hallucinating, and he's threatening about his family, killing them." The caller said the rest of the family had been locked out of the house.

The caller indicated that the family wanted him to go to the hospital. The 911 operator stayed on the line and connected the caller to paramedics. The caller then said the person was her brother and he thought someone was trying to poison him. She said there were no weapons in the house—only kitchen utensils. The decision was made to send police and an ambulance to stand by. She said she would meet police at the house. The call went out that the person was "EDP (Emotionally Disturbed Person)." His identity was given as Ki Yang. His physical description and other information gleaned from his sister were also given out on the radio. The dispatcher also said that medics were en route.

Saint Paul Officers Mike Tharalson and his partner Shannon Sills responded to the call. They were met by four to six members of the Yang family. They spoke to Yang's son Chong. He indicated he had lived with his father until three days prior when his father changed the locks. Chong requested that officers break into the house so he could retrieve some of his clothes and other property. Chong was asked if Ki had threatened anyone or had committed any crimes. The response was, "No." Tharalson told them that he had no authority to break into the house. Tharalson notified his sergeant of the situation.

Family members then climbed up an exterior stairway and onto the roof of the back porch. They were able to speak to Ki through an upstairs window. Tharalson joined the family members but was told that Ki "doesn't like police." Tharalson stayed back from Ki's sight. They were speaking in Hmong, but Tharalson could tell from the tone Ki was using that he was not going to cooperate with the family and let them in the house.

When Tharalson came down from the roof, he noticed a family member had a tire iron-like tool and was trying to open a door or window. He made it clear that the police could not break into the house but stated he would stand by if one of them did. Two female members of the family said they saw Ki with a gun. Chang told them it was only a BB gun. When asked if he was sure, Chang said, "Yes." The porch window leading to the kitchen was broken, and a family member climbed in and opened the back door. Tharalson followed the family into the house.

Tharalson asked if Ki would come downstairs to them. He was told, "No, he won't … it will be no problem." Suddenly, the person ahead of Tharalson in the living room shouted, "They there? He is." Tharalson did not see Ki immediately, but heard him tell the family to "get their stuff and get out."

Tharalson looked into the living room and saw Ki about fifteen to twenty feet away. He saw what looked like a weapon in his left hand that he was holding down low. Ki had a "sickle like" instrument in his right hand held high over his head in a threatening manner. Ki shouted at Tharalson, "You better get out of here" and began advancing toward him.

The weapon appeared to have a two- to three-foot handle with an eight- to ten-inch long blade at the top. Believing the gun was a BB gun, Tharalson focused on the weapon in his right hand. Tharalson yelled at family members to "get out" and told Ki to, "Drop the weapons." Tharalson had his .40-caliber Glock out and was retreating to the back door. He could tell that the family was scattering, but he was concentrating on Ki.

Ki refused to stop or put the weapons down. Tharalson told investigators later, "Yang's eyes were fixed on me and not on the family members running by him." When he reached the back door, a large plastic garbage pail prevented the door from opening all of the way. Ki advanced to about six to eight feet from Tharalson. When he continued to advance, Tharalson fired four rounds at him. He did not stop. Tharalson continued backing up onto the porch but missed the door due to focusing on Ki, who was still coming with the weapon over his head. When he was about three feet away, Tharalson fired two more times. Ki fell to the floor.

Tharalson exited the porch and watched to see if Ki moved. Sergeant Kellerman who had arrived and Sills ran to check on Tharalson. After determining that he was not injured, medics were called in to check on Ki. Family members were exiting the upstairs window, as they apparently ran upstairs when the shooting began. Ki was taken to the Ramsey County Medical Center where he was pronounced dead. An autopsy determined he had been hit by three of the six rounds fired at him. There were no drugs or alcohol in his system.

Officer Sills related the same status of the call. She added that once inside the house, Tharalson told the family to "get what you need." She then heard Tharalson shout, "Gun, get out." Family members began screaming. She grabbed two of them and pulled them outside. She never saw Ki Yang, but she heard shooting and thought that it was Yang who was shooting. She then saw Tharalson on the porch who appeared to be pushing an Asian male away from him. She radioed that shots were fired and requested additional officers.

Investigation determined that Yang had been having mental problems for ten to fifteen years. He had been hospitalized many times with police involvement. Family members said he was fine with medication, but he had not been taking it. A family member later said that he told Tharalson that Ki had a Hmong "tsaus." When asked to draw a "tsaus," a family member drew a sickle-type weapon.

A Ramsey Count grand jury returned a no bill on January 29, 2003. The family of Ki Yang filed a lawsuit against the Saint Paul Police, claiming that the department did not adequately train officers to handle those with mental illness properly and that lack of training contributed to the death of Yang. The lawsuit was dismissed on April 13, 2006.

Chapter Ten

The Unexpected Can Happen
aka Accidental Shootings

I

There is always a chance of danger when working undercover or in a decoy assignment. This proved to be true for a Minneapolis police decoy operation in the early morning hours of Thursday, September 21, 1984. The unit consisted of seven officers and one sergeant. The members of the unit alternated as the decoy, the "eyeball" or backup and the arresting officer. All of the officers worked in plain clothes and at times used cosmetics, wigs or other clothing to change their appearance. There had been a high number of thefts and robberies from persons in certain areas of Minneapolis, and the unit concentrated in those areas.

Bill Hinz, a thirty-eight-year-old officer, was assigned to the unit, and it was his turn to be the decoy. He was parked, sitting in a fairly new four-door Oldsmobile. The vehicle was parked at an angle partially on the sidewalk with the lights off, parking lights on and the car turned off. Hinz splashed whiskey on his face and clothing prior to parking the car. In addition, he also swished whiskey around in his mouth and left an opened bottle of whiskey in plain site on the console between the separated front seats.

The lid was off to allow the odor throughout the vehicle and to give the appearance of a passed out intoxicated individual. Hinz normally would put the keys in his sock and open the door enough to put in interior light on. This time, however, just as he came up from stashing his keys, he saw a vehicle stopping and opening the driver's door. He slumped forward over the steering wheel and partially to the right side of the front area. Sgt. David Niebur and Officer Bill James were across the street in an unmarked van and had the "eyeball." Two additional officers were a block away in an unmarked unit.

The individual who got out of the car and was later identified as twenty-two-year-old Sal Saran Scott approached Hinz's vehicle. He asked Hinz if he was okay. Hinz ignored him, and he asked two more times. Hinz played drunk and unresponsive. Scott then went back to his car, backed it up past Hinz's car and put it in a parking lot of a nearby business.

When Scott returned to Hinz's car, he first spoke to him through an opened window. He then opened the door and began shaking Hinz. He continued to ask him if he was okay. Hinz began to fake snoring as if he was asleep. Scott continued to poke him. Scott then went to Hinz's billfold in his left rear pocket. He then asked him where the keys were located. Hinz faked snoring again. Scott then grabbed Hinz's left hand and struggled. However, he was successful in removing a gold ring which had a large red stone in it. Scott continuously asked Hinz if he was okay and said he had to get the car out of the way "before the cops come."

Scott became more intense in his search for the keys as he started feeling down Hinz's legs below his knees. He tried twice to push Hinz across the front seat out of the way toward the passenger seat. Hinz hit the brake light twice to signal the "eyeball" that a crime had occurred. Scott began looking through Hinz's jacket and removed a pocket calendar from his shirt pocket. Realizing the persistence of Scott, Hinz began to become more responsive before he found the keys or looked closely at the calendar as it would identify him as an officer. Scott had been "working on" Hinz for approximately five minutes.

Scott told Hinz they should get out of the car and walk around. He pulled Hinz from the car. As he pulled on him, Hinz fell to the ground near the back of the car. Scott stumbled with Hinz and was over him momentarily before pulling him to his feet again. He then pushed Hinz up against the side and roof of the car. Hinz continued to play his role, neither resisting nor assisting.

As Hinz was still being pushed against the car, he heard Officer James shout, "Police officer." Hinz quickly turned and saw James in the middle of the street. He heard James getting closer and telling Scott to "freeze." Scott, who was still pushing Hinz, suddenly spun from Hinz toward James. Hinz heard what he believed to be a muffled sound of a shotgun discharging. Hinz was sprayed with blood and noticed Scott had fallen on his back to the pavement. He turned and saw James throw his shotgun to the street and say "Shit."

Bill James, a thirty-eight-year-old officer with sixteen years' experience, was watching in the "eyeball" van. He and Sergeant Niebur realized Hinz was in trouble. They called for the backup unit. James ran out of the van with his issued double-barreled .12-gauge shotgun toward Hinz and Scott, leaving the door open for Niebur. He saw Scott pushing Hinz against the car just back of the opened driver's door. About twenty feet away he yelled, "Freeze, police." James was pointing the shotgun at Scott. Scott turned and looked directly at James.

James shouted, "Police, put your hands on the car!" Scott appeared to be complying. James began walking and placed the shotgun in a port arms position—left hand on the port stock and right hand on the grip. James looked at Hinz and when James was about two feet from them, Scott turned and lunged at James. James felt and heard the shotgun discharge. Scott immediately fell to the pavement. James saw that Scott had been shot in the head. He exclaimed, "Shit," and threw the weapon down, breaking the stock. He heard Niebur behind him call Code 3 for an ambulance on his radio.

The call was recorded at 2:19:57 a.m. Scott was dead at the scene. His blood alcohol was .00. James did not recall if his safety was on or not. Later, tests by firearms experts could not get the weapon to discharge by any means other than pulling the trigger.

Previously, while James was chasing two people fleeing from a stolen car, he slipped on the snow and accidentally discharged his weapon. One of the individuals fleeing was struck by the bullet. That person did not have life-threatening consequences and recovered. James was shot during roll call in 1975. A weapon was accidentally discharged, and James was hit in the groin area. James was off work for almost two years before being cleared to return to work.

When this shooting was reported in the Minneapolis newspaper, the homicide investigator for Minneapolis Police received a telephone call from a Ramsey County (Saint Paul) Deputy Ed Whitledge. Whitledge called to report that he had been assaulted by Scott while he was an inmate on January 24, 1981. Scott had been booked for a theft. He stuffed toilet paper into the toilet, causing the toilet in his cell to flood. When he was requested to stop urinating on the floor, he told Whitledge to, "Go fuck yourself and come in and get me if you think you can." When Whitledge and another deputy attempted to remove him from the cell, he assaulted Whitledge and ripped his shirt. Whitledge was aware of other deputies having problems with him while at Ramsey County jail. Ironically, Whitledge was involved in a fatal shooting on January 22, 1994.

The Hennepin County Attorney's Office presented the case to a grand jury, and a no bill was returned on October 2, 1984.

II

Law enforcement officers are well trained, and very seldom are there accidental discharges. Unfortunately, an accidental discharge happened early on Thanksgiving Day, Thursday, November 28, 1991.

Brent Stanfield, owner of a large yellow twenty-six-thousand-pound gross vehicle weight moving-type van, was letting his truck warm up on a cold night. Stanfield started the vehicle and returned to the All-Stars Sports Bar and Grill in the City of Spring Park in one of the western suburbs of the Twin Cities. He was back inside for about ten minutes when he saw his truck leaving the parking lot. Stanfield chased after it and the driver, later identified as twenty-four-year-old Richard Krueger. Krueger swerved the truck at Stanfield and accelerated it out of the parking lot. Stanfield ran back into the bar to call 911 and report it stolen. It was now 12:48 a.m.

The call went out immediately, and two officers from the City of Orono saw the truck proceeding on Hennepin County Road 15. Officer Mark Erickson, a thirty-nine-year-old with thirteen years' experience from the South Lake Minnetonka Police Department, heard the radio call and chase while in his department's station. He proceeded to his squad to assist the Orono officers.

The fleeing truck proceeded south and west on County Road 15 and turned south onto County Road 19 toward the City of Excelsior, entering the jurisdiction of South Lake Minnetonka. Erickson joined in the chase. During the pursuit, the truck was traveling at high speeds and at times was being driven in the oncoming lane of traffic. All of the police squads had emergency lights and sirens activated. The truck continued ignoring the pursuit and eventually crashed through a fence into a tree and snow bank near the Tonka Terrace Shopping Center in the City of Shorewood. The truck was apparently stuck.

The two Orono officers and Erickson tramped through the snowy field and surrounded the front of the truck. They repeatedly yelled for Krueger to come out of the truck with his hands up. The officers were shining their flashlights into the cab and could not see anyone. They were close to him when he crashed and knew no one had exited the cab and fled.

The commands from the officers brought no response from within. Erickson approached the truck from the passenger side with his 9-mm pistol drawn. Erickson was able to open the passenger door. Apparently Krueger was hiding in the cab with his head toward the passenger door and his feet under the steering wheel. Erickson had his weapon in his right hand. He began to climb onto the running board. With his left hand he grabbed the handle next to the door used to pull oneself up to the cab. His foot was on the running board which was partially covered with snow and ice. He slipped as he was just getting up, and his weapon accidentally discharged.

Erickson later told investigators his first reaction was that someone else might have fired a weapon, because he did not realize it was him who had fired. He then felt around in the dark and found Krueger on the seat bleeding. It was determined that Krueger was struck in the chest with the bullet exiting out the back of his neck. He was dead at the scene. The radio call of a shot being fired was at 12:55 a. m.

Krueger had been cited five times in the previous five years for alcohol-related driving offenses. His license was under suspension at the time of the shooting. Krueger was living alone and unemployed. His latest arrest for drunken driving was ten months previous in the City of Orono.

On December 19, 1991, a Hennepin County grand jury decided that the fatal shooting of Krueger was accidental and no charges would be forthcoming against Erickson.

III

Minneapolis Police Sgt. John Rouner was on routine patrol in his marked squad working alone around 1:55 a.m. on Saturday, April 29, 2001. It was a pleasant night and he had his window opened about halfway. He was eastbound on 31st Street when he heard five or six shots coming from the alley in the 3100 block of Clinton Avenue South. Rouner immediately aired the information about the shots. Other officers in the Third Precinct of Minneapolis were dispatched to assist in the area of East 31st Street and Clinton Avenue on the city's south side. He turned his headlights off and made a U-turn in the alley.

Rouner saw a male walking in the alley. He put his spotlight on him and ordered him to the ground at gunpoint. Sgt. John Pielow arrived and assisted him. The person was handcuffed and questioned. He told the officers he lived in the area and had exited his house to check on sounds of shots being fired. His identity and address were verified. Finding no weapon, fired casings or live rounds on him, this individual was released and told to return to his residence.

Rouner and Pielow then heard a radio transmission from Officers Darrin Waletzki and Gregg Mihelick in Squad 321 that they were trying to stop a Chevrolet Camaro they saw leaving the area. The vehicle would not stop. Believing the vehicle was involved in the "shots fired" call, Pielow and Rouner responded.

Officers Waletzki and Tim Costello later told investigators that when they saw the Camaro leaving at a high rate of speed, they turned in behind it and activated their emergency lights to get the vehicle to stop. The vehicle began driving faster and ran a stop sign, turning southbound on 4th Avenue South. In the 3300 block of 4th Avenue the Camaro showed down to approximately five miles per hour and began to pull over to the side of the street as if to stop or as if the passengers were going to jump out and run. As the officers came up to the Camaro, it took off at a high rate of speed and went through the stoplight at 34th Street.

The officers continued chasing the vehicle and observed it hitting the curb and going up on the sidewalk. They were proceeding south at speeds up to seventy miles per hour and were going through red lights. The Camaro turned west on 42nd Street and stopped at 3rd Avenue South. It appeared as though the occupants were either throwing something out of the vehicle or attempting to exit the car. The car again pulled away at a high rate of speed and turned northbound on 3rd Avenue. They went through another red light at eighty miles per hour. As the officers cleared through the lights at 38th Street, they observed the Camaro crash into one parked car on the east side of 3rd and one on the west side of the 3700 block of 3rd Avenue.

The Camaro hit the car on the east side so hard it flipped onto its top.

The front of the Camaro was extensively damaged. The second car hit was turned completely around, facing the opposite direction from the impact. Before approaching the Camaro, Waletzki called for rescue and an ambulance Code 3 because of the severity of the impact.

Pielow was approaching from the north, and the squads arrived at the crash scene at the same time. Costello went up to the driver's side. Pielow and Waletzki went to the passenger side. Both had their weapons drawn due to the original call of shots fired and the obvious attempt to evade officers during the chase. The passenger-side window was completely gone, apparently caused by the collision. They gave repeated commands to the passenger to show his hands. It appeared to them he was leaning toward the center console and reaching for something either there or in the driver's seat. They made the decision to attempt to bring his hands out of the car by reaching in through the missing window. Waletzki reached in the car with his left hand, holding onto his gun with the other while he continued to give commands to see his hands.

Waletzki grabbed the passenger's right shoulder in an attempt to turn him so his hands would be visible to him and Pielow. Pielow also reached in to grab the man. As Pielow pulled the passenger, his weapon discharged hitting the man in the lower neck and upper chest area. Paramedics arrived within seconds and immediately began medical attention. He was transported to Hennepin County Medical Center.

On Tuesday, May 1, 2001, the passenger identified as twenty-one-year-old Efrain P. Depaz died from the accidental shot. He had been on life support since the chase and shooting. Fidel Depaz, brother of Efrain, told investigators his brother would only let someone drive his car if he had not been drinking. The driver, twenty-two-year-old Israel Rosas-Olalde, had been drinking less and was driving. In May, Rosas-Olalde pleaded guilty to fleeing a police officer and was sentenced to sixty days in the Hennepin County Workhouse and three years' probation. He also faced deportation.

On September 27, 2001, a Hennepin County grand jury declined to indict Pielow in the shooting death of Depaz. It was determined the shooting was accidental. A lawsuit was initiated by the family of Depaz. On May 3, 2002, the Minneapolis City Council voted to give the Depaz family two hundred thousand dollars to settle the wrongful death suit.

IV

It can be argued that this incident was *not* an accidental shooting. I agree that the officer shot the person at whom he was aiming. However, the officer mistakenly shot a citizen who was attempting to take a weapon from an assailant who had already shot others. Therefore, I am calling this an accidental shooting.

December 3, 2001, started out as a very violent day in the City of Saint Paul. At 8:30 a.m., a thirty-four-year-old man was driving his car down the street in the north central area of the city. While at an intersection, he was shot twice by an unknown assailant. The shooter fled, and the victim drove to a nearby fire station. He began honking his horn, and paramedics soon came out and attended to him. He was transported to a nearby hospital.

About ninety minutes later, police received the first of many 911 calls about a shooting in the backyard of a residence less than a mile from the first shooting. Witnesses working in the area saw a man pointing a gun at a thirty-five-year-old man. The victim was begging the man not to shoot. The assailant said, "Shut up," and shot the man in the head.

The assailant, later identified as twenty-six-year-old Carlos Scott, ran about two blocks away and pounded on the door of a home trying to get a ride to elude police. The person would not open the door. Scott then went to a car occupied by forty-six-year-old Charles Craighead and his fiancée, Joyce McDougle. Craighead, a house painter, was in the area to speak to a homeowner about a painting job. Scott came up to the car and pulled a gun on Craighead. Craighead jumped out of his car and began to struggle with Scott for control of the weapon.

Responding officers were given a description of the assailant from the most recent shooting as a black male, about five feet six inches and weighing about 150-160 pounds. When the first officer, forty-one-year-old Michael Lee, arrived, the two were still fighting for control of the weapon. He shouted three times for the two to put the gun down. When the gun pointed toward Lee, he fired his .12-gauge shotgun, hitting both men. Scott was seriously injured, and Craighead later died at the hospital.

A 911 call during the incident with Craighead said, "The one who has the gun is not the guy, he's not the bad guy now." It was related that the "good guy" had taken the weapon from his attacker. The message which went out to officers eight seconds later was, "One of the males took the gun away from another male." It is not believed Lee heard this transmission as police tapes show that Lee had left his squad and did not get the message. Eight seconds later the same caller said, "The police shot the wrong guy."

In April, 2002, the family of Craighead filed a lawsuit against Lee and the City of Saint Paul. The lawsuit contended that Lee violated Craighead's civil rights by using deadly force without good reason. The Saint Paul Police Department was also faulted for not effectively training, supervising, and disciplining officers who had used excessive force in the past.

On May 19, 2002, a Ramsey County grand jury cleared Lee of any criminal fault in the death of Craighead. In December 2005, the Saint Paul City Council approved a four-hundred-thousand-dollar settlement regarding the lawsuit of Craighead's death. In November 2006, Police Chief John Harrington made a posthumous presentation of the department's Award of Valor, the highest honor bestowed on a citizen, to Craighead's family and fiancée.

Chapter Eleven

It May Look Real
aka Replica Weapons

I

It was not warm at 1:30 a.m. on May 8, 1985, in Lakeville, Minnesota. One would be surprised to hear that a person was trying to break into occupied trailer homes dressed only with a ski mask and pair of boots, but that was indeed the call to Lakeville police that early morning. A frantic caller told the dispatcher that a man had attempted to break into her home at the Queen Anne Mobile Home Court. Four officers responded to the complex and searched for the suspect but were not able to locate him.

Two of the officers left and thirty-year-old Sgt. Scott Johnson and twenty-nine-year-old David Bellows remained in the area. They had been taught in a training session that suspects conceal themselves very effectively and are usually able to hear officers conversing. Sergeant Johnson loudly announced in effect, "I guess the guy took off. We might as well go." They drove out of sight and stopped.

The same woman called back around 2:15 a.m. She said that the man was pulling himself up on the outside window sill and peeking into her house. She was extremely upset and reported that he was only wearing a ski mask and black boots.

Johnson and Bellows were dispatched again. They had stayed nearby so were able to walk back from where they were parked. They saw the man, later identified as thirty-year-old Jack McNamara, between two trailer houses. They identified themselves as police officers and ordered him to stop. McNamara fled, and the officers pursued him over a barbed-wire fence that separated the trailer park from Interstate 35. It was a clear, star-filled night. However, the only light was from a single yard light in the trailer park area. McNamara stopped, turned in a crouching position and pointed a handgun at them.

Both officers heard a report (sharp sound resembling a shot) and a flash. Johnson and Bellows were twenty-five to thirty feet away standing beside each other. Bellows was on Johnson's left. Bellows is six-foot-five and Johnson around five-foot-nine. Bellows, after hearing what he believed to be a shot, saw Johnson (out of his peripheral vision) drop. He believed Johnson had been hit by the shot. Bellows fired all six rounds in his .357-caliber revolver. McNamara fell to the ground. Bellows was surprised when he turned to check on Johnson as he was beginning to stand and had not been shot. When Johnson heard the shot, he immediately crouched to a kneeling position one knee. Johnson stated that his instinct told him "to get as small as I could." He fired three rounds from his .357-caliber revolver. Bellows said he did not hear any of Johnson's rounds being fired.

It was determined that McNamara was carrying a metal cap gun which looked like a Luger. Investigation revealed that McNamara apparently drove to the trailer park from his home—also a trailer park—about two miles away. His clothes were found in a tool shed in Queen Anne Park about two blocks from the home of the woman who had called police. Other residents had also seen McNamara trying to break into other homes. No one in the complex knew him. It was never determined why he had come to the trailer park and acting so strangely.

A Dakota County grand jury returned a no bill in June 1985 regarding the shooting.

II

Who would think that at 3:30 on a Monday afternoon arresting a person for drunk driving would lead to a shooting where someone was killed? That is exactly what happened in South Saint Paul on May 11, 1987.

This incident began when the South Saint Paul Police Department responded to a local truck stop to check on a supposedly drunken individual who was attempting to leave in his car. When the officer requested the man, later identified as twenty-nine-year-old Mark Sinclair, to exit his vehicle, he refused. That officer, Patrolman Larry Snaza, notified his supervisor, Sgt. Greg Mohrland. Two additional officers arrived, and Sinclair's seventeen-year-old girlfriend immediately exited the vehicle when asked. Sinclair eventually got out of the car. Sinclair gave the officers three different names. The decision was made to take him to police headquarters to determine his identity. Sinclair was put in the backseat of Mohrland's squad. Mohrland did not search or handcuff Sinclair.

Sergeant Mohrland began driving to police headquarters. Captain David Vujovich was ahead of Mohrland in his squad, and Snaza followed in his. While en route, Mohrland looked in the rearview mirror and saw Sinclair pointing what he perceived to be a small black weapon at Mohrland's head. Mohrland slammed on his brakes, throwing Sinclair into the metal screen separating the front and back seats. Mohrland turned the car off, grabbed the keys and ran from it. As in all marked squads, there are no handles in the back seats that would allow someone to exit. All three officers attempted to negotiate with Sinclair to surrender his weapon. One of the officers went unnoticed to the opposite side and opened the door. He tried unsuccessfully to wrestle Sinclair from the squad.

Sinclair exited the squad himself and swore at the officers. When he pointed the weapon at Captain Vujovich, Sergeant Mohrland fired his .357-

caliber revolver. It struck Sinclair in the stomach. He died approximately two hours later at a local hospital. An autopsy determined that he died from a single gunshot wound to the abdomen.

Investigation determined that the weapon in Sinclair's possession was a small dark cigarette lighter. It looked like a .25-caliber semiautomatic handgun and was about three inches long. When questioned after the shooting at the police department, Mohrland's girlfriend was told that Sinclair had something that looked like a derringer. She immediately told police that it sounded like Sinclair's cigarette lighter. However, she claimed she had not seen it that day. She added that she had thrown the lighter in a garbage container because it did not work. She did not see Sinclair retrieve it.

She was in Snaza's squad following Mohrland's squad when she saw Mohrland stop and exit it. She heard radio transmissions in the squad that Sinclair had a weapon. She saw Sinclair get out of the squad with the three officers standing around him. She could not hear what was being said. She saw Sinclair point at one officer and saw all three officers point a weapon at him. She claimed Sinclair dropped his hand and began walking around. She was unable to see what he was doing at the time she heard the shot because his back was to her.

Sinclair was also known as Mark A. Rowe. He had been arrested two days earlier by a nearby police department on an outstanding warrant issued on March 5. The warrant was for probation violation of an earlier drunken driving matter. That drunken driving charge was the second one he had had in a five-year period. Sinclair's employer at a local freight company said Sinclair had recently come to work intoxicated to complete papers to get paid from a recent hauling assignment. Sinclair had also been arrested in Louisville, Kentucky, for being drunk and for making terroristic threats. His employer posted his bond and told him he would not get any new hauling assignments until he had completed an alcohol abuse program.

On the day of the incident, Sinclair began drinking beer early in the day.

He had gone to look at a semi-tractor he was considering buying. Apparently, in addition to drinking beer, he had been sipping on a bottle of rum he had in his truck. Other friends told authorities that Sinclair liked to pick fights. They also said he hated cops and often talked about fighting with them.

Sinclair would not have been shot if he had refrained from alcohol. All he had to do was tell the officers that it was a lighter and throw it down. Apparently, he was too intoxicated to clearly understand the consequences. Mohrland was cleared by a grand jury. However, he left the department on a medical retirement within two years of the shooting.

III

Twenty-four-year-old Mark Richards, according to his girlfriend and relatives, had purchased a Luger pellet gun to scare people away from his girlfriend's car that was always parked on the street. Police had no idea that was the case when a radio call went out to Minneapolis officers around 8:00 p.m. on Friday, August 21, 1987, regarding "man with a gun." Additional information was that a Hispanic male had threatened several kids with a gun and that person was sitting on the steps of a residence still holding the gun in his hand.

Minneapolis Officer James Wilson responded to the call. He happened to have his wife as a ride-a-long in his squad that night. As he approached the area, a young male came running toward his car waving his hands. He said that the man threatening him was still holding the gun and sitting on the steps of a house. Wilson had the boy get in the back seat of the squad and started down the street. As Wilson approached the house where the man was sitting, the man stood up. The boy pointed the man out to Wilson and said, "That's him." Wilson notified other responding squads of the exact address.

As he got closer, Wilson saw what he believed to be a .22-caliber handgun. The man, Mark Richards, had his gun hand fully extended while walking toward the street. Wilson saw Officer Pete Jackson park his squad up the street and exit with his shotgun. As Wilson removed his shotgun and exited the squad, he heard Jackson shout commands to Richards to stop and put down the weapon. Wilson caught up to where Jackson was located. Richards continued walking and paid no attention to the officers' demands. Wilson saw a person across the street on the boulevard, and Richards was walking directly at him with his arm and gun pointing at him. Richards would not stop or respond to the officers as he continued toward the person. Wilson believed Richards could grab the person as a hostage and take cover behind cars parked on the street. Wilson then fired his .12-gauge shotgun once.

Jackson furnished investigators with the same information regarding the call. When he exited his vehicle, it appeared to him that Richards was "totally focused" on someone across the street. It was the young boy he later walked toward. Jackson called for Richards to put down the gun and could hear Wilson doing likewise. Jackson felt that Richards was determined to shoot the young boy as he walked toward him and did not look away at any time. Jackson, fearing for the young boy's life, fired his .12-gauge shotgun once. He heard Wilson fire almost simultaneously, and Richards fell to the street.

It was determined during the investigation that Richards had the gun to scare people. He was wearing headphones and listening to music at the time of the shooting. He should have heard the officers' demands. Witnesses one block away heard the officers calling for him to put the gun down. He also could see both officers, as they were in full uniform. On the steps where Richards had been sitting was a mostly consumed bottle of Jack Daniel's whiskey. Witnesses said they had seen Richards sitting on the steps drinking prior to the shooting.

Richards was determined to have died from multiple wounds from the shotgun's 00 buck. There was no blood alcohol for Richards noted in the police file. Both officers were cleared by a Hennepin County grand jury.

IV

An innocent forty-three-year-old woman pulled her van into a garage at her apartment on the south side of Minneapolis around 1:30 p.m. on Tuesday, August 23, 1995. A witness saw her park her vehicle and open the door to remove groceries. The witness said, "I saw her one second and then the next second she's running toward me covered in blood." The woman had both hands on her throat and was bleeding profusely. She was rushed into the apartment building, and 911 was called. A description of the assailant was given. When the call was dispatched, the assailant's clothing description was described as "unique."

A two-person Minneapolis police squad was driving through a nearby alley when the call was dispatched. A man fitting the description of the woman's attacker was challenged by the officers. The man, later identified as twenty-two-year-old Teru Dakkar McSwain, aka Teru Dakkar Jollif, immediately sprinted away from the officers. Officer Andrew Aspin jumped from the squad and pursued McSwain. After a short chase, Aspin confronted McSwain in a face-to-face standoff. McSwain pointed what appeared to be a handgun at Aspin. After repeated commands to drop the weapon, Aspin fired his .45-caliber pistol. McSwain was hit three times in the chest and later died during surgery at Hennepin County Medical Center. McSwain was wearing a shoulder holster, and the weapon was an authentic replica of an automatic handgun, but this one only fired BBs.

Homicide investigators found a knife with a blade almost four inches long next to McSwain. The knife had the victim's blood from the stabbing. That woman recovered from her wounds and told homicide investigators that McSwain said nothing to her when he approached her. He just walked up and cut her throat. She did not know him and had never had any contact with him to her knowledge. Investigators also determined that he had been responsible for the death of a young woman in the same neighborhood the previous week. No motive for the murder or assault was ever determined.

Aspin was cleared by a Hennepin County grand jury.

V

A Minneapolis 911 operator began receiving calls around 8:30 a.m. on Wednesday, December 8, 1999. The callers said there was a man was walking and waving a gun in the vicinity of Washington and Cedar Avenue South just east of downtown Minneapolis. There was also a call that the man entered a building and threatened someone with a gun.

Four Minneapolis squad cars responded to the area. Officers found the man walking with what appeared to be a gun in his hand. They began following him. The man, identified as forty-two-year-old Rocco A. Dandrea, continued walking along railroad tracks and a then to a bicycle path just off the Interstate 94 exit to 5th Street. Initially there were no bystanders nearby, so the police officers took several minutes trying to coax him to put his weapon down. The officers kept shouting over and over for him to, "Drop it. Drop the gun."

Two veteran officers were among the officers responding. Fifty-year-old Sgt. Mike Green and fifty-six-year-old Steven Sworski were two of the officers trying to get Dandrea to put his gun down. They were flanking him for approximately one-half mile as he walked. Not far from the Hubert H. Humphrey Metrodome, a bicyclist neared Dandrea's shooting range. The officers called for him to stay back, but he continued in the direction of Dandrea. Dandrea then pointed his weapon at the man on the bicycle. Green fired one round of 00 buck from his .12-gauge shotgun, and Sworski fired twice from his 9-mm handgun. Medics responded. Nine minutes after the shooting, Dandrea was declared dead at the scene.

The Minnesota Bureau of Criminal Apprehension (BCA) conducted this investigation. A witness told BCA investigators that he saw police following Dandrea and heard them shouting very loudly for him to drop the gun. He said Dandrea just kept walking and paid no attention to the officers who were yelling and almost surrounding him. The witness said Dandrea "just kept walking straight ahead."

It was not determined why Dandrea would not stop. He had the weapon in one hand and a cassette player in the other, with headphones in his ears. The officers were shouting loud enough to override any music. Additionally, officers stated they were walking in his line of vision continually trying to get his attention. There should have been no doubt that the police wanted him to stop. His weapon was an exact replica of a German Luger.

The BCA obtained a search warrant for Dandrea's apartment. When one walked into it, it seemed like something out of a movie. Apparently, he was a *Star Trek* fan. There was a mock cockpit and screen made from tinfoil that looked like the *Star Trek* spaceship *Enterprise*. There were makeshift antennas like those seen on United States space missions in different locations around the apartment. There was also a military uniform with captain's bars on the shoulders.

On May 22, 2000, a Hennepin County grand jury cleared the officers.

VI

No matter the circumstances or age of the person killed by police, there are always questions. It is more difficult when the person killed is a young boy, especially if he had a replica weapon. This was the situation on Sunday, October 24, 2004.

Minneapolis Officer Scott Mars was working in the Fourth Precinct during the early morning hours of October 23 and 24. He was working in a marked squad car with his partner Doug Lemons. About 11:35 p.m. they received a call of shots fired in the area of 26th and Newton Avenue North. They stopped about one block away and shut the squad off to listen for anything relating to the "shots fired" call. Mars heard a loud gunshot that seemed about a block away. He radioed the information as he and Lemon exited the squad. They continued toward the sound through an alley just south of the location.

From the alley, they observed a large party at 2019 26th Avenue. They suspected the shots might have come from someone at the party. They decided to conceal themselves behind two large wooden boxes and trash cans to watch the party for any criminal activity. They were able to see several young males and females inside the house through windows. They heard loud music and loud conversations. After approximately twenty to thirty minutes, several partiers around the ages of fifteen to twenty came outside in front of the house and appeared to be arguing. Mars felt like a fight was about to break out.

Mars was able to hear some of the discussion taking place. He heard, "What are you gonna do, nigger? What are you gonna do?" He then saw four or five males approach a group of other males. He also heard a female voice shout, "Mookie, don't do it! Don't do it, Mookie!" While Mars was watching this activity, he received a radio transmission that 911 had just received a call that there was a black male with a gun at 2019 26th Avenue North, the house they were watching.

Mars and Lemons started moving toward the front of the house. As they approached from the back yard, Mars could hear arguing and screaming. There was a privacy fence to the east of the residence so they could not see what was happening in the front. Mars saw another Minneapolis squad approaching from the west. He could hear sounds of people scattering northbound away from their direction. They were able to see that officers had stopped and were talking to people at the house. They decided to walk back to their squad.

After they returned to their squad, they returned to patrol duties on 26th Avenue. Another "person with a gun" call came in close to the original address. Mars believed it was possibly related to the incident they had watched at the house. Mars continued in the squad and could see several people in a group moving eastbound on a nearby street. Dispatch aired a description of the person with a gun. The description was a black male, age of fourteen-sixteen and wearing a red jersey. While he was receiving the radio description, Mars turned east on 30th Avenue. He saw two males running east on the north side of the street. One of the two matched the description. Mars believed this to be the person with the gun. The other male was wearing a white T-shirt.

Mars immediately exited his squad and ran after the individual matching the description. Mars began shouting, "Police, stop. Show me your hands."

Mars ran into an alley and continued to issue the same commands. Mars was able to see that his right hand was in his front waist area out of his sight. He could see his left hand swinging back and forth in a normal running manner. Mars was thinking at that point that the person was trying to conceal a weapon in his right hand.

Mars continued to chase and cry out his commands. In fact, one command was, "Stop. I know you have a gun." The suspect ran into the yard at 3027 Knox Avenue North. As he ran up a small mound in the front yard, he encountered a chain-link fence and started to slow. Mars stopped on the mound with his flashlight in his left hand and his 9-mm Beretta in his right. The suspect still had his back to Mars. Mars yelled, "Show me your hands."

The suspect replied, "I have a gun," and started to move his left shoulder around toward Mars. As he was moving around, Mars saw a chrome handgun near his right thigh. He spun completely around and raised the gun. Believing he was going to be shot, Mars fired two rounds. He saw the suspect drop to the ground, and the gun flew through the air. Mars radioed that shots had been fired and gave his general location. He heard Lemon calling for him and was able to direct him to his location. Lemon stayed with the suspect, and Mars went to the area where he saw the gun go. It was across the fence in the yard next door on the grass. He kept a visual on the gun but did not enter the yard. Sgt. Mike Young came to the scene. Mars told Sergeant Young that he did not lose sight of the suspect in the red jersey once the chase began.

Lemons described the same information up to the time of the chase. Lemons chased the suspect in the white T-shirt. He caught up to him and was able to get him on the ground. He searched him for weapons and looked around the area to see if he had dropped one. He believed that Mars was probably chasing the person with the gun. He told the person on the ground to stay there as he ran to catch up to Mars. He heard Mars say, "I know you have a gun." He then heard two shots. Lemons cried, "Where are you?" Mars responded, and Lemon ran to where Mars was located. Lemons said he would cover the suspect while Mars looked for the gun. Mars quickly located it in the adjacent yard. Lemons gave their address and called for an ambulance. Sergeant Young arrived before the ambulance and rendered first aid.

Officer Peter Hafstad responded to the scene and was directed by Sergeant Young to go with the ambulance to Hennepin County Medical Center. Hafstad took possession of the suspect's clothes.

A Crime Lab Unit officer collected a Marksman Repeater Air Pistol from the yard at 3023 Know Avenue North. It was processed for latent fingerprints. One latent print on the underside toward the end to the barrel was identified as the left middle finger of the suspect, identified as fifteen-year-old Courtney Jaquez Williams. An autopsy revealed that Williams was hit by both rounds fired by Mars.

A thorough investigation was conducted by Minneapolis Homicide Unit. The first person to call 911 said the weapon was chrome-plated and the person was threatening others with it. The person with the gun was described as a black male, five-foot-six or seven inches tall, slender build, red jersey and fifteen to twenty years old. Another 911 caller described fifteen to twenty kids arguing and one aged fifteen or sixteen who was seen pulling a gun out of his pants. A witness on Knox Avenue heard someone shouting, "Stop. Get down" and then two shots. Another witness on Knox heard someone shout, "Halt" or "Stop" and then two shots. A third person on Knox heard something about "freeze or ya know…put hands up or whatever" and then two shots. A seventeen-year-old female at the original house party told investigators that she saw Courtney pull the weapon out of his waistband and let people hold it. She held it and said it "looked like a .45-caliber pistol, but it wasn't, it was a BB gun." She said Courtney had it the last time she saw it. She said police showed up at the house and everyone ran away. She learned on Monday that police had shot Courtney.

As in most cases like this, the media publishes numerous comments from the community activists who constantly criticize law enforcement. Comparisons to the Tycel Nelson case fifteen years earlier were made. During the 1990 shooting of Nelson, individuals accused police of cleaning the weapon when no fingerprints were found on it. When a fingerprint, as in this case, was found, they claimed that it only showed that he touched the gun at some time.

Twenty people were called to testify at a Hennepin County grand jury on February 3 and 4, 2005. The grand jury determined there was not enough evidence to charge Mars with any criminal violation, and a no bill was returned on February 4, 2005.

Chapter Twelve

Earning Some Extra Money
aka Off Duty Employment

I

Police officers, especially in the metropolitan area, have the opportunity to work "off duty" for extra money. Officers work in various capacities while doing so. Some of the assignments are at sporting events, financial institutions, lodging facilities, shopping centers and a variety of other commercial establishments.

The Pursuit Hometel (low-rent hotel) on the south side of Minneapolis was a rather unique place with four separate buildings. In June 1988, the owner decided it would be advisable to have police officers work part-time during their off-duty hours. The shifts would be 4:00 p.m. to 2:00 a.m. and 5:00 p.m. to 3:00 a.m., with one officer on each shift. The overlapping hours were for the safety of the officers. The officers were to stop people from climbing over the surrounding fence and entering rooms which were vacant or from staying in rooms with regular tenants. The officers had a master key to all areas in the buildings. Officers would be allowed to enter rooms with the key after knocking on the door and identifying themselves. These checks were to make sure vacant rooms did not have squatters and to make unregistered guests leave.

Certain tenants who were expelled from the building would be listed in the "no return" book. These people would also have been served with trespassing notices. The desk clerk or police officers would be the persons to put names in the book. The trespassing notice would also be taped on the window in the lobby. Any person who was a threat to other tenants would also be on the list. Alcohol was not allowed on the premises or in any room. Tenants would be tagged and removed if they continued to violate the policy.

Officers began working at Pursuit on July 15, 1988, seven days per week. There were approximately twenty-five Minneapolis officers working there. Numerous arrests for burglary and trespassing were made, as well as identifying those with outstanding warrants. Several individuals were also taken to Detox. The owners were having difficulty making expenses. One employee told an officer that he was to accept as many tenants as possible to help gain revenue. Strange things can happen with an attitude like this.

Officers Stacy Niebur and Alissa Clemons volunteered to work at Pursuit. Both were fairly new officers and were trying to earn some extra money. Around 6:30 p.m. on September 6, 1988, they were working together when they noticed a woman, Cassandra Harris, outside the building holding thirty-year-old Tom Jennings to keep him from fighting another man. The officers intervened and were told by Jennings that it was none of their business. When asked for identification, Jennings said, "For what?" He eventually gave his name. Clemons asked the desk clerk if Jennings was known to her. She had his complete name and date of birth. While Clemons was inside, Niebur checked on the other men outdoors and sent them on their way. Niebur was attempting to get information from Harris, and she told her, "Quit fucking with us." Both Harris and Jennings appeared to be intoxicated. They were registered at Pursuit, and policy dictated that they were not allowed to stay there or come back.

They requested a squad to transport the two to detox. They were informed no squad was available for transporting. Since Detox was only two blocks away, they decided to walk the two there. They were standing on the steps of Pursuit and started to handcuff Harris. Harris was calling Clemons a "nigger bitch" and Niebur "honky bitch." Jennings, who had been sitting on the steps, jumped up and said, "Get your fucking hands off her [Harris]." Jennings kicked at Niebur. She used her chemical spray to control him, and they were able to handcuff the two.

The officers started walking the two to Detox. They continued to curse the officers and fell to the sidewalk, refusing to walk. They would call to other intoxicated friends to assist them. The shouting was creating a scene and drawing a crowd. Someone in the crowd yelled, "Get the bitches." Dispatch was called to cancel the Detox reservation and to request a squad to transport the two to jail for disorderly conduct. When Jennings was taken away, he told the officers that he would find them and "get them." Because of this problem, a trespass notice for Harris and Jennings was completed and given to the desk clerk at Pursuit. They would be denied staying at Pursuit or even being on the property.

On September 12, 1988, at 5:00 p.m. Niebur and Clemons were again working at Pursuit. They saw Harris and Jennings walking up the stairs to the front door. The couple was stopped and told that a trespass notice had been filed so they were not allowed to stay there. Harris told the officers that they had talked to the owner's son-in-law, and he told them that they could return. The officers went in to check on the notice and could not find it. They attempted to check with the son-in-law, but he was unavailable. About 5:15 p.m., one of the co-owners came out of a meeting and spoke to the officers. She said she was unaware of the previous problem and told the current desk clerk that Harris and Jennings were not to be allowed in any room at Pursuit as of that date.

Around 6:30 p.m., Jennings and another male were seen loitering in front of one of the Pursuit buildings. Both were advised of the loitering notice and asked to leave. The two went across the street and pointed their fin-

ger as if pulling a trigger at the officers. The officers went across the street
and asked, "What's the problem?"

Jennings said, "You're gonna get killed." He was advised that if they continued acting the way they were, they would be arrested for making threats.
As Niebur and Clemons were walking away, Jennings said, "Die, Ike and
Dyke." When they turned to look at him, he ran inside the building. The
two officers did not chase him. They returned to the Pursuit complex.

Around 8:15 p.m. and after making rounds, they decided to make sure
that Jennings was gone from the room he had previously occupied. There
was no sound coming from the room. Niebur knocked on the door and
called, "Police." She then put the master key in and unlocked the door. Niebur
was on the right and Clemons on the left side of the door. The door swung
left to right. Clemons could see into the room first. The room was completely dark. Clemons took out her flashlight and moved it around the room.
Clemons realized that someone was in the bed lying on his right side facing the door. The bed was in the center of the far wall. Clemons yelled, "Who's
that?" There was no answer. She then shouted, "Jennings?"

He answered very loudly, "What?" Clemons directed him to, "Get out
of the bed, 'cause you know you're out of here." Jennings got out of bed, and
Clemons told him to come over to her. The light from the hallway, as well
as Clemons' flashlight, lighted the room. Clemons saw something in Jennings' right hand. She shouted, "Police. Drop it!" She pulled out her weapon
with her right hand and continued to shine her flashlight with her left.
Clemons saw that it was a knife in his hand and called for him to put it
down. Believing that Jennings was going to stab either her or Niebur, Clemons
fired two rounds from her .357 revolver that was loaded with .38-caliber
ammunition. Jennings fell about three to five feet from her.

Niebur then yelled, "Get your hands up." That was when Clemons noticed that there was another male in the room. The second person was searched
and handcuffed. The man said that he was "dozing" and did not see Jennings
with a knife. An ambulance was called. Jennings expired prior to the arrival

of medical personnel. A brown-handled knife with a folding two-inch blade was recovered about three feet from Jennings. Two twin beds had been pushed together to form one bed, and a small television set was sitting on the chair near the bed. There were clothes scattered about in plastic bags. Two empty malt liquor cans were located on the floor next to the TV.

An autopsy determined that both rounds entered Jennings in his chest area. One shot lacerated his heart and lung. A Hennepin County grand jury returned a no bill on October 11, 1988. Clemons has since left law enforcement. Niebur is now the Chief of Police at a Minneapolis suburb.

II

Saint Paul Police Officer David Timm was working at the Hampden Park Food Cooperative on Raymond Avenue during the evening of October 12, 1993. Unfortunately, three young men had a different idea about what to do that evening. Nineteen-year-old Kia Lor, eighteen-year-old Bruce Teng Thao and sixteen-year-old Pha Vang were up to no good that night. They wanted to get some money that night. However, their plan was not to work— it was to commit an armed robbery. Apparently Lor and Thao picked up Vang. Lor asked Vang if he wanted to do an "AR." Vang knew that to be an armed robbery and did not contest the idea. Lor drove to his residence to get his .357 revolver. Lor told Vang that he had robbed the targeted store previously and that it was "easy."

Ten months previously, in December 1992, Hampden Co-op was robbed by four men wearing ski masks just before closing at 9:00 p.m. An attempt was again made in January 1993 just prior to closing. However, it was unsuccessful as the doors had already been locked. The Hampden Co-Op decided that it was time to hire an off-duty police officer. There was some controversy from board members of the cooperative because they were opposed to an armed person. Those opposing said that if a robber came into the store demanding money, the employee should just give it to him. When David Timm was hired, he told board members that he would use his weapon to protect himself or others if necessary as Minnesota statutes provide.

At almost 9:00 p.m., Lor drove his vehicle to the co-op and parked it. The three young men entered the co-op, with Lor leading the way. Vang and Teng were immediately behind him. All three were wearing handkerchiefs (bandanas) or other clothing items over their faces to hide their identities. Timm was off to the side of the entry in full police uniform talking to an acquaintance when they entered. Apparently, none of them had thought to check out the co-op to see if there was security.

Lor, according to witnesses, began calling out, "Hit the floor. Get on the fucking floor." A forty-two-year-old man and his daughter were standing near the checkout area. He stated that the robber pointed his gun at him and daughter as if to encourage him to hurry to the floor. He heard one of the robbers shout, "Where's the cash register?" About the same time, Vang, who later confessed to his participation, saw Timm and immediately exited. He told investigators that he did not believe Timm saw him.

The witness heard shouting and saw one robber who was waving his gun back and forth point his gun at Timm. One shot rang out. He saw Timm struggle with that robber, later identified as Teng, and his gun fall to the floor. The weapon discharged as it hit the floor and the round came close to the man and his daughter. Another shot rang out, and Teng fell to the floor. Timm called to the man to "get out of the store" while pointing to the rear exit. Timm ran out the front door in pursuit of the fleeing robbers.

Timm later told investigators that he was standing about seventeen feet from the cash register talking to someone when he heard Lor come into the store yelling to "get down." He saw a man and a little girl go to the floor. Timm announced that he was a police officer and told the robbers to put down their guns. One of the robbers fired at him. Timm fired his 9-mm Glock at one of the robbers. They began to wrestle, and Timm fired his weapon again. The robber's gun fell as he went to the floor. Timm told the customers to get out the back door as he ran out the front. He saw Lor run across the street by a tree as if he was using it to hide. For some unknown reason, Lor started across the street directly at Timm. Timm fired again, and Lor fell to the street. Timm ran back into the store and told an employee to call 911. Timm indicated that when he first exited the store he thought he saw someone running away to his left. A witnesses walking in the area came forward and verified that someone had run away. That person was identified as Vang. When he was arrested, he confessed to that robbery and six other armed robberies that had occurred during the past year. He told officers that he did not have a weapon in the co-op robbery. He said that he "would have killed the officer" had he been armed.

Medical assistance arrived, and both Lor and Teng were taken to the hospital. Both died at the hospital from gunshots to the upper body.

Timm, the oldest officer involved in a fatal shooting at age fifty-nine, was the wrong person to confront with a weapon. Timm was an excellent shot and one of the Range Masters for Saint Paul Police.

It was also determined that Lor had been arrested twice preciously on weapon violations and was a member of the Cobras youth street gang. Teng had quit attending school prior to the shooting.

Timm was cleared by a Ramsey County grand jury.

III

This shooting incident occurred while the officer was off duty but not getting paid. Jeffrey Johnson, a seventeen-year-old high school student, had been a Minneapolis Police Explorer for three years. He wanted to become a police officer and was participating as a ride-along with Officer Paul Moen on Saturday, November 6, 1993. Johnson had been riding with Moen who was assigned to the Fourth Precinct, an area that covered the northwest side of Minneapolis. This particular precinct handled some of the most violent crimes in the city. There were numerous homicides in the area, and drug dealing was also a major problem. Moen was taking Johnson home in his personal vehicle, a 1993 red Isuzu pickup truck, at the end of the shift.

Johnson related to homicide investigators that he was going to his residence with Moen about 11:40 p.m. As they approached his home, he saw two black males physically fighting near the street. Moen pulled behind a car parked in front of Johnson's house. One of the two fighting started jogging toward them in the pickup. As he reached the vehicle, Johnson recalled Moen saying, "He's got a gun."

The young man, later identified as twenty-one-year-old Phillip Gonzales, turned and yelled, "Fuck you," and fired the gun at the person with whom he had been fighting. He then turned and pointed the gun at Moen.

Johnson stated that he went for cover by opening his passenger door and crouching on the street next to the opened door. He heard three shots that sounded much louder than the ones Gonzales had fired. Johnson looked up and saw him still standing with his gun aimed at Moen's head. He then saw Moen fire several shots at Gonzales. Gonzales fell to the street. Johnson then heard more shots coming from the direction of the other man. Moen got out of his vehicle to see if he could see where the other man had gone. He came back to Johnson and said that the other one had run away. He asked Johnson if he was okay.

Neither Moen nor Johnson was injured. Johnson said he would run into his house and call 911. Moen said he would call from his cell and Johnson heard him say "Emergency, officer needs assistance." He gave the location and address to the 911 operator. Moen then checked on Gonzales. Johnson also checked him and did not believe he was breathing.

Fifty-three-year-old Paul Moen was a twenty-four-year veteran of the department at the time of the shooting. He related to investigators that he was almost at Johnson's house when he saw three black males fighting. He went past them and made a U-turn to pull in front of Johnson's house. Johnson asked him if they should call 911 about the fight. He saw one of the men running away and felt it would not be necessary to intervene. He had rolled down his window in an attempt to hear what was happening. The lighting conditions were excellent. In addition to his vehicle's lights, there was a street light directly above them.

Johnson was about to get out of the pickup when Gonzales came running near Moen's truck and stopped. Moen watched him reach into his waistband and pull out a handgun. He took a few steps and then turned and shot in the direction of the other two males. Moen stated that he "became alarmed" and pulled his duty weapon, a Beretta 9-mm pistol, from his holster. He was still wearing his full Minneapolis police uniform with a jean jacket open in the front over his shirt.

Gonzales appeared to become aware of Moen in his pickup. Before Moen could identify himself as an officer, Gonzales turned and aimed directly at Moen's face. After seeing Gonzales fire at the others, Moen feared for his and possibly Johnson's life. He fired his weapon three or four times. Gonzales starting leaning forward and the barrel of his weapon started to lower. Gonzales made "eye contact" with Moen and started to raise the weapon in an upward movement. Moen estimated that Gonzales was only five feet or so from him. He extended his weapon out the open window and fired again until he began to fall. Moen saw him hit the pavement and the gun fall from his hand. He heard shots coming toward him from the direction of the other two men who had been in the fight. Moen fired one shot in the direction of the two. He then grabbed his cell and called 911. He stated that he was still talking to 911 when squads arrived and secured the scene.

When the duty Sgt. Mike Fossum arrived at the scene, he checked Gonzales, who was about four feet from Moen's pickup. He was obviously dead. Fossum cancelled the medical response. Gonzales was wearing a black pullover shirt, blue jeans, and black suede tennis shoes. At his feet was an Essex Arms .45-caliber pistol. Four fired casings were near the body. Investigators ran the license of a vehicle that neighbors said was unfamiliar to them. It was registered to a female in the suburb of Brooklyn Park. The lady told police that the car was being used by her boyfriend Phillip Terrell Gonzales. She had not seen him for several hours.

It was determined that Gonzales had numerous contacts with law enforcement dating back to 1988. The charges included discharge of a firearm, narcotics, theft, and disorderly conduct. He had been sentenced to forty-four months of conditional non-confinement and had recently been released from prison in St. Cloud. The handgun in his possession had been reported stolen in Saint Paul on January 10, 1993.

An autopsy was conducted and determined that Gonzales died from multiple gunshot wounds to the head and chest. There were seven entry wounds, and any of them could have caused immediate death. The keys to his girlfriend's car, a bag of crack cocaine and one marijuana cigarette were on his person.

Johnson's mother was interviewed by police when she arrived home just after the shooting. She saw all of the police cars and Gonzales' body in the street. Her son told her that Moen had possibly saved his life. She related that her twenty-year-old son had been killed in 1990. He had been stabbed by someone trying to steal his vehicle parked in the alley behind their house. In July 1993, one of Jeffrey's friends was shot in their front yard. He survived, and that incident increased Jeffrey's desire to be a police officer.

A Hennepin County grand jury returned a no bill on February 16, 1994. Tragically, Moen died of a heart attack while on duty wrestling with a suspect on July 1, 1995.

IV

On March 23, 1996, Minneapolis Officers Jonathan Beecham and Dwayne Walker were working from 10:00 p.m. to 3:00 a.m. at the Riverside Supper Club on the north side of Minneapolis. The Riverside was a large establishment with a huge parking lot.

Four friends, two males and two females, decided to go to the Riverside to dance. When they pulled into the parking lot, the car stopped. Carlos, who owned the car, opened the hood to check on the car. While he was looking under the hood, he yelled at his friend Kisha to try to start it. It still would not start, so he tried to move the cables to the battery. He heard a voice say, "It's a jack, mother fucker. Don't move." Carlos saw two black males. One ran up to him and put a gun to his head. The other one grabbed his friend Wayne who had been in the car with him.

The robber put a "9-mm or .45 auto" to his right temple. The robber said, "Mother fucker, where's it at?"

Carlos said, "What, man?"

The robber said, "Mother fucker, the money." The robber was patting Carlos' front pocket at the same time. He took some cash that Carlos had in his pocket. He pulled out Carlos' identification from his other pocket and then returned it. The robber continued searching his shirt pockets, back pockets, and jacket. Carlos had just cashed his weekly paycheck and believed that he had between $450 and $500 dollars in cash. Carlos could hear the other robber demanding cash from Wayne and Kisha. He heard Kisha say that she had no money.

The man told her, "Shut up, bitch." Carlos then heard four or five shots.

The person robbing him said to the other robber, "What the fuck you shoot for?"

The other person said, "Fuck these niggers."

Kisha told investigators that after the car stopped she had to go to the bathroom. She exited the car and did "her thing." As she stood to pull up her pants, she heard a "dude" near Carlos say, "Give me your money, mother fucker." She then heard some shots. She said she could not see Wayne and assumed he was down on the ground as another robber was talking to him. The robber by Carlos walked toward her and said, "Bitch, where's the money?" She said she had no money and told him to check her purse in the front street. The robber then asked her for a kiss. He kissed her on the cheek and then ran away.

Wayne had almost the same story. He said he got out of the back seat and asked a person nearby for some help. The next thing he recalled was hearing gunshots and a person telling him to give him money. He took out his wallet and gave it to the man. He was told to get on the ground and some-one fired a round near his head.

Tina, the fourth person in the car, recalled some guys in hooded sweatshirts and carrying guns came up to the car. They announced a robbery. She took off running toward the entrance of the Riverside and heard gunshots. She yelled that there was shooting in the parking lot. She heard more shots and went back to check on her friends. Carlos said that they had stolen five hundred dollars from him. Seconds later they saw a guy lying on the ground. Carlos pointed at him and said, "He took five hundred dollars from me."

Beecham and Walker were just inside the entrance about 1:40 a.m. when they were approached by a female who told them, "They're out there shooting." They radioed the police dispatcher that shots had been fired and immediately ran to the parking lot.

Beecham followed about five to ten feet behind Walker. He heard Walker call to the black male, "Let me see your hands." About that same time he saw a black male running away from them. The man had a gun in his right hand. Walker started to pursue the person running away. He could hear Walker yelling for the man to stop.

Beecham saw the first suspect begin to trot away in a slow jog and then sprint through the parking lot. Beecham was running parallel with the first suspect in the parking lot while also trying to watch Walker in his pursuit of the second suspect. He saw the second suspect swing his firearm in the direction of Walker. He saw Walker shoot at the man. He saw the man turn to run and then fall to the ground. Beecham then focused on the first suspect. He saw him get into the passenger side of a car. He radioed the description of the car. He saw that responding squads had cut off the getaway car. Beecham ran to the car and identified the passenger as twenty-one-year-old Eugene Clanton.

Walker told investigators that he saw a small blue car (owned by Carlos) with the driver's door open and an individual on the ground next to the door. Walker thought that the person on the ground may have been a shooting victim. Two other people were standing by the car. He saw a black male walking away from the car. Walker called out his identity and told the person to stop and raise his hands. He then saw another black male run from the car. As the man began to run, he heard a woman scream, "He just shot him."

He then heard a male yell, "Stop him. He just robbed me." Walker began pursuing that man.

Walker shouted at the man to "Stop," and "Raise your hands." He saw a handgun in the man's right hand. He called for him to "Drop the gun" numerous times. The suspect stopped, turned toward Walker and pointed the gun at him. Walker fired his Beretta 9-mm numerous times at the man. The man turned and ran about fifteen to twenty yards before collapsing to the ground. Walker held the suspect at gunpoint and told the victims of the robbery who had come to his area to keep their distance. Walker handcuffed the man. Numerous Minneapolis officers arrived and assisted him. A .38-caliber revolver was found next to the suspect.

Carlos told police that he heard the police who ran into the parking lot yell, "Freeze," when the robbers started to run. When the officer quit shooting, he heard one of them (Walker) say, "We got one." He went to that officer and told him that the person down, "He got my money. They just robbed me." Walker told him to back away and remove his hands from his pockets. Other officers arrived and put him in a police car. He was identified and interviewed. Wayne told police that he stayed on the ground and did not see anyone well enough to identify them.

Carlos's car had three holes in the windshield and one in the driver's side mirror. Four .380 casings were found next to the car. A .380 Smith and Wesson handgun was found in the parking lot under a car in the area where was chasing Clanton. The casings found were examined and determined to have been fired from the recovered weapon. Clanton denied any involvement. When told that his clothing was going to be checked for gunshot residue, he said he had been to a local gun range. When asked the name and location of the range, he responded, "I can't remember." He was later charged and convicted of robbery and attempted robbery.

The suspect who was shot and killed was twenty-eight-year-old Keith L. Jackson. Jackson was originally from Missouri, graduating from high school in 1986. He attended the University of Nebraska in Lincoln for two years. He eventually received a license in cosmetology and moved to Minneapolis. An autopsy determined that Jackson was hit by four rounds. One in his forehead proved to be fatal. He had three hundred dollars in twenties and a total of $316 in paper money in his pocket.

The driver of the getaway car told police that he knew Jackson had a .38-caliber revolver that night, but he denied knowing that Clanton and Jackson were going to rob anyone. He heard shots from the location where they had gone and then saw Jackson running. He said he saw Jackson fall, and Clanton jumped into his car at the same time. He figured they had done something wrong and just wanted to get out of the area. He was stopped by police cars before he went very far.

A no bill was returned by a Hennepin County grand jury on May 16, 1996.

V

Thirty-eight- year-old Edina Police Officer Jeffrey Elasky was working a security detail at the Best Buy Company's warehouse in Edina on Thursday, August 15, 2002, from 3:00 to 11:00 p.m. He was not in uniform, wearing blue jeans, T-shirt and carrying his weapon in a fanny-pack holster.

Elasky decided to take his lunch break at 8:20 p.m. He left the Best Buy building en route to a Subway nearby on Industrial Boulevard. It only took him less than three minutes to get to the Subway. He drove his personal car and parked directly in front of the store. He saw a red Chevrolet Impala as he pulled into the lot. That was the same type of vehicle that an Edina police reserve officer he knew drove, and he wondered if he was in the Subway. He could then see through the glass that he was in the Subway.

There were two Hispanic employees working behind the counter. The reserve officer and another white male were the only other customers in the store. Elasky and the reserve officer made small talk while the sandwich was being prepared. The officer got his food and sat down directly across from the cash register. The other person took his food to the back of the store's eating area. A white female came in behind Elasky and ordered a sandwich. Two white males and a white female then entered the store. One of the Hispanic employees was having language difficulty understanding what one of the new customers ordered. The other employee left the cash register to assist.

Elasky stood with his back to the cash register and was talking to the officer while he was eating. They were only about three feet apart. All of a sudden a black male, later identified as thirty-year-old Lamont Scott, entered the store and pulled out what appeared to be a blued semiautomatic handgun from inside his coat or waistband. He started walking toward the customers. He was about five to ten feet inside the store. Scott was pointing the handgun at everyone in the store and yelling, "Get on the fucking ground, this is a robbery." He said it twice.

Elasky recalled that there was another person entering about the same time as Scott. Elasky felt the two might have been together. The other person was a white male in his late teens or early twenties. He had a jersey with the number 24 on it. He did not see a weapon in that person's possession. Elasky told investigators another reason he believed them to be together was, "If he would have been a customer and would have seen the gun in the black guy's hand, a normal person would have run."

The other customers were backing away from the man with the gun toward where Elasky was standing. Scott continued waving the gun at them still screaming, "This is a fucking robbery. Everybody on the ground."

Elasky told investigators later, "Several things were going through my mind. I was scared that I was going to die and the customers would be next. I was wondering how I was going to get my firearm out of my fanny pack holster without him shooting me first."

Elasky crouched behind the cash register and took his Smith and Wesson .40-caliber pistol from the holster. He did not think Scott saw him. Customers were screaming and going to the floor. Elasky believed that "we were all going to die." As the customers in line behind him were going down, Scott pointed the gun at him and screamed at him, "Get on the ground." Scott was about ten to fifteen feet from him. He then took a couple of steps toward him and swung the gun in his direction. Elasky stood up from behind the counter and fired two shots. Elasky did not announce his identity as a police officer. He said, "I didn't have time. I believed he was going to shoot me so I shot first."

Elasky saw one round hit Scott in the upper right chest. He spun around and ran out the front door heading northeast. The white male with him ran by Elasky to the back office area. Elasky was hollering, "Police—Stop." He yelled at the reserve officer to call 911 to get help and an ambulance. The other customers were screaming and crying. He told the people still in the store that he was an Edina police officer and pulled out his badge so they could see it. He continued to cover the front and back doors as he was not sure where the two had gone.

Edina Officer Vik Konters arrived, and together they checked the back office area. The back door was open and the white male was gone. More officers arrived and went outside looking for the suspects. Elasky felt that he should go back in the Subway because he was not in uniform and had no ballistic vest. Before getting to the door, he heard officers shouting, "Put your hands up." He turned and saw Scott. The officers continued yelling at him and he was not moving. Elasky approached Scott with another Edina officer. He saw a gun in the grass about three feet from Scott's left hand. Scott was taken by ambulance to Hennepin County Medical Center where he was pronounced dead. Elasky was taken to a nearby hospital for a blood test.

The second robber, nineteen-year-old Anthony R. Marcum, fled to the nearby TGI Fridays restaurant. He went into the restroom and changed clothes. He was identified by customers at the Subway and TGI Fridays and taken into custody.

Scott had felony convictions for narcotics and armed robbery. He had a warrant for his arrest in California at the time of the robbery. Marcum also had a record. However they were all juvenile and unavailable. Marcum was sentenced to eight years in jail for attempted robbery of the Subway and for an earlier robbery of the same Subway. He also admitted to another robbery with Scott in St. Louis Park. Marcum remains incarcerated at the Minnesota maximum prison at Oak Park Heights with a possible release date of November 25, 2008.

A Hennepin County grand jury returned a no bill on January 26, 2003.

Chapter Thirteen

Who Says Drugs Are Okay?
aka Drug Related Matters

I

Drug dealers never seem to learn. When you have people coming and going from a residence at all hours of the day and night, you are going to attract attention from the neighbors and police. This was the case at 2901 3rd Avenue South in Minneapolis. Police informants had made several purchases of cocaine and crack at the six-unit apartment building. There were three apartments upstairs and three down. The concern for police was apartments 5 and 6 upstairs (apartment 4 was unoccupied).

Just after midnight on July 15, 1987, patrol officers stopped a suspicious vehicle for a traffic violation. The man in the vehicle was questioned by officers, and he told them that the woman in his car had approached him on a nearby street requesting twenty dollars for a "blow job." The man claimed he was a cab driver by profession and was aware that the address where he let the woman in his car was a known drug and prostitution house.

The officers then removed the woman from the car to question her. She could not produce any identification and clutched her purse. Fearing that she might have a weapon, the officers asked her to allow them to look in it. She complied. The officer found two twenty bills, makeup, and a pill. As the officer started to walk her back to his squad, she stated, "I can help you guys. I know what you are looking for in that house [2901 3rd Avenue]. I just made a buy about two hours ago. There is crack cocaine being sold there. Those people ripped me off, I want to cooperate with you guys to bust them."

Narcotics officers were contacted, and she was taken the Third Precinct where they could interview her. She was willing to make a "controlled buy." The information she gave was that there were always several people in the two upstairs apartments and the occupants always had weapons. She further indicated that there were always lookouts. Usually, one would be outside and one on the second floor to inform of "unauthorized" visitors. The lookouts were also supposedly armed. She was given two "marked" twenty-dollar bills and made a controlled buy of crack cocaine. The Emergency Response Unit (ERU) was called after a Hennepin County judge signed a search warrant.

It was decided that a ruse was needed to gain entry to the apartment building due to the lookouts. The ruse would be an officer disguising himself as a pizza delivery person in order to get control of the outside lookout. Thirty-six-year-old Bob Thunder had been working in full uniform in a squad in the north Fourth Precinct. He and his partner were asked if they wanted to work some overtime in the Third Precinct. Thunder's partner declined, but Thunder volunteered. He was told to change into street clothes and that he would be acting as a pizza delivery man. He was also told there would be a narcotics warrant after he gained entry. He secured his off-duty weapon, a .357 revolver issued by the department. When he met with the officers organizing the warrant, he asked about how to conceal the weapon rather than keeping it on his belt. A light jacket would look suspicious in the July heat. The decision was made to actually put the weapon in an empty pizza box. He went with an officer to a local twenty-four-hour police hangout called the Pizza Shack. He was given an empty box and access to one of the employee's vehicles used to deliver pizza.

The officers met a few blocks away to finalize the execution of the warrant. Thunder was told that he was to wait until the other officers and ERU were in position. Then he was to "neutralize" (control) the lookout at the front door by placing him under arrest. Another officer was going to do the same to a lookout a block away on a bridge. When everyone was in position, Thunder and a female narcotics officer (as the passenger) would drive to the front of the building. Thunder was going to approach the door along with the female officer following him. As they approached the building in the car at 3:25 a.m., he received a radio transmission that there was a male standing on the steps. Thunder exited the car with the pizza box in his left hand and his gun in an opening in the box with his right.

He approached the man on the steps anouncing "Pizza Delivery." When asked by the man where he was going, he answered by saying "upstairs." When he got to the first step, he threw down the pizza box and yelled, "Police officer, freeze." The lookout was ordered to put his hands in the air. As Thunder started up the steps, the lookout, later identified as thirty-one-yeear-old Gerald "Bud" Whitten, began backing away to a darkened area. As Whitten was doing this, he went into a crouched position. Thunder yelled for him to show his hands. Whitten came up from the crouched position with a gun in his hand. Fearing for his life, Thunder fired once from about four feet. Whitten slumped backwards. Realizing that he had shot Whitten, Thunder shouted to call an ambulance. Other officers ran past him to carry on with the search. There were additional gunshots fired by police at the lookout upstairs. No one was injured. One suspect jumped out the second-story window and was immediately caught by officers covering the back. That man had no weapon. However, he did have $357 and the two marked twenty-dollar bills. A total of three males and two females were arrested.

Whitten died at the scene from a gunshot wound over his left eye. Next to him was a Smith and Wesson Model 60 .38-caliber revolver. A weapon recovered in the upstairs search was a Smith and Wesson 9-mm stolen from Bill's Gun Shop on November 27, 1985. Cocaine and crack cocaine was seized during the search as well as other drug paraphernalia. One of the men arrested told police, "All I does is smoke a little reefer once in awhile.'"

One woman told police, "I don't know nothin' about no dope." She also claimed that she never saw anyone with a gun or selling drugs. She said that someone came upstairs yelling, "The police is coming."

A Hennepin County grand jury returned a no bill on August 4, 1987.

II

Occasionally, a police department will have to conduct an investigation in another jurisdiction and a shooting will occur. This is exactly what happened on Tuesday, November 21, 2000, when Saint Paul Police had to conduct a shooting investigation by Minneapolis officers occurring in Saint Paul.

Officer Dave Garman of the Minneapolis Police Department was working as a plain-clothes officer in the Community Response Team (CRT) unit. Sometime in the late summer of 2000 he met a person known to him only as "Mike," later identified as Michael Ivory. The two had a conversation that eventually turned to marijuana. Ivory told Garman he could "hook him up" with marijuana. Sometime later, possibly late September, the two met again. Garman was actually off duty eating at Mickey's Diner in Saint Paul. They again talked about various things, including marijuana. Garman gave Ivory his work cell number.

On November 21, 2000, Ivory called Garman and told him he wanted to sell Garman some marijuana. Ivory described the quantity and price of the marijuana for sale. A deal was made for Garman to purchase one half pound of marijuana for seven hundred dollars by a friend of Garman. Ivory wanted the sale to take place at Mickey's Diner in Saint Paul as "his guy" did not want to go into the City of Minneapolis. While Garman was talking to Ivory on the telephone, it sounded like a white man talking in the background. (The cell phone used by Ivory was later determined to be listed to

Jimmy Fye of Saint Paul.)

Discussion about who to look for at Mickey's Diner took place. Ivory said that they would be in a small blue car. Ivory called twice saying they were in Mickey's parking lot and wondered where Garman's friend was located. The decision by Garman's group was to make a buy/bust and not allow them to leave the parking lot.

Thirty-one-year-old Mike Kaneko, an Asian male, was the officer to make the purchase. He was equipped with a body transmitter. Kaneko knew what Ivory looked like and had a description of the car. However, he did not have any information regarding Ivory's friend. Kaneko called the Saint Paul Police narcotics unit to make sure they were not working on suspects at Mickey's Diner nor were there undercover officers working as drug dealers. Kaneko made certain his body transmitter was operating and that his backup officers were on site in the parking lot. He waited a few blocks away for a Saint Paul squad to arrive.

After meeting the Saint Paul officers, Kaneko and his partner, Kara Abbas, proceeded in his undercover vehicle to Mickey's Diner. As he came into the lot, he saw a van in the lot which looked like it was part of the drug transaction. He parked near the van and transmitted the license number to backup. He went in the parking lot and parked. No one approached his vehicle. Shortly, a vehicle matching the description given to him pulled in behind him. Ivory got out of the blue Toyota and came up to Kaneko's pickup and entered the passenger side. Ivory told him the man wanted to do the transaction elsewhere. Kaneko told him he did not want to move and wanted to talk to his friend.

Kaneko went to the blue car and spoke to the driver, later identified as twenty-nine-year-old James C. Fye. Kaneko talked to Fye through a rolled-down window. Fye said he had the marijuana in the car, but he wanted to leave because there were too many police in the area. Kaneko and Fye continued to discuss the purchase.

At that moment, the van in the parking lot began to exit. Kaneko asked

Fye if he knew the people in the van and whether it was involved in the deal. Fye said it was not. The backup officers drove into the lot behind the exiting van. Kaneko saw Officer Scott Ramsdell exit the backup vehicle and begin approaching Fye's Toyota. Kaneko could see Ramsdell's badge displayed in the middle of his chest with his gun out. Ramsdell started shouting, "Police. Police."

Kaneko looked at Fye and he appeared to have a "startled or panicked" look on his face. Fye dropped his hand between the seats and shifted the car into reverse. Fye quickly backed up and swung the car around. Kaneko said other officers ran to the Toyota and shouted, "No, no, no, stop, police." Kaneko stepped away as he was supposed to be arrested along with Fye. Fye continued ahead to the west exit of the parking lot.

Officer Ramsdell was in front of Fye's car. He was struck by the Toyota in his legs causing him to lose his balance and fall onto the hood. Kaneko saw Officer Aaron Morrison approach the passenger side of the car and holler, "Stop." Ramsdell slid off the car and it appeared as though Fye was going to run over him. The vehicle lunged forward again. Kaneko moved to the rear passenger side of the vehicle. Kaneko heard gunshots and muzzle flashes. He could see glass breaking out of the Toyota.

The Toyota continued out of the parking lot to the street. Kaneko heard more gunfire, but could not see Ramsdell. Kaneko told investigators he believed that Ramsdell was being dragged by the Toyota, or he was dead from being hit by it. Kaneko ran out onto the street and fired one shot from his .40-caliber pistol. The car stopped across 7th Street next to the median in the middle.

Ramsdell told investigators he was part of the arrest team. He had met with the Saint Paul officers also. The Saint Paul officers were given a radio to monitor Kaneko's conversations. He and Morrison drove by Mickey's parking lot and saw Kaneko's undercover pickup with the blue car matching the suspect's vehicle behind it. They also saw a maroon van in the lot.

They listened to the conversation between Kaneko and Fye. Fye mentioned that he had the marijuana in his trunk. The decision was made to arrest him, so they drove to the west entrance to the lot. They could see Kaneko talking to a white male in the blue car. They also saw other arresting officers from Minneapolis blocking a maroon van from leaving the east entrance of the lot.

Ramsdell had his badge clipped to his shirt, and Morrison had his badge hanging from a chain around his neck. Ramsdell took out his gun and approached the car, shouting, "Police. Shut off the car. Step out of the car." Morrison walked up to the driver's side and Ramsdell started to walk behind the car to get to the passenger side. Kaneko was backing away from the car. Ramsdell could see Fye make eye contact with Morrison, and then the car started moving in reverse. The tires started spinning, and Ramsdell had to jump away from the car. As the car was backing up, Ramsdell saw Morrison react as if he had been struck by the car.

Fye had the car in a position to go out the west entrance (not an exit) to the street. Ramsdell was directly between the car and the street. The car was not moving. Ramsdell had his gun out and trained directly on Fye. He was yelling, "Minneapolis police." Ramsdell was about fifteen feet in front of the car when he saw the tires begin to spin and come at him. The car hit him, and he went up on the passenger side hood. He started to fire his gun with his right hand at the driver while on the hood of the car. The car continued toward the street. Ramsdell rolled off the hood on the passenger side while he continued firing more shots. The car then went down West 7th Street on the wrong side of the street. Ramsdell continued firing at it.

The car stopped in the street, and all of the officers approached it. An ambulance was called. Fye was dead at the scene. Ivory was hit and taken to Regions Hospital where he recovered with no complications.

Ivory spoke to investigators. He related the same story about meeting Garman, known to him only as "D." Ivory contacted Fye, whom he had known since 1995-96 when they were incarcerated together at Faribault prison. Arrangements were made to sell a half pound of marijuana to one of D's friends for $750 at Mickey's Diner at 6:45 p.m.

When Fye and Ivory drove by Mickey's, Fye thought there were cops around. They went into the lot anyway and parked behind the pickup that they were to meet for the deal. Ivory went to the pickup and told the "Chinese guy" that his friend wanted to leave the area. The guy got out of his pickup and came back to talk to Fye. Ivory was surprised when Fye told him the marijuana was in the truck because Ivory had seen him put it in his coat pocket when they left Fye's house. Ivory said something about seeing a couple of white guys coming and they were going to get robbed. Fye threw the car in reverse as Ivory saw a white guy coming up on his side of the car. Ivory told Fye that he wanted out, but "things were happening too fast." Fye straightened out the car and stepped on the gas. Just as they were about to exit the parking lot, he heard shots being fired at them. The person on his side of the car shot first. Ivory believed the first shot was the one that hit him in the shoulder. Ivory was also hit in the forehead with the round exiting at the top of his head (a glancing wound that did not penetrate the skull). Another shot was a "through and through" to his right shoulder causing no major damage.

Ivory claimed he did not hear anyone yell that they were police nor did he see any badges. Ivory admitted he was the "go between guy" for about ten or so deals involving Fye selling marijuana. Most of these were small twenty-dollar bags. Ivory knew that Fye used methamphetamine and saw Fye shoot up a syringe of it before they left his house to do the sale.

It was determined at autopsy that Fye had three entrance wounds. Recovered from his person and Toyota were zip-type plastic baggies containing marijuana, methamphetamine, and cocaine. Fye had a criminal record dating back to 1979 for robbery, assaults, burglary, illegal drugs and parole violation.

A Ramsey County grand jury cleared the officers. A civil suit was filed against the City of Minneapolis, Minneapolis Police Department, and the three officers for using excessive force, negligent training of their officers, and violation of the Fourth Amendment by Fye's family. The suit was dismissed with no money being awarded on August 4, 2004.

Mike Kaneko is now a special agent with the BCA.

III

Police officers know that drug transactions are always dangerous. Whether it is a "buy/bust" or a search warrant for drugs, officers are alert to the paranoid demeanor of the individuals involved. This shooting incident started long before the actual day that the shooting occurred. On February 11, 2003, a Hennepin County deputy assigned to the narcotics squad met with a Confidential Reliable Informant (CRI). The CRI told the deputy that a black male about twenty-six to twenty-seven years old, five-foot-eight, stocky build with numerous gold teeth that he only knew as "Chase" was dealing illegal drugs. Chase lived in an apartment building at 6806 63rd Avenue North in Brooklyn Park. The CRI had two cell numbers to reach Chase for the purchase of drugs. The CRI was able to identify Chase from a photograph as twenty-eight-year-old Antonio Demetrice Harvey. Harvey was well known to local law enforcement.

Arrangements were made to have the CRI make a drug purchase from Harvey. On February 13, 2003, a purchase of 6.6 grams of cocaine was made by the CRI from Harvey. There was discussion between the two about making a purchase of a larger quantity of drugs. A search warrant was obtained, and a search of his vehicle was conducted. Only a small amount of marijuana was found. Harvey admitted that the marijuana was his, and it was also determined that he had an outstanding warrant for a driving violation. His brother, Maurice Harvey, was with him and there was also an outstanding warrant for him. Both appeared in court and were released.

On March 12, 2003, deputies met with the CRI to arrange another purchase of cocaine from Antonio Harvey. A controlled buy of 27.8 grams of cocaine was made at the apartment building of 6806 63rd. Again, there was a discussion about purchasing a larger quantity of drugs.

After numerous calls back and forth, the purchase of eight ounces of cocaine from Antonio was arranged for March 25. Numerous officers, including a surveillance team watching Harvey, were involved in the proposed "buy/bust." Harvey and the CRI met throughout the day while a surveillance team observed them. It was finally determined that the CRI would pay seven thousand dollars for the eight ounces. With Harvey during the meetings was his friend Robert Lane.

Surveillance had Antonio and Lane returning to a house on Upton Avenue North in Minneapolis. During surveillance at that address, another black male arrived. He was wearing a red baseball cap, multi-colored polo shirt and light pants. This person was identified as thirty-year-old Roderick Harvey. Officers were now aware of three individuals possibly involved in the transaction, and all were wearing distinctive clothing. This was related to the officers involved. A call to Antonio at 4:15 p.m. determined that the CRI and Harvey would meet in the parking lot of the Brooklyn Park apartment in twenty minutes.

Because this was to take place in Brooklyn Park, narcotics officers met two Brooklyn Park Police Department (BPPD) marked squads to explain the proposed plan to arrest Harvey after the transaction was completed. The marked squads would be used to let Harvey know that law enforcement was involved and it was not a "rip off" by another drug dealer.

At approximately 4:50 p.m. surveillance officers saw Antonio and Lane exit the Minneapolis residence and enter a tan-colored Buick. Both were wearing the previously described clothing furnished to other officers. Roderick Harvey also left dressed the same and entered a silver Kia. They drove away in tandem in the direction of Brooklyn Park. Surveillance was not continued. The CRI called Antonio around 5:57 p.m. and was informed that they would meet in the parking lot in approximately seven minutes. The surveillance team for the arrest near the parking lot observed the CRI parking his GMC pickup in the parking lot. A few minutes later the Kia entered the parking lot. About five minutes later the Buick was seen driving in the area as if conducting a counter-surveillance.

The CRI was wearing an electronic monitoring device and transmitted that a black male wearing a red baseball cap was approaching his vehicle. The surveillance team saw the person and knew it to be Roderick Harvey, supposedly not involved in the transaction, carrying a white plastic bag from a drug or convenience store. Roderick entered the pickup through the passenger door.

The monitored conversation determined that Roderick had four ounces of cocaine. The CRI said that he was waiting for Chase and the deal was for eight ounces. Roderick said he had four ounces and demanded to see the money.

The following is a partial transcript of the discussion between Roderick and the CRI that was being monitored:

CRI: I'm telling you that's where the money is

Roderick: I'm fittin' to kill ya man

CRI: I know and I don't want to die

Roderick: Stop

CRI: I'm telling ya

Roderick: Stop screaming

CRI: Okay, I'm telling ya, I don't want to die…please don't shoot me

Roderick: I don't care about goin' to jail

CRI: I know, I…

Roderick: I'm going to kill you. Are you da po po, If you da po, are you da police?

CRI: No, I'm not

Roderick: Where da money at?

CRI: I'll grab it…can I grab it?

Roderick: No

CRI: Please?

Roderick: No

CRI: You can come right with me

Roderick: Hey, if you move one more time, I swear on my life, I'll kill you. If you drive me crazy once. They're comin'…So you the police…

CRI: No, I'm not. I am not the cops. Please, please, don't shoot me, Please, I'm not.

When hearing what was happening to the CRI, the officers in the two BPPD squads immediately went to the CRI's pickup with lights and sirens activated. Hennepin County Deputy John Seery was in one squad as the passenger. BPPD Officer Jennifer Foster also raced to the scene with BPPD Officer Chris Donahue. Deputy Seery could see two individuals in the front seat of the pickup. A white male was in the driver's seat, and a black male was in the passenger seat. Seery exited the squad and yelled for both of them to put their hands in the air. The passenger jumped over the driver and exited out the driver's door away from Seery.

Seery saw a gun in his hand. He yelled for him to drop the gun. Roderick fled with Seery following him. Roderick went past a couple of cars and then turned pointing the gun at him. Seery fired his .40-caliber pistol. He believed that he hit him. However, Roderick turned and ran away. Seery continued to shout commands for him to drop the weapon. He stopped and turned toward Seery with the gun, so Seery fired again. Roderick then ran around a corner of a garage out of his sight.

Seery was hesitant to go around the corner because he feared Roderick might be waiting to shoot him. He was then joined by other officers. Seery peeked around the corner and saw Roderick lying on his side on the ground. Seery and the other officers started to go toward him, continually calling for him to drop his weapon. Seery could see that the slide on the gun appeared to be jammed and Roderick was trying to work it so he could fire it. Seery moved closer, and Roderick suddenly turned the weapon at him. Seery fired again and heard other officers firing their weapons. Roderick dropped his weapon and Seery ran up and kicked it away from him. Another officer came up and handcuffed him. Yet another officer "gloved up" and put gauze on his wounds. An ambulance was immediately called.

BPPD Officer Chris Donahue saw Roderick exit the CRI's vehicle with

Seery chasing him. He heard two or three shots and saw Roderick fleeing around the corner of a garage out of his sight. He caught up to Seery, and they both cautiously went around the corner. He saw Roderick lying on the ground with the gun in his hand. He yelled for him to drop it. He could not tell for certain but it appeared that the gun had malfunctioned as he was attempting to reload it. Roderick turned the weapon toward them. Donahue began firing at him, as did other officers who had caught up to them.

BPPD Officer Robert Roushar was working in the area in a marked squad. He heard the BPPD squads who were helping transmit that the suspect had a gun and heard the two squads go into the Groves Apartment parking lot with lights and siren. He followed and saw Donahue and Seery chasing a black male. He heard shots being fired. He left his squad and ran up to the garage corner where he had seen the suspect and officers run. He saw a suspect on the ground and officers yelling for him to drop the gun. The suspect seemed focused on Seery and Donahue. He pointed his gun at them. Roushar then fired his .40-caliber pistol at him.

The last person involved in the shooting was thirty-three-year-old Deputy Richard Palaia. His assignment that day was to be part of the surveillance team in a van which would arrest the suspects following the buy. He was with three other Hennepin deputies in the van. He heard the panicked conversation by the CRI and the mention of the gun. The van followed the two marked BPPD squads into the parking lot. He saw Seery chase Roderick around the corner of the garage. He heard the gunshots. He caught up and went around the corner. He could see Roderick with the gun in his hand pointing at his own head. He yelled for him to drop it. Roderick pointed it at Seery and Donahue. Palaia fired his .40-caliber handgun twice.

About two minutes after the BPPD squads entered the parking lot with the lights and siren activated, two Hennepin County vehicles saw the Buick that Antonio and Lane had been seen driving when they left Upton Avenue driving away from the apartment. The car was stopped and they were arrested. Four children were in the backseat of the Buick: two six-year-old boys, one nine-year-old boy, and a two-year-old girl.

Crime scene investigators determined that Roderick fired one round at the officers and the weapon jammed. He was shot before he could fire again. It was not determined who fired the fatal shot, as more than one round could have been fatal. Police records revealed that Roderick had pleaded guilty to fleeing police in Minneapolis in 2001. He was wanted at that time for robbery and was found hiding in a woman's closet. He was sentenced to one year in jail, but the sentence was suspended.

All of the officers were cleared by a Hennepin County grand jury.

IV

The vicinity around Franklin Avenue and Park Avenue near Lake Street in Minneapolis has a reputation involving criminal activity. There are prostitutes walking the streets as well as drug activity and an occasional homicide. Officers are especially alert to possible drug transactions.

Around 4:45 a.m., on Friday, October 10, 2003, Minneapolis Officers Jamie Conway and Charles Greaves were in their marked squad proceeding northbound on Park Avenue (a one-way) near 22nd Street. Officer Greaves noticed two individuals standing by a parked car. It appeared to Greaves that the two were conducting a drug deal. Greaves shined his spotlight on the two. One of the men started walking north from the car. The other man stuffed something in his waistband and proceeded to walk south from the car. Both officers tried verbally to make conversation with the man walking south.

Conway told investigators later that when they asked the man to come over to the squad to talk to them, he said, "What for?"

After that response, Conway said, "Just come over and talk to us." The man, later identified as twenty-one-year-old Walter K. Collins, took off running. Greaves backed up the squad the wrong way on Park Avenue in an attempt to follow him. Collins then made a quick turn eastbound through a hedge. Conway saw that Collins had his left hand tight to his waistband with his right arm swinging in his running motion. Conway believed he had a gun tucked in his waistband. Conway exited the squad, drew his 9-mm pistol and gave chase. He had his gun in his right hand and flashlight in his left.

Conway was several feet behind Collins when he made a sudden change of direction. He had been running east and then turned to go southwest. When he made the turn, Conway saw him remove a gun from his waistband with his right hand. Conway yelled for him to get on the ground four or five times. Conway was gaining on him and cutting off his escape route. Conway told investigators later that when he got closer "he looked directly at me and began to raise the handgun toward me. Fearing that the suspect was going to shoot me, I fired my service weapon at him." Conway saw him take a few more steps and then fall to the ground. The weapon flew about three or four feet from him. Conway stood over the weapon and covered Collins until Greaves caught up to him. Conway was not certain whether he had hit Collins or if he had just fallen on his own.

Conway stated that as Greaves was handcuffed, Greaves said Collins had been hit in the arm. Collins looked up at Conway and noticed blood on his lips. Greaves then removed the handcuffs and checked for wounds in order to administer first aid. Conway said at some point during that time Greaves radioed for an ambulance, Code 3. Conway retrieved first-aid supplies and attended to Collins. Other officers soon arrived and took control of the crime scene. Paramedics and other medical personnel arrived to examine Collins. Conway was taken to the hospital for blood and urine samples per departmental policy.

Greaves related to investigators that after he radioed that Conway was giving chase, he heard Conway shout, "Get down." He then heard two shots. Greaves then pulled into the driveway of the Phillips Eye Institute and saw Conway holding a suspect who was lying on the ground at gunpoint. Greaves exited his squad, and Conway yelled for him to call an ambulance because he might have shot him. Conway was standing near a weapon on the ground. Greaves called for an ambulance and then handcuffed Collins. He noticed that he was spitting blood. He took the cuffs off so his breathing would not be restricted and began rendering first aid. He had to cut off his shirt to locate the wounds. When medical personnel arrived, he let them continue.

Greaves went back to the area where they first saw Collins on Park Avenue. He found a black holster for a handgun. He notified the Hennepin County crime scene team which was processing the shooting scene. The holster was a black nylon Uncle Mike's brand. Next to where Collins had fallen was a model JS, Stallard Arms, Inc. 9-mm pistol. The weapon was traced to a sporting goods store in El Paso, Texas. No further information regarding the purchaser could be found. In the parking lot near the shooting was a black-colored magazine that fit the weapon. The magazine was partially loaded and close to it was one live 9-mm Spear brand round. Three fired shell casings from Conway's weapon were also located near the parking lot.

An autopsy determined that a bullet entered at the outer right portion of the right upper arm with the exit on the inner portion of the right upper arm. Another entrance wound was in the right under arm to the chest. The pathologist believed this would be consistent with the person being struck while his arm was in an extended position. The medical examiner found two scars from apparent bullet wounds earlier in his life.

Collins had been arrested for an aggravated robbery near the location where he was shot. The charges were dismissed when the victim failed to show up for trial. He had been the victim of two shootings, one in January 2002 and one in June 2002.

A Hennepin County grand jury returned a no bill on April 4, 2004.

Chapter Fourteen

Call It Whatever You Like
aka Miscellaneous Crimes

I

This shooting is the very first one that occurred in the twenty-five-year study. A carrier was delivering newspapers on his route when he heard sounds like glass breaking at a townhouse complex. He called the Burnsville police, who responded about 5:20 a.m. on Saturday, January 3, 1981. One officer went to the front of the townhouse and two to the back. The two in the back saw a person with a flashlight moving about in the house. The officers also spotted a broken window in the back of the house. Officers set up waiting for the intruder to come out. The officers rotated at the back of the house near a privacy fence by the patio. It was at least ten degrees below zero, and the officers rapidly got cold.

As seventeen-year-old Gregory Knodel opened the patio door and emerged, Officer Stephen Baker identified himself and ordered him to stop. Knodel screamed and raised a fourteen-inch piece of metal, probably used as his pry bar, as he charged Baker. Baker fired his revolver four times, hitting Knodel three times. He died at the scene. Jewelry, coins, and a prescription bottle of Valium belonging to the residents were found on his body.

Subsequent investigation by authorities determined that the metal piece in his hand when charging the officers was part of a longer piece. The other part of the metal was in a vise at his father's residence miles away. It appeared as though he had recently cut it with a hacksaw. Knodel had been with friends earlier that night and was using a city directory to call numbers in the area to determine if people were home. He told his friends that if no one answered, he would know that the owners were probably gone for the holidays and he would be able to burglarize the residence.

Knodel was AWOL from the Army at the time of the burglary. Baker was cleared by a Dakota County grand jury. However, the city was sued and did make an undisclosed settlement with his family. Officer Baker, who had previously been with the Los Angeles County Sheriff's Office, left the Burnsville Police Department to become a corporate jet pilot. Flying airplanes professionally was something he had been doing on a part-time basis.

II

A call came into the Brooklyn Center Police Department on Wednesday, October 28, 1981, at 3:05 p.m. that a suspicious vehicle was in the parking lot of a complex where a series of auto thefts had occurred. Officer David Grass responded and observed two individuals by a GMC pickup truck running in the parking lot. He lost sight of them as they both went into the apartment building at 3311 North 53rd Avenue.

Grass entered the building and saw an individual later identified as eighteen-year-old Gerald Lavalle banging on the door of an apartment. He had a long-barreled weapon that Grass knew to be either a rifle or shotgun. Grass, who was not seen by Lavalle, backed out of the building and called for assistance. Officer Dennis Flaherty responded to his call for help.

The 911 operator received another call at 3:15 a.m. The male caller said there were two people in the hallway of that apartment building banging on an apartment door and one had a weapon. This information was furnished to the officers who had remained outside. For some unknown reason, Lavalle decided to leave the building. When he came out by himself, the two officers twice yelled at him to, "Freeze, drop the weapon."

When Lavalle brought the weapon up and pointed it toward the officers, they both fired their .357 revolvers at him. Emergency responders arrived and transported him to nearby North Memorial Medical Center. He subsequently died at 2:30 p.m. that afternoon.

The weapon in Lavalle's possession was a .20-gauge shotgun purchased on December 11, 1978. There was one empty shell in the chamber of the gun, and the magazine was full of live rounds. It never was determined if Lavalle fired his weapon. The officers did not recall if he fired at them (possibly due to them firing the revolvers). Neither of the officers was injured.

A Hennepin County grand jury returned a no bill on November 24, 1981.

Grass remained with the department, and Flaherty became the Executive Director of the Minnesota Police and Peace Officers Association. He later worked in the office of the mayor of Saint Paul.

III

Joycelyn Robertson was at her home at 1829 North Girard when she called 911 on Wednesday, January 31, 1996. Minneapolis Officers Gerald Wallerich and Dan Ortiz were dispatched to the apartment at 12:57 a.m. for "unknown trouble." When they arrived, Joycelyn Robertson told them that her ex-husband from Chicago had found her and threatened her. Her husband was not there at the time of the report. She related that she had moved from Chicago with her friend Kesha Williams and had been in Minneapolis only forty days. Joycelyn said she had two children ages two and six months. Kesha had three children ages four, two, and six months. The officers took the report and left.

Derek Ferguson told police he came home to the apartment from work around 1:30 a.m. and discovered that all of the adults in the house had been drinking. Apparently Kesha and Joycelyn had been talking about him, and Joycelyn said that Derek had been using drugs. Derek asked Joycelyn if she had said that, and she denied it. Kesha "got really pissed" and they began arguing. Derek said he took Kesha into another room to "settle her down." They heard Joycelyn call someone a "bitch." Kesha went to ask whom she had called bitch. They began wrestling. Derek broke up the fight.

The two women started fighting again. Kesha had thrown an air freshener can at Joycelyn, and she responded by throwing two glasses back at her. They started fighting in the kitchen. Derek grabbed Kesha and took her into the bathroom. He tried to lock her inside, but she got out. The two continued arguing, and Kesha went back to the kitchen and got a pair of scissors. Kesha had blood on her hands from getting cut by the glasses thrown at her. Derek said he took the scissors away from her.

Apparently, sometime during all of this Robertson was able to call police from her room. While she was on the phone with 911 around 2:15 a.m., Williams hollered "bitch" at her and told her what she was going to do to her. Robertson called 911 three times and told the operator that they better send the police because she was "going to go out there and kick her [Williams'] ass." Robertson was told that the police were on the way, but she told the operator, "I can't wait."

While in her room, Kesha went back into the kitchen and started throwing dishes out of the sink onto the floor. She also grabbed a knife. Joycelyn stayed in the room while Kesha sat in a chair yelling at her to come out of the room. Derek said that he was aware Joycelyn had called the police at least two times. According to Derek, Kesha also knew she had called and told her, "We fought before and there was no police."

The police responded again, and Derek let Officers Wallerich and Ortiz in the apartment. The two officers had been told by dispatch that there were people physically fighting and there were knives and guns involved. The officers saw broken glass all over the kitchen floor, and there was a "burning odor." They saw Kesha sitting on a futon-type chair in the living room. Blood was observed by the officers on the wall and floor. Officer Wallerich asked Kesha what had happened as he saw cuts on her wrist.

Kesha did not answer him. She reached down between the wall and her chair. She came up with a knife in her right hand. Joycelyn came out of her room and said to Kesha, "You're a silly bitch." Kesha grabbed the knife that she had put on the floor and quickly went toward Joycelyn. Everyone yelled for her to stop. Wallerich yelled twice for her to put the knife down.

Kesha kept advancing toward Joycelyn, who was holding her baby and said, "Bitch, I'm going to kill you." Joycelyn backed into the bedroom closet and pulled a bamboo door across in front of her. Kesha attempted to stab Joycelyn two or three times. Wallerich fired one round from his 9-mm pistol, and Kesha fell to the floor.

Scott Hamilton was also in the apartment and helped Derek break up the fights between the two women. He later told investigators that he did not hear the police tell Kesha to drop the knife. He claimed the police called Kesha a "ho" (whore) and told her, "Stop, ho," and, "Ho, don't make me shoot you." He said the police officer shot her twice. He also said he did not see Joycelyn "holding no baby."

Witnesses, other than those in the apartment, were vital to the officer's version of the events. One witness heard commotions in the apartment and called 911. He said he heard what he believed to be a police officer yell, "Drop the knife" and then a shot. Another impartial witness heard "throwing of items crashing" and men sounding like there were breaking up a fight. That witness thought it was women fighting as he heard, "I'll kill you, bitch."

An autopsy determined that Kesha was killed by the one shot. The round went through the third rib into the right chest. It went through the right lung and aorta, stopping in the left lung. Joycelyn was treated for two cuts on her hand. She admitted to police that they had been drinking and arguing. However, she could not recall why they were arguing.

A Hennepin County grand jury returned a no bill on April 9, 1996.

IV

Why would someone attempt to injure a police officer over something as simple as being told to leave a motel room? Brooklyn Park police had to confront such a situation at the Northwest Inn on Monday, March 29, 1999.

Sixty-five-year-old Donald Richter had checked into the Northwest Inn and paid cash for four days, but he had stopped paying. It is the policy of the inn for cash customers to pay in advance. The problem began on Friday, March 26. According to employees at the inn, Richter had threatened at least two room-service employees during the week. He also made threats to the front desk manager when asked to leave. The police were called that Friday. Richter, the manager and police had a discussion regarding the situation. Richter did not appear violent and was not arrested. The comments made by Richter were determined to be not exactly threatening. It was decided that security and the manager would accompany service employees when they went to Richter's room.

Richter did not pay his rent on Monday and displayed a temper tantrum toward the employees. Police were again called.

Thirty-four-year-old Officer Kent Cleveland and twenty-four-year-old Christopher Donahue responded. Donahue had only four months as a licensed officer and was in field training with Cleveland. They went to Richter's room on the second floor to tell him that he was being evicted and would have to leave. The room exited immediately out into a hallway balcony overlooking the reception area.

The officers were just inside the door trying to reason with Richter. He became very upset and irrational. He charged the two officers with a screwdriver in his hand. They retreated out the door and were against the short wall of the balcony. Rather than fall to the first floor and in fear that they might be stabbed with the screwdriver, both fired their .40-caliber Glocks. Richter fell to the floor and was declared dead at the scene when medical personnel arrived.

Investigation determined that Richter had previously been living at a senior citizen complex in Forest Lake for over five years. Residents of that complex told investigators that Richter had been gone for a week prior to the shooting. Many said that he did not like to socialize with residents. Residents felt he was apparently having some personal problems in his life. He was known to have at least four grown children.

It was never determined why Richter was so outraged or what prompted his behavior. On October 20, 1999, a Hennepin County grand jury cleared the officers.

V

At 6:13 a.m. on August 22, 1999, the Lac Qui Parle County Sheriff's Office received a call from the nearby Chippewa County Sheriff's Office that someone had entered the residence of a couple in Lac Qui Parle County. While in the residence, the person pointed a weapon at the husband and wife demanding money.

Lac Qui Parle Deputy Ron Halvorson was notified and responded to the residence at 6:47 a.m. The crime had occurred in his jurisdiction, and he came to take a complete report. The sixty-nine-year-old husband and sixty-two-year-old wife told the deputy that they were sleeping when they were awakened just before 6:00 a.m. by someone in their bedroom. At first, they thought it was their grandson who stayed with them on weekends. The man told them he did not want to hurt them. The woman turned the light on and was immediately told by the intruder to turn it off. It was fairly dark in the room, but they could tell he had a shotgun. The man started to get out of the bed and was told to stay in it. The intruder was pointing the gun at him. The intruder asked for money, alcohol and if they knew where he could find a job. The man told the couple that he "farmed up north." He indicated he needed the money to help feed his two kids. The couple believed the man was intoxicated and stated that he occasionally took a drink from what they thought was a bottle of hard liquor. The man would take a drink and then set it down on the dresser at different times while in the room.

They estimated that he was in the room for five to ten minutes. He told them to stay in the bedroom and then left. They heard the front door close, but they did not hear a vehicle leave. A .12-gauge shotgun belonging to their grandson and a Ray-O-Vac black plastic flashlight was determined to be stolen. They described him as a white male about twenty to twenty-five years of age. He was six feet tall with a stocky build and wearing blue jeans and a dark-colored shirt.

Halvorson was still investigating the scene when he heard radio traffic in the City of Montevideo asking for the description of the intruder. Halvorson got the impression that Montevideo police had an incident transpiring which corresponded with his case. Halvorson left the residence of the robbery at 7:49 a.m. to acquire gas for his squad in Montevideo. After returning to his vehicle, he heard radio traffic about a meeting of law enforcement behind the Montevideo VFW. When he called Chippewa County dispatch on the telephone, he discovered there was a report of an armed man at the Deb Serna residence in Montevideo. It sounded very similar to the suspect whom he was investigating. He decided to go to the VFW to inform officers there about his investigation.

Discussion at the VFW determined that Chippewa County received the original call regarding the home invasion at 5:30 a.m. An officer from Montevideo initially responded, because it was just outside of the city, and found that the intruder was gone. It was then determined that the crime took place in Lac Qui Parle County and that was when Halvorson was called. Around 7:00 a.m. the Chippewa County dispatcher received an anonymous call that there was a male with a shotgun at the Deb Serna residence near Casey's convenience store in the south area of Montevideo.

Montevideo Officer David Jerve went to the convenience store in an effort to locate the caller and/or learn more about what was being reported. He was unable to locate the caller. However, he did obtain a description of the white male using the phone. The man was accompanied by a white female. Jerve was familiar with the area and that Victoria Serna's residence was about two blocks away. He also knew that Victoria had a daughter, Debra, who resembled the female with the male making the call at Casey's. Jerve went to the Serna residence to place it under surveillance.

Jerve requested help from Chippewa and Lac Qui Parle Counties to assist. Numerous calls were made to the residence, but no one answered. Officers wanted to determine if they had a hostage situation or an assault taking place. Finally, officers were able to contact Victoria's son, Dean Serna. He told officers that his mother and her grandchildren were away from the residence and that he believed Debra and her daughter Kirbi might have been staying at the residence.

A gray Oldsmobile was parked in the yard of the house. The license was run and officers went to the registered owner's home and determined that the car had just been stolen. The owner had no idea why it would be parked in Serna's yard.

Based on the anonymous phone call, the description of the male at Casey's, the stolen vehicle in the yard, the description of the home invasion in the county and the lack of response to the residence, it was decided to make an entry into the Serna home to determine if people were being held hostage or were the victims of an assault.

Officer Jerve, Officer Clark Weber, and Chippewa Chief Deputy Douglas Hodge made up the three-person team who entered the residence. Entry was made through an unlocked back door at 9:30 a.m. The officers were unable to locate the suspect on the first floor, but they did find thirteen-year-old Kirbi. She told the officers that her mother was upstairs with the suspect. The three then proceeded to the door of the upstairs bedroom where Kirbi said they were located. Jerve was the lead officer with a body bunker. He tried the door and found it slightly open. He pushed the door open and was immediately confronted by an armed individual, later identified as thirty-two-year-old Ronald E. Sears, pointing a shotgun at him. Jerve fired his 9-mm handgun five times at Sears. Sears fell to the side of the bed. He was handcuffed, and the shotgun was secured. Serna was hit by bullets fragments and immediately taken from the residence to get medical attention. A second ambulance was cancelled because Sears was dead at the scene.

Serna was interviewed at the hospital. She said Sears came to the residence early that morning. He pointed a shotgun at her and Kirbi. He threatened to kill them. He assaulted her once and was in the process of assaulting her again when the officers entered the residence. Sears heard the officers coming up the stairs. Sears told her to get up and close the door. She went to the door but left it slightly ajar. As she closed the door, she was able to see police officers in the hallway with what she described as a "shield" with the word "police" across the front. She indicated she was frightened and did not know what to do. She returned to the bed where Sears was. The door opened, and Sears raised the shotgun at the police. She believed that Sears fired first and then police. She ran out of the room to find her daughter.

Deputy Halvorson was outside of the house as backup. He looked into the stolen car in the yard. He saw a flashlight that matched the description of the one stolen from the Lac Qui Parle couple. Later, the shotgun in possession of Sears at the time of the shooting was identified as the one owned by the couple's grandson. It was also determined that the grandson and daughter of the home invasion worked for the same construction company as Sears. However, they did not know him. Sears' mother lived about a block away from the Serna residence. Alcohol was a factor in the shooting.

Officer Jerve was cleared in the shooting.

VI

Reports of the events leading up to this fatal shooting are varied. This shooting started with a burglary of a rural residence in Mahnomen County in northern Minnesota. There were several weapons among the items stolen. The weapons included shotguns and a lever-action Browning .308 rifle with ammunition.

The Clearwater County Sheriff's Office received a call late afternoon on Saturday, May 14, 2005. The caller was from North Dakota and related to

Deputy Gene Harmon that his niece was living with an individual in Mahnomen County by the name of Franklin Brown. The caller said his niece had been forced by gunpoint to strip naked to show that she had not stolen anything from him. She was forced to do this in front of two of his male friends. Harmon advised the caller that he needed to personally talk directly to the victim in order to get a statement. Harmon said he was just getting off duty and his niece could contact any deputy to give a statement.

Deputy Harmon was awakened at 5:30 a.m. on Sunday by a dispatcher who mistakenly believed that he was the deputy on call. The dispatcher apologized and told him that Franklin Brown had been taken to the hospital, but she would contact the deputy on call.

When Harmon arrived for his shift at 9:00 a.m., he discovered that Brown had requested an ambulance at 5:30 a.m. because he had somehow hurt his neck. After being discharged from the hospital, Deputy Larry Olson had given Brown a ride back to his residence. It was also determined that Mahnomen County was requested to avoid any further contact with him as they were working on getting a search warrant for his residence regarding the stolen guns. Harmon and Chief Deputy Paul Brehm had conversations during the day regarding information needed for the search warrant. The ambulance call to Brown's residence earlier assisted in determining information about the property and the layout of the residence.

Around 2:00 p.m., Brehm advised Harmon that the warrant was being signed by a local judge and that officers would meet a short distance from Brown's residence at the parking lot of the old Lake Ray Lodge at 3:00 p.m. The Lodge had been destroyed by fire and was about one-quarter mile into Mahnomen County. Officers from Mahnomen County, Clearwater County, White Earth Tribal Police and two Minnesota State Troopers arrived to discuss individual assignments and strategy for executing the warrant. Brehm showed the participants the warrant that included a description of the shotguns and rifles suspected to be at the residence. It was decided that Harmon's vehicle would be the first onto the property with a marked squad so anyone could see that it was a law enforcement vehicle. Harmon was to drive around to the back of the residence and provide cover. Brehm and other Mahnomen deputies would be the first armed officers into the house, with others coming in after them. As Harmon pulled around to the back, he heard Deputy Mike Erickson call on the radio that he had seen Brown in a window.

Brown's residence was a story and half. The upstairs was a loft with stairs going up to the back of the house. Harmon exited his squad and discovered there was only one entrance. He walked completely around the house and could hear officers inside yelling, "Search warrant, search warrant, get down." Harmon went to the entrance. The two White Earth Tribal officers were there and entered with him. Harmon saw one of the troopers near what they believed to be the bathroom door. He then went into the living room where he saw Mahnomen County Deputy Doug Krier with his gun out and Mahnomen County Deputy Jennifer Reemer with her stun gun out. Brehm had a Ruger mini-14 .223 rifle pointed toward the loft. Krier was grabbing large pieces of cloth hanging down from the rafters that were covering the loft area. Harmon moved around the other deputies and began walking up the stairs to the loft. He was able to look through an area approximately a foot square into the loft.

Harmon could see in the far corner of the loft that there was a bed with someone sitting on it. It appeared to Harmon that the person was moving around in the bed like he was trying to get at something. Harmon had a stun gun in his hand and activated it. When activated, a laser is turned on to aim it. Harmon pointed it at the person, later determined to be Brown, and fired. As Brown turned toward him, he saw the Browning lever-action rifle pointing at him. He recognized it because he had previously owned one. Brown was racking the lever of the rifle as he was swinging it around. Harmon, in that split second, could tell that the stun gun was not having any effect. He dropped it and pulled his handgun.

Brown was swinging the rifle around at a downward angle at the deputies below. Harmon heard a gunshot and out of the corner of his eye saw debris come from the floor. Brown started to turn toward Harmon and was working the lever of the rifle again. Harmon, knowing that his bullet-proof vest would not stop a .308 round and fearing for his life, fired at Brown with his .40-caliber handgun. Harmon could hear other shots being fired. When the shooting stopped, Harmon could see Brown lying on the bed with his hands still on the rifle. Harmon proceeded to the bed and reached over him and grabbed the sling of the rifle to remove it from him. Deputy Krier, also an EMT, came up to check on Brown.

Brehm had a little different perspective of the incident. He was going to be the first to enter the home. As they approached, he heard the radio transmission that "He's standing in the window" and Brehm could hear him "take off running."

The door was kicked open and Brehm along with Krier entered the house. They began yelling, "Sheriff's office, search warrant."

Brehm did not see Brown or anyone else in the house except law enforcement in the main area. He saw a narrow stairwell leading to the loft area above them. The officers kept yelling who they were and their purpose. He then heard Deputy Reemer yell, "Let me see your hands." Brehm did not see anyone. He then saw Krier reach up and pull a cloth that appeared to be a privacy curtain for the loft bedroom. About this same time, Harmon came around Brehm and started up the stairs to the loft on Brehm's right side. When the curtain was completely off, Brehm saw Brown from the waist up. He recognized Brown from the photo at the briefing. Brehm shouted, "Sheriff's department, search warrant."

Brown yelled back, "Get out of my house! Get out of here!"

Brehm then cried, "He's loading a gun." He also recalled Harmon holler, "Gun," as he heard a stun gun being fired. The stun gun sounds like a .22 being fired, and Brehm could see the wires attached to the gun.

Brehm then saw Brown point the weapon toward the stairs where they were standing. He fired his weapon. The weapon fires a three-round burst with each trigger pull, but Brehm pulled the trigger so quickly the first time that only one round fired. He then fired three-round bursts three more times. Harmon was also heard firing at this time. The shooting stopped, and Brehm saw Harmon continue up the stairs and take the rifle from Brown's reach. Krier went up to check for Brown's vital signs and announced that he was dead.

One of the White Earth Tribal officers at the scene was interviewed and substantiated all of the shouting, announcing who they were and the purpose of entering the home. He also heard Brown calling to the officers to leave. He recalled hearing Reemer cry, "Gun, he's got a gun," and other officers holler, "Drop the gun." He then heard the stun gun being fired, and that was followed by numerous other shots. This officer also related that he had arrested Brown for driving while intoxicated, driving a stolen car, and assault. He had also taken a report of Brown being a victim of an assault.

An autopsy determined that Brown died from multiple gunshot wounds. His blood alcohol was .18, and he had marijuana in his system. A grand jury determined that Brehm and Harmon were justified in the shooting of Brown on June 28, 2005.

Table 1
Weapons Used by
Suspects Shot by Police

Type of Weapon	Number of Officers Shooting (Percent Rounded)	Number of Fatalities
Handgun	94* (47 percent)	53
Shoulder weapon	22* (11 percent)	11
Knife/Edged weapon	41 (20.5 percent)	24
What appeared or was said to be a handgun, knife, or other deadly weapon (bat)	24 (12 percent)	15
Automobile	16 (8 percent)	6
Accidental (Suspect Unarmed)	3 (1.5 percent)	3
Total	**200 (100 percent)**	**112**

*One suspect pointed a shotgun at the officers and was shot. He then went to his handgun. Two individuals, one in rural Minnesota and one during a metropolitan area bank robbery, used a .223 rifle to begin shooting at the officer(s) and then changed to a 9-mm handgun. Two individuals were shot when they attempted to get a handgun away from the police. One wrestled away an officer's weapon and shot two officers; however, the weapon was retrieved by the officer and used to fatally shoot the person. Another took an officer's handgun, but was shot by two other officers and that officer using a shotgun. One unarmed person was accidentally shot while fighting with officers as he was being arrested after robbing a decoy officer. Another officer accidentally discharged his weapon as he slipped on a wet running board of a stolen truck striking the suspect as he lay hiding across the seat.

Table 2
Number of Officers at Shooting Scene Firing a Weapon at the Suspect

Number of Officers	Number of Incidents	Number of Fatalities
6	3	3
4	5	5
3	10	10
2	28	28
1	61*	63*
Totals	**110**	**112**

*There were two separate events where only one officer shot a weapon and two individuals died.

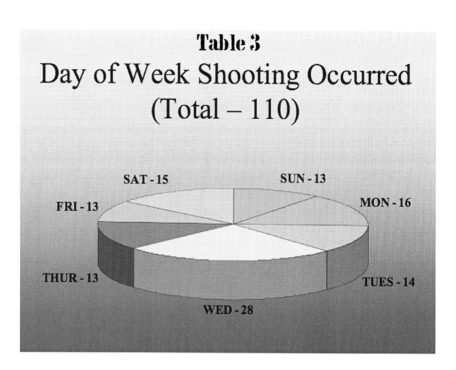

Table 3

Day of Week Shooting Occurred
(Total – 110)

SAT - 15   SUN - 13
FRI - 13   MON - 16
THUR - 13   TUES - 14
WED - 28

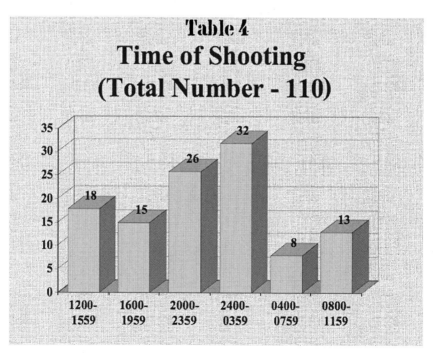

Table 4
Time of Shooting
(Total Number - 110)

Time	Number
1200-1559	18
1600-1959	15
2000-2359	26
2400-0359	32
0400-0759	8
0800-1159	13

Table 5
Type of Weapon

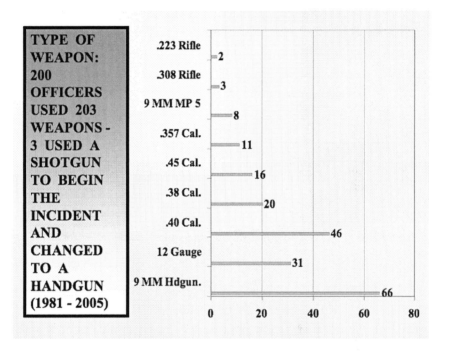

TYPE OF WEAPON: 200 OFFICERS USED 203 WEAPONS - 3 USED A SHOTGUN TO BEGIN THE INCIDENT AND CHANGED TO A HANDGUN (1981 - 2005)

.223 Rifle	2
.308 Rifle	3
9 MM MP 5	8
.357 Cal.	11
.45 Cal.	16
.38 Cal.	20
.40 Cal.	46
12 Gauge	31
9 MM Hdgun.	66

Table 6—Firearms Discharges by Minnesota Law Enforcement Officers Resulting in Death 1981–2005

Date	Day	Agency	Deceased				Officer			
			Name	R/S	Age		Name	R/S	Age	Exp
3 Jan 81	Sa	Burnsville PD	Gregory Knodel	W/M	17		Stephen Baker	W/M	34	11
12 Aug 81	W	Minneapolis PD	Melvin Johnson	W/M	51		David Niebur	W/M	39	14
							Mike Carey	W/M	28	6
26 Aug 81	W	Minneapolis PD	Eugene Mehl	W/M	20		Ted Boran	W/M	38	15
							Art Gooselaw	W/M	35	12
							Pete Heeren	W/M	35	11
							Tom Peterson	W/M	31	8
28 Oct 81	W	Brooklyn Center PD	Gerald Lavalle	W/M	18		Dennis Flaherty	W/M	30	8
							David Grass	W/M	32	10
19 Jan 82	Tu	Minneapolis PD	Donald Haynes	B/M	32		Jerry Larson	W/M	33	10
							Ron Johnson	W/M	28	6
							Greg Zipoy	W/M	29	7
18 Jan 83	Tu	Faribault PD	Russell Lambert	W/M	46		Robert Basel	W/M	32	4
17 Dec 83	Sa	Minneapolis PD	Rigoberto Prieto Cuellar	Cu/M	23		Mike Green	W/M	34	11
							Charles Dodge	W/M	31	6
3 Aug 84	F	Hennepin County SO	Gerald Heft	W/M	43		Steven Peterson	W/M	35	13
21 Sep 84	Th	Minneapolis PD	Sal Scott	B/M	22		Bill James	W/M	36	9
9 Jan 85	W	Sauk Rapids PD	Michael Rahrlien	W/M	24		Doug Brinkman	W/M	23	3
3 May 85	F	Kittson County SO	Robert Stewart	W/M	40		Craig Spilde	W/M	34	10
8 May 85	W	Lakeville PD	Jack McNamara	W/M	30		Scott Johnson	W/M	30	11
							David Bellows	W/M	30	5

Firearms Discharges by Minnesota Law Enforcement Officers Resulting in Death 1981–2005 (cont'd.)

Date	Day	Agency	Deceased			Officer			
			Name	R/S	Age	Name	R/S	Age	Exp
18 Jul 85	Th	Saint Paul PD #	Eric Schmieg	W/M	21	Richard Schmidt	W/M	57	30
17 Dec 85	Tu	Saint Paul PD	Erick Ware	B/M	26	Kenneth McIntosh	B/M	37	10
						Richard Munoz	His/M	30	8
16 Jan 87	F	Minneapolis PD	Hosie Walton	B/M	54	Bruce Johnson	W/M	38	14
						Steve Day	AmI/M	30	6
11 May 87	M	South Saint Paul PD	Mark Sinclair	W/M	29	Gregory Mohrland	W/M	39	11
25 Jun 87	Th	Saint Paul PD #	Scott Winder	W/M	27	Eugene Polyak	W/M	28	3
15 Jul 87	W	Minneapolis PD	Gerald Whitten	B/M	31	Bob Thunder	AmI/M	41	11
21 Aug 87	F	Minneapolis PD	Mark Richards	W/M	25	James Wilson	W/M	33	10
						Pete Jackson	B/M	30	7
6 Nov 87	F	Minneapolis PD #	Kerry Howk	W/M	35	Donald Heitland	W/M	47	18
						Mike Sundstrum	W/M	45	20
						David Peterson	W/M	47	20
12 Sep 88	M	Minneapolis PD	Tom Jennings	B/M	30	Alissa Clemons	B/F	25	2
19 Mar 89	Su	Dakota County SO	Larry Hill	B/M	49	Todd West	W/M	29	2
22 Jun 89	Th	Chippewa County SO	Dennis Ostenson	W/M	42	Joe Linneman	W/M	36	10
						Kelly Aalfs	W/M	31	11
15 Nov 89	W	Inver Grove PD	Ba See Lor	A/M	13	Kennerh Murphy	W/M	54	20
			Thai Yang	A/M	13				

Firearms Discharges by Minnesota Law Enforcement Officers Resulting in Death 1981–2005 (cont'd.)

Date	Day	Agency	Deceased Name	R/S	Age	Officer Name	R/S	Age	Exp
16 Apr 90	M	Blue Earth County	Daniel J. Lynch	W/M	25	Willis Purvis	W/M	36	12
18 Sep 90	W	Saint Paul PD	Fred Weed	W/M	27	Michael Hinzman	W/M	37	11
22 Sep 90	Sa	Saint Paul PD	James Ludwig	W/M	34	Charles Anderson	W/M	51	25
						Joe Strong	W/M	33	10
1 Dec 90	Su	Minneapolis PD	Tycel Nelson	B/M	17	Dan May	W/M	28	6
13 Jul 91	Sa	Brainerd PD	Barry Peterson	W/M	26	Tom Pfingsten	W/M	33	6
12 Oct 91	Sa	Bloomington PD	Theresa Lindquist	W/F	40	Leonard Anderson	W/M	43	20
						Phil DeGia	W/M	35	9
28 Nov 91	Th	So. Lake Minnetonka	Richard Krueger	W/M	24	Mark Erickson	W/M	39	16
9 Feb 92	Su	Minneapolis PD	Theodore Bobo	B/M	24	Colin Koski	W/M	27	3
						David Ulberg	W/M	26	3
						Mike Hentges	W/M	32	4
						Charles Dodge	WM	39	15
29 Jul 92	W	Brooklyn Park PD	Donald Gross	W/M	49	Terry Huntington	W/M	43	12
						Jeff Jindra	W/M	33	11
						Steve Pearson	W/M	33	8
						Kent Blum	W/M	36	5
						Steven Baker	W/M	26	4
2 Dec 92	W	Minneapolis PD#	Earnest Dean-El	B/M	30	Jeff York	W/M	27	1
13 Dec 92	Su	Eagan PD	Dennis Seiz	W/M	43	James Theilen	W/M	32	5
						Dan Mason	W/M	25	4
						Brad Jurgens	W/M	32	3

Firearms Discharges by Minnesota Law Enforcement Officers Resulting in Death 1981–2005 (cont'd.)

		Deceased				Officer			
Date	Day	Agency	Name	R/S	Age	Name	R/S	Age	Exp
27 Dec 92	Su	Beltrami County	Delwyn Dudley	AI/M	43	Steve Kovacic	W/M	36	10
4 Apr 93	Su	Brooklyn Park PD	John Bertelsen	W/M	28	Steve Palmquist	W/M	28	5
						Steve Pearson	W/M	33	9
28 Apr 93 Ω	W	Minneapolis PD	Dale Johns	AI/M	26	Jeffrey Drew	W/M	50	25
26 Jul 93	M	St. Cloud PD	Duane Breitbach	W/M	33	Tom Schlieman	W/M	31	5
						Mark Moline	W/M	28	1
		Waite Park PD				Arlan Schermerhorn	W/M	30	9
26 Aug 93	Th	Minnesota DNR#	Donald Polcyn	W/M	42	Grant Coyour[1]	W/M	38	16
		Moose Lake PD				Bruce Manty	W/M	50	25
12 Oct 93	Tu	Saint Paul PD	Kai Lor	A/M	19	David Timm	W/M	59	24
			Bruce Teng Thao	A/M	18				
6 Nov 93	Sa	Minneapolis PD	Phillip Gonzales	B/M	21	Paul Moen[2]	W/M	52	23
22 Jan 94	Sa	Ramsey County	Shawn Mettler	W/M	20	Edward Whitledge	W/M	42	6
						Tom Haltiner	W/M	47	15
1 Feb 94	Tu	Dakota County SO	Gerald Giesler	W/M	37	Luther Klug[3]	W/M	33	4
						Brad Jeska	W/M	31	6
						Todd West	W/M	33	6
2 Mar 94	W	Minneapolis PD	Donald LaPoint	AI/M	32	Mark Osland	W/M	29	5

Firearms Discharges by Minnesota Law Enforcement Officers Resulting in Death 1981–2005 (cont'd.)

Date	Day	Agency	Deceased Name	R/S	Age	Officer Name	R/S	Age	Exp
8 Apr 94	F	Minneapolis PD	Calvin Sam	AI/M	49	Joel Kimmerle	W/M	30	4
						Tammy Diedrich	W/F	31	6
13 Apr 94	W	Minneapolis PD	Steven Cole	W/M	23	Curtis Graff	W/M	32	5
						David Pleoger	W/M	24	1
12 Jun 94	Su	Anoka PD	Wilma Brown	AI/F	43	Ed Egly	W/M	38	11
10 Aug 94	W	MN State Patrol	Mohd Ahmad Hasan	Ir/M	47	Scott Trautner	W/M	29	8
						Kenneth Drevnick	W/M	36	15
		Roseville PD				Loren Rosland	W/M	31	10
						Robert Ebert	W/M	47	18
		Maplewood PD				David Arnold	W/M	49	27
		Oakdale PD				Eugene Johnson	W/M	40	15
25 Jul 95	Tu	Washington County SO	Charles Lesnau	W/M	17	Lonnie Van Klei	W/M	37	7
22 Aug 95	Tu	Minneapolis PD	Teru McSwain	B/M	22	Andrew Aspin	W/M	39	10
27 Sep 95	W	Grand Rapids PD	Gregory Glynn	W/M	37	Brent Bradley	W/M	32	11
						Frank Scherf	W/M	37	16
		Itasca County SO				Dean Scherf	W/M	31	6
						Joseph Skofich	W/M	41	17
		St. Louis County SO				William Henegmon	W/M	44	23
						Randall Lehman	W/M	46	24
29 Jan 96	M	Benton County SO #	Thomas Kantor	W/M	26	Nancy Wiggin	W/F	34	2
31 Jan 96	W	Minneapolis PD	Kesha Williams	B/F	21	Gerald Wallerich	W/M	33	6
23 Mar 96	Sa	Minneapolis PD	Keith Jackson	B/M	31	Dwayne Walker	B/M	28	6

Firearms Discharges by Minnesota Law Enforcement Officers Resulting in Death 1981-2003 (cont'd.)

Date	Day	Agency	Deceased			Officer			
			Name	R/S	Age	Name	R/S	Age	Exp
20 Apr 96	Sa	MN State Patrol	Adam Hotkiewicz	W/M	19	Curt Karges	W/M	27	6
12 Jun 96	W	Rushford PD	Scott A. Omodt	W/M	24	Sam Stensgard	W/M	40	12
						Andrew Ochs	W/M	24	1
25 Aug 96	Su	Saint Paul PD	Freddie Bowen	B/M	52	Steve Anderson	W/M	29	6
						John Wright	W/M	42	12
						Jeff Winger	W/M	30	9
						Carl Schwartz	W/M	41	8
6 Nov 96	W	Saint Paul PD	Robert Benson	W/M	39	David Sohm	W/M	39	17
						Julie Harris	W/F	28	1
						Tom Perzichili	W/M	28	4
						Vince Martin	B/M	33	5
28 Apr 97	M	Saint Paul PD	Demetrius Hill	B/M	18	Gerald Vick[4]	W/M	33	6
22 Oct 97	W	Hennepin County #	Gerald Lehn	W/M	30	Gary Johnson	W/M	43	19
21 May 98	Th	Saint Paul PD	Teng Xiong	A/M	30	Brad Schultz	W/M	33	9
24 July 98	F	Crow Wing County	Mike Truchinski	W/M	41	Dennis Lasher	W/M	34	6
4 Mar 99	Th	St. Louis County	David Sanders	W/M	43	Charles Burns	W/M	49	24
						Jodi Kangas	W/F	29	6
29 Mar 99	M	Brooklyn Park PD	Donald Richter	W/M	64	Christopher Donahue	W/M	25	1
						Kent Cleveland	W/M	35	14

Firearms Discharges by Minnesota Law Enforcement Officers Resulting in Death 1981–2005 (cont'd.)

Date	Day	Agency	Deceased Name	R/S	Age	Officer Name	R/S	Age	Exp
5 May 99	W	E. Grand Forks PD	Brian Hangsleban	W/M	49	Brian Cheney	W/M	23	1
						Curtis Graff	W/M	37	11
13 May 99	Tu	St.Cloud PD	Kevin Hartung	W/M	33	Tom Schlieman	W/M	37	10
6 Aug 99	F	Minneapolis PD (Hancock, MN)	Robin Emmert	W/M	37	Tim Hanks	B/M	33	6
						David Clifford	W/M	35	6
22 Aug 99	Su	Montevideo PD	Ronald Sears	W/M	32	David Jerve	W/M	44	14
8 Dec 99	W	Minneapolis PD	Rocco Dandrea	W/M	42	Mike Green	W/M	50	27
						Steven Sworski	W/M	56	30
13 Apr 99	M	Duluth PD	Donald Herold	W/M	65	Daniel Fogarty	W/M	38	15
14 May 00	Su	Minneapolis PD	Sean Hayes	W/M	34	Tim Costello	W/M	25	3
						Jeff Kading	W/M	24	Days
						Brandy Steberg	W/M	28	3
						Gene Stuker	W/M	28	2
						Jeff Werner	W/M	28	7
3 Jun 00	Sa	Woodbury PD #	Perry Parks	W/M	42	Michael Pomeroy	W/M	39	17
13 Jun 00	M	Minneapolis PD	Barbara Schneider	W/F	49	Sarah Saarela	W/F	35	5
						Bill Palmer	W/M	29	6
11 Sep 00	M	Dakota County SO	Walter Kangas	W/M	52	Tom Hooper	W/M	34	10

364

Firearms Discharges by Minnesota Law Enforcement Officers Resulting in Death 1961–2005 (cont'd.)

			Deceased			Officer			
Date	Day	Agency	Name	R/S	Age	Name	R/S	Age	Exp
1 Nov 00	W	Minneapolis PD	Alfred Sanders	B/M	29	Matt Blade	W/M	32	11
						Hein Dinh	A/M	26	4
						Valarie Goligowski	W/F	40	11
		Minneapolis Park				Lupe Herrera	His/F	46	18
						Steve Manhood	W/M	41	3
16 Nov 00	Th	Edina PD #	David L. White	B/M	30	Bill Moir	W/M	49	23
						Scott Kuyper	W/M	36	12
						James Rygg	W/M	29	7
21 Nov 00	Tu	Minneapolis PD	James Frye	W/M	29	Aaron Morrison	W/M	28	3
						Scott Ramsdell	W/M	30	3
						Mike Kaneko	A/M	31	6
29 Mar 01	Th	Fridley PD	Timothy Golden	W/M	33	Tom Swanson	W/M	31	8
						Jason Cardinal	W/M	28	6
2 Apr 01	M	Minneapolis PD	Demitreus Sesler	B/M	27	Brandy Steberg	W/M	29	4
						Jason King	W/M	32	8
29 Apr 01	Sa	Minneapolis PD	Efrain Depaz	Hi/M	21	John Pielow	W/M	49	16
27 May 01	Sa	Duluth PD	James Balen	W/M	43	Martin LeRette	W/M	49	18
23 Jun 01	Sa	Mille Lacs County SO	Robert Crawford	W/M	72	James Osowski	W/M	37	13
						Bill Hawley	W/M	40	19
29 Jul 01	Su	Minneapolis PD #	Abdullah Simmons	B/M	15	John Ochs	W/M	32	10
30 Jul 01	M	Beltrami CountySO #	Mark Patch	W/M	26	Greg Winskowski	W/M	47	22

Firearms Discharges by Minnesota Law Enforcement Officers Resulting in Death 1981–2005 (cont'd.)

			Deceased			Officer			
Date	Day	Agency	Name	R/S	Age	Name	R/S	Age	Exp
8 Aug 01	Tu	Scott County SO #	Thomas Opalinski	W/M	34	William Vendel	W/M	38	5
3 Dec 01	M	Saint Paul PD	Charles Craighead	B/M	46	Michael Lee	W/M	41	13
10 Mar 02	Su	Minneapolis PD	Abu K. Jeilani	B/M	29	Joel Kimmerle	W/M	38	12
						Jim Jensen	W/M	36	13
						Hein Dinh	A/M	27	6
						Justin Merten	W/M	31	6
						Michael McCarthy	W/M	34	8
						Vickie Karnik	W/F	35	15
1 Aug 02	Th	Minneapolis PD	Martha Donald	B/F	60	Melissa Schmidt[5]	W/F	35	9
15 Aug 02	Th	Edina PD	Lamont Scott	B/M	30	Jeffrey Elasky	W/M	30	9
2 Sep 02	M	Saint Paul PD #	William Hayek	W/M	19	John Linssen	W/M	32	10
						Mark Nelson	W/M	26	3
						Pete Crum	W/M	35	10
27 Sep 02	F	Saint Paul PD	Ki Yang	A/M	46	Michael Tharalson	W/M	33	9
2 Oct 02	W	Rosemount PD #	Shane Lynner	W/M	38	Jewell Ericson	W/M	40	17
28 Dec 02	Sa	Saint Paul PD	Walter Dochniak	W/M	22	Cort Baumgart	W/M	31	6
						Ann Anderson	W/F	26	4
						Shawn Shanley	W/M	29	3
25 Mar 03	Tu	Hennepin County SO	Roderick Harvey	B/M	28	John Seery	W/M	38	6
						Richard Palaia	W/M	32	5
		Brooklyn Park PD				Chris Donahue	W/M	28	8
						Robert Roushar	W/M	31	8

			Deceased			Officer			
Date	Day	Agency	Name	R/S	Age	Name	R/S	Age	Exp
7 May 03	W	Minneapolis PD	Eric Netters	B/M	31	Mark Bohnsack	W/M	28	5
13 May 03	Tu	Anoka Country SO #	Erik Nylen	W/M	29	Dustin Reichert	W/M	31	6
22 May 03	Th	Olmsted Country SO #	Calvin Barrett	W/M	43	Jason Christensen	W/M	32	6
10 Oct 03	F	Minneapolis PD	Walter Collins	B/M	21	Jamie Conway	W/M	31	7
9 Dec 03	Tu	Wadena PD	Kenneth F. Lessley	W/M	43	Tom Crawford	W/M	43	16
3 Jan 04	F	Saint Paul PD	Johnnie Rodgers	B/M	54	Charles Sims	B/M	34	6
30 Jan 04	F	Fergus Falls PD	Leslie Fredrickson	W/M	52	Kile Bergren	W/M	30	9
						Jess Schoon	W/M	30	7
13 Apr 04	Tu	New Hope PD	Ron Adamson	W/M	50	David Friskney	W/M	37	13
2 Jun 04	W	St. Louis Park PD #	Todd Hubbell	W/M	34	David Smith	W/M	43	13
						Siar Nadem	W/M	27	3
		Golden Valley PD				Dean Kettner	W/M	48	26
24 Oct 04	Tu	Minneapolis PD	Courtney Williams	B/M	15	Scott Mars	W/M	31	8
24 Dec 04	F	MN State Patrol	Rodney Miller	W/M	45	Chad Mills	W/M	27	7
22 Jan 05	Sa	Minneapolis PD	Benjamin DeCoteau	AI/M	21	Mark Beaupre	W/M	38	15
15 May 05	Su	Mahnomen County	Franklin Brown	AI/M	21	Paul Brehm	W/M	50	30
		Clearwater County				Eugene Harmon	W/M	46	20

Firearms Discharges by Minnesota Law Enforcement Officers Resulting in Death 1981–2005 (cont'd.)

		Deceased				Officer			
Date	Day	Agency	Name	R/S	Age	Name	R/S	Age	Exp
18 May 05	W	Chisago County SO	Robert A. Peterson	W/M	31	Justin Wood	W/M	27	5
1 Aug 05	M	Minneapolis PD #	Ricky Redin	W/M	47	Jason Walters	W/M	32	12
						John Engle	W/M	33	10

[1]Killed in line-of-duty during aircraft accident on June 11, 1999
[2]Died in line-of-duty from heart attack assisting another officer on July 1, 1995
[3]Killed in line-of-duty by intoxicated driver on July 17, 1996
[4]Killed in line-of-duty by armed assailant on May 6, 2005
[5]Killed in line-of-duty during fatal shooting of armed suspect on August 1, 2002
— Officer firing weapon or other officer(s) assaulted/injured during the shooting by fists, club, vehicle, knife, or firearm.

Index

About the Author

Larry C. Brubaker was born on December 4, 1944, at Havre, Montana. He received his early education and Bachelor of Science degree in Montana. After teaching and coaching for three years, he began a career with the Federal Bureau of Investigation (FBI) on April 12, 1971.

Following his initial training at the FBI Academy, Quantico, Virginia, Agent Brubaker was assigned to the Portland, Oregon, field office. Subsequent assignments took him to Detroit, Michigan (1972–1979) and Minot, North Dakota (1979–1984). He was assigned to the Minneapolis office of the FBI in July 1984.

While employed by the FBI, Brubaker had numerous assignments. He was a polygraph examiner for eight years and coordinated the training program for the states of North Dakota, South Dakota, and Minnesota. Brubaker served as a crisis negotiator for over twenty years and trained many local negotiators during his career. In addition, he was the area's representative to the FBI's National Center for the Analysis of Violent Crime. He served as a counselor for the 173rd session of the FBI National Academy. He was a charter member of the International Homicide Investigators Association in 1987 and remains an active member. He is also a member of the Minnesota Sex Crimes Investigators Association and the Northwest Chapter of the FBI National Academy Associates.

During his tenure with the FBI, he taught various violent crime topics throughout the United States, Canada, and at the FBI Academy, Quantico, Virginia. He has also taught at the International Law Enforcement Academy, Budapest, Hungary. He has appeared on numerous local radio and television news reports. He has been interviewed on National Public Radio, Primetime Live, 48 Hours, MSNBC News, Discovery Health Network, and Langley Production's Court TV.

Brubaker received his Master of Arts from Saint Mary's University, Winona, Minnesota, in 1993. He retired from the FBI in June 2000 to become the Regional Corporate Security Manager for Unisys Corporation, Eagan, Minnesota. In June 2006 he left Unisys Corporation and created his own company: Applied Consulting and Training LLC. Brubaker has provided expert witness testimony for Minnesota law firms regarding the use of deadly force, false reports to law enforcement, sexual assaults and interviewing. Presently, he serves as an adjunct professor at Winona State University, Saint Mary's University, and Hamline University.